State Trooper:

America's State Troopers and Highway Patrolmen

TURNER PUBLISHING COMPANY
Paducah, Kentucky

Turner Publishing Company
412 Broadway • P.O. Box 3101
Paducah, KY 42002-3101
(270) 443-0121

Turner Publishing Company Staff:
Publishing Consultant: Keith R. Steele
Project Assistant: Charlotte Harris
Designer: Heather R. Warren

ISBN: 1-56311-613-8
Library of Congress
Control #: 2001089731

Limited Edition
Printed in the USA

Featured writer: Marilyn Olsen

Special thanks to PS-Publishers, 1816 Ivy Oak Square,
Reston, VA 20190 for permission to use some of their
cruiser photos.

TABLE OF CONTENTS

Troopers representing various states at the United States Capitol.

Chairman Rhinebarger meeting with President William J. Clinton at the White House.

THE WHITE HOUSE

Washington

June 21, 2000

Warm greetings to the members of the National Troopers Coalition.

America owes a lasting debt of gratitude to the men and women of our law enforcement community. Each day, you put your lives at risk to protect us, ensuring the safety of our families and our homes. Thanks to your efforts, we have started to turn the tide on crime, and it is now down for a remarkable seventh year in a row. Our communities are the safest they have been in a generation - with more community police on our streets and fewer guns in the hands of criminals.

Across America, neighborhood by neighborhood, hope for a safer future is being restored, and I salute all of our nation's state troopers and highway patrol officers for your steadfast dedication to this vital mission. Best Wishes for continued success.

May 1998, Chairman Rhinebarger and 1st Vice Chairman Michael Muth presenting U.S. Attorney General Janet Reno a plaque from the NTC for her support of State Troopers and Highway Patrolmen.

Office of the Attorney General
Washington, D. C. 20530

Mr. Scott Reinacher
Chairman
National Troopers Coalition
112 State Street, Suite 1212
Albany, New York 12207

Dear Mr. Reinacher:

Law Enforcement officers have one of the most difficult yet rewarding jobs in America. Our Nation's state troopers and highway patrol officers have played an important role in making our communities a safer place to live and work. Your willingness to put your lives on the line to uphold the rule of law represents the highest form of public service.

As I travel around this nation, I see firsthand the positive impact of your efforts. On behalf of the Department of Justice, thank you for your continued service to our country.

Sincerely,

Janet Reno

Janet Reno

Publisher's Message

When one stops to think about what makes the United States of America a great nation, the men and women of America's law enforcement come to mind. After all, what benefit would there be in fighting victorious battles abroad and defending against an outside enemy only to be defeated from within our own borders by lawlessness? To further highlight this crucial role of America's law enforcement, we are privileged to offer this tribute to the National Troopers and the men and women who have served as state troopers nationwide. This volume attempts to tell the real story of America's highway patrol, state police and state troopers in a way that properly recognizes the thousands of troopers who serve and sacrifice on a daily basis throughout our nation.

Our sincere appreciation goes to Jim Rhinebarger, Scott Reinacher and Mike Muth with the National Troopers Coalition, and the board of directors who shared our vision and supported this historic project. Marilyn Olsen, editor of Indiana's Finest magazine contributed to the project with her dedicated research to provide a nationwide historic overview of state police.

Most importantly, we appreciate the response of each state's police and families who submitted histories, personal experience stories and photographs to make this book possible.

Now, as a salute to all state patrol troopers and their families, we present with great pride and honor, this volume, *State Trooper: America's State Troopers and Highway Patrolmen.*

Dave Turner
Turner Publishing Company
President

Keith Steele
Turner Publishing Company
Publishing Consultant

"Turner books capture the heart and soul of their subjects. They are poignant, informational, insightful and more." — Craig W. Floyd, chairman, National Law Enforcement Officers Memorial Fund, Inc.

Turner Publishing Company is the country's leading publisher of law enforcement and military books. Some of our recent publications include: *Maryland State Police; San Diego Sheriffs; Alabama State Troopers; National Organization of Black Law Enforcement Executives (NOBLE); National Law Enforcement Officers Memorial; St. Paul Police; FBI National Academy; New Mexico State Police; Portland Police; New York State Troopers; Los Angeles County Sheriffs; Michigan State Police; Former Special Agents of the FBI; Baltimore Police; Massachusetts State Police; Blue Knights; Forgotten Heroes of Dade County, Florida; Drug Enforcement; Rhode Island State Police; Savannah Police; Jacksonville, Florida Sheriffs; Oklahoma City Police; Chicago Police; Utah Highway Patrol; Milwaukee County Sheriffs; Baltimore County Police; Orange County, Florida Sheriffs; Oklahoma Heroes*

Chairman's Message

It is with great pride and honor that I serve as chairman of the National Troopers Coalition, whose purpose is to provide preferred services by elevating the standards of policing and to promote the professionalism of state police officers and highway patrolmen.

Contained within this history book one will read about the eminently trained and respected state police and highway patrolmen both past and current, who arc truc heroes. The traditions that they continue to honor are truly indicative of the pride instilled during their training and the continued excellence while serving in state law enforcement.

The history contained in these pages is only a fragment of the vast histories that each state police and highway patrol has traveled. The chronicles will also disclose the superior accomplishments achieved throughout the years and the work performed daily by our nation's troopers.

This publication will also serve to educate the general public and law enforcement professionals on the history and the duties on this nation's state police and highway patrolmen.

Sincerely,

Scott L. Reinacher

The National Troopers Coalition

by Marilyn Olsen

Like many fraternal organizations, the National Troopers Coalition began with a social event. In the early 1970s, Thomas J. Iskrazycki, President of the State Troopers Fraternal Association of New Jersey, thought that troopers from surrounding states might enjoy the chance to get together on an information basis to compare cars, weapons, working conditions, salaries and pensions, as well as simply to get to know one another better.

So he invited them all to a picnic.

Similar events were held for six or seven years. In 1977, Richard Whelan, President of the State Police Association of Massachusetts suggested that a more formal organization be formed among troopers of the New England states. The first meeting was held in Framingham, Massachusetts in September. Representatives from Massachusetts, Rhode Island, Maine and Connecticut attended. They drew up by-laws, wrote a constitution and names the organization Northeast Regional Troopers Coalition, NERTC.

After several meetings, they began to publish the Trooper News Letter and expanded its circulation beyond the east coast to all the states that had associations.

Soon, many states became interested in forming organizations similar to NERTC and quarterly regional meetings were held across the country. The name was changed to the National Troopers Coalition, NTC, incorporated, for legal purposes in New York.

According to Article III of the bylaws, the purposes and powers of the NTC are:

1.   a continuing effort to better police services to the public

2.   to stimulate mutual cooperation between state police associations throughout the nation

3.   to elevate the standards of policing throughout the United States and promote the professionalism of the state police officers

4.   to assist member state police associations in achieving the best possible equipment, salaries, pensions, fringe benefits and working conditions

5.   to provide a vehicle through which state police associations may disseminate factual data for the purpose of collective bargaining and legislative lobbying.

Within ten years, the NTC grew from a four-state organization to a membership of 43 states representing nearly 44,000 state police and highway patrol officers nationwide. Today, NTC membership includes representatives from 48 associations (three states have two associations) and represents more than 45,000 troopers.

A History of State Troopers

by Marilyn Olsen
editor, *Indiana's Finest*

Chairman Thomas J. Iskrzycki presenting a plaque to Mrs. Ronald Reagan at the White House.

Introduction

Although every civilization since the dawn of time had imposed order by one method or another, the system of policing that would develop in the United States had its origins during the reign of Alfred the Great who ruled England in the late 10th century.

During this period, the peace was maintained by the mutual pledge. Groups of 10 families were organized as a "tithing." Generally, one man in the tithing was given the responsibility of compliance with the law. If any one member committed an offense, all could be fined. Tithings were organized into groups of 100, led by a constable. These groups of 100 were concentrated into geographical areas known as "shires," with a "shire-reeve," appointed by the king to serve as chief law enforcement agent. Wrongdoers were generally brought before the local landowners who dispensed punishment as they saw fit.

In the 11th Century, law enforcement became an around-the-clock responsibility as night patrols were added. These constables and night watchmen were also expected to serve as firefighters. The office of justice of the peace was created to supervise this force. As in the US seven hundred years later, this system was generally sufficient to serve a predominately rural area where everybody knew everybody else.

Although there was no nationally recognized and uniform code of laws, over the centuries, the system known as "common law" had evolved. Common law, as distinguished from local laws which might be very specific, covered crimes such as murder that everyone could agree were wrong.

By the 18th century, as towns grew into cities full of strangers and immigrants from other cultures, crime became more random and more violent. The sheriffs, constables and local watchmen who had kept the peace for hundreds of years in rural areas and small towns were simply overwhelmed by the complexity of urban law enforcement.

Henry Fielding (the author of Tom Jones) was appointed as Magistrate of London to solve the problem. He organized a force known as the "Bow Street Runners." This force was given the power to break up criminal gangs and make arrests.

To further emphasize the presence of the police, in the mid-1700s, for the first time, police officers began to wear uniforms.

British Home Secretary Sir Robert Peel is credited with establishing the first "modern" police system in 1829. Under his leadership, The Metropolitan Police Act was passed. It set up two commissioners who established regulations for the hiring, training and supervision of the agency. Twelve principles of policing were developed:

1. The police must be stable, efficient and organized along military lines.
2. The police must be under government control.
3. The absence of crime will best prove the efficiency of police.
4. The distribution of crime news is essential.
5. The development of police strength, both by time and area, where and when a crime has occurred or may occur is essential.
6. No quality is more indispensable to a police officer than a perfect command of temper. A quiet, determined manner has more effect than violent action.
7. Good appearance commands respect.
8. The selection and training of proper persons are at the root of efficient law enforcement.
9. Public security demands that every police officer be given an identifying number.
10. Police headquarters should be centrally located and easily accessible to the people.
11. Police officers should be hired on a probationary basis before permanent assignment.
12. The keeping of crime records by police is necessary to determine the best distribution of police strength.

However, it would be many years before these principles made their way across the Atlantic and were adopted by police forces in the United States.

The Evolution of Policing in the US

Although within a hundred years, our ancestors would begin arriving from all corners of the world, the first to arrive in any number came from England in the 1600s. They had left the old world to start a new life in a more hospitable social environment. But, like all creatures of habit, they brought along the elements of society with which they were familiar — English as a common language, black frock coats, skirts with lots of petticoats, a preference for meat and potatoes and a system of law enforcement.

The system of law enforcement practiced by most of the earliest colonists was based on the English common law. Under common law, serious crimes (felonies) were distinguished from less serious ones (misdemeanors). A judge presided over a court where serious crimes were tried before a jury. The jury heard the case and determined guilt or innocence. If the accused were found guilty, the court determined what the punishment would be. Less serious crimes were adjudicated by justices of the peace or magistrates.

But the laws and punishments often varied considerably from what they had been in England. Those colonies that were essentially theocracies, for example, based their local laws on the tenets of their religion. And sentences, as we all remember from reading The Scarlet Letter, often consisted of humiliating the guilty who failed to see the error of their ways to the satisfaction of those handing out the punishment.

In most of the colonies, the governor appointed a sheriff (the American version of the "shire reeve"). This individual usually had a variety of responsibilities including locating offenders, managing the jail and serving as coroner. The sheriff was then, as now, a county official.

In the larger towns and cities volunteer watchmen and constables had what we would now call patrol duty. They walked the streets at night to protect citizens from robbers, looked after the security of businesses and sounded an alarm when there was trouble.

In the earliest days, as in England, constables and watchmen were generally sufficient to maintain order. But by the mid-1800s, the crush of immigrants into what were becoming major American cities simply overwhelmed these untrained and unorganized volunteers, as well.

While some cities considered bringing in the military to keep the peace, most preferred to establish a full-time paid police organization.

In 1844, New York became one of the first states to give its cities and towns the right to organize police departments. Baltimore, Boston, Chicago, Cincinnati, Newark, New Orleans and Philadelphia soon followed. And, in what was to differentiate American policing from British policing forever, in 1854 the Philadelphia police began to carry guns.

Although these forces adopted the principles developed in England by Sir Robert Peel, they were, compared to the British police, still unprofessional. Rather than following a clear chain of command up to a commissioner, these early departments quickly became part of the local political machine with appointments and dismissals made at the whim of the party in power.

In some instances, this system had its advantages. Despite, or perhaps due in part to, the patronage nature of their job, often, these early officers were models of what we now know as "community policing." They were the center of social welfare for the neighborhood they patrolled, solving family disputes, making sure the hungry were fed and the poor taken care of. Police "paddy wagons" even doubled as ambulances. More importantly, by being a full-time, identifiable presence, they served as a force for order. At last, in most neighborhoods, there was someone specific to go to to report a disturbance, file a complaint or seek help.

Unfortunately, as politicians continued to dominate the police, the good that was done was often overshadowed by the bad and before long many city police departments were riddled with graft and corruption.

To bring objectivity back to policing, the Pendleton Act was passed in 1883, establishing a civil service commission to oversee entrance examinations, promotions, and grievances within police agencies. But even after the Act went into effect, police were still often poorly trained and supervised. There were countless reports of police brutality and ineptness in solving crimes.

While the East was becoming more urbanized and police forces becoming more structured, the West was still, well, wild. Seldom, if ever in human history had so many people moved in such numbers to settle so vast an unknown (at least to them) territory. They quickly overwhelmed the indigenous people who lived in scattered tribes and did not have the single military force that might have helped them stage an effective resistance.

Legend and scores of cowboy movies would have us believe that the settlers who did not survive were killed by renegade bands of Indians. In fact, a great many died of disease, in childbirth, or simply as a result of living in a sod house with poor sanitation and few amenities or any kind. Furthermore, the social climate in which most settlers had grown up was absent from their new home. There was no local police chief who knew most of the people in the town. Law enforcement was left up to the sheriff, who often had a territory of several hundred miles to patrol. When trouble broke out, the sheriff had to assemble whatever posse he could from the citizens of the nearest town.

The only other presence was that of the US Marshals who enforced federal law in the absence of any other type of criminal justice system. When the citizens were unhappy with the law as it was enforced (or not enforced), they often formed "vigilance committees" which were often little more than mobs who were quick to mete out justice as they saw fit. In frustration with the lack of an established police force, some citizens chose another alternative. In Wyoming in 1892, for example, cattle ranchers feuding with farmers over livestock grazing rights hired 25 professional gunfighters from Texas to help them in their feud with the farmers.

Outlaws like Frank and Jesse James, the Dalton boys and Billy the Kid robbed stagecoaches transporting gold back east. To protect their assets, bankers and the railroads also hired private police organizations like the Pinkerton Detective Agency. But they, too, unencumbered by the law, were pretty much free to get their man by whatever means it took.

As towns in the West became bigger and more settled, full-time police agencies were hired and courts set up to handle disputes. But, in many ways, the die was already cast for the problems that would continue across the country from that time forward.

"Loyalty to the weapon that had helped the colonists win the Revolution and allowed pioneers to brave the frontier remained fervent. Guns were firmly rooted in the American tradition. They had come to symbolize freedom, independence and power, attributes that have often been used to describe America, a nation born and sustained with the help of gunfire."

Meanwhile, in the South, life for many wasn't all that much different from life in the middle ages. Powerful white families owned huge tracts of land, maintained by slaves or poor white sharecroppers. Local towns, populated by middle class whites, existed in part at least to service the plantations. "Free" blacks had scarcely more rights than slaves. As in the East and West, county sheriffs were free to deputize posses when the need arose. But the sheriff was an elected officer, beholden to the only eligible voters, white men. And the white men with the most power and money generally decided how the law would be enforced.

After the Civil War, when the South was occupied by federal troops and governed by northern "carpetbagger" administrators, civil policing was basically suspended, with the army filling the void. The control exercised by the army and northern interlopers combined with the deep-seated feelings over the loss of the war gave rise to the Ku Klux Klan and other secret white supremacist organizations.

By the turn of the century, the United States faced a number of challenges. While the question of what to do to solve these problems would vary from state to state, the solution as to how to solve them would be the same: creation of the state police.

Labor Unrest

One of these problems was labor unrest. Throughout the latter part of the 19th century, the American economy had been growing at a record pace. Inventions such as the sewing machine, harvesting machine, high speed printing press and typewriter had changed American farms and factories forever. By 1890, for the first time, the value of industrial goods was greater than agricultural goods and workers flocked to the cities to find higher paying work. Although jobs were plentiful, workers, especially those who worked for large corporations, were becoming increasingly discontented. From 1880 to 1900, nine million immigrants landed on American shores and many workers feared that they would be replaced by this continuous influx of immigrants who would often work longer hours for less pay.

Others found their jobs being eliminated as machines began to replace manual labor.

Many also became bitter at what they saw as an increasing disparity in wealth between themselves and the owners.

In many industries, companies fed these fears by opposing trade unions, firing workers who joined and refusing to bargain with unions. In this atmosphere, strikes were inevitable.

In 1877 a railroad strike shut down two-thirds of the nation's railways. Violence erupted in Maryland and Pennsylvania. Workers were shot and railroad properties sabotaged. In 1892, seven people were killed in a steel strike in Pennsylvania. In 1894, federal troops were called in to break a strike against the Pullman Company near Chicago.

In the early 1900s, unions staged a series of violent strikes at the nation's coal mines, iron mills, textile factories and railroad yards. The magnitude of such strikes quickly overwhelmed the ability of local police officers to contain the violence. Faced with these strikes, the states tried a variety of tactics.

To provide protection to the coal and steel operators, the Pennsylvania state legislature granted police powers to the Coal and Iron Police, but they were little more than untrained thugs hired by the operators. In 1902, during the Great Anthracite Strike, 140,000 Pennsylvania coal miners walked off the job causing such a coal shortage that President Theodore Roosevelt finally intervened. He sent in federal troops.

Michigan dealt with labor unrest and lawlessness by calling in the state militia.

In West Virginia, strikes in the coal mines resulted in the National Guard being called in, martial law declared and a military tribunal created.

While local police were often involved in providing police protection during strikes, in some cases, local police could not be called out to settle a strike because the police were the ones striking. Such was the case in Boston on September 9, 1919 when 75% of the city force walked off the job.

While the private security forces and state and federal militias often quelled the violence when local police could not, there were many problems associated with using them. Private security forces, paid for by management, stopped the violence but did so by brutalizing the strikers. The military, both state and federal, had the power to stop the violence, but, as soldiers, had no training as peace officers. They had been taught to destroy an enemy by force, not prevent violence. In addition, settling domestic disputes was not their primary objective. States such as Michigan suddenly found themselves without the option of the militia when it was called to active duty in World War I.

The problem was the need for a permanent professional police force, trained to keep the peace that could be mobilized in sufficient

Uniformed Troopers and detectives with confiscated booze during Prohibition, 1924.

Illegal Liquor

A second problem was illegal liquor.

Alcohol for consumption and currency has been as American as apple pie since Colonial days. Even the Puritans, who preached against almost every other kind of pleasurable activity did not outlaw drinking. During the last half of the 18th century, the going price for a muscular slave was twenty gallons of whiskey. Distillers regularly paid a higher price for grain than millers did and babies were often given rum in their bottles to quiet them down. By the 1830s, the consumption of alcohol had reached an estimated 10 gallons per capita per year.

Although there had always been those who advocated temperance, they remained a small minority until the 1850s when a move toward limiting the sale of alcohol, if not prohibiting it altogether, began. In 1851, Maine prohibited the manufacture and sale of "spiritous or intoxicating liquors" that had no medicinal use and by 1855, twelve other states had followed suit.

Although there was not much temperance activity during the Civil War, as soon as the war ended, the rapid increase in saloons (one for every 400 people) by 1870, caused a renewed focus on the problem. In 1873, thousands of women joined the "women's war" against liquor, a battle that was still being waged at the turn of the century.

By 1916, 23 of the 48 states had anti-saloon laws. These laws presented a special challenge to law enforcement, particularly when, during WWI, additional states enacted wartime liquor prohibitions. Since some states were "wet" and others "dry," bootleg-

ging liquor across state lines became a booming industry.

The 18th Amendment to the Constitution, adopted in 1919, went into effect in January 1920 prohibiting the manufacture, importation, transportation or sale of alcoholic beverages nationwide. The Volstead Act, that defined how the new law was to be enforced, made violations of the law federal crimes. The Jones Act of 1929 further stiffened penalties.

Many states also passed laws related to alcohol and the enforcement of these laws added significantly to the workload of local law enforcement personnel. In Columbus, Ohio, in 1929, for example, arrests for violations of liquor laws were 10 times that of arrests for auto theft and 20 times the rate for arrests for robbery. In Virginia, liquor violations dominated all other forms of felony.

Making liquor illegal, of course, did not make it any the less desirable to many Americans. So in addition to coping with liquor laws, local agencies found themselves facing a new and much more menacing problem- organized crime.

Gangsters like Al Capone quickly stepped in to meet the needs of this lucrative market, happily adding bootlegging to its repertoire of other illegal pursuits. And lucrative it was. In 1927, Capone's Chicago-based organization alone realized a $60 million profit.

The illegal liquor business was also deadly. From 1923 to 1926, 215 Chicago gangsters killed each other in competition for the business. From 1919 to 1933, 164 police officers died in the line of duty in Chicago, nearly one officer every month for 15 years.

Local law enforcement agencies, sometimes working with federal agents, were also often involved in shutting down "blind pigs" and speakeasies. But the result was often a Catch 22 situation for them. Many citizens,

contemptuous of the law in the first place, simply ignored law enforcement's efforts and the establishments were up and running again almost as soon as they were shut down.

In some cases, local newspaper reporters served as go-betweens, warning speakeasy operators of impending raids based on tips from law enforcement officers who were careful to spread enforcement around so as not to harm any one proprietor too much. Even when offenders were arrested, they often used their connections in local government to receive little if any punishment. Enforcement efforts became a largely ineffective deterrent.

In many areas, drunkenness before and after Prohibition was not treated as a serious offense.

"The police tended to treat the ordinary drunkard with a kind of amused, vacant paternalism. It was important to arrest drunks, sober them up and keep the streets in shape for respectable people. Often, the police infantilized drunks, who were mostly laborers, and often immigrants; they treated their offenses with malicious humor. This was also the attitude of the newspapers, when they reported the goings on in police court. It was, in a sense, a big joke. Laughing at drunks and skid row bums was one way to avoid taking the problem seriously."

When Prohibition was repealed in 1933, organized crime and criminals did not go away. They merely shifted the focus of their enterprise to gambling, prostitution and drug trafficking. Court records from 1920 to 1930 show that Prohibition agents concentrated their efforts on those they could not shake down - the poor, the barely literate, the recent immigrants least able to defend themselves. The wealthy were virtually immune from prosecution, as were bankers and wealthy entrepreneurs responsible for establishing lucrative contracts with bootlegging investors, often with the complicity of congressmen.

And, as importantly, in this era of widespread police corruption, the problem of enforcing what liquor laws were enacted following Prohibition became state laws. The solution would be the creation of the state police.

Violent Criminals

While urban organized crime bosses like Al Capone specialized in bootlegging, prostitution, gambling and drugs, smaller, but no less dangerous gangs of violent criminals terrorized rural areas robbing banks, gunning down citizens and police, and fleeing across county lines out of the jurisdiction of local law enforcement agencies.

During the late 1920s and early 1930s, Kansas became a haven for criminals such as Bonnie and Clyde, Pretty Boy Floyd, Ma Barker and Alvin Karpis. Between 1932 and 1934, Bonnie and Clyde, alone, killed 10 law enforcement officers from four states.

numbers to make an impact. The solution would be the creation of the state police.

Bank robbers like John Dillinger and the lesser known Brady and Easton gangs were also knocking over Midwestern banks at the rate of one a day. The 1920s and 1930s were also two of the deadliest decades in law enforcement history. An average of 169 law enforcement officers a year died during the 1920s and 165 a year during the 1930s.

While stiff federal laws had been passed relating to these violent criminals in May 1934, these crimes became federal crimes only when the criminals escaped across state lines to avoid prosecution or killed a federal officer. Bank robbers continued to have a heyday rushing across county lines and out of the jurisdiction of the sheriff yet staying within the state, thus eluding federal officers.

The public, many of whom who had been more tolerant of the escapades of criminals during Prohibition, had had enough. They were ready for a professional police agency with statewide jurisdiction.

The solution to this problem would be the creation of the state police.

Growth and Mobility

In addition to the mobility of criminals, the growth and mobility of the population as a whole became a problem for law enforcement. In 1860, the US population was just over 31 million. By 1900 it had more than doubled to 76.2 million and by 1910 it was more than 92 million. Railroads expanded from 30,000 miles of track before the Civil War to 270,000 miles in 1900.

When most people lived in small towns, the local police chief actually knew most of the population. When something happened — a burglary, a runaway teenager, a hit and run accident - the chief or town marshal probably had a pretty good idea who the offender was. But as towns grew into cities and people moved more frequently, communities became considerably less tight knit.

Local enforcement officers of the time were, by today's standards, amateurs. All were elected by the citizens of towns and counties and, not surprisingly, many officers were part of the local political machine. There were few, if any, specific qualifications in most cases. In many areas, it wasn't even necessary for the sheriff to be able to read or write. Little, if any, training was available. Most officers learned their craft on the job or through an informal apprenticeship to an experienced officer. The sheriff or town marshal depended as much on gossip as anything else to solve crimes.

The problem of mobility experienced in small towns was greatly magnified in cities. Cities quickly responded by creating not only large police departments, but by beginning to specialize. Detective squads were organized in Boston in 1846, New York in 1857, Philadelphia in 1859 and Chicago in 1861. By the early 1900s, urban police departments were beginning to experiment with fingerprint identification and other forensic tools. But, unfortunately, many city police departments became corrupt, and the tools of local politicians. In any event, the jurisdiction of city police only extended to the city line. What expertise they did have — politics aside — was not available to the many people who still lived in America's small towns and rural areas.

On Tuesday, October 29, 1929, the American Stock Market crashed and with it the decade that had been known as the "Roaring Twenties." Although only 5% of Americans owned stock, nearly all would be affected by the crash within a few years. As the economy slowed, workers were laid off. From January 1930 to January 1931, unemployment grew from four to eight million. In 1931 another 3 million people lost their jobs. By 1933, 16 million Americans were out of work.

Of particular interest to law enforcement was the fact that an estimated 500,000 young men and women had left home and were roaming the countryside. Then, as now, rootless teenagers were the perpetrators of many crimes.

In both cities and small towns across America even the best local law enforcement forces could no longer cope with the numbers of people on the move. They needed an agency with state-wide jurisdiction. The solution would be the state police.

Automobile Traffic

The increase in automobile traffic was another factor in the creation of the state police.

Although the first gasoline powered automobile had been invented by Karl Benz in Germany in 1885, for more than 20 years, the automobile was a novelty affordable to only the very rich. But in the early years of the twentieth century The Ford Motor Company changed all that. Between 1903 and 1908, Ford developed a series of cars, designating each model with a letter of the alphabet, beginning with A. By the time the company got to the Model N, a small, light four-cylinder machine, the unit price had dropped from more than $2,500 to $500 and this mechanical marvel was within the reach of most families. In 1908, General Motors had also begun producing automobiles offering buyers a choice among Buicks, Cadillacs, Oldsmobiles and Chevrolets. By 1925, buyers could also choose a Chrysler.

Americans took to the roads in huge numbers. In 1900 there were only 8,000 automobiles in the US. By 1905, that number had grown to 77,000, by 1910 to 450,000 and 1920 to more than 8 million. Local police agencies were quickly faced with hundreds of auto crashes, drunk driving violations and a new crime - auto theft.

Most states enacted laws relating to ownership, driving age, and speed limits in various locations and circumstances. Sixteen generally became the minimum age for operating a motor vehicle but a driver's license, as such, was not always required. In New York in 1910 the law required all drivers to "drive in a careful and prudent manner and at a rate or speed so as not to endanger property, life or limb. Any speed over 30 mph if persisted in for a quarter mile or more was presumptive evidence of careless, imprudent driving. The statute also made hit and run a felony."

The local police now had dozens of new laws to enforce. And, for the first time in history, average otherwise law-abiding Americans were faced with the likelihood of committing a crime.

In some states, like Alabama, the first highway patrol officers were also given responsibility for providing driver's license testing. Early tests included a driving examination, knowledge of highway rules and "attitude toward law and highway safety." Driver's licenses then, as now, were issued for a specific period of time and files were kept of each driver's record of offenses.

Throughout the 1920s the cities continued to grow and access to cities also became easier thanks to the automobile. Millions of Americans settled in suburbs created either when cities expanded to include small towns or new "subdivisions" were built.

The advent of the automobile also brought with it a new and more dangerous way for the intoxicated to violate the law. Most states made it at least a misdemeanor to operate a motor vehicle while intoxicated and many imposed more severe penalties for subsequent offenses

WANTED

JOHN HERBERT DILLINGER

$10,000.00
for the capture of John Herbert Dillinger or a reward of

$5,000.00
for information leading to the arrest of John Herbert Dillinger.

or causing bodily injury or death to someone else while driving under the influence.

Most of these laws were state laws. States that did not already have a state police found that they now needed one.

Vigilantes and Hate Groups

By the time state police agencies were founded, the tradition of taking the law into one's own hands was also well established. Indeed, the laws that have always protected the right of Americans to gather peacefully in a "good" cause, have also protected those whose motives may be much different.

There is little doubt that America has always been (and still is) a violent society. Although there was actually very little violent crime in Colonial settlements, the punishment for even the most petty offense was violent - often a public whipping. In Salem, Massachusetts in 1692 , a vigilante group publicly executed 19 townspeople who were thought to be witches.

While slaveholders were not allowed to murder their slaves, they were certainly allowed to beat them and many did, publicly and frequently. During the 1780s Colonel Charles Lynch, from whom we have derived the term "lynching," regularly rounded up wrongdoers and dispensed his brand of justice under a large tree in his front yard.

In the West in the 1800s citizens had taken the law in their own hands basically because there was no one else to do it. The posse, although a legal law enforcement entity, was often little more than an angry mob. The justice posses dispensed was often swift and violent. It was not unusual for a posse to catch a criminal, try him and hang him all on the same day.

The West wasn't the only place where violence was a fact of every day life. Between 1884 and 1900, more than 2,500 Americans (more than were legally executed) were lynched by their fellow citizens. The majority of those killed were African Americans in the South.

The term "vigilante," had actually first appeared in San Francisco during the 1850s when groups of citizens formed "vigilance committees" to try to contain the huge increase in crime brought on by the gold rush. But perhaps the most infamous of all vigilante groups was the Ku Klux Klan, a white supremacist group founded in Tennessee in 1865 by some bored ex-confederate soldiers. (see sidebar).

The "whitecappers" were a variant of the Klan. Originating in southern Indiana in 1887, the movement spread quickly. Unlike the Klan, the whitecappers were not racists, but rather moral crusaders and women were often members. In one celebrated incident, twelve members of the Women's Christian Temperance Union in Osceola, Nebraska in 1893, donned their white hoods, and flogged "certain young ladies" whose activities they considered immoral.

By the early 1900s, it became obvious that states would continue to have problems with vigilante and hate groups. Unfortunately, in many communities, in every part of the country, local hate groups like the Klan often had the support, if not encouragement of local law enforcement. And because the crimes these groups committed — murder, arson, battery — were state crimes, the federal government had no jurisdiction over them.

If hate crimes were to be stopped, it would take a state police agency to do it.

Politics

Because law enforcement officers at all levels were appointed by local government officials, it is not surprising that from the beginning law enforcement in the United States was tied to politics and prone to corruption.

One early state police publication said: "In the very early stages of police work, officers were selected on the basis that 'it takes a crook to catch a crook' and the major difference between the underworld and the police was the difference between public and private enterprise. Politicians secured valuable aid from their allies in the world of vice and gangsterism and wanted police forces that would cooperate rather than obliterate anti-social forces. As long as the taxpayer was purchasing protection which he never obtained, police work could not reach the dignity of an established profession."

While the most famous example of police corruption was probably that of the New York City police during the administration of "Boss Tweed," the problem was by no means limited to New York, or even to large cities. As long as jobs depended on patronage, those with the power to hire would be able to command both who was hired and what they did once employed.

In the late 1800s, The Lexow Committee in New York found that in "most precincts of the city, houses of ill-repute, gambling houses, policy shops, pool rooms and unlawful resorts of a similar character were openly conducted under the noses of the police." In general, brothels were subject to "blackmail," and the police permitted "professional abortionists to ply their awful trade."

To clean up these corrupt forces, many cities made their police agencies part of the civil service system and by 1915, 122 of the nation's 204 largest police departments were regulated as such.

The influence of politics was by no means eliminated from the police, but it was clear that the public at least wanted its future police agencies to maintain as much distance as possible. What the states really needed was a professional and objective state police.

Lack of Coordination Among Agencies

Ironically, as the nation grew, the problem in many states became not too little law enforcement, but too much. "As cities grew with their attendant criminal problems, city police systems were inaugurated and expanded until there were hundreds of county and municipal police authorities seeking to stem the growing tide of criminal depredations, all of them acting independently and with very little correlation of effort."

Postal inspectors, the Secret Service and the Treasury Department had both interstate and intrastate authority, but they could act only when violations of federal laws were committed. "As far as murderers, bank robbers, kidnappers, forgers, arsonists, rapists and other major crimes were concerned, the crossing of the state line was a virtual sanctuary, subject only to the uncertainties of extradition from a distant state if the pursuit actually enlisted enough cooperation to secure a capture."

As is detailed later in the section on communications, even when these agencies wanted to coordinate efforts, because they had only the most rudimentary radio systems they had no really effective way to communicate in anything like a timely manner.

Even where there were sufficient numbers of police officers of one kind or another, in many instances they simply did not have the right resources or organization to meet the growing and changing challenges of twentieth century policing. The answer for the states would be a state police force.

Police Brutality

As long as there have been police, it was assumed that at least some force is necessary to control criminals. Although by the 1800s in most cities police personnel stopped short of public whipping or lynching wrongdoers. the "third degree" was common up to the end of the 19th Century. Police routinely beat and tortured criminals with metal pipes and fists to elicit confessions. Later, after the public began to complain, many police switched to bright lights and rubber hoses that didn't leave visible marks — but the intent was the same.

One of the problems was the military mindset. Police agencies in cities organized along semi military lines behaved, in many ways, like soldiers. But there was supposed to be a difference.

"Police were intended to be different from the military, which uses deadly force against an enemy that threatens national interests. Police are generally expected to use limited force, when force is needed, although not against an enemy."

As John Alderson said in his 1985 book, The Listener, "The difference between the quasi-military and the civil policeman is that the civil policeman should have no enemies. People may be criminals, they may be violent, but they are not enemies to be destroyed."

Yet, because of these tactics, by the early 1900s many citizens were more afraid of the police than they were of criminals. It became apparent that a new type of police officer with a better knowledge of how to handle violent behavior was needed. That new type of police would be the state police.

The Need for Professionalism

To address the many of the problems that all communities were facing regarding their police forces, by the mid 1800s, rule books and codes of conduct for police were beginning to appear.

With the switch to civil service status came the need for qualifications by police, but by today's standards, they were fairly forgiving. Some rules were made primarily for the sake of appearances. In Chicago in 1861, for example, mustaches were prohibited, a proper style for beards was outlined and all patrolmen were required to eat with forks.

Although all officers had to pass the civil service requirement, other than that, most departments demanded only a height and weight requirement and an elementary education.

August Vollmer, the Berkeley California Town Marshal is credited with at last bringing professionalism to US police in the early 1900s. Among other things, he put his patrolmen in cars, installed a radio communications system, developed a crime lab and a system of classifying criminals via their modus operandi, established a police school and recruited college educated men to be police officers. Later as Los Angeles Police Chief he required all officers to undergo intelligence tests as a basis for promotion. He advocated cooperation between social agencies in the police in dealing with juvenile delinquency and campaigned for more humane conditions for prisoners. It was his belief that drug addiction was a medical, not a police problem.[5] In the ensuing years some, but certainly not all, of his ideals became reality in American police departments.

All of these factors combined to vividly illustrate the need for a much more sophisticated and professional police force with state-wide jurisdiction. Gone forever were the days when the locally elected sheriff with virtually no training, scanty if any communication system and no forensic lab could hope to combat the growing numbers and sophistication of the states' criminals.

In 1923, in a speech to the General Assembly, Missouri Governor Arthur M. Hyde said: "The best machinery for law enforcement by state authority yet devised is a state police force. Such a police force can be trained. It is not hampered by county line. It can police and protect the state highways. Its sole reason for existence would then be to enforce the law equally and equitably in every county of the state, and without fear or favor to protect every citizen in the exercise of his right to life, liberty and property."

The Creation of the State Police

Later in this book, the history of each of the state police agencies is presented in detail. Because they were formed over a period of nearly 50 years and each responded to the specific needs of that state at that time, it is not possible to present a universally accurate picture. Yet, there were, and continue to be, common threads that join them all.

Qualifications

Although many agencies would be embroiled in politics for years to come, as state police were created, in general, the patronage system disappeared. True, many departments continued to insist that officers declare their political affiliation, but most at least tried to maintain a political balance. All recruits, regardless of their political views, were required to meet certain standards.

In some states only single men were allowed to apply and serve. Most states had an educational requirement. Most also had age, height and weight requirements. Men generally had to be at least 5'9" tall, weigh at least 150 pounds and be between the ages of 21 and 35. All also had to be in good physical health, free from venereal diseases, "organic and functional defects" and "of good moral character." Most were interviewed, investigated, their references checked and fingerprints verified with

Ohio State Trooper.

The first Indiana State Police posts were built in 1937 by the WPA at a cost of $16,494. Two are still in use today.

Georgia troopers Mink and Forehand.

Range at Headquarters.

Academy class, Mapes Hall.

the FBI. Some, but not all states also required a period of state residency.

One early state police recruitment brochure advertised for "men with the patience of Job and the judgement of Solomon, possessing the knowledge of an attorney, the movements of an athlete, the concern and skill of a physician, the training of a social worker, an engineer, a psychologist, a chemist, a sportsman and a gentleman — all in one dynamic personality."

In addition to physical, mental and moral requirements, most departments also regulated what an officer could do off-duty. Most, for example, could not enter taverns (except in performance of duty) or associate with persons of questionable character. Charges could be brought against officers who were known to frequent "disorderly houses," gambled or sought public office.

In most states, troopers also had to agree to live anywhere in the state and many faced frequent transfers, sometimes as often as every six months.

All state police agencies were (and re-

main) semi military organizations and as such, officers were subject to a much stricter supervision than other state employees. Men assigned to a barracks often could not leave unless they had the commander's permission.

Men would have to agree to live in the barracks for at least a few days a month and be on-call 24-hours a day. The average workday was generally 12 to 16 hours and most officers worked six days a week or in revolving shifts. As crimes and periods of heavy traffic tended to occur on holidays, few troopers were given time off to spend them with their families. Some troopers on duty at a roadblock slept in their cars, with local farmers bringing them food and others often camped out in fields and forests.

But the stringent requirements paid off.

Wrote one early state police publication, "As careful selection by competent police officers has begun to weed out the treacherous and ignorant and training and science has put scientific instruments for arriving at the truth in the hands of men capable of using them, integrity has replaced deceit, public service has

supplanted scandalous public graft and social ethics have triumphed over special privilege. With these steps, police work has arisen as an eagerly sought and honorable profession."

A Paramilitary Organization

Although early-on most states had recognized the limitations of having their state-wide law enforcement needs met by the military, most saw the advantage of a force that was organized like the military. Although the agencies would provide a wide variety of services, the states wanted their state police to follow the same basic procedures. Reports and forms would be standardized and officers would follow a printed set of standard operating procedures (SOPs) that would be consistent across the state.

The state police would wear uniforms and be subject to inspections by superiors. They would also use rank to designate authority, following, in general the system used by the military.

And, perhaps most importantly, they would follow a chain of command. Each officer would be directly accountable only to the person holding the next highest rank. The buck would stop with the man at the top, who, himself, generally reported directly to the governor of the state. Although some agencies quickly became known as "the governor's police," at least they were free from the influences and temptations of local political machines.

Training

Stringent training was another thing that set the state police apart from all other police agencies of the time. While many other police officers had merely to pass a few physical tests and learn how to shoot a gun, the state police in every state underwent at least several weeks of rigorous instruction.

Since they were a para-military organization, most were trained like soldiers. They slept in tents, were awakened early, marched to and from meals and classes, wore uniforms, saluted senior officers and learned to say, "Yes, sir!" Like soldiers they also did calisthenics, learned to shoot a variety of firearms and had to pass inspections of their living facilities and gear. They would also follow the military model, designed to impress recruits with the need to conform to the norms of the organization and follow orders. Individuality was discouraged. Competency according to the rules was praised.

But there the similarity ended. Unlike soldiers they were not being trained to destroy a foreign enemy. The people they would encounter in their profession would be fellow citizens and they needed to be compassionate to the innocent and understand the guilty. They would also need to learn how to avoid the temptations the job would present.

As an early state police publication said, "In their training for police work, the rookie officers study social evils leading to the creation of outlaws, as well as abnormal psychology of the crime of passion, the feeble minded, the psychopathic or the insane type and the person who simply cannot adjust himself to difficult circumstances. In the study of the job ahead, state policemen consider the widely developed lures of commercialized vice, with its attractions of distorted movies, reams of spurious sex literature on the news stands, vicious marijuana cigarette peddlers in the high schools, slot machines, pool ticket rackets and other gambling devices."

Although most state police recruits received considerably more initial training than local law enforcement officers, rookies were also put on a year's probation during which time they would essentially apprentice with an experienced officer. After that year, they and their fellow officers, unlike almost all other police agencies at the time, would undergo refresher courses on a regular basis for the rest of their career.

The State Police Uniform

Many state police agencies were hastily organized and often underfunded, so often the early troopers were required to buy their own uniforms and sometimes their own guns. Since many of them rode horses or motorcycles, the uniform often consisted of a wool jacket, breeches and high boots. In some instances, this uniform was designed not so much for practicality as for appearance as many departments modeled their uniform after that worn by the Royal Canadian Mounted Police.

Because the state police were a new force, it was important that the public easily recognize who they were. Thus, except in the coldest weather, many early troopers did not even wear overcoats. Those riding horses or motorcycles without windshields had to insulate their uniforms with folded newspapers to keep from freezing to death as they sped down the highway. In the summer they sweltered under a thick wool jacket.

Eventually all agencies provided uniforms for their troopers. Most uniforms were gray, blue or green to distinguish police officers from members of the military. George Chandler, the first superintendent of the NYSP is said to have chosen gray because it was a mixture of black and white, symbolic of good and evil Chandler felt that each trooper would meet in his travels.

Whatever its color, the uniform consisted of a distinctive hat, jacket, breeches or trousers and boots. Motorcycle officers often also received heavy leather gloves and leather jackets. Some, like the Delaware State Police uniform, included putters and high shoes and a Stetson hat.

As one early state police publication said, "Troopers wear the distinctive uniform for three reasons: to identify the man to the public, to represent authority and to publicize the presence of a police officer as a deterrent to wrong doing. While the uniform may be feared by the guilty, it also exists for the safety of the upright."

Officers were also generally issued a .38 caliber revolver, a pair of handcuffs and often a shotgun. In what was considered a radical move at the time, New York State Police Su-

New Mexico State Police, Service School. 1937.

Louisiana Troopers.

Louisiana State Troopers.

Ohio State Highway Patrolman helps small child.

Louisiana State Trooper.

1931 Model A. Ford, Arizona Highway Patrol car.

20

erintendent Geroge Fletcher Chandler ordered
s men to wear their pistol on a belt outside
eir uniforms. Afterwards many had cross-
aw holsters, others had swivel holsters worn
1 the side of the shooting hand.

In some states the uniform reflected the
atus of the officer. In New Mexico, for ex-
mple, patrolmen with less than five years on
e job (known as junior patrolmen) wore uni-
rms with silver buttons and trim. After five
ears they became senior patrolmen and wore
old buttons and trim.

As the use of motorcycles diminished, tall
oots and breeches were replaced by trousers
d dark shoes, although many officers still
ore wool uniforms in both winter and sum-
er. It wasn't until after World War II that
ost agencies provided troopers with lighter
eight uniforms for summer and warmer over-
oats for winter.

Although the "Smokey the Bear" or cam-
aign hat is the hat most commonly identified
being a state trooper hat, early troopers wore
variety of headgear. Some agencies wore
garrison" hats, some Stetsons and others even
raw hats.

Nothing, however, was more distinctive
each agency than its shoulder patch. Al-
ough some states have changed patches over
e years, all wore them proudly from the be-
inning.

raffic

Regardless of what form a state police
gency would eventually assume, all agencies
ad, and continue to have, one responsibility
common — traffic. As one early state po-
ce publication put it, "No war need be more
eared that the daily battle in our streets and
ighways. Death strikes indiscriminately at
en, women and children, the weak, the help-
ess or the aged. The conflict knows no battle
ne, for tragedy can strike anywhere."

While Americans were prepared to accept
asualties in war and most were largely unaf-
ected by deaths among violent criminals, the
eaths of ordinary citizens like themselves and,
orse yet, innocent family members, was
omething else again.

By the 1930s, traffic deaths had ex-
eeded the numbers of soldiers killed in
World War I. By 1937, there were 40,000
eaths a year on the nation's highways and
e country's state police were largely given
e responsibility of doing something about
is alarming trend.

It quickly became apparent that the role
f the state police officer would involve far
ore than a fast car and a ready ticket book.

Each state police officer was taught to
anage traffic, administer first aid, investigate
n accident, comfort the wounded, administer
runkometer tests and, above all, act quickly,
almly and courteously.

Louisiana State Police.

Once out on the road, he was expected to
enforce speeding laws, but to do so with professionalism. He had been taught that "a
courteous reminder of traffic regulations
corrects more bad driving practices and wins
more friends for law enforcement than were
ever favorably influenced by bludgeoning
tactics."

Most early state police had the option of
issuing either a traffic citation or a warning
ticket to any person stopped for speeding. And,
as now, records were kept and penalties could
be imposed on a repeat offender. Likewise,
suspensions for drivers could result from the
accumulation of too many tickets.

Some state police officers were also responsible for testing drivers for licenses and
although the requirements varied from state to
state, they included mental examinations,
physical tests, knowledge of the rules of the
road and a driving test.

Whereas in the earliest days of traffic enforcement, bribes to local law enforcement
officers were common, most states soon set up
a procedure for fines to be handled by justices
of the peace or other courts. State police of-

ficers were specifically barred from receiving
a "cut" of any fines assessed.

In 1932, Northwestern University in cooperation with the International Association of
Chiefs of Police created a Traffic Institute,
whose main focus was (and is) to study the
causes of traffic accidents and train police officers in traffic safety and accident investigation. State police from across the country attended these schools and returned to their communities to share the information with local
agencies.

In the late 1930s most states also enacted
specific traffic requirements. Pedestrian responsibility was outlined, hitch hiking curbed,
reckless homicide and reckless driving defined.
Many state police agencies even produced
booklets explaining these new laws in "plain
language."

Violent Criminals

Although crime had always been a problem in the early 1920s and 1930s, it was, in
the minds of many, becoming an epidemic. It

was estimated that "during every minute of the day and night the forces of the underworld extort $28,500 from American citizens — a total of $1.7 million every hour and $15 billion every year. But money was only part of the problem. In addition one in 84 people suffered injury or death as a result of criminal activity every year. There were 152 robberies, 850 burglaries, 2,307 thefts and 488 car thefts every day."

Then, as now, the greatest number of offenders were males between the ages of 18 and 25. Nineteen year olds were consistently the most violent. Overall, the ratio of male-female criminals was nine to one, although women committed almost as many larcenies and auto thefts as men.

Then, too, most criminals were from the "lower social ranks," and the earliest state police officers recognized the correlation between crime and poverty. The repeat offender was a problem, as well.

Although apprehending criminals was the primary mission of early troopers, crime prevention was certainly a secondary goal.

Many early highway patrol officers had been strictly that. They could chase down speeders, but could not arrest a criminal unless he had also committed a traffic offense. In the early 1930s, as lawlessness following the repeal of Prohibition rose, most states granted their state police officers full arrest powers.

These powers, combined with the newly implement state wide radio system, allowed them to provide for the first time what became an invaluable service — the coordination of local and county agencies in the pursuit of criminals.

As a robber fled from county to county, the state police radio system mobilized troopers, city police and sheriffs and roadblocks were set up. If the criminal fled across the state line, the trooper could continue in hot pursuit, secure in the cooperation of the state police in the next state. If necessary, state police could also alert federal officers and a nation-wide manhunt could begin.

Criminal Identification

The creation of an "Identification Section" by the state police represented another move toward interagency cooperation in most states. Just as the establishment of a state wide police radio system greatly enhanced the ability of all agencies to apprehend fugitives, the identification system at last provided a central clearing house for identification of the state's increasingly mobile criminals.

In most states at least one officer in each geographical district was trained as a fingerprint expert. Any officer, local, county or state, could call upon this expert to collect fingerprints at a crime scene, send them off to the state police fingerprint file for comparison or even on to the FBI.

The War on Drugs

Although enforcing laws relating to illegal liquor had been one of the major factors in the creation of the state police, most agencies quickly became involved in enforcement of drug laws as well.

In the mid 1920s, marijuana began working its way up from Mexico. As today, teenagers were the primary target of drug dealers and soon "reefer" was almost as common as beer at teenage parties.

Most states quickly passed laws regarding the production, distribution, possession and use of this drug and the state police were pressed into service in an enterprise most still pursue today.

Logistical Support

As state police agencies geared up for the war on crime and traffic, like most "armies" they realized the need for logistical support. Although some contracted out these services, most soon added garages, mechanics, warehouses and quartermasters to their force. Then, as now, these functions, while under the supervision of uniformed officers are now primarily civilian functions.

Records & Accident Reports

When traffic deaths began mounting, citizens looked to the state police to make their roads safer. Early on, state police agencies realized that accomplish this task, they would need to know just where, when and by whom these accidents were occurring and see if they could establish patterns around which to launch prevention campaigns.

Most states passed accident reporting laws. A dollar figure was attached and a deadline set for filing the report. If a state police officer was on the scene, he, too, submitted a report. This accident record information was made available to citizens, the courts and insurance companies.

Within a year or so, most departments had amassed tens of thousands of reports that were analyzed, coded and the data punched onto cards. Tabulating machines provided a statistical picture of accidents in the state. Most states put his information to immediate use assigning officers to the areas where the most

Georgia State Patrol headquarters.

accidents were occurring. The concept of "selective enforcement" was born.

Then, as now, the accident records department of most agencies was supervised by a state police officer but most of the personnel were civilians.

Criminal Reports

Before 1900, very few records on crime were kept. Maine, Massachusetts and New York were the first states to collect crime statistics and in the early 1900s, the International Associations of Chiefs of Police created a Committee on Uniform Crime Reports. In 1930, the US Attorney General designated the FBI to serve as the national clearinghouse for data collected by the Uniform Crime Reports project.

By then, most states with state police agencies had also been collecting information on criminals both from state police officers and other law enforcement agencies in the state. Generally, the criminal record contained both the details of the crime and arrest and a fingerprint card. These files were made available not only to state police officers but also to other law enforcement agencies. In some states a "limited" criminal history was (and is) available to employers and individuals on whom the file is being kept.

Communications

In the early part of the century, as today, time was of the essence in catching criminals. Literally every minute counted, as the robber or murderer committed his crime, jumped in his car and sped off to parts unknown. Yet, because even a rudimentary radio system was still years away, time was actually the enemy of the first state police.

Some of the very first state police officers received their messages by mail and the criminals escaping from them had, at the least, several days head start. Other troopers received messages passed along by local sheriffs, which often wasn't much faster.

Troopers on horseback, like those in New York, fanned out in pairs from substations created in rooming houses or hotels established in each county. If an emergency arose, a call would be placed to the next stop and a message left for the patrol. Local telephone operators informed everyone on the party lines along the route to flag the patrol down and call them in. An arrangement was made with the telephone company in 1921 that anyone could pick up a telephone and ask for the New York State Troopers. Needless to say, there wasn't much in the way of confidential information in those days

Officers on patrol in the early 1920s could at least maintain contact with the post or barracks by telephone. But when the post wanted to contact an officer, it would have to call a

store or gas station along the officer's route. In some states, the officer made routine stops at a predetermined time. Some have opined that this practice was the origin of the police connection to doughnuts, as phones in bakeries were especially handy since they tended to be open late at night and early in the morning.

In other states, a proprietor would raise a flag or other signal and the officer would know that a message was waiting. In Delaware, 42 gas stations were selected and their telephone numbers printed in the Wilmington Evening Journal. Anyone who wanted to see a police officer would call the nearest station and the attendant would put up a red flag. The officer would then stop to see what the problem might be. Patrolmen in Kansas were instructed to listen to a commercial radio station in Topeka to receive information.

In 1923, the Pennsylvania State Police installed the nation's first statewide police radio telegraph system which remained operational until 1947.

In 1927, the Pennsylvania State Police established public radio station WBAK in Harrisburg and in 1933 began operating its own AM radio station and in 1930. WRDS in Michigan created the first State Police radio system. In the late 1920s, the Connecticut State Police installed the first FM three-way mobile statewide stem in the world.

By the early to mid-1930s, most police agencies had installed a low watt AM radio band that transmitted from a 200 foot tower next to the transmitting station. Transmitting stations were connected by dedicated wire lines that provided transmitter and receiver control, voice transmission and private teletype communications. At least one licensed radio operator was on duty 24-hours a day, seven days a week, including holidays.

While the AM radios were a definite improvement, they still presented security problems. "Just about anybody could listen to the broadcasts," said Dispatcher Jerry Bushore who began service with the Indiana State Police in 1940. "The public and even the gangsters could listen in to what we were saying."

The transmitting stations also housed a radiotelephone transmitter and receiver to communicate with mobile and base radio units, including intrastate and interstate radio telegraph communications. The communications center was generally referred to as "Dispatch."

In some states, the dispatch room had a large map of the state with more than 3000 lights identifying various areas around the state including barracks or posts and other government buildings. Officers from other agencies were identified by different colored lights.

"When we would dispatch a trooper somewhere, we would put the light on dim," said Fletcher Hancock, the Chief Clerk of the Indiana State Police who operated such a system in 1935. "Then when he arrived, we would push the plug all the way in and the light would

Maryland State Police. TFC Roland C. Cothorne II.

be bright. The white lights gave the location of the troopers. The red lights meant emergency."

Dispatch rooms were also often equipped with "teleautograph" machines, connected to the motor vehicles bureau. The operator would write a request for information with a special pen attached to an electrically operated moving arm that produced the request and answer on paper tape at each location, allowing for electrical transmission of actual handwriting.

In the late 1930s, teletype machines began to appear in state police radio rooms. Developed to comply with Federal Communication Commission regulations prohibiting the rebroadcast of police bulletins, the teletype was provided as an auxiliary service of the telephone company. The teletype not only allowed person- to- person messages to be sent, but also the same message to be sent to more than one destination simultaneously. A permanent typed record of the conversation was produced.

Even with the teletype in place, many departments continued to operate a CW (Morse Code/Network) because it was generally cheaper to operate than commercial telephones. Although a good operator could send and receive code at 40-50 words a minute, dissemination of information was still one-way. Troopers could receive information, but until two-way radios were installed in 1941, could not respond. An early form of facsimile transmission was also used, sending a printed tape to the patrol officer in the car.

The first mobile radio installations were made in the 1940s. Still, they were far from perfect. In bad weather there was still so much static it was difficult to hear what was being transmitted. And even in good weather, troopers found that they often had to go to the top of a hill so their signal would go through.

By the mid 1940s, state police radio stations housed transmitters for several frequencies and the height of transmitting towers was increased from 200 feet to 300-400 feet. In some states, three-way radio equipment was being tested, connecting the radio stations, patrol cars and aircraft.

In November, 1945, the first coding system (later to become the 10-code system) was created.

In the late 1940s, most agencies switched to the FM band. Many agencies assigned call letters to their stations, similar to commercial radio stations.

By the early 1950s, 3,000- watt power amplifiers began to replace the 250- watt transmitters and repeater stations were being installed to strengthen incoming signals and eliminate dead spots.

In the late 1950s, Virginia, Arizona and Indiana became the first states to install state-wide microwave systems, which provided both telephone and teletype communications. The microwave was a "closed" radio system" transmitting point-to-point in a much more economical manner than commercial telephone lines. .

In the mid 1960s, the National Law Enforcement Telecommunications System (NLETS) was created and in 1968, departments were linked with the National Crime Information Center (NCIC), providing for the first time, nearly instantaneous access to information on wanted criminals nationwide.

In 1970, most agencies upgraded microwave systems to more than 400 channels and two-frequency mobile radios were replaced with four-frequency scan units. Officers were also issued the first mobile radio extension systems (MREs) which for the first time allowed officers to maintain communications with the post and other cars when out of their cars

During the 1970s, most state police departments implemented statewide computerized filing systems as well as portable/mobile radio repeater system and mutual aid communications networks. Some also created a communications network developed between the state police and amateur and citizens band radio organizations.

Now, most states are also connected to a wide variety of information services through the Internet and E-mail and most now have Web pages, providing both other agencies and the public with up-to-date information. In the testing stages are global positioning devices for patrol cars.

With all the communications capability, however, problems continue to plague departments who have not fully converted to the 800 MHz system. Some cars have low band, some high band, some 800 MHz. In many cases, officers find it possible to communicate best by going back to the technology of the 1930s and simply use their phone.

Investigations

Although Edgar Allen Poe is credited with sparking the American public's interest in detective work in his stories The Gold Bug and Murder in the Rue Morgue, detectives and their stories were not a new concept in law enforcement. They had existed for years in Europe where certain constables who chased down criminals were known as "thief takers." Their job was to get property back to the owner — for a price, no questions asked.

Allan Pinkerton was probably the first detective most Americans knew anything about and he is sometimes credited with laying the foundation for the science of criminal investigation.

As they were being created, most state police agencies, with the exception of those whose responsibility was strictly highway patrol, started an investigations bureau.

While the patrolman wore a uniform to make his presence known, the detective, even from the first was primarily a plainclothes officer. As one early state police publication put it,

"The plainclothesman lives and acts behind the scenes. He does not exhibit the shining mark of his authority as does the uniformed officer. His salary may not be commensurate with the amounts of which his talents might earn in business or industry. He does not and cannot live the life of the ordinary private citizen. His greatest recompense is the love of the work. He gains immeasurable satisfaction from his share in the task of ferreting out the unfortunate, but godless human derelicts whom J. Edgar Hoover eloquently terms 'the rats.' And, if a state police detective or any other officer worthy of this job fails to get his man, it is usually an honest failure, for he wants to succeed with a completeness fully equal to that desired by the public whom he serves."

Fire Marshal Detective investigating arson scene.

1950's: Note dual shoulder belts and dash mounted speedometer.

The State Police Crime Laboratory

Although the most famous crime lab in history was probably the living room of Sherlock Holmes and Doctor Watson at 224B Baker Street in London, the first real crime lab was established in Lyon, France in 1910 by Edmond Locard, a physician, who convinced local police to use the scientific method to investigate crime. Locard believed that individuals could not enter an area without leaving something behind or picking up something from the scene. Locard's Exchange Principle was the beginning of the study of "trace evidence."

Using Locard's Principle and other early techniques, the first real crime lab in the United States was created in 1923 in Los Angeles by August Vollmer. As State Police agencies were formed across the country, most quickly set up labs of their own, using all the state-of-the-art technologies of the time.

Hypnosis and "truth serum" were apparently used occasionally, but word association was a much more common test. Single words were spoken to a suspect who was asked to reply with the first word that came to mind. Investigators noted not just the word but also kept careful track of the time it took to reply. Hesitation was considered a sure sign of guilt.

Bloodstains, poisons and stomach contents could be examined at most labs, although many agencies relied on the toxicology labs of nearby universities. Suspect packages could be X-rayed before being opened, as could bodies to see if there were any bullets lodged within.

"Ultra violet ray machines," were used to examine fraudulent checks and fingerprints on cloth or paper could be "developed" under the violet ray after being sprayed with silver nitrate.

Teeth marks, tire patterns, "jimmy marks" and even the dead faces of executed or murdered men were preserved by the process of "moulage reproduction," in which a thin plastic was poured over the item or face. Moulage had replaced plaster of Paris which was found to be so heavy that it often destroyed the evidence it was trying to preserve.

Early state police crime labs also often built four by five view cameras piece by piece and distributed them to troopers in the field. Mug shots were taken by these Graflex cameras and the film developed in darkrooms located in barracks or posts as well as at the central lab. In 1939, the Indiana State Police constructed the first color mug shot by placing four negatives from a graphic camera together to create a color separation. The photo was produced by lithography.

Many police detectives in the 1930s also experimented with the new scientific technique of developing a "modus operandi." Some

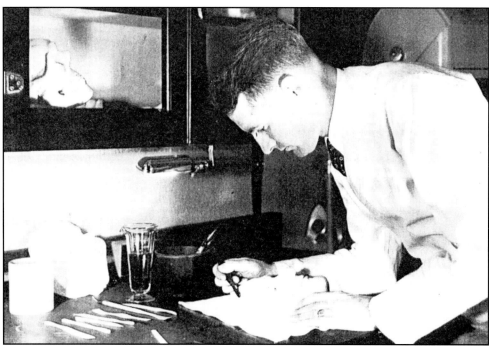
Finishing a death mask of Harry Singer, executed murderer.

1940's Michigan State Police fingerprint technicians.

states created a mechanized modus operandi system in which felonious acts were divided into their constituent elements, tabulated on a card for that particular type of crime and filed under categories. A detective on the trail of a criminal could place the cards in a sorting machine and be presented with a ready list of suspects.

The book "Questioned Documents" written by Albert S. Osborn in 1910 provided the basics for the establishment of a questioned documents section at even the earliest state police crime labs. From the beginning scientists could testify as to the identity of criminals from handwriting samples and spot attempts at forgery. They could even lift handwriting from the indentations left on pages below, compare documents written on type-

writers and decipher alternations in checks and other legal documents.

As in all areas of forensic science, questioned documents examiners have greatly increased the accuracy of their craft through the use of technology. Today the Electrostatic Detection apparatus is used to produce a visual image of indented writing on transparency film. The Video Spectral Comparator allows examiners to examine documents through infrared illumination and spot the slightest differences in inks and papers.

Although early in the 1900s Caesar Lombroso and Angelo Masso had suggested that both blood pressure and respiration changed markedly in reaction to stress and could thus be used as indicators of guilt or innocence, they were not able to create a device to consistently and accurately measure these activities. In 1932, Professor Leonard Keeler of Northwestern University law school succeeded where Lombroso and Masso had failed and the first practical and reliable polygraph was developed. State police labs were quick to add these machines to their store of forensic tools and continued to use pretty much the same machine to the present, although now many are replacing them with laptop computers.

The science of toxicology was founded by Mathieu Orfila a Spaniard teaching medicine in France, who, in 1814 published the first scientific treatise on the detection of poisons and their effects on animals.

In 1901, Dr. Karl Landsteiner discovered that blood could be grouped into different groups (A, B, AB and O). Dr. Leone Lattes, a professor at the Institute of Forensic Medicine at the University of Turin in 1915 devised a simple procedure for determining the blood group of a dried bloodstain a technique that he applied to criminal investigations. Both toxicology and serology were both a part of early crime labs and continue to be an important tool in the detection of crime.

In 1941, a mobile crime laboratory, the first of its kind by a police agency was put into service in Illinois. Since then all state police crime labs have vans equipped with state-of-the-art (and some not so state-of-the-art) equipment. With them, crime scene technicians can stay at the scene of the crime as long as is necessary, collecting and cataloging evidence that will later be taken to the lab for analysis.

While fingerprint identification is still the most definitive means of identification, there are still limitations to its use. Criminals can often avoid leaving any fingerprints, even at the scene of a major crime. Fingerprints are also often difficult to collect. Even in a very violent crime like a rape or murder, the ensuing struggle may have left fingerprints smudged or incomplete, or, if a body is left out in the weather or in water, the fingerprint evidence may have been washed away. So even though there are now millions of fingerprints on file and sophisticated computer technology to match them, it is still often difficult to find enough fingerprint evidence at a crime scene to be conclusive. But not so with DNA evidence. At almost any crime scene at least something can be collected — a hair, a drop of blood, saliva or other bodily fluids.

In the early 1990s, most state police crime labs began acquiring both the technology and the scientists necessary to process samples of DNA.

Although in the first years DNA matches were responsible for confirming identification of a local suspect who was already apprehended, there was no database with which to compare the sample collected with those criminals within the state or across the nation who were most likely to have committed the crime.

In the mid-1990s, the Convicted Offender Database Program was created. Now anyone entering a correctional institution in most states will submit a sample of DNA and those samples will be entered into a database, available to any law enforcement agency in the country through the Combined DNA Index System (CODIS). The system is maintained by the FBI.

It had been possible for many years to match a bullet with a gun with nearly 100% accuracy microscopically examining the marks in the barrel (lands and grooves) with the evidence on the bullets. Both are as unique as fingerprints on a person. Firearms examiners had also been able to determine the distance which a firearm was from a target, the trajectory of a weapon (the science of ballistics) and the meaning of powder left on skin or clothing. But, unfortunately, such a match could only be made when the examiner had both the bullet and the gun. In 1995, however, the national Drugfire database, created by the FBI, went on- line. Using it, state examiners can now identify all spent cartridges recovered from crime scenes with similar cartridges entered by agencies across the country, thus, greatly increasing the chance of catching today's more mobile criminals. The Integrated Ballistics Identification System (also known as Bulletproof and Brass Catcher), developed by the Bureau of Alcohol, Tobacco and Firearms and Forensic Technology of Montreal, Canada also matches expended bullets and cartridges. A similar database, the FBI's General Rifling Characteristics file gives state agencies access to more than 14,000 specimens from the FBI's Standard Ammunition file and CD Rom images of more than 5,000 firearms in the FBI's Reference Firearms Collection.

Today there are more than 300 public crime laboratories in the US, more than three times the number operating in 1966. Four major federal crime laboratories have been created to assist in the investigation and enforcement of criminal laws that extend beyond the jurisdictional boundaries of state and local forces. The FBI maintains the largest crime lab in the world at its headquarters in Washington, D.C. The DEA maintains a lab that is responsible for the analysis of drugs seized in violation of federal laws regarding the production, sale and transportation of drugs. The Bureau of Alcohol, Tobacco and Firearms has responsibility for analyzing alcoholic beverages and documents relating to tax law enforcement as well as for examining weapons, explosive devices and related evidence received in conjunction with the enforcement of the Gun Control Act of 1968 and the Organized Crime Control Acto of 1970. The US Postal Inspection Service labs offer expertise to any local agency.

The FBI's National Crime Information Center is now being converted to NCIC 2000 which will give officers with computers in their police cars the ability to transmit and receive text data as well as photos and fingerprints.

The State Police in World War II

As the entire nation prepared for the upcoming war, state police agencies found themselves not only fighting crime and patrolling the roads but pressed into service to assist the civil defense and help communities cope with the changes in society that would inevitably result.

Although most state police officers were exempt from serving in the military, some states conducted additional recruit classes, appointing only married men with dependents to increase the odds of deferment. Even so, most agencies experienced shortages of men as the war progressed and officers enlisted in the military. Ohio swore in an auxiliary force of 2,800 American Legionnaires. Utah created a force of 350 volunteers called "Deputy Highway Patrolmen." Still, most Troopers who served during the war found themselves working many extra hours. As in other organizations, women also assumed jobs formerly held only by men. In Arizona, three of the patrolmen's wives became Patrol dispatchers.

By the beginning of 1940, most state police agencies were called upon to train civilian Civil Defense volunteers, provide security for war production plants and be prepared to defend the state against enemy attack.

The US government also requested that most state police agencies survey the state's factories to determine their importance in national defense programs. State police were also asked to provide escorts for army convoys crisscrossing the states to army posts, naval bases and airfields. Troopers were provided to facilitate these moving columns by clearing the road ahead, securing the cooperation of municipal authorities and advising as to routes to be taken.

In addition to traffic duty, state police officers also worked with the FBI checking on the records of suspected "alien enemies." State police officers also assisted the military in tracking AWOL soldiers and performed night patrols around vital defense areas.

Security was increased at state police radio rooms and a revolver was furnished to the civilian dispatchers. Civilian dispatchers were also photographed and fingerprinted by the military when they worked together at any location. State police were also asked to work with other state agencies to stagger working hours, to produce more efficient use of mass transport, enforce speed reduction and prevent loss of time to industrial workers going to and from defense plants. They were also asked to construct charts showing highways and entrances to defense plants for emergency use and enforce vice laws. Fingerprint experts from the state police were pressed into service taking, classifying, identifying and photographing defense plant workers. State police also worked with the FBI to investigate all incidents of "un-American activities" and gave demonstrations and lectures on air raid control, air raid warden's duties, bombs and gas warfare. State police and state highway personnel surveyed all highway bridges and completed reports detailing their exact location and type of structure. They also gave special attention to any indication of sabotage or damage done to telephone company installations. They even did a survey of funeral parlors to determine the number of privately owned ambulances. In many states, state police ran scrap rubber campaigns, collected aluminum pots and pans and delivered them to smelters.

They even lectured speeders on the unpatriotic nature of wasting tires. A pamphlet issued by the Indiana State Police declared "Each time a motorist turns a wheel in unnecessary driving, he must realize that it is a turn of the wheel against our soldiers and in favor of Hitler."

Motor Carrier Units

As early as the 1930s, some state police agencies had assumed the responsibility for enforcing laws relating to trucks. (In other states this responsibility became — and remains- that of officers of the state highway department, officers in a separate division of a department of public safety, the state's revenue department or a variety of other agencies).

But where it was a state police responsibility, the real work of motor carrier officers was not really to start until after World War II was over and commercial vehicles again took to the road in record numbers.

In the early 1950's the National Defense Interstate Highway Network was created and police agencies across the country were asked to place an emphasis on patrolling the multilane freeways that would soon crisscross every state. As the highways were completed, all states not only experienced a tremendous influx of truck traffic, they found that trucks that had been developed during World War II were bigger and heavier than their pre-war counterparts. Many states responded by enacting laws increasing penalties relating to the height, width, length and gross weight of vehicles moving on the public highways. In many states, the burden of enforcing these laws fell to the highway patrols.

Unfortunately, this added responsibility coincided with a similar increase in automobile traffic and troopers in those states found that they simply could not continue to catch speeders, work accidents and crimes and measure and weigh trucks. Many of these states responded by creating a Motor Carrier unit. In many cases such a unit was composed primarily of civilians.

These "weigh clerks" manned permanent scale inspection stations and patrolled the road with portable scales. Often, however, they had little enforcement authority. They did the physical work of crawling under vehicles, writing the necessary reports and filling out forms for arrests and warnings. Then they had to find a trooper to actually issue the ticket.

The first weigh stations were small buildings with a platform scale out front that required each truck to put each axle on the scale one at a time to be weighed. This was a time consuming process that resulted in long lines of trucks losing valuable time as they waited their turn at the weigh station.

In the 1970s, most weighmasters were finally given enforcement powers. The weighmaster could then follow up on arrests, appear in court and give testimony.

In 1979, the Motor Carrier Safety Assistance Program (MCSAP) provided federal funding for overtime, equipment and facilities for motor carrier personnel.

This was a godsend for most departments as deregulation of the trucking industry in the early 1980s resulted in the creation of a myriad of federal and state laws pertaining to trucks and interstate transportation of goods.

By the early 1990s, weigh stations were equipped with an electronic Weigh in Motion (WIM) system allowing trucks entering the weigh station to be scanned at speeds of 20 to 40 mph and their weight calculated instantly. Those in compliance could be waived through the station and be on their way in minutes, freeing personnel to concentrate their inspections on the few trucks that were out of compliance. Many weigh stations now also include inspection buildings where a truck can pull inside over a pit and an inspection may easily be accomplished whatever the weather.

Today in most states with designated motor carrier personnel, the function is still largely civilian and in many states, unlike sworn members of the agency, women comprise 50% or more of personnel.

Motor carrier inspectors who are not sworn police officers attend several weeks of training, some portions of which, like defensive driving, duplicate those received by troopers. They study first aid, water safety, court requirements and all the rules and regulations with which truckers must comply. By statute in most states motor carrier inspectors must also be re-certified each year. Most motor carrier agencies also train specialists to inspect hazardous materials haulers for compliance and do inspections of vehicles after an accident to assure that safety violations did not exist.

Many motor carrier personnel are also trained as accident reconstructionists, specializing in accidents involving truck crashes.

Because the interstate system was created at the beginning of the cold war, a major

New York State Police forms of patrol.

consideration in its design was its military use. The original plans stated that one mile in every five be straight. These straight sections were to serve as airstrips in the event of war or other emergencies. Although few military aircraft land on the interstates, an occasional private plane does, so motor carrier accident reconstructionsists sometimes find themselves working an airplane crash.

Motor coach and school bus safety are also responsibilities of most motor carrier personnel who inspect thousands of school busses each summer and work to keep unsafe motor coaches off the road.

Paperwork compliance, once a source of confusion to even the most experienced haulers, has become high tech. Laptop computers linked with form readers streamline the process and a national computer system now links states with a variety of agencies involved in the trucking industry.

Catching Speeders

When troopers were first given the responsibility of catching speeders, they didn't have much to work with. In the 1920s and 1930s, the standard procedure upon observing a speeder was simply to catch up with him,

follow him for awhile, clock his speed, then pull him over and issue whatever the state required. In some states, like Arizona, patrolmen gave out large red tickets that were supposed to impress the drivers with the seriousness of the infraction.

But whatever the result, the pursuit itself posed several problems. In order to "clock" the vehicle effectively, the officer had to get close to it. That often meant executing a U-turn and accelerating around other cars in order to nab the offending car. Often by the time the officer got to the vehicle the driver had either seen the officer and slowed down or turned off at a side street and disappeared.

Once behind the vehicle, the officer also had to remain at a constant distance from it for a long enough period to establish that the vehicle was indeed speeding. On a lonely country road this wasn't all that difficult. But in city traffic or on busy roads, there was nothing to stop another vehicle from cutting in between the officer and the car he was clocking or, again, to stop the astute driver from simply slowing down. But this was the system the state police used until after World War II.

The only variant on simply "pacing" a car was the speed trap, the first of which were created by some of the more enterprising troopers who put two rubber hoses on the highway

and used a stopwatch to time how fast cars crossed over them.

It wasn't until the early 1950s, that highway patrol officers had a really efficient way to catch violators — radar.

Radar

Radar, the acronym for radio detection and ranging, was developed by several scientists over a period of nearly 100 years. British physicist James Clerk Maxwell was the first to notice the behavior of electromagnetic waves in 1864. In 1886, German engineer Christian Hulsmeyer using Maxwell's principle, was the first to design a device that could detect an object by radio echoes. Hulsmeyer's goal was to find a way to avoid collisions at sea. In 1922, Italian inventor Guglielmo Marconi also constructed such a device.

The first practical radar system was developed in 1935 by British physicist Sir Robert Watson-Watt and at the beginning of World War II, engineers from the US and Britain worked closely together to develop military applications for radar. Their discovery was used extensively during the war

The first radar units to be used by state police were the stationary radars, mounted in

Ohio State Trooper serves speeding ticket.

police cars or held in the officer's hands. Police agencies were quick to adopt the use of these devices that now allowed the officer to station himself by the side of the road, aim the radar unit at the car and immediately get a reading. Unfortunately, unaware of the consequences of prolonged exposure to microwave radiation, many officers who had mounted the units next to their heads or who rested the units in their laps when not in use, suffered some severe health consequences. In some states, these radars are now outlawed.

Mobile radar was a major improvement. Officers with these radars could use the device whether the police car was moving or not. If moving, the device would also record the speed of the patrol car for comparison.

Some states also experimented with photo radar, a system in which a stationary radar unit was attached to a computer and a camera. If an approaching motorist was exceeding the speed limit, the camera, which was equipped with a date stamp, took a picture of the front or rear license plate. The photo was then sent to the motorist along with the ticket. Radar was also used by teams of officers, one clocking the offender and radioing ahead to an "interceptor officer" waiting down the road to arrest the speeder.

Vascar

In the 1960s, Arthur N. Marshall, a Richmond Virginia real estate broker, invented the Visual Average Speed Computer and Recorder (VASCAR) which worked on the formula that distance divided by time equals velocity. The compact device enabled troopers to accurately clock the speed of vehicles as they met the trooper on the highway as well as vehicles approaching from the rear. With VASCAR, the speed of the officer's car is irrelevant to the reading. VASCAR allows the officer to clock a motorist's speed from a moving patrol car and unlike radar, VASCAR cannot be detected by a "fuzz buster" or similar device.

As soon as VASCAR units became widely available, they were also used by teams of officers, one in an aircraft and one on the ground. White lines were painted on the highway a quarter mile apart. A trooper on the ground positioned his or her car just past one of the lines. The pilot with the VASCAR unit flew in lazy circles over the lines. When he spotted a suspected speeder, he recorded the time the car crossed the white lines and then radioed the description of the vehicle to the trooper on the ground who issued the ticket.

In 1979, the VASCAR plus, the fourth generation of VASCAR devices was made available. The new units eliminated down time, stored multiple distances and could be used as evidence in "following too closely" arrests.

Lasers

In some states, Troopers are now issued laser units. Although they currently cost about four times as much as radar, they have the advantage of being able to accurately measure not just the speed of the patrol car and the speeder, but also the exact distance in between. The laser's 4 foot wide beam also allows it to more accurately pinpoint a vehicle in a crowd of others, although since like radar the beam is invisible, there is no real way to be sure. Although it may be some time before most highway patrol officers have lasers, they are now being widely used by accident reconstructionists and emergency response personnel.

The Stop Stick

Between 1989 and 1991, 924 people were killed as a result of police pursuits. This number concerned Indiana State Trooper Ken Greves. Working with engineer Dan Olive, Greves invented the Stop Stick, a triangular shaped styrofoam bar, 36" long and 3" on a side with 72 hollow spring steel quills with pointed tips imbedded in the bar. Officers equipped with the Stop Sticks can now place it on the highway in the path of the vehicle being pursued. The stick will deflate the tires without causing the driver to lose control of the car at speeds of nearly 80 mph.

The Video Camera

In 1991, viewers across the country tuning in their evening news watched in horror and fascination as Los Angeles Police Officers brought down motorist Rodney King. While many police agencies had already been experimenting with the use of video cameras, interest was suddenly renewed as the impact of having such vividly documented proof of just what went on at a routine police stop became crystal clear.

It also became apparent that while citizen taping of such an incident could be valuable, it could also be risky. Such taping would be random at best and prejudicial at worst, as there was nothing to stop a citizen from either editing the tape or shooting it selectively.

So police agencies, particularly state police agencies, who routinely stop so many cars, began installing the instruments. Now, thanks to the availability of federal grant money to purchase them in most states, they are relatively commonplace and have proven to be an extremely useful tool. Most are automatically activated as the car's roof lights go on, recording the stop from the beginning. The cameras' autofocus and zoom features allow for a wide range of coverage and apertures automatically adjust to nighttime and poor weather conditions. A time and date stamp, which cannot be altered without detection, appears on each frame

The wireless body microphone the officer wears also records all conversation, leaving little doubt as to who said what to whom.

Although mounted on the frame near the windshield, most video cameras can be removed to be used outside the car or swiveled to record what is going on in the car's interior — a feature many officers use when transporting a member of the opposite sex to avoid any accusations of sexual harassment.

Videotapes are especially valuable in instances where there has been resistance on the part of the motorist or when a drunk driver has been stopped and, the next day, may not remember just what went on. "When they sober up they may have convinced themselves that they were greatly wronged by the stop," said one trooper, "but you show them that tape and there just isn't much doubt about what happened."

Videotapes are also being accepted more frequently as evidence in trials. The jury may not choose to accept the word of the police officer, but they can scarcely argue with something they see with their own eyes.

Aviation

Although some state police agencies had experimented with the use of aircraft as early as the 1930s, most did not use aircraft on a regular basis until after World War II. Following the war, not only were surplus aircraft available, but also many trained pilots eager to use these skills in a peacetime job.

Soon, state police pilots were pressed into service flying medical supplies to disaster areas, directing traffic at large public events and transporting state officials. By the late 1950s, state police pilots were also using aircraft on regular patrol of the highways and Gil Holt of the Indiana State Police developed a system of using the VASCAR for clocking ground vehicles from the air still widely in use today.

Following the Vietnam War, most agencies added helicopters to their fleet. The maneuverability of helicopters made them indispensable for rescues in congested areas, at the scene of traffic crashes and in crowd and traffic control. By the early 1970s, many agencies maintained their own hangars and became FAA certified to do their own repairs. In the late 60s, the Maryland State Police started using Bell helicopters for law enforcement and medevac operations. Transporting critically injured patients from the highway to trauma centers within the "golden hour" became a national model.

In 1983, the Virginia State Police purchased two helicopters and have since worked closely with local volunteer fire rescue squads. It remains the only private/public cooperative medivac unit in the nation.

State police aircraft have also been widely used in the "war on drugs." Both fixed wing

Ohio Highway Patrol helicopter on patrol.

Virginia Bomb tech, Randy Dyer.

and helicopters began working with the Drug Enforcement Agency, state national guards and conservation agencies, in the annual eradication of marijuana. In the early 1990s, most state police agencies equipped helicopters with thermal imaging devices now widely used to locate indoor marijuana growing operations, in manhunts and to search for missing people.

By the mid-1990s, most agencies were also training emergency response personnel and divers to jump from the helicopters onto the tops of buildings, into water and at a remote crime scene.

Special Weapons and Tactics Riot Control

Many state police agencies had been formed to help control crowds or strikers during periods of labor unrest, and most have continued to do so in one way or another since. In some areas, industrial strikes continued to be the problem. In other areas, it has been prison riots. In fact, in some states the posts were located near the prisons specifically because there was always someone there who could quickly mobilize a trained and armed police force.

During World War II, the need for riot control was replaced by other priorities. Beginning with the mid-1960s, however, it became obvious that this skill would be again be needed as student dissent and civil rights issues dominated the nation's cities and campuses. State police agencies began to form teams of specialists.

Explosive Ordnance Recognition and Disposal

Dissent relating to the Vietnam War in late 1960's resulted in bombings at campuses across the nation. A worker was killed in an underground bombing at the University of

Wisconsin and other bombings like those attributed to the Weather Underground followed as dissidents discovered that there was nothing like a bomb threat to attract media attention to themselves and their cause.

Although the military had many trained explosive ordnance disposal personnel in its ranks, the Posse Comitatus Act prevented them from testifying in civilian courts. So police agencies had little choice but to train their own personnel and state police agencies, with their state-wide jurisdiction, became the obvious agency to be involved.

Although the military could was not able to participate in these operations, it was willing to provide the training. In 1968, the US Naval School for Explosive Ordnance Disposal at Indian Head designed the first three-week course specifically for police officers and in 1971, the Law Enforcement Assistance Agency (LEAA) developed a three-week Hazardous Devices School (HDS) for police personnel in Huntsville, Alabama at the Redstone Arsenal.

After attending training, Explosive Ordnance Disposal (EOD) team members were certified not only to identify and render safe a wide variety of explosives, they were also qualified to testify in court. Unfortunately, once they were trained, EOD team members found that there was very little equipment for them to use. Most had to make do with their bare hands, a pocket knife, a grappling hook and a rope. "We'd hook up the device, get back at what we thought was a safe distance and just give the line a big yank," said Indiana State Police EOD team member John Mull.

Because little was available commercially, some agencies built their own tank-like vehicles to contain explosive devices. Later, most teams were issued portable Bendix X-Ray units which were replaced by the Golden X-ray. With this device they could at least see what was inside a suspicious package before they attempted to move it.

In addition to the high profile events like campus bombings, EOD teams were also called

upon to remove old dynamite from farms, dispose of military souvenirs dating back to the Civil War and examine suspicious packages received by civilians. Many also helped remove dangerous chemicals that had been stored in public buildings (like school basements) during the cold war as part of the Civil Defense effort.

During the next decade personnel known as Explosive Ordnance Reconnaissance (EOR) members were added to the teams. These personnel were trained to recognize explosives, but not to recover or detonate them, to deal with bomb threat situations and to secure an area where an explosive material or device was found until the appropriate personnel could get there.

In more recent times, EOR and EOD teams have joined drug enforcement officers in disposing of caches of ethyl ether, dynamite, plastic explosives, and a variety of other dangerous substances found in raids of clandestine drug labs.

Most state police EOD/EOR team members are still sent to the Bomb Data Center at Redstone for training. Commanders of such units attend the FBI's Bomb Squad Commander's Conference every 18 months.

Today's EOD/EOR are much better equipped than their predecessors. Most units have Kevlar(bomb suits that include arm protection, gloves, heavy boots and a plexiglass face protector. Units also have an X-ray unit, a tool kit and disrupters (water cannons). Some agencies also have robots that can be operated remotely so that the team member can always remain at a safe distance from the "improvised explosive device." Such robots come equipped with a 360-degree panning video camera, hydraulic arm with a mechanical hand and voice receiver.

Although the bomb squads in the movies routinely blow up every bomb they find in a spectacular display of smoke and fire, state police EOD teams only do so as a last resort. In most cases, they clear the area, x-ray the device, and disrupt it with the water cannon. Said one EOD member, "A great big bang is the last sound you ever want to hear."

Emergency Response Teams

Along with EOD/EOR teams, most state police agencies also formed emergency response teams. While containing riots had required primarily large numbers of well armed men with a lot of patience, post-war law enforcement was to demand a good deal more. Although ERT members are equipped with high powered rifles and other special gear, the primary emphasis is on training. Although most are volunteers, they put in long hours every year making sure their skills are sharp.

Today ERTs participate in marijuana eradication, VIP security, high profile drug buys, service of felony warrants, execution of high profile or dangerous warrants, work with hostage negotiators, provide courtroom security, transportation of high risk prisoners and provide security at special events.

Underwater Search and Recovery

Since the beginning, most state police organizations assisted local law enforcement agencies in water search and rescue operations. But, except for their sense of touch, pike poles and boat hooks were about all the equipment most water rescue teams had. Although the self-contained underwater breathing apparatus (SCUBA) had been invented in the 1940s, it was not used outside the military until the late 1950s. When it did become available, many agencies were quick to train personnel in its use. Although a few of the members of the early Underwater Search and Rescue Teams had military training, most were volunteers simply willing to give it a try.

Without scuba equipment, early divers could only dive down for the few minutes they could hold their breath. With the equipment, because they could stay down for much longer, they were able to dive deeper. Thus, it became necessary to also train them in hyperbaric chambers. Because these divers also faced many more risks, most departments sent them to schools organized by the National Association of Underwater Instructors (NAUI).

In addition to the wet suits the divers first wore, many soon added dry suits for use in cold water or deep diving. And, since every second counts in attempting a water rescue, divers were trained to be out of the police car, into the suit and other gear and into the water within minutes.

In addition to rescue, most state police divers were also trained in underwater recovery of evidence — most in finding even the smallest item, like a bullet, in black water, i.e. water where visibility is nearly zero. Such courses take upwards of 160 hours and divers drill as often as once a month to keep their skills sharp.

Virginia Scuba Coordinator Mike Berry.

In more recent years, state police divers have also trained with emergency response teams, learning to jump from helicopters into oceans, lakes and rivers, perform a rescue and be pulled back into the helicopter, often with a struggling victim in tow.

Hostage Negotiation

Although hostage negotiation of some form or another has been going on for as long as people have held hostages, the political unrest of the 1970s made most state police agencies aware of the need for a team of specialists to deal with these highly visible and volatile situations. Hostage negotiator Tom Davidson of the Indiana State Police recalls a particularly horrible incident from his own experience in which a man barricaded himself in a house with his infant child. "He begged for the chance to talk to his mother," said Davidson. "Because we did not yet fully understand the intricacies of a negotiation, we brought her in. As soon as she got on the phone, the hostage taker said, 'Here, Mom, this is for you,' and

proceeded to shoot both the infant and himself."

It became apparent that both because of the complexity and duration of such a stressful situation, highly trained teams needed to be formed to handle them. Most departments recruited volunteers from their ranks and contacted the FBI to conduct schools on this subject. Today's hostage negotiators are now able to preserve the life of victims, citizens the police and suspects. "We are not there to treat their illness, solve their family problems or save their souls," says Davidson. "We are there to provide short term intervention."

The Year 2000 and Beyond

What will the challenges be for the state police in the year 2000 and beyond?

Violent Juveniles

In August, 1998, the citizens of Chicago watched in horror as the local television stations reported that the suspects in the murder and sexual molestation of an 11-year old girl were two boys, aged 7 and 8. While for years state police officers have known that teenagers and young adults were the most likely to commit crimes, even they are shocked by the increasing numbers of criminals even younger.

There are now 40 million American children age 10 or younger and many experts feel they form a "vast reservoir or tomorrow's potential criminals." In 1995, FBI director Louis J. Freeh warned, "The ominous increase in juvenile crime coupled with population trends, portends future crime and violence at nearly unprecedented levels."

While violent juveniles, often involved with gangs and drugs were once considered primarily the problem of city police, as they move onto the highways and into the suburbs and rural areas of the country, they will pose an increased challenge to the state police.

Vigilante Groups and Hate Crimes

Although experts disagree on what causes people of one race, ethnic group, sexual orientation or religion to violently attack those who are different than themselves, hate groups show no sign of disappearing. While the federal government has expertise in dealing with hate groups, the acts committed by them — arson, battery, murder- are ordinarily state crimes and thus not in federal jurisdiction. In addition, groups like the Ku Klux Klan, often choose to stage their rallies on state property so as to attract maximum media attention.

Thus, in the next century the job of policing such groups will continue to fall to the state police.

The War on Drugs

All state police agencies, whether they are strictly highway patrol or are full-service agencies, will continue to be at the front line in the war on drugs. Local police agencies will probably continue to make the greatest numbers of arrests because they are the closest to the users at the end of the distribution line. But the state police will be increasingly involved in working with both these local agencies and the federal government to get to the source of the problem.

As experience has shown, money alone cannot solve the problem. The federal government has already thrown billions of dollars at it, and, if anything, the illegal drug business is bigger than ever.

What will be required will be more training in interdiction, eradication and intelligence. The state police cannot ever hope to outspend drug traffickers, in the 21st century, their only hope will be to outsmart them.

Image

Whatever else it may have accomplished, televised coverage of the O.J. Simpson trial clearly illustrated that there has been a change in public attitude toward the police.

Community policing advocates argue that the problem is that police have isolated themselves from the public by spending the majority of their time in cars and only responding when called. Others contend that the problem is the "few bad apples" that have made everyone in uniform look bad. Yet others maintain that the problem is that the police are still a predominately white male force in a multicultural society. Another factor may be the tendency of police personnel to operate in a closed social network.

While the truth is that probably all of these are factors to some extent, the result has been that there is an increased distance between the public and the police — particularly the state police, whom the public sees less frequently than local police officers.

As a result the state police officer no longer enjoys automatic respect. Motorists are increasingly rude and uncooperative. The testimony of police officers is no longer automatically believed by juries. And, increasingly, citizens arc bcginning to win suits against state police officers for a wide range of complaints from the very serious to the very silly. Even the state police, who have always been considered the premier law enforcement agency in most states, have seen their image tarnished.

Multiculturalism

During a routine traffic stop, an Indiana State Trooper who had been trained in interdiction suspected that the car he had just pulled over might contain drugs. Because the trooper was alone in the patrol car, he asked the driver to step out of the vehicle. After the officer patted him down, he asked the motorist to kneel on the pavement with his hands behind his back. To his astonishment, the driver began to shake uncontrollably and burst into tears. Only after bringing in a fellow trooper who spoke Spanish did the trooper learn that the motorist, a recent immigrant from Central America, assumed that once in that position, he was about to be executed.

Whereas once the scene enacted on this Midwestern interstate would have happened only in a state that bordered Mexico, today troopers are likely to encounter people from all over the world from a wide variety of cultures with a similarly wide range of attitudes about the police. Some, like this motorist, will find any encounter with the police a major trauma. Others victims in accidents or crimes, will simply need help and someone who can understand what they say.

Safety

Today's population is better armed than ever before. In 1970, there were 203.7 million people and an estimated 104 million firearms in America — one gun for every two people. Today, the ATF estimates that Americans own 140 million rifles and shotguns and 60 million handguns — 200 million weapons - and that more than 50% of households have at least one gun. Unfortunately, a larger percentage, particularly those who are at the age when they are most likely commit a crime, also have a violent mindset. This trend will be of particular concern to highway patrol officers who are the most likely of all police officers to face a stranger in an isolated place, alone.

Dealing with Unsolvable Problems

As they have since the beginning, the public still looks to the state police to solve their problems. Whether it is a rude motorist who cut them off at a stoplight or a domestic battery, the first reaction is to get on the cell phone and call the state police. In an increasingly less stable society, however, it has become harder and harder for the police to solve people's problems. Limited by stricter laws regarding their behavior, spread thin by sheer numbers of calls, state police officers can often, at best, only lend a sympathetic ear or provide a temporary respite. They appear, the problem stops, they leave, it starts again. The police have responded, but they have not solved the problem.

Unfortunately, the public sees this as a lack of action, particularly in an era when the government has chosen to spend increasing amounts of money on enforcement and put a larger percentage of its citizen in prison than any other country on earth.

State police officers, of course, are also frustrated by this situation. Time and time again they see the bad guys back on the street almost before they have completed the paperwork. Even if they have the discretion to take a batterer to jail without the victim pressing charges, it is not unusual for the batterer to return and kill his or her spouse — generally in front of the children.

As Edwin J. Delattre, the author of Character and Cops: Ethics in Policing says, "They are ground down by danger, resentment of criminals who prosper, perceived failure of social service and criminal agencies and the daunting repetitiveness of their work. Some drift toward despair over the violence, suffering, hopelessness, ignorance and self-destructive behavior they encounter day after day. Some are ineffective-even dangerous — because they become cynical, convinced that policing is a daily battle of 'us against them.'"

Are There Solutions?

The state police, like all public police officers, are in the middle of the criminal justice system. They don't make laws, determine guilt or innocence or administer punishment. Yet, ironically, they are the public servants in the process who most often deal directly on a day to day basis with the people who are most affected by laws — law breakers and victims.

Thus, it is simply not possible for the state police to effect solutions. All they can do is develop strategies to protect the majority who follow the rules from the minority who don't.

What strategies will be the most effective in the 21st century?

Re-evaluation of the Role of the State Police

All state police agencies are now at least 50 years old. As the new century approaches, many are finding that while the agency was relying on traditional law enforcement methodologies, the society was changing. Thus, in the years ahead, many agencies will be assuming a wider, or narrower, range of responsibilities, depending on the role they will play. Some agencies which have had responsibility for both criminal investigations and highway patrol will be evolving those areas into more distinct functions. Others will be combining hitherto separate functions into one department. Yet others will be taking the responsibility for areas such as investigations and media relations out of the districts and forming teams or task

forces who will specialize in white collar crime, pornography, violent crimes, crimes against children and so on. As one superintendent recently said, "We can no longer afford to be all things to all people. We cannot assume that because we have always done our job one way that that is the most effective way to operate in the future. Our job has always been to provide the best law enforcement possible to the citizens of the state. We must do whatever it takes to do that."

Attraction and Retention Quality People

Unfortunately, even as most agencies are raising the educational qualifications of recruits, they cannot offer the same level of compensation as private industry or even county and city police agencies. While in the past, most people joined the state police because of its reputation as the state's premier law enforcement agency, that alone may not continue to be enough. The availability of jobs in a booming economy, the lure of a salary several times greater than the state can afford to pay as well as more generous benefits may well override any benefit the state police can offer. The challenge will be to provide other incentives so that state police agencies attract and keep not just numbers of people, but the right people.

State police agencies must also work diligently to achieve diversity. Because many state police agencies have had responsibility in rural areas, they have tended to attract officers from rural areas and thus have, in many states, remained a predominately white male

organization. Even if the actions of white officers are consistently fair and unbiased, they may still continue to be seen as racist if the percentages of minorities remain low. White officers will continue to be accused of "targeting" minorities and unnecessarily harassing them. Even where affirmative action quotas cannot be set, states must continue to set goals for minority hiring. Similarly, state police agencies must continue to seek out female recruits.

Politics

Because state police are state agencies, they will always be subject to the political agendas of the people who pay their salaries. But, because the agency must act consistently over many administrations, it must have clear and consistent policies that are communicated on a regular basis to its employees, to the citizens and to the media.

Keeping Officers Safe

In the past, the effort to keep officers safe meant primarily giving them a gun and some body armor and advising them to watch their back. In today's increasingly violent age, much more will be required. The officers with the most direct contact with the public must not only have the weapons to protect them once they come face to face with an angry citizen, but computers and data bases to allow them to know who they're dealing with before they ever get out of the car.

From the first day they enter the police academy to their last day on the job, they must also receive excellent training for the wide variety of roles they play.

Taking Advantage of New Technology

In addition to in-car computers for the officers on the road, state police agencies must begin to use technology to enable them to do their job more quickly and more effectively. Because state police officers can no longer assume that their testimony will be believed by a jury, officers will need to depend more on video cameras, videotaped preliminary interviews and other tools to help them better document everything they do.

Agencies must take advantage of websites and e-mail to allow citizens to report crimes or give information on-line. They must also use these resources to educate the public about how to make themselves and their communities safer, alert them to the presence of dangerous criminals like sexual predators and wanted fugitives and allow them access to information in a way that is both convenient, cost effective and anonymous.

Louisiana Air Support Unit, Bell Long Ranger IV helicopter

Implementing Better Communications Systems

Most police agencies have known for years, that, despite the many improvements, their communications systems were, for the most part, inadequate.

When flight 800 crashed into the Atlantic Ocean on July 17, 1996, more than 50 police agencies responded. "The scene was chaotic," said Bill Nagel, Deputy Director of New York City Emergency Management. "There were at least 1,500 personnel, a hoard of reporters and not one press officer. There was no way for individual agencies to communicate with one another. Cellular phones quickly became useless and there was no common radio frequency."

A similar situation existed following the crash of American Eagle 4184 in a cornfield in Lake County, Indiana. Fifty-four agencies responded, each with its own agenda and communications setup. Said Dave Perkins of Indiana State Emergency Management, "Often the only way to communicate was just to walk over to whatever command post you needed to talk to."

Although the investigation of major catastrophes like airplane crashes is usually the responsibility of federal agencies, establishing the command posts and communications network often falls to the state police. For disasters like the crashes of Flights 800 and 4184 and the day-to-day work of the nation's state police officers, preparation for the 21st century must include a significant improvement in communications equipment.

Learning to Work More Effectively with Other Agencies

There may have been a time when law enforcement agencies could work alone, when they could hoard information, compete with other agencies for arrests, and maintain separate and closely guarded databases. If that time ever existed, it is certainly long gone now. With crime and the fear of crime on the rise, the numbers of violent criminals increasing and the costs of technology enormous, there is no choice. All law enforcement agencies from the lone town marshal in a town of 250 people to the FBI must now find ways to pool resources, share information and work together.

Enlisting Community Support

Although most state police agencies could, and still can, count on the moral support of the people in their communities, in the 21st century, they will need to explore ways the community can help in a more tangible way. "We must learn to ask for what we want," Criminal Justice Assistant Professor Kenna Quinet told 500 representatives from 200 different law enforcement agencies in Indiana in December 1997. "We need to convince the public that we can't do the job alone anymore. We need to ask our vendors, our schools and colleges, the business people in our home towns what they would be willing to contribute to the fight against crime in their communities."

Using Civilian Review Boards More Effectively

In the past, many state police civilian review boards were primarily ceremonial — visible only when handing out valor awards or promotions - or reactive —serving as a sounding board for the administration when something went wrong. As agencies will be subjected to greater and greater scrutiny in the future, they need to use their civilian review boards to serve as a liaison with civilians. Boards must become more visible, promoting the positive aspects of the agency to the public and taking greater responsibility in issues relating to policy and discipline.

Working More Effectively with the Media

In the past it was often sufficient to just assign someone from every barracks or post to answer the questions posed by the local media. That is no longer enough. In an era when the public demands instant information, state police agencies must train experts within the agency in this specialized field whose primary responsibility will be to proactively place positive stories about the state police. Each trooper must also be trained to work with the media, so that he or she will always give the appropriate response, no matter what the situation.

Helping Officers Cope

As recent events have shown, the public may no longer hold politicians to a higher standard than other citizens. But even as many people become less respectful, more violent and just plain meaner, they still expect the police to be consistently helpful, courteous and patient. As mentioned earlier, that's not easy. While we can't expect people to change, if police are to avoid losing their "best and brightest," they must, in the years ahead provide not just physical, but emotional support. Experimental programs like critical incident stress debriefings, offering counseling and support groups to both officers and their families and giving administrators the training to identify problems with employees early must be continued and expanded.

It's Not Getting Any Easier

It's not getting any easier to be a state police officer. Whether the officer is a highway patrol officer, an investigator or and administrator, every officer will find his or her job a bigger challenge in the 21st century.

While there is still controversy about whether or not there are more crimes, there are still plenty of them and there is little doubt that many crimes are much more violent.

State police agencies will no doubt continue to struggle with the limitations of low pay and an aging infrastructure, while the drug trade puts billions of dollars in the hands of teenagers.

Adult white collar criminals, using increasingly sophisticated technology will continue to cost the American people more each year than crimes committed by all the burglars, robbers and car thieves put together and will continue to be much harder and more time consuming to catch.

Even as state police agencies become more professional and better trained, the media will continue to sensationalize every mistake the state police make.

Although the population will continue to grow in all areas of the country, there is little hope that state police agencies will be able to keep pace. Yet the public, as it always has, will continue to expect a state police officer to respond to their every call day and night, 365 days a year.

The brochure advertising for state police officers in 1933 may not have been so far off the mark when it asked for "men with the patience of Job and the judgement of Solomon, possessing the knowledge of an attorney, the movements of an athlete, the concern and skill of a physician, the training of a social worker, an engineer, a psychologist, a chemist, a sportsman and a gentleman — all in one dynamic personality."

How the State Police Became Troopers

George A. Chandler, the first superintendent of the New York State Police, is credited with giving state police officers the title, "trooper." Although he had no police experience, prior to being chosen superintendent, Chandler had a distinguished career both as a medical doctor and military officer. Although he had hoped to take his mounted cavalry regiment into World War I, Theodore Roosevelt convinced him, instead to take command of the New York State Police, with the under-

Louisiana Troopers.

standing that should Roosevelt decide to organize another "Rough Rider" troop, Chandler would be a part of it.

In anticipation of this eventuality, Chandler organized the New York State Police like a cavalry troop. He required that they meet the qualifications of soldiers, be similarly trained and wear uniforms that would distinguish them from other police agencies of the time.

But, most importantly, for all state police officers who followed, he decided to call his officers "troopers," a designation that is still given to most state police officers today.

"We're gonna make Dillinger look like a piker."

The short, sad lives of
Alfred Brady, James Dalhover
and Clarence Lee Shaffer

Alfred James Brady, Rhuel James Dalhover and Clarence Lee Shaffer, Jr., all native Hoosiers, were troublemakers from the start. By age 24, Brady had served 180 days at the State Farm. Before they were even teenagers, Dalhover had spent 16 months in reform school and Shaffer had already begun stealing and stripping cars.

By age 20, Dalhover had become a moonshiner and served 100 days in jail, had escaped in a stolen car and been sentenced to two years at the New Mexico State Penitentiary. Paroled after 13 months, he was returned to the Kentucky State Reformatory and served an addition two years for assault with intent to kill.

By the time these three met and decided to pool their talents, there was little doubt that they were up to no good.

The gang officially formed in 1935. Their first operation was a theater robbery that netted them each $4.

From then on, every Saturday night they set out for a series of robberies, favorite targets being grocery stores, filling stations and drug stores. It is estimated that in less than 18 months, the gang committed more than 150 robberies. To aid in the getaway from these robberies, they began a series of auto thefts, often ordering startled motorists out of their cars at gunpoint and leaving them stranded on county roads as they roared off toward another job.

By now, fancying themselves major crime figures, they began bragging that they would "make Dillinger look like a piker" and began accumulating an incredible stash of firearms. Eventually they would routinely carry more than 30 guns with them in their car wherever they went.

In February, 1936, they added murder to their criminal repertoire, allegedly after being awakened from a sound sleep in their car in Anderson, Indiana by a local policeman. "What are you doing here?" asked the officer. "Killing coppers, that's what we're doing," they replied and they shot him dead before he had time to draw his gun.

Reveling in their success, the gang routinely took off on long, wild car trips to New Orleans to establish a base of operations and then back to Ohio for the weekend to rob a jewelry store. To Baltimore, where another base was set up and back to Ohio, Indiana and Illinois for more robberies.

Often, Brady gang robberies involved big shootouts with storeowners, innocent bystanders and police. In March, 1936, during a jewelry store robbery, a store owner jumped on Brady's back and began wrestling with him. Another member of the gang began shooting wildly at the two of them with Brady and the storeowner alternately popping up from behind the display case yelling, "Don't shoot, it's me!"

Soon after, the gang robbed a grocery store crowded with customers. A young clerk came up the stairs from the basement. Without hesitation, Brady shot him dead and pushed the body down the stairs.

During another jewelry store robbery, two local policemen unknowlingly pulled up and parked right in front of the getaway car while one officer went into the local dimestore. As members of the gang emerged from the store with pillowcases full of jewelry, Brady went up to the policeman and held a gun on him while another member of the gang went back into the store for another bag of jewelry. The second policeman, emerging from the store, began firing, the getaway car sped off and a great gun battle ensued. The gang escaped but one member was wounded.

The local doctor reported the gunshot wound to the Indianapolis Police and when gang members returned, another gun battle ensued and Indianapolis Police Sergeant Richard Rivers was killed.

In the spring of 1936, both Brady and Dalhover were arrested in Chicago while trying to fence some jewelry. Shaffer was arrested in Indianapolis and all were brought to the Hancock County Jail to await trial for the murder of Sergeant Rivers.

On October 11, they grabbed the sheriff who was delivering their breakfast, took his .38 revolver and escaped in a stolen car.

By this time, literally dozens of law enforcement agencies were looking for the gang, including the FBI. The gang fled to Baltimore, where, in less than a month, Shaffer and Dalhover met and married tow sistersdespite the fact that Dalhover was already married and had two children back in Indiana.

Using Baltimore as their base, they continued their trips back to Indiana to commit robberies. Although the Brady gang seemed to have been among the most disorganized of all bank robbers in history, their impetuousness and total disrespect for the law also made them among the most dangerous.

On May 23, 1937, when they had driven from Baltimore to Sheldon, Illinois, only to find that the bank they intended to rob was out of business, they "ran the roads" until they located a bank in Goodland, Indiana and robbed the bank of $2,528.

Speeding away from the bank, they passed Indiana State Police officer Paul Minneman and local deputy sheriff Elmer Craig checking a parked vehicle. The gang opened fire, missed both officers and sped off down a county road.

Minneman and Craig loaded their guns, jumped in their police car and, with no police radio to keep them in contact with other officers, these two rookie officers, alone, took off after one of the most notorious gangs in U.S. history.

Tire tracks led directly to a country church and Minneman and Craig followed. As they got out of the car to examine the tracks, a blast of automatic rifle fire downed both officers. Emerging from behind the church, Shaffer stood over the barely conscious Minneman and fired a round of bullets into the officer lying helpless in the mud, then stripped him of his gun belt and .38 Colt service revolver. Brady located the terrified and injured Craig who had run to the shelter of nearby trees. "Should I finish him off?" yelled Shaffer. "No, let him suffer," Dalhover replied. And with that the gang reached into the patrol car, took the first aid kit and fled.

Although Craig survived his wounds, sixty-four hours after the shooting Paul Minneman became the first Indiana State Police officer to die in the line of duty.

A neighbor woman, who lived across the street from the church also received injuries as a result of jumping into her well when she heard the gunfire.

The Brady gang returned to Baltimore to spend the loot. By this time, the manhunt for the gang had intensified to such a degree that the file on the Brady gang was in literally every police agency in the country. A $1500 reward was offered for any information on the gang furnished to the FBI.

On the run, the gang drove to Bangor, Maine where they had been told they could buy firearms with no questions asked. But when they asked the clerk for a Thompson Machine Gun, the clerk told them to come back and informed the local police. Special agents replaced store clerks, sharpshooters crouched on nearby roofs and everyone waited. When Dalhover walked into the store and said, "Got my Tommy?" he was seized, searched and relieved of a .45 and a .32 Colt.

Wondering what was taking so long, Shaffer peered into the store and saw the agents handcuffing Dalhover. Shaffer drew his gun and fired through the front door wounding a special agent. Others fired back and Shaffer fell dead on the sidewalk.

Meanwhile, more agents surrounded the car and ordered Brady to surrender. Yelling, "Don't shoot, I'll get out," Brady lunged out of the car, drew a gun and started firing. Agents returned fire and Brady, riddled with bullets, fell in the middle of the street, Paul Minneman's .38 Colt service revolver clutched in his dead hand.

Dalhover, the gang's only surviving member was executed in 1938 for the murder of Trooper Minneman and buried in a cemetery not far from his hero, John Dillinger.

Alfred Brady, whose primary goal in life was recognition for his flamboyant and glamorous lifestyle, was buried, unclaimed, in a pauper's grave in Bangor, Maine.

Predecessor Agencies:

Three agencies are generally credited with serving as the models for what became the state police.

The Texas Rangers

In a sense, the nation's state police were first formed in 1823. Stephen F. Austin, who had been contracted to recruit settlers to Texas, was having a problem with raids by Comanche, Tonkawa and Karankawa Indians. Under Mexican Law, he was authorized to assemble a company of men to supplement those already under the command of Moses Morrison. He called for "ten men to act as rangers for the common defense." During the next 50 years these rangers, were organized and disbanded as needed. The force was composed of men from a wide variety of backgrounds and cultures. An early historian remarked that they could "ride like a Mexican, trail like an Indian, shoot like a Tennessean and fight like the devil." Most served as unpaid volunteers.

Several of the Ranger companies were mustered into the federal service to act as scouts for the US in the 1846 war with Mexico. The Rangers are said to have fought with such ferocity that they were known as "Los diablos Tejanos," the Texas devils. During the Civil War, the Rangers provided frontier protection. In the 1870s, the Rangers were again activated to cope with lawlessness, this time lawless Texans: outlaws, train robbers and cattle rustlers. Although the law authorized 20 men to a Ranger company, it was said that for "one riot, one ranger" was sufficient. About the Rangers Captain Bill McDonald is credited with saying "No man in the wrong can stand up against a fellow that's in the right and keeps on a-comin."

During Prohibition, the Rangers served as a border patrol, intercepting burro trains of bootleg liquor from Mexico and capturing smugglers. During the 1920s and 1930s the Rangers also raided gaming halls, smashed drinking establishments and when the jails overflowed, were said to handcuff prisoners to telephone poles.

Even after the Highway Patrol was created in 1927, the Rangers continued to operate. Texas Ranger Frank Hamer was among the officers who shot and killed Clyde Borrow and Bonnie Parker in Louisiana that same year.

In 1935, The Texas Rangers were moved from the Adjutant General's Department, the Highway Patrol was moved from the Highway Department and a single state police force was created under the Department of Public Safety. The rangers were charged with enforcing the law with emphasis on felony crimes, gambling, narcotics, riot suppression and locating fugitives.

Today the force, headquartered in Austin, has more than 100 members recruited from the ranks of the Department of Public Safety. Rangers do not wear uniforms but are equipped with firearms, and sophisticated communications equipment.

The Arizona Rangers

During the Civil War the Army of the Confederacy developed plans to capture what is now Arizona and New Mexico, ensuring that the flow of gold would continue to move undisturbed from California through Texas to the rebel forces in the South. In August, 1861, this force: all volunteers- was organized in West Texas. Its three companies were known as the Arizona Volunteers, the Arizona Guards and the Arizona Rangers. The plan was abandoned in 1862, but a territorial ranger force, whose primary job was to fight Indians and protect supply routes and settlers, continued for the next 20 years.

In 1885, the ranger companies were disbanded and reorganized as the Arizona National Guard. Many such groups were formed in the next few years, but most were known as Arizona Rangers. Again, their primary mission was to protect settlers from Apache attacks. By 1901, although the Apaches were no longer a threat, outlaws, rustlers, thieves and killers were, and the legislature appropriated enough money to pay a captain $120 per month, a sergeant $75 and 12 privates $55. Each man also received $1 a day per diem.

Although each ranger was issued a badge, there was no uniform and most rangers preferred to keep their badge out of sight until an arrest was being made. Each ranger rode about 400 miles a month. According to their charter, the rangers could pursue a felon out of state or into Mexico, where they were then required to turn the suspect over to the local agencies. During their brief existence, the Rangers nabbed 14 murderers, more than 100 rustlers and 93 robbers. They are also credited with returning 400 goats that had somehow ended up 600 miles from their owner.

In 1909, however, the Territorial Legislature repealed the Rangers Act of 1903, accusing the governor of using the rangers as his personal police force. But their official demise didn't stop the force from acting. A ranger named Redwood was reportedly still chasing rustlers five days after he was no longer employed.

The Royal Canadian Mounted Police

Like the Texas Rangers, the Royal Canadian Mounted Police were created to provide law and order to a nation expanding into new frontiers. Although hunters and settlers had

1929 Riot Squad (Michigan). The Patrol car was confiscated.

been moving west in Canada for many years, there was no official law enforcement agency to protect them and most simply took the law into their own hands. In 1873, after a group of wolf hunters killed a number of native women and children in an altercation with the Assiniboine Indians, Prime Minister St. John A. Macdonald began recruiting for a mounted police force. In 1885, the newly formed North West Mounted Police were assigned to police the construction of the Canadian Pacific Railway, handling labor disputes and enforcing gambling and liquor laws. In the 1890s, the NWMP faced a new challenge as Tagish Charlie and George Carmack discovered gold and the Klondike Gold Rush began. The NWMP was increased from 19 to 285 men in the next three years to cope with the influx of miners.

In 1904 the force was renamed the Royal Northwest Mounted Police, not only riding horses but also traveling by dogsled to remote outposts in the northern areas of the country.

In 1920, the NWMP was combined with the Dominion Police to form the Royal Canadian Mounted Police.11

Police Firearms

Prior to the advent of interchangeable parts in the first half of the nineteenth century — a concept pioneered in New England for the production of firearms — the constables, marshals, sheriffs and other law enforcement officers in the British colonies and nascent United States used the same hand-made flintlock muzzle loading small arms that everyone else used. Flintlock actions gave way to percussion cap ignition in the decades before the Civil War, and mass produced firearms provided the first recognizable "models" as we now understand such products.

Law enforcement long guns during the muzzle loading era, whether flintlock or percussion cap, were either rifles — that is, firing a single projectile — or shotguns. Muzzle loading double-barreled shotguns were common, but heavy enough to be confined to guard duties.

The degree of precision of metal fabrication attainable by the 1830s allowed Samuel Colt to engineer his six-shot revolvers, initially with percussion caps igniting black powder. These weapons still required each chamber to be individually loaded, but the law enforcement officer thus armed had the assurance of at least five shots (or six if he foolishly loaded the chamber on which the hammer rested) before having to reload. Famous Colt models of this era included the single action Walker and Army pistols, and were usually .36 to .44 caliber, but sometimes smaller.

The popularization of self-contained cartridge weapons at the end of the Civil War displaced the inferior muzzle loading technology in law enforcement as quickly as constrained public budgets permitted. The single action Colt Peacemaker was famous in the West, mostly chambered in .44 or .45 calibers. The repeating long guns of choice were the lever action Henry and, later, Winchester. The Winchester Model 1894 is still in wide civilian use a hundred years later.

With the development of double action revolvers, most prominently by Smith & Wesson, and slower-burning "smokeless" powders in the last quarter of the 1800s, smaller pistol calibers became practical for law enforcement use, especially in more densely populated urban areas where errant shots could endanger innocent bystanders. Although some light revolver cartridges like .32 caliber were used in large cities, the de facto standard which emerged for law enforcement was .38 caliber, specifically the .38 Special.

Gun designers, most notably John Browning, produced the first "automatic" repeating weapons for military use around the turn of the century. The US Army adopted Browning's legendary Colt model 1911A1 as its official sidearm (the date is part of the model number) chambered in .45 ACP. Law enforcement interest in these new automatic designs was limited until the advent of Prohibition and the adoption of WW-I surplus military arms by bootleggers and gangsters. Most flamboyant of these weapons was the Thompson submachine gun, nicknamed the "Tommy Gun" in press accounts, chambered in .45 ACP. Law enforcement selectively adopted these same long guns, in addition to their now-classic pump-action shotguns, as the need arose to battle gangsters. For sidearms, however, various models and barrel length .38 Special revolvers were nearly ubiquitous.

In the decades following WW-II there was a steady migration from .38 Special revolvers to similar equipment chambered for the new .357 Magnum cartridge. This new cartridge offered increased kinetic energy, and therefore stopping power, without requiring police marksmanship training methods to change much at all. Isolated departments and agencies used semi-automatic pistols, especially the Army Colt 1911A1, but these weapons had the significant disadvantage of being single-action. It was not generally regarded as safe to carry such a pistol with a round chambered and the hammer "cocked & locked," so this made the pistol dangerously slow to be ready for use in a deadly-force situation.

During this same post-war era, European law enforcement agencies had never been as completely dependent on double action revolvers as had American departments. European gun engineers had steadily pursued double action semiauto designs, and the standard sidearm of the Wehrmacht was the 9mm P-38. Improved double action designs emerged from civilian manufacturers, notably the Browning Hi-Power model. By the 1960s, European gun manufacturers, such as Glock, Sig-Sauer, Baretta and others had greatly improved safety mechanisms in these pistols, to the point that law enforcement officers could safely carry their sidearm with a round chambered and the safety engaged. Chambering of these European models was nearly always 9mm, mostly 9X19, but sometimes in the "short" cartridge designated in the US as ".380".

With the designers having solved the speed of deployment and handling safety issues of double action semiauto pistols, they now represented superior technology to the revolvers in nearly universal law enforcement use in the United States. As long as none of the cartridges misfired, these semiauto pistols had more than twice the shot capacity and were faster to fire and reload than the old police revolvers. As in Prohibition, the crooks also had some influence on department's equipment selections as they increasingly adopted these modern semiauto designs.

American police agencies and departments rapidly switched to semiauto sidearms in the 1970s and 1980s, many initially to 9mm models because of the European example. Dissatisfaction with the kinetic energy and stopping power of the 9X19 cartridge was al-ways present in American departments, however, and grew with experience. This led to mixed policies and standards, and research to find more suitable semiauto cartridges for law enforcement use. With the FBI's support, the 10mm cartridge was developed, but it proved to be overpowering for many departments. There was, and is, a resurgence of interest in the classic .45 ACP cartridge for police applications, but of course in a modern pistol design. But a compromise cartridge design has emerged — the .40 S&W — which grows steadily in popularity, since it provides more power than 9mm, more capacity than .45 ACP, and is easier to shoot accurately than 10mm. Leading manufacturers of double action semiautos, including Glock, Sig-Sauer, Baretta, Smith & Wesson, Ruger and others, offer models for law enforcement chambered in all the above calibers.

Most modern police departments still provide officers with shotguns — usually sturdy, reliable pump action models from Mossberg, Remington and many others. "SWAT" team armaments, however, more closely resemble military commando squads than officers on routine patrol. Fully-automatic assault rifles (Colt M-16, H&K, Uzi, FLN, etc.), elaborate telescopic and/or laser sights, night-vision systems and other expensive exotica are commonly provided for these high-risk personnel to use in hostage incidents, drug raids and other such paramilitary missions. A few major urban police departments have begun equipping beat officers with assault rifles — Los Angeles is an example — in response to well-publicized firefights with felons.43

Drunkometer/Breathalyzer

As early as 1933, Indiana University Medical Center biochemist Dr. Rollo N. Harger had conduct a police school that trained 40 police officers each year to recognize drunk drivers and use existing equipment to conduct chemical tests and educate the public. "The extent of physical and mental impairment caused by intoxicants long has been a subject of debate,"Harger wrote. "It is frequently argued that a few drinks will stimulate an individual, give him keener perception, convert him into a more alert driver."35 Harger's goal was to establish scientifically that this was not the case and to provide police officers with a way to accurately test for intoxication that would also be acceptable as evidence in court.

In the mid-1920s, Harger had developed reliable blood and urine tests for determining the amount of alcohol in the body. But these methods were not only complicated, it took from several hours to several days to get the results. Recognizing that police personnel would need the information more quickly, his theory was that a breath test would be better, since it was the easiest body material to obtain.

In the mid-1930s, he had little trouble recruiting volunteers to participate in his tests. Subjects were give three drinks of 90 proof whiskey at 45 minute intervals, tested for alcohol concentration and asked to sort a series of cards. The tests proved that reaction time doubled when the level of alcohol reached .15%.

The next step was to develop an instrument police officers could use to determine the level of alcohol. Fortunately, along with being a superb teacher and chemist, Harger was also an inventor. In 1937, he created a machine he and his colleagues jokingly called the Drunkometer. The local Literary Digest referred to it as Harger's "Gin Gadget" but the name Drunkometer stuck.

To use the Drunkometer, the suspect was required to inflate a balloon. His breath would travel into the mechanism and the potassium permaganate solution would turn from "wine color" to amber. When the color change was complete, the chemical in the test tube at the right of the machine would have absorbed its full quota of alcohol. The test tube was then sealed and sent to the Indiana University medical center to be weighed. The increase in weight was in direct ratio to the degree of intoxication.

It was immediately put to use by the Indiana State Police and Indiana became the first state in the nation to authorize the use of chemical tests to determine the specific level of intoxication.

In the late 1940's some agencies began using a variant of the Drunkometer called and

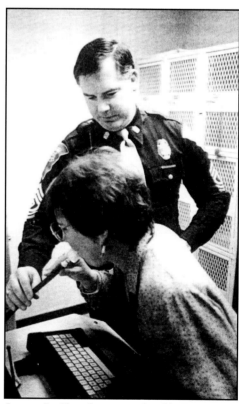

Sergeant Davidson demonstrates how blood alcohol levels are determined in 1992. He and Indina's Finest editor, Marilyn Olsen, are pleased to report that she tested .001.

Intoximeter, which also used chemicals to determine the level of alcohol in a person's blood via a breath test.

Robert Borkenstein, head of the ISPs laboratory who trained ISP troopers on the use of the Drunkometer for many years was continually frustrated by the fact that because it required careful measurements of chemicals and the individual officer's ability to correctly judge the chemicals' color, results were often inaccurate. In 1954, Borkenstein invented the Breathalyzer. The Breathalyzer works on the concept that alcohol fades the color of potassium dichromate. The subject breathes into a cylinder that traps air from the lungs. The air is passed through an ampoule of potassium dichromate in a solution of water and sulphuric acid. If alcohol is present and fades the chemical, a galvanometer indicates the degree of fading. The operator then balances the galvanometer reading by moving a light bulb inside the machine and the adjustment is automatically recorded in figures representing the percentage of alcohol in the blood. Portability was an additional improvement. The Breathalyzer could be taken to the scene of an accident and plugged into the cigarette lighter of the trooper's car.

In the late 1950s, the National Safety Council produced an "alcoholic influence report form" to serve as a guide in performing field sobriety tests. In addition to noting the size of the pupils of the eyes, the ability of the suspected drunk driver to keep his balance, walk and turn, bring his finger to his nose or pick up coins, the officer was encouraged to have the subject repeat the words, "electricity, Methodist Episcopal and Around the Rugged Rock the Ragged Rascal Ran."

Diversity

Although state police agencies were not racially integrated until the 1950s, local police agencies had hired black officers as early as the 1880s.

After Reconstruction, black police officers were assigned duties primarily in black communities to keep other blacks in line. The agencies for whom they worked gave officers carte blanche to use physical force in doing so and many black officers "earned notorious reputations." A photo taken of Robert William Steward in the late 1880's shows him and his white colleagues, "with their shirts off and in a pose symbolizing their readiness to do battle with criminals on the streets." Hugh Allen, the first African American considered for a police job in St. Louis was also hired primarily for his physical prowess even though he achieved one of the highest scores on the St. Louis police exam.

Ira L. Cooper of St. Louis was appointed in 1906 as one of the department's "negro specials." A college graduate, he became the

department's first African-American sergeant, was put in command of a squad of black detectives and listed in "Who's Who in Colored America." He was credited with solving many crimes among them a bank embezzlement scheme conducted by a black porter, whom white detectives were convinced could not have done the job because "blacks did not have the intelligence to commit such crimes." After his death in 1939, one city official remarked that 'but for his color he would have been made chief of the department."

In his book, Black Police in America, from which much of the information in this section was taken, W. Marvin Dulaney says, "African Americans had to define their position as law enforcement officers in a racist society that usually regarded them as 'blacks in police uniforms,' rather than as police officers who happened to be black."

During the 1940s and 1950s many southern cities began hiring black police officers not only to patrol black communities and prevent crime, but also to improve race relations. In 1950, Marshall Jenkins, president of the Houston chapter of the Texas Negro Peace Officers' Association said, "The old Negro officers were placed on the force with no training and used force and violence to take the place of training, but today's officers are carefully selected and highly trained, not only in handling prisoners, but in methods of treating the public."

Throughout the 1950s and 1960s, black officers began to form associations such as the Guardians, the Afro American Patrolmen's League and in the mid 1970s, the National Order of Black Law Enforcement Executives (NOBLE). These black police executives lobbied state and national legislatures for both increased police professionalism among all officers as well as an end to racism at all levels of law enforcement.

Between 1950 and 1957, the Illinois State Police hired 25 minority officers under the merit system. By 1975, there were 52 black male officers and 43% minority (black and Spanish surname) males on the department. In 1968, Robert Patton was promoted to Captain in the Illinois State Police, becoming the highest ranking black officer in any state police force in the US.

Most other state police agencies began hiring black officers during the 1960s, but often only after protracted lawsuits. Even today, on most state police departments, African Americans represent a small percentage of the force.

Women Become Police Officers

Women first joined America's police forces in the 1840s as jail matrons. The first woman to have the title police officer was Marie Owens of Chicago, the widow of a Chi-

Michigan's first female troopers, Noreen Hillary (L) and Kay Whitford (R).

cago patrolman. Appointed in 1893, she did not have arrest powers, but like other women officers for the next 70 years served primarily as a social worker. When Alice Stebbins was given arrest powers in 1910, her duties were still limited to working with women and juveniles.

By the end of World War I there were 300 policewomen, among them Georgia Robinson appointed in 1916 to the Los Angeles Police department. (Preserve and Protect p.40) Robinson's appointment was a landmark in several ways. Not only was Robinson the first African American woman police officer, her duty, to refer young black women to social agencies rather than arrest them was one of the first attempts by the LAPD to attempt to provide services to the black community and dispel the idea that African Americans were naturally predisposed to crime. (Black Police)

In 1935, a separate bureau was created in the New York Police Department for policewomen.

Throughout the 1950s and 1960s, women regardless of their color were appointed to police departments in increasing numbers, but their responsibility was limited. They were generally assigned to work in community relations positions, with women or juvenile offenders. In 1950, even after Vivian Strange became the first black woman to be promoted to police sergeant, she was assigned to be a community relations officer.

In 1952, five women were hired as policewomen in Abilene Texas and issued navy blue wool dresses with yellow piping on each side, navy shirts, black ties navy blue fore and aft hats and a badge that said Police Woman. They couldn't make arrests and did not carry handguns. If they saw something wrong, they had to call a "real police officer." "We were meter maids, but they called us policewomen,"said Lucy Owens. "Mostly, they wanted us to keep those cars moving around the post office and the court-house."

It wasn't until 1968 that Indianapolis Police Department officers Betty Blankenship and Elizabeth Coffal became the first women assigned to patrol duty

"Two interrelated factors led to the use of women as patrol officers. The first was the 1972 amendment of the Civil Rights Act of 1964 which extended the act's coverage to public employees and prohibited job discrimination on the basis of sex. The second was an investigation conducted by the Police Foundation in the early 1970s on the performance of women patrol officers. In general, the studies found that women officers carried out their duties effectively and in fact were less likely than their male counterparts to engage in unbecoming conduct. The only variance from the performance of male officers was that they made fewer arrests and gave fewer traffic citations." In 1972 15 women in the Policewomen's Bureau who had been assigned to precinct desk jobs at the NYPD, volunteered to go on patrol. In 1973, the title policewomen was finally abolished and both male and female members of the department were called police officers. (NYPD website).

Although the percentage of women, black or white, on state police forces remains small, African-American women have probably benefited the most from the increased hiring of women as police officers. By 1990 more than 35% of the women police officers employed in the United States were African Americans and black women constituted 30% of all African American police officers as opposed to 15% of all police officer who were African American.

The Ku Klux Klan

Started by six men in Pulaski Tennessee in 1865, the Ku Klux Klan was at first just an "elaborate game for grown men who like to wear eerie costumes and ride at night on horseback." But soon it turned into a vigilante organization. Ex Confederate General Nathan Bedford Forrest served as head of this group, composed primarily of other ex-Confederates soldiers. The aim of the Klan was threefold: to strike back at the federal Reconstruction government, to put the blacks " back in their place" and to chase the white carpetbaggers back north. "They saw themselves as defenders of the white man's way of life, protectors of their women and saviors of their land and property. To them, it seemed that the Yankees were anxious to turn everything south of the Mason Dixon Line over to illiterate blacks, so

the Klan became a way for the upper class southern whites to strike back." In 1869, the federal government ordered the Klan disbanded. But whippings and lynchings of blacks continued.

In 1915, Thomas Dixon, Jr.'s book, *The Clansman*, was made into the movie, Birth of a Nation and interest in the Klan was revived. William J. Simmons, a former Methodist minister was made Imperial Wizard. "I went around Atlanta talking to men who belonged to other lodges about the new Ku Klux Klan," said Simmons. "The Negroes were getting pretty uppity in the South about that time." "This was a time when people wanted something to belong to, and the Klan, with all its mystery, pomp and pageant offered them their money's worth."

During World War I, the Klan gained even more strength, expanding its list of enemies to include Germans, Catholics, socialists and union leaders. But blacks continued to be the primary target for violence. In 1919, more than 70 blacks were lynched and 14 publicly burned. By the early 1920s, the Klan claimed more than 5 million members. In 1920, Edward Young Clark assumed leadership of the Klan, in a deal that gave him 80% of all the money he could raise from new members. Soon local Klan organizations (Klaverns) were springing up in Indiana, Ohio, Pennsylvania, New Jersey, New York and Maine.

To join and be "naturalized" recruits paid a ten dollar "klecktoken." Four dollars went to the "kleagle" who brought in the recruit, one dollar to the king kleagle of the region and fifty cents to the local grand goblin. The remaining $4.50 went to Atlanta headquarters and was divided among the imperial wizard and his imperial promoters.

In 1940, the Klan joined the German American Bund and staged a large rally in New Jersey. In 1944, unable to pay its back taxes, the Klan disbanded again.

The end of racial segregation in public schools, however, brought renewed interest in the Klan and by 1965, Klan membership was estimated to be 40,000. Today it is difficult to estimate the exact size of the Klan as there are now many organizations all claiming to be Klans of one kind or another.

Even today, rallying in white sheets and hoods, Klansmen often appear on state property. The steps of the state capitol is a favorite location because it always guarantees good media coverage. And so, in most states providing a police presence at Klan rallies becomes a responsibility of the state police, a continuing drain both on funds and manpower. Last year, for example, it cost the Indiana State Police nearly $200,000 in overtime to separate the Klansmen from the anti-Klan protestors and all of them from harming the merely curious. When the costs of other Indiana police agencies were added the figure rose to $650,000.38

Fingerprinting

The science of fingerprint identification was invented in 1881 by Alphonse Bertillon. He had created the first "mug shot" file by taking pictures of French criminals and collecting them at the Bureau of Identification in Paris and making them available to police officers and witnesses to crimes. Although 291 criminals were identified the first year the program was in effect, Bertillon felt that too many criminals were eluding police by simply changing their appearance.

To further refine the identification process, Bertillon developed a statisticaly-based system of identification of criminals based on body measurement. His Bertillon System was widely used by police agencies for more than 20 years.

Meanwhile, in England, scientists Sir William Herschel and Sir Francis Galton, discovered that the tiny ridges on the fingertips were distinctive to each individual and that nothing in age, mutilation, acid, could permanently alter them. As importantly, they found that the grease from the fingers left a finger print on the surfaces it touched and that such prints could be matched with those of the individual to place him at the scene of the crime. Fingerprint experts, however, continued to be known as Bertillon experts.

In 1900, the first fingerprint convictions were obtained in France, England and the US and in 1904, St. Louis established the first fingerprint bureau in America after seeing a demonstration of the technique at the St. Louis World's Fair. In 1906, Joseph Arthur Faurot followed suit compiling the first fingerprint file for the New York City Police Department. A system for filing fingerprints according to the position of arches, loops, whorls and composites was developed by Sir E.R. Henry, Director of Scotland Yard. In 1934, the FBI created a national fingerprint file in the US. By the mid-1930's it became legal in most states to require people to be fingerprinted as part of the booking process following an arrest. In Illinois the Henry fingerprint system eventually replaced the Bertillion system.

As word of the effectiveness of fingerprinting spread, celebrities such as John D. Rockefeller, Jr. Guy Lombardo and Walt Disney had themselves fingerprinted amid widespread publicity and soon ordinary citizens were flocking to state fair police booths to have their fingerprints voluntarily placed on file.

In the 1980s, the FBI created the Automated Fingerprint Identification System (AFIS), a computerized database of fingerprints from across the country. Those agencies requesting a match enter the sex, race, age and other information of the suspect. Then the computer scans the "10 print card" and produces an image of each print on the screen magnified from the one inch or so print on the card to ten or twenty times that size. The AFIS computer, that can scan 650 fingerprints per second, compares the print to the more than 700,000 or so it has on file and comes up with the four or five its system thinks are the closest. The human fingerprint examiner then does a manual exam to verify the computer's choice.

In November, 1995, the FBI began converting 32 million master fingerprint cards to digital images, creating the Integrated Automated Fingerprint Identification System.

Killed in the Line of Duty

Patrolling our state highways can be one of the most dangerous jobs in law enforcement, but it is also one of the most important tasks an officer can be asked to do. Just consider that more than 40,000 people die in automobile accidents each year in our country more than the number of persons killed by homicide or drugs combined. Fortunately, the highway fatality figure has declined dramatically over the past decade and much of the credit is due America's 45,000 state troopers who put their lives on the line daily to make our roads safer.

The first state law enforcement officers to be killed while performing their duties were Captain Thomas G. Williams and Privates Wesley Cherry, J.M. Daniels and Andrew Melville of the Texas State Police. One the afternoon of March 14, 1873, the four officers arrived in the town of Lampasas, Texas, to help clean up what had become a wild and violent frontier settlement. When they entered one of the local saloons and attempted to make an arrest, a shoot-out erupted and the four officers were all mortally wounded. More than three years later, the persons charged with killing the four state police officers stood trial. The jury is said to have acquitted them "without even leaving their seats to reach a decision."

Four hundred thirty state troopers have been killed in automobile accidents, 225 in motorcycle mishaps. The first to die behind the wheel of a car was New York State Trooper James N. Skiff, who collided with a trolley car on May 25, 1920. Car crashes are a unique hazard of the job when you are a state trooper. In fact, traffic accidents are the single greatest cause of trooper deaths, followed by firearm assaults, which account for 405 state police fatalities.

Drunk drivers killed more than 50 state troopers.

Texas highway patrolmen H.D. Murphy and Edward B. Wheeler had the unfortunate distinction of being two of the 10 law enforcement officers killed by outlaws Bonnie and Clyde.

The first female trooper to die in the line of duty was Frances I. Galvin of the Colorado State Patrol who was struck by a car. (Craig Floyd March 1997, American Police Beat)

Arizona Peace Officers Memorial. This brass sculpture, a tribute to Arizona peace officers who gave the ultimate sacrifice while protecting the citizens of Arizona stands near the State's capital in Phoenix, Arizona.

Ohio State Highway Patrol.

Bibliography

Anderson, Kelly C., *Police Brutality*, Lucent Books, San Diego, CA 1995

Bartollas, Clemens and Michael Braswell, *American Criminal Justice, An Introduction*, (second edition), Anderson Publishing Co., 1997

Bechtel, H. Kenneth, *State Police in the United States, A Socio-Historical Analysis*, Greenwood Press, Westport, CT. 1995

Behr, Edward, *Prohibition, Thirteen Years that Changed America*, Arcade Publishing, New York, NY 1996

Bender, David, *Crime*, Greenhaven Press, San Diego, CA, 1998

Bintliff, Russell, *Police Procedural, a writer's guide to the police and how they work*, Writer's Digest Books, Cincinnati, OH 1993.

Borkenstein, R.F., *Chemical Tests for Intoxication*, Indiana State Police, 1949

Carpenter, Michael J., *Green Mountain Troopers: Vermont and Its State Police*, PTR Publishing, Shaftsbury, VT, 1997

Cox, Mike, *Silver Stars and Six Guns*, Texas Department of Public Safety, txdps.state.tx.us

Cretors, Fred, *Sentinels for Safety*, Indiana State Police, Indianapolis, IN 1940

Crime, A Serious American Problem, Information Plus, Wylie, TX, 1994

D'Angelo, Laura, *Hate Crimes*, Chelsea Publishers, Philadelphia, PA, 1998

Dolan, Edward F. and Margaret M. Scariano, *Guns in the United States*, An Impact Book, New York, NY, 1994.

Donzingner, Steven R., *The Real War on Crime*, Harper Collins Publishers, Inc., New York, NY, 1996

Dulhaney, W. Marvin, *Black Police in America*, Indiana University Press, Bloomington, IN 1996

Durham, Jennifer L., *Crime in America*, AABC-CLIO, Inc., Santa Barbara, CA 1996

Eiserer, Tanya, *First Policewomen Little More Than Meter Readers*, www.texnews.com/local97/3blue08037.html

Floyd, Craig, Chairman, *National Law Enforcement Officers Memorial Fund*

Freidman, Lawrence M., *Crime and Punishment in American History*, BasicBooks, New York, NY 1993

Ferguson, Tom, *Modern Law Enforcement Weapons & Tactics*, DBI Books, Inc., Northbrook, IL

Golay, Michael and Carl Rollyson, *Where America Stands*, 1996, John Wylie and Sons, New York, NY, 1996.

Higgins, Will, "Klan Rallies Create Big Bills for Taxpayers," Indianapolis Star, March 29, 1998

Illinois Labor History, www.kentlaw.edu/ilhs/curriculum.html#6

Indiana State Police, 1921-1937, Indiana State Police, Indianapolis, IN 1937

Landau, Elaine, *Armed America*, Julian Messner, a division of Silver Burdett Press, Inc. Simon & Schuster Inc., Englewood Cliffs, NJ, 1991

Lutholtz, M. William, Grand Dragon: *D.C. Stephenson and the Ku Klux Klan in Indiana*, Purdue University Press, West Lafayette, IN 1991

McCord, Monty, *Cars of the State Police and Highway Patrol*, Krause Publications, Inc. 1994

Moss, Geroge Donelson, *America in the Twentieth Century*, (Third Edition), Prentice Hall, Upper Saddle River, NJ 1997

Olsen, Thomas F., *Evolution in Law Enforcement Small Arms*, Indianapolis, IN 1998

Police Women's Bureau, The, www.ci.nyc.ny.us/nyclink/html/nypd/3100/retro-37

Rowland, Desmond and James Bailey, *The Law Enforcement Handbook*, Nethuen Publications, a division of the Carswell Company Limited, 1985

Royal Canadian Mounted Police, www.RCMP-grc.gc.ca.

Saferstein, Richard, PhD., *Criminalistics, An Introduction to Forensic Science*, (Sixth Edition), Prentice Hall, Upper Saddle River, NJ 1998

To Serve and Protect, Turner Publishing Company, Paducah, KY 1995

United States History from 1865, Addison Wesley Publishing company, Menlo Park, CA, 1986

Winters, Paul A., *Policing the Police*, Greenhaven Press, Inc., San Diego, CA 1995

Wright, Richard A., *West of Laramie, A Brief History of the Auto Industry*, www.com.wayne.edu/staff/wright/autohistory/oo.html

Special Stories of State Troopers

*Taken from submitted material, the following pages feature (in random order)
stories, personal experiences, news articles and historical accounts.*

Alabama State Troopers are involved in all natural disasters.

DUI: Head On Into Traffic

by Michael S. Payne, Alabama

One night while patrolling the Interstate (I-85), my dispatcher advised me of a vehicle traveling north in the southbound lane. I was about eight miles from the location of the possible DUI suspect. I responded code 3 (lights and siren) to attempt to make contact with the violator. An off-duty Notasulga Police Officer (Officer Bradley) was riding with me that night. He stated "He's right in front of us." I said "Where?" He stated "In front of us." What had occurred was the suspect vehicle was actually traveling south in the north bound lane. His vehicle head lamps had blended with the south bound traffic. It was hard to tell he was coming head-on toward my patrol car. I stopped in the center of both lanes with my blue lights on in an attempt to stop the subject. The violator slowed down to about 30 mph. The violator and I looked eye to eye, then he accelerated very quickly. I advised the dispatcher that I was 10-100A (hot pursuit/attempting to elude). The violator was running about 95-100 mph in the left lane (fast traffic lane) of the north bound traffic lanes. Fortunately, all the traffic we encountered was in the right lane and all pulled off the road. The chase lasted about 3-4 miles when the violator came around a curve with a downgrade slope. There were two 18 wheelers side by side. Both trucks hit their brakes and the violator turned into the median at 95 mph. I slammed on my anti-lock brakes then turned into the median. Both trucks passed without hitting anything. The violator started spinning 360 degrees in the median. After spinning three complete times, the violator's vehicle came out of the median and crossed the north bound lanes of traffic. The violator's vehicle hit a guardrail head-on and flipped completely into the air and made one revolution. The vehicle flipped several times down a 400 feet embankment. I stopped my patrol car in the median and called for an ambulance. I then ran over to the guardrail and jumped over it. When I got down to the violator's vehicle, it was resting on its right side. The suspect was sitting in the car. I asked if he was all right. He advised "Yes." I then told him his car was smoking and was possibly going to catch fire. I told him, if he could, to get out of the car. The suspect climbed out of the car. We both climbed the embankment to the top at which time, I told him he was under arrest for DUI, reckless endangerment and whatever other offenses I could think of. I finally charged the suspect with DUI, reckless endangerment, speeding, attempting to elude, driving on the wrong side of the road and driving with a suspended driver's license. The violator was transported to the hospital and released. I then took the suspect to jail.

This occurred my first year as an Alabama State Trooper. As I look back on this situation, I remember praying that the violator would not hit anybody while traveling head-on into traffic.

A Modern Day "Sgt. Preston"

Reprinted from Pacific Northwest Law Enforcement News, November 1959

On November 1, 1959, the 6'5", 230-pound sergeant, Gene Morris, became the only state police officer in the entire Alaska Northwest, an area of more than 200,000 square miles. A kind of modern day "Sergeant Preston." A former professional baseball player, Morris batted back and forth between police work and baseball after an injury to his pitching arm made full-time baseball impossible. He came up to Whitehorse, Yukon Territory, as an engineer with Standard Oil in 1944 and then to Fairbanks in 1945. Morris went back to the States in 1948 and for two years alternated as a baseball manager in the summer and a policeman in the winter in Iowa. In 1950 he heard of an opening on the Highway Patrol in Fairbanks and gave up full-time baseball for good. And so the modern day "Sergeant Preston" took off for the north country with a couple of guns, a pair of handcuffs, a sack full of baseball bats and gloves and an old woolen baseball jersey.

"They Always Get Their Man"

Reprinted from Pacific Northwest Law Enforcement News, 1960

While the slogan, "They always get their man," has long been identified as referring to action of the RCMP, Trooper Thomas C. "Tommy" Roberts, oldest member of the Anchorage detachment from point of service, and trail-roughened, is not convinced that the slogan should be solely applied to that agency.

Informed that an assault had been committed in remote Lime Village, an Indian settlement, Roberts volunteered to bring out the suspect. He flew to within 10 miles of the village and completed the journey on foot. Then, due to landing gear failure, he was forced to bring his man out on foot to Sparrevohn, a distance of 35 miles, where air transport service was available.

A Notification To Remember

by Laurel Norris, Sergeant
Arizona Department of Public Safety
Criminal Investigations Bureau

I was at home asleep when I received the call-out at 0615 hours. It was Saturday, May 15, 1982. I was a two-year veteran with the Arizona Highway Patrol assigned to District 10, area one, which encompassed a 100-mile area southwest of Phoenix, Arizona. Call-outs were not unusual for our area and neither were fatal accidents. This would be my first fatal involving out-of-state travelers.

As I approached the accident scene on State Route 85, affectionately called Bloody Buckeye Road, I saw a semi-tractor trailer and a light tan Ford sedan blocking the westbound traffic lanes. I was the second trooper to arrive on the scene and was immediately told there were three fatalities. Looking at the tan Ford, I wondered how three lives could have perished with so little exterior damage. The tan Ford sedan was facing south off the roadway with the rear wheels resting in a dirt ditch, the left side of the vehicle looked unblemished. As I walked around the front of the vehicle, I saw the devastation. The entire right side of the vehicle had been peeled away like a sardine can. There were three bodies still trapped in the vehicle, the driver, front passenger and the

A notification to remember.

left rear passenger. A fourth passenger who had been sleeping in the right rear position had been flown to the hospital in critical condition. Although the driver of the semi-tractor had not been physically injured, mentally he was shaken by the totality of the deaths.

I completed my investigation at the scene and released the bodies to the county mortician. From the written documentation gathered, I was able to ascertain that the deceased driver and one of the passengers were the father and aunt of the injured passenger, but the third deceased passenger was a mystery and her identification did not match her driver's license photo. The three deceased individuals showed residency in Texas and the injured passenger was in the military, stationed in California. The hospital advised the fourth passenger was in a coma with extensive internal injuries; they were not sure if he was going to pull through.

Working from our Communications Center in central Phoenix, I set out to identify the mystery passenger and to make death notification to the appropriate parties. Our policy dictates that a death notification is to be made in person by a law enforcement agency. Since all three of the deceased were from out of town, I was tasked with identifying the nearest law enforcement agency to their residencies, and asking that agency to make the death notification. I was able to obtain the phone number of the police department in a small town in Texas in which the deceased resided. I contacted the department and spoke with a dispatcher who was the only person in the office at noon. I explained I had three local residents who had been killed in an auto accident in Phoenix, Arizona, and needed an officer to confirm their identities and make the death notification to the next-of-kin. I also requested the officer to contact me back with the information on who had been notified and at what time. I gave the dispatcher my name and call back number and proceeded to wait for the return phone call.

Approximately 15 minutes later, I received a phone call from a woman in Texas who stated she had been advised by the local police department that her father had been in an accident in Arizona and that she was to call me. I verified that her father was the driver and she confirmed the identity of the passengers, including her father's girlfriend, the third passenger. She then asked me for details of what had happened; at this time I figured she had already been told her father was deceased. This was a big mistake on my part, as I started to explain that he was killed because he fell asleep at the wheel, crossed the center line and was struck practically head-on by a semi-tractor trailer. The next thing I heard has haunted me for years; there is no mistaking the blood-curdling scream of someone who has just been told unexpectedly of the death of a loved one. To my horror, I heard the phone drop and the distant screaming of a woman in pain. I felt so helpless and shocked at what had happened,

then the anger set in as I realized the local police had only told this woman to call me, they had not made the death notification in person, nor was there an officer at her residence at the time she called me.

I immediately contacted the local department and demanded an officer respond to the woman's residence as I had no idea what her condition was or if she needed medical assistance. Within 10 minutes, an officer contacted me from the residence; the officer had found two distraught women and had to request medical assistance for one of them.

I learned a very valuable lesson that day and recognized that not all agencies receive the same level of training in all aspects of law enforcement. Do not assume anything and ask to speak with the officer at the residence first, before you talk to the next-of-kin in an out-of-state death notification.

I still live with the horror of that woman screaming into the phone and the helplessness I felt that fatal night. The fourth passenger did survive and recovered fully. He had just graduated from military boot camp; his father and aunt had picked him up to return to Texas for a two-week leave, before he was sent on overseas.

Civilian Ride-Along Helps Trooper

by Laurel Norris, Sergeant
Arizona Department of Public Safety
Criminal Investigations Bureau

Working the swing shift (1800-0200 hours) seems to be the most sought after shift for civilian "ride-alongs." I guess they figure it is the most likely shift for something exciting or dangerous to happen. As a female Highway Patrol officer I was routinely tasked with handling requests from civilians wanting to "see what it was like" to be an officer. I was a two-year veteran with the Arizona Highway Patrol stationed in Avondale, which is a suburb west of Phoenix, Arizona that encompassed a two-lane State Route and a four-lane freeway. Since the freeway was not completed, most of my activity centered around the State Route, which ran through several small towns and communities.

On September 6, 1982, I was two hours into my shift when I picked up a young female, 18 years of age civilian ride-along. It was around 2100 hours when I picked up Sandy (fictitious name) and began explaining the responsibilities of a civilian rider. Normally, I would accomplish this task while at a substation or parked in the patrol vehicle. But, since the night was young and Sandy was eager to see what being an officer was all about, I elected to explain the responsibilities as I drove. As I traveled westbound on State Route 85 through the small community of Cashion, I had just finished explaining how important a triple nine code was when I noticed a vehicle parked

on the roadway, facing eastbound in the traffic lane with all its lights off. Several moving vehicles nearly ran into the parked vehicle as I was negotiating my patrol car eastbound to notify travelers of the impending hazard. I positioned my marked patrol car behind the parked vehicle and activated my overhead emergency lights and rear flashers. After approaching the vehicle and identifying that it was not occupied, I heard a male voice off in the distance. An elderly man approached walking with a fast gate, and as he passed my location he stated that he had just stopped to get directions and would be on his way directly. I asked the individual why he had stopped and parked on the roadway when he could have, and should have, pulled into the gas station where he obtained directions. His only reply was he was not from around here and just stopped for only a moment.

At this time, I told the driver I needed to see his operator's license and vehicle registration. The elderly subject removed his wallet from his rear pants pocket, opened the wallet and while still holding the wallet displayed the license in clear plastic just long enough for me to take a quick look at it. I asked Mr. Smith (fictitious name) to please remove the license, to which he refused, stating I had seen enough and that he needed to get on his way. Mr. Smith was informed that either he could show me his license properly now or at jail facility. Mr. Smith became very agitated over this and continually stated how he needed to be on his way as he was already late and attempted to get into his vehicle in an effort to leave.

As I grabbed Mr. Smith's arm to keep him from entering his vehicle, the fight was on. Now mind you, I do not condone elderly abuse, but when you have an 82-year-old man in a wrist lock and bent over the hood of your patrol car, you would think he would be a little passive. Not Mr. Smith; not only was he cussing up a storm, he was attempting to kick me, and strike me with his free hand. I didn't know whether to laugh at how ridiculous a sight it must be to manhandle an 82-year-old man or to cry at the thought that if I pressed too hard I could end up breaking Mr. Smith's arm. As I held Mr. Smith against the patrol car and attempted to get him to calm down, I noticed a crowd was gathering outside the local bar. It didn't take long to realize I was the center of attention, and that there were bets being made by the drunken crowd on who was going to win in the struggle.

It had only been a matter of minutes since this whole situation began to unfold with Mr. Smith when I recognized a familiar sound off in the distance. I heard sirens blaring in every direction possible and wondered what was happening and now I was going to miss out on whatever it was because of Mr. Smith's obstinacy.

As I focused my attention back on Mr. Smith and attempted to handcuff him before he hurt himself, or I hurt him, I realized the sirens were getting closer to my location. The next time I looked up, I observed several squad cars from the sheriff's office, local police departments and Highway Patrol skidding up to my location. A half a dozen officers exited their vehicles with guns drawn as the crowd in front of the bar vanished in a cloud of dust. I now had Mr. Smith secured with handcuffs when the first officer approached me and asked what was the triple nine situation? I was flabbergasted to learn that Sandy, my civilian rider, had called in a triple nine over the radio. As soon as my fellow officers learned that the triple nine was for an 82-year-old man who refused so show his license, I was ridiculed and embarrassed to the fullest. It wasn't until one of my fellow officers attempted to place the arrested Mr. Smith into the rear of my patrol car, that everyone fully understood the problems Mr. Smith was capable of causing. Mr. Smith refused to keep his feet in the vehicle when the officer tried to close the door and then he kicked the door open and attempted to get out. After four attempts to get Mr. Smith into the vehicle by himself, the officer requested assistance with holding Mr. Smith down while the doors were closed; it took a total of four officers to secure Mr. Smith.

Mr. Smith was transported to the Maricopa County Sheriff's Jail facility where he continued to resist officers during his booking process. Mr. Smith had to remain restrained throughout the process and during his arraignment proceedings. Mr. Smith was charged with creating a roadway hazard by parking on the roadway and resisting arrest.

An additional fall-out from this arrest was that a fellow officer burned up her patrol vehicle's engine attempting to respond to the triple nine call. She was so upset with me when she found out it wasn't a legitimate call because she had destroyed her new patrol car for nothing. A positive note was the dispatcher handling the radio that evening complimented the civilian rider for her calm voice and accurate description of my location which allowed responding units to find me.

I now explain the difference between requesting a backup and calling a triple nine situation to all civilian riders prior to placing the patrol car in gear.

Who Will Help The Kids

by Laurel Norris, Sergeant
Arizona Department of Public Safety
Criminal Investigation Bureau

Working undercover narcotics is not everyone's bag, and least of all mine. I had spent the first five years of my career in uniform patrolling the highways of Arizona, a year instructing at the State Academy, three years protecting the governor of our state, and two years working administrative positions. But one of my least-liked experiences came when

I was offered an opportunity to work street narcotics. I had always wondered whether I could handle the stress and strain of working an undercover assignment. My first concern was, would I burst out laughing the first time someone attempted to sell me dope? I had always found it very humorous when I heard how someone had walked up to an undercover officer and openly sold them narcotics. My first attempt at buying narcotics was a sobering experience.

My narcotics partner had been dealing with a women for nearly a year. She was a small-time user, but a middle person for larger quantities of dope. My partner figured she was the perfect doper for me to use, as she was low volume and a low safety risk. We had spent a week rehearsing my cover story, "I don't use marijuana, I just wanted to buy a small amount as a birthday gift for my sister who uses regularly." It sounded believable and I felt comfortable playing such a role.

As we drove up to the apartment building I became very nervous and was hoping the contact wasn't home. As we sat in the car waiting for me to build up the courage to go in, our doper walked around the corner of the building, recognized my partner and waved. I started to panic as she looked very familiar to me; I wasn't sure if I had gone to school with her or if I had arrested her before. My partner told me it was too late now, we had to go since she had seen us. As I exited the vehicle, my partner introduced me, and the doper's immediate response was, "You look familiar, where did you go to school?" I wasn't sure whether I should tell her the truth and take the chance that she also went there and would remember me, or to lie and choose another school. I was hating this assignment immensely. I told her the truth and was relieved to find out she had not attended the same high school.

We all walked to her apartment which was on the second floor and barely furnished. The doper immediately took my partner off to the side and started to conduct business; she was in need of cash and wanted to sell him some crack cocaine. I sat on the couch and watched an 18-month-old lying on the floor and playing with kitchen utensils. There was also a 2-year-old wandering in and out of the living room.

My partner wasn't interested in making any purchases that night and tried to get the doper to sell me some marijuana. The doper was so desperate to make a big sale, she tried to convince my partner that the crack cocaine she had to sell was very high quality. She suggested her 14-year-old son smoke some of the crack in an effort to show the burning purity. Both my partner and I stated that wasn't necessary, but she insisted, and her son was more than eager to perform the task. A 16-year-old girl came out of the bedroom and became irate that she wasn't selected to smoke the crack. I

was flabbergasted, this woman had a 14-year-old son and a 16-year-old daughter who were already junkies. The 2-year-old and the 18-month-old were also her children. If she was actively encouraging the older kids to use drugs, what chance did the two younger kids have growing up in such an environment?

The day we busted her was the only day the doper acknowledged her two younger children and expressed a concern of what was going to happen to them. Child Protective Services was contacted and responded. All four kids were taken into state custody, but the doper eventually received full custody.

I no longer work undercover narcotics; it is too draining mentally and it is frustrating to see the type of lives dopers live and the revolving doors of criminal justice.

I Buried An Indian

by Officer D.A. Schroder

I have been an officer with the Arizona Department of Public Safety for approximately 25 years. My first day of the 18 week DPS academy was September 14, 1972. Three weeks prior to graduating the available duty stations for the state were posted. One of the duty stations was Oraibi. Not one of my 40-member cadet class put in for Oraibi, most of us had never even heard of it before. Anyway, I was asked by Colonel Tom Milldebrandt, head of the Highway Patrol Bureau if I would volunteer to take this duty station. I told the colonel that I would let him know the next day. That night I looked Oraibi up on a state map and learned that it was on the Hopi Indian Reservation in northern Arizona. After graduation in January 1973, I moved to Oraibi. The nearest DPS officer or town was Winslow and it was 80 miles to the south.

I found the Hopi people to be gracious and I was welcomed by most of them. However the first Hopi Indian that I told was under arrest tried to fight me. It was like being the new kid in a bad part of town, he had to try me out. After that first arrest, I guess the word got around because no one tried to fight me again.

From the time that I accepted this duty station I decided that I would strive to respect the Hopi's beliefs, heritage and traditions as long as it wasn't contrary to the laws I swore to uphold. The following details, about one rainy Sunday night in late August of 1973 resulted in me gaining the total respect of the entire reservation.

I had gone off duty at 1500 hours that day and was at Bruce Powell's house for dinner. Bruce was the manager of the Babbitt's trading post in Oraibi. A rain and lightening storm moved into the area approximately 1700 hours.

At about 1845 hours the Oraibi village chief knocked on Bruce's front door. He related: A young Hopi woman had walked t his house, from about four miles south of the village. She told him that her husband had been out hunting rabbits with his rifle and she thought he had been struck by lightning, but she wasn't sure. The chief asked Bruce and I if we would go find the young man and retrieve the body, if it were true.

Most of the Kachina dances performed by the Hopi people are their way of praying for rain for their crops, as they have no irrigation. They believe the "Rain God" is the good spirit and lightning is an evil spirit. If someone gets struck by lightning their belief is that the evil spirit enters the body and then is transferred to anyone who touches the body.

After getting directions to the area where the young Hopi male was hunting Bruce and I drove his Blazer to the area.

Approximately two hours later we found the 22 year old Hopi lying face down approximately 100 yards east of his pickup, still clutching a 22 rifle. After I rolled the body over I pried the rifle out of his hands and noted that his hands had sustained an electrical burn, his teeth appeared to have been pushed outward, all the laces on his boots were split and the toes of his boots were blown out from the inside. Bruce and I placed the body in the back of his Blazer and drove to the church, which was on main street in the Oraibi village.

The village medicine man, who was performing prayer ceremonies at the deceased's home, was notified that we found and retrieved the young man, that he had been struck by lightning and that he was deceased. We stayed with the body, outside the church, as the Hopi believed that the evil spirit would also enter a building if he were taken inside. Then we were requested to transport the body to the Indian hospital in Keams Canyon (27 miles to the east) so the doctor could pronounce him dead, for insurance purposes.

We arrived back at the church, with the body at 0200 hours. At 0530 hours we were requested to take the body up on the side of the hill behind the deceased parents home where we found a 51 diameter by 6' deep hole had been dug. At the direction of the medicine man Bruce and I prepared the deceased for burial: the body was laid on a new blanket, we tied prayer feathers in his hair and on his shirt over his heart, a new complete set of clothing, right down to underwear was placed around him. We were instructed to wrap the blanket around the body, we tied a new rope around the blanket above his head, spiraled it around the blanket then tied it around the blanket below his feet. I then climbed into the grave, Bruce lowered the body into the hole and I laid the body in the bottom. We then shoveled the dirt back into the hole. The 22 rifle and other personal effects of the deceased were placed on top of the grave.

For the next three hours Bruce and I participated in a purification ceremony, performed by the village medicine man, to drive the evil spirit out of our bodies and his Blazer.

For the rest of my assignment in Hopiland I received numerous personal invitations to various Hopi ceremonies. When the word got around the reservation that I was transferring numerous Hopi people attempted to convince me to stay.

I have never regretted volunteering for this duty assignment. The experience and knowledge I gained over my first 19 months on the Highway Patrol was immeasurable.

Arizona Highway Patrolman D.A. "Dave" Schroder #1176. Photo taken on the Hopi Reservation in 1973 by a newspaper reporter out of Winslow, AZ.

"If Necessary, Lay Down My Life..."

The Newhall Incident, California: 25 Years Later

The words Newhall and tragedy became forever synonymous on April 6, 1970. On that day four young California Highway Patrol officers lost their lives in a four and a half-minute gun battle that left four women widows and seven children, ranging in age from nine months to four years, without fathers. The tremor that rolled through the CHP and, in fact, all law enforcement, spoke of grief for lost comrades and their suffering families, of organizational concern with the urgency of rethinking high risk stop procedures, of humility imposed by such a catastrophic event, and then, the iron resolve to prevent a reoccurrence.

The 25th anniversary of this sad day was observed in April 1995, at the present Newell Area office, where a brick memorial pays tribute to Officers James Pence (6885), Roger Gore (6547), Walt Frago (6520) and George Allen (6290). The Memorial once stood at the former Newell Office, but was rebuilt at the new site about one mile from the scene of the slayings, which occurred in a restaurant parking lot just before midnight.

Officers Frago and Gore had been alerted by radio of a vehicle carrying someone who had brandished a weapon. They spotted the car, fell in behind, called for backup, and began the stop procedure. When the subject's vehicle had come to a halt in the parking lot, the driver was instructed to get out and place his spread hands on the hood. Gore approached him and Frago moved to the passenger side. The right door suddenly swung open and the passenger sprang out, firing at Frago, who fell with two shots in his chest. The gunman, later identified as Jack Twinning, then turned and fired once at Gore, who returned fire. In that moment the driver, Bobby Davis, turned and shot Gore twice at close range. Both officers died instantly.

When Pence and Alleyn drove in moments later, they could see neither suspects nor downed officers, but immediately came under fire. Pence put out an 11-99 call ("officer needs help") then took cover behind the passenger door. Alleyn grabbed the shotgun and positioned himself behind the driver side door. Both officers were mortally wounded in the ensuing exchange, and one subject was hit.

Suspects, Jack Twinning and Bobby Davis, escaped, later abandoned their vehicle and then split up. For nine hours officers blanketed the area searching for the killers. Twinning broke into a house and briefly held a man hostage. Officers used tear gas before storming the house, but the suspect killed himself using the shotgun he had stolen from Officer Frago. Davis was captured, stood trial and was convicted on four counts of murder.

Bobby Davis was sentenced to die in the gas chamber, but in 1972 the California Supreme Court declared the death penalty to be cruel and unusual punishment and, in 1973, the court modified Davis' sentence to life in prison. For many years he was incarcerated at Folsom State Prison, but was last known to have been moved to Pelican Bay State Prison, the home of California's most notorious criminals.

In the weeks immediately after the four deaths, the emotionally charged follow-up investigation sometimes lingered on faultfinding, but ultimately achieved the desired catharsis, a completely revamped set of procedures to be followed during high-risk and felony stops, with emphasis at every step on officer safety. If there can be such a thing as a silver lining in a cloud this dark, it would be the renewed focus on officer safety, a concern still uppermost even 25 years later.

At the 1995 Memorial Ceremony, family members and colleagues of the dead officers joined dignitaries and Highway Patrol officers who didn't know the four men, but whose lives have been influenced by that fateful night in 1970. Officers Walt Frago, Roger Gore, James Pence and George Alleyn will live forever in that special place of memory which the Highway Patrol reserves for those who have given their lives while on duty. These four remain unique because their memories evoke a sorrow never quite put behind us, and the knowledge that their sacrifices ultimately made the Highway Patrol stronger, wiser and more resolute.

Trooper Ernest J. Morse
Connecticut State Police

High profile cases kept Connecticut State Police in the national spotlight throughout the 1950s. On February 13, 1953 Ernest J. Morse, age 31, was on patrol on the Wilbur Cross Parkway when he spotted a car reported stolen in Brookline, MA. Morse pursued and stopped the car. As he approached the car, John Donahue fired a shot and struck Morse in the abdomen. Several minutes later, a carload of sailors from the Groton Sub Base found Morse lying near his car still conscious. Morse whispered portions of a license plate number to the sailors, and directed them to use his radio to call for help. Morse died less than an hour later. Donahue was spotted again, a chase ensued, shots were exchanged and Donahue was captured.

Trooper Russell Bagshaw
Connecticut State Police

On Wednesday, June 5, 1991, at about 3:00 a.m. Trooper Russell Bagshaw, age 28, of Manchester, Connecticut, was executed in an ambush style shooting after he stopped at a North Windham gun shop to check the build-ing. A four year veteran assigned to Troop K, Trooper Bagshaw interrupted a burglary at the store, and died of multiple gunshot wounds before he could use the radio or exit his cruiser. A firefighter driving by the gun shop minutes afterwards, saw the cruiser with its strobe lights on and stopped at a pay phone to call the store owner and ask whether there was an alarm at the shop. When the shopkeeper replied that the alarm had not gone off, the firefighter returned to the shop. He found Trooper Bagshaw slumped over the wheel. The firefighter then used Trooper Bagshaw's portable radio and began calling, "Officer down! Officer down!" Several minutes later, troopers began arriving.

It was clear that the incident had begun as a burglary at the gun shop, during which more than 20 weapons were stolen. After launching one of the most aggressive investigations in state police history, detectives began combing the area, and developed information that a gray Volkswagon Rabbit was seen pulling out of the shop driveway around the time of the shooting. A witness was able to provide enough of a description for a composite drawing. Troopers from around the state traveled to North Windham to help in any way. Departments from Massachusetts and Rhode Island offered to do what ever they could.

Sergeant Steven Fields had been at the shooting scene from the onset, and was ordered home to get some rest. He stopped at a tavern in Jewett City on the way home at about 1:00 a.m. the next morning, and was harassed by a patron, Terry Johnson, age 21, of Mansfield. Johnson directed some racial remarks at Sergeant Fields and made some comment that it was "too bad" he wasn't "in that cruiser." In short order, Johnson was arrested and charged with Breach of Peace in what first appeared to be an unrelated incident.

In what can only be described as a bad move, Johnson's arrest got a number of people thinking. Trooper Keith Hoyt of Troop E looked at the composite drawing and remarked that it looked similar to Terry Johnson. He also remembered Johnson drove a gray Volkswagon Rabbit that had been registered to Daniel Parker of Mansfield. State Police Detectives Michael Guillot and John Szamocki dove into Johnson's background and began interviewing everyone he was known to associate with, including Donald Williams of Jewett City. Williams promptly told the detectives that Terry Johnson had admitted to "killing a cop."

Donald Parker and his wife Wendy were interviewed, and Parker reported that Terry Johnson had been staying at his home since November. Parker also reported that he sold his Volkswagon Rabbit to Terry Johnson. Other pieces began to fall into place when Mrs. Parker said she had seen Terry Johnson come home some time after 3:00 a.m. on Wednesday morning. On Thursday afternoon State Police Detectives Thomas Davoren and Lawrence Gibeault located the gray VW at the Johnson family home in Griswold. They interviewed Terry's brother Duane, age 18, and during that interview, Duane provided the details of how he and Terry had burglarized the gun shop. Before the interview was over, Duane would name his brother as Trooper Bagshaw's killer.

On Friday at about 1:30 a.m., Col. Raoul Ouellette addressed the media and reported that state police were executing arrest warrants on Terry and Duane Johnson for the murder of Trooper Russell Bagshaw as he spoke. In less than 48 hours, the department had identified and arrested the two men responsible for the most cold-blooded violence ever leveled at a Connecticut State Trooper.

In a surprise turn of events, Terry Johnson pleaded guilty to the capital felony murder before the trial began. In May 1993 he was ordered put to death in the state's electric chair. Most legal experts predicted that if Johnson was to be executed, the appeal process would take five to 14 years before exhausted. His brother Duane was tried and also convicted of capital felony murder in 1994. In November of 1997 the state Supreme Court overturned that conviction, ruling that there was no evidence that Duane Johnson intended to kill Trooper Russell Bagshaw, since his brother pulled the trigger. The court let stand a felony murder charge and ordered the Superior Court to re-sentence Duane Johnson for that crime. On November 14, 1997 Duane Johnson was re-sentenced to 60 years in prison for felony murder.

Reprinted with permission from Connecticut State Police Academy Alumni Association 90th Anniversary Year Book, Meriden, CT.

Sgt. W.F. Black
Georgia State Patrol

The first Georgia State Patrol Trooper killed in the line of duty was Sgt. W.F. Black. Black and Trooper Bass Farr were on patrol a few days before Christmas 1940, near the town of Ringgold in north Georgia. The two troopers stopped a vehicle driven by an escapee from Missouri, on a lonely two-lane road.

The escapee waited, gun in hand, while Black approached the vehicle. In the dark, there were two quick flashes from the escapee's handgun. The first hit Black in the groin, knocking him backward, and the second hit him in the chin and chest as he fell to the pavement. Farr quickly tried to get Black to a hospital in Chattanooga, Tennessee. Unfortunately, Black died somewhere around the Tennessee-Georgia state line.

Armed with full arrest power, Georgia and Tennessee State Troopers searched for the escapee. The troopers became involved in a chase with the suspect on Christmas Day around 5:00 p.m. The suspect crashed his vehicle, but again eluded police. However, he was apprehended about one hour later as troopers tracked him.

Complacent No More!
Submitted by Tfc. Larry E. Bray, Maryland State Police

On March 6, 1978, I was working the 3:00 to 11:00 p.m. shift in the northern patrol sector of Cecil County. This sector was a rural area, consisting of the small community of Rising Sun, which at that time had about 700 residents. Rising Sun was your typical Small Town, USA.

Troopers working this predominately rural area enjoyed a close working relationship with the local citizens. Troopers assigned to this patrol sector handled such typical calls as accidents, occasional domestics, bar fights, thefts, and breaking and enterings. The volume of calls was much less than many adjacent sectors. I had been a trooper for approximately eight years and had grown accustomed to working in this quiet community. I suppose I had become a victim of that condition that police officers commonly refer to as "complacency." Most of the calls I handled had become almost routine in my mind, dealing with the same individuals every weekend, responding to the same complaints. Little did I know that on this particular day, about four hours into my shift, I would experience an ordeal that would change my attitude of "complacency" completely and forever.

At the time, the town of Rising Sun had a police force of three full-time officers. Officer Daniel Benham was on duty this night. Danny and I had become good friends and had come to rely on each other in the performance of our police duties also. There were no boundaries between us. The old saying, "one riot, one trooper," was still the norm with the Maryland State Police, and you were expected to handle your calls accordingly.

At approximately 2200 hours, Danny contacted me via radio in reference to an assault complaint at the Rising Sun Hotel, and requested I respond for back-up. When I arrived, I contacted Danny, who had been conversing with several people on the establishment's parking lot. It had been determined that a subject was presently inside the hotel with a shotgun and he had been pointing the gun at patrons in the hotel. It was also known that the weapon was loaded as the subject was seen loading and ejecting the shells while inside the bar. Unfortunately, troopers working the road at that time didn't have today's luxury of a Tactical Assault Team or negotiators available to handle this type of situation.

Danny and I immediately started clearing the hotel of the remaining patrons as their safety was of primary concern. We had observed the suspect standing with his back to the door against a knee wall which separated the poolroom and the bar area. We entered the building from the side entrance. Danny and I had decided that he would take up a position just inside the door and provide cover while I attempted to approach the subject from the rear

using the knee wall as cover. With my service revolver drawn, I approached the suspect and when I was within a foot of the subject, I announced "Police," and ordered him to put the gun down. He suddenly turned around, pointing the weapon at me. My first instinct was to shoot, however, there were two employees still in the building, and Danny was nearby. I immediately grabbed the barrel of the shotgun and a struggle ensued, causing the shotgun to discharge. Somehow, no one was injured from the blast as I was able to keep the weapon pointed to the floor. After the shotgun discharged, the subject continued to struggle, grabbing my legs and forcing me backwards. After taking the weapon from the subject, he was finally subdued and taken into custody.

Later investigation revealed that the subject was emotionally distraught and enraged over marital problems. The subject was charged with attempted murder, assault, and weapon charges.

This entire incident lasted probably only seconds, but it seemed like an eternity. Everything seemed to be in slow motion. I learned a valuable lesson from this incident: take every call seriously, nothing is ever "routine" about our profession, and above all don't become "complacent." The experience certainly reminded me of the dangers of being a police officer, and how quickly any situation can become serious.

I thank God that neither Danny, any of the civilians in the bar, nor I were struck by the shotgun blast, and that we were all able to go home that evening to our families.

Mother's Day
by Cpl. Boyd N. Trantham, Maryland State Police

It was Mother's Day, May 12, 1984, and I was working the night shift. Riding along with me on this night was a long time friend and state police cadet named Joe Barker whom I had known from high school. Ever since, we wanted nothing more than to join the Maryland State Police and both realized just how lucky we were to have fulfilled our dreams. We had no way of knowing that in just a few minutes we would be put through an ordeal that we would remember for the rest of our lives.

A short time after midnight we were dispatched by the barrack duty officer to an assault and battery in progress on a rural back road in the county in which we were working. While en route, we were notified that our response was now upgraded to "code one." Rarely ordered, this code is given only in the most urgent cases when someone's life is imminently at risk. Needless to say, this heightened our senses as we sped closer to the scene of the assault, and I took the extra precaution of informing Cadet Barker of the location of my .38 caliber back up revolver in the event that the situation got out of control. And out of control it would soon become!

As I approached the location of the call, I instinctively turned off my lights and siren to avoid any detection by the suspect or suspects at the scene. As we crept closer to the scene I could faintly observe some movement off to the side of my patrol car but could not tell exactly what it was. I quickly turned my spotlight in that direction and could not believe what I saw. Holding a large metal object high above his head, the suspect was striking repeated blows at a man who was laying on the ground beneath him. At first I was unsure that it was even a human body due to the severity of the assault, but soon discovered that this was the suspect's father who was being beaten nearly to the point of decapitation.

I quickly exited my patrol car, drew my .357 magnum revolver, and ordered the suspect to halt. As he disappeared behind my car,

I again ordered him to halt. No sooner had I done so, the suspect frantically charged me with his weapon held high above his head just as he had done moments before. As fire flew out of the muzzle of my weapon, the suspect continued to charge directly toward me with his weapon in hand. I immediately fired a second round which caused the suspect to collapse to the ground in front of me. Believing the ordeal to be over, I watched with amazement as the suspect got to his feet and once again charged me with the weapon with which he had just killed his father. As he continued his assault, I fired for a third time causing him only to falter slightly as the bullet struck him. As I raised my revolver for the fourth and what I hoped to be the final shot, the unbelievable occurred. I pulled the trigger and nothing happened. The gun was jammed! The suspect was now right on top of me as we both tumbled to the ground.

"Shots fired! Shots fired!" filled the radio waves as Cadet Barker, who could not believe what was happening, frantically called for assistance. Fellow troopers and deputies were responding, but I knew it would be some time before they arrived due to the rural area of the call. Meanwhile, I was briefly able to get away from the suspect who was still very much alive and still chasing me with his weapon trying to kill me. I now began to call for Cadet Barker to get my back up weapon as I could literally hear the swings of the suspect's weapon cutting the air as it narrowly missed my head. While running as fast as my body could take me, I tried to inspect my revolver in an attempt to find the reason for the malfunction. I said to myself, "You're out of ammo," but as I reached for my speedloaders, I realized that this was not the problem. I now knew that my only chance to stay alive was to somehow get back to my cruiser and my other weapon.

By this time, the suspect and I were over 200 yards away from my cruiser, and he was still right behind me. Exhaustion began to set in as I could hear the suspect, still close behind me, finally collapse to the ground. Over all the commotion I could hear Cadet Barker screaming my name as he was running toward me with my .38 revolver and flashlight. Believing, for a second time, the incident to be over, I told Cadet Barker to return to my patrol car to make sure help was on its way. I could not believe it when I noticed the suspect get to his feet once more and mount another charge toward me with his weapon raised. I again ordered the suspect to drop the weapon and surrender, but as before, he ignored my warnings and lashed toward me. I fired a single shot from my .38 and the suspect fell to the ground, his weapon still in hand. I quickly ran over to him and removed his weapon and hoped that this would finally be the end.

By this time, Cadet Barker had pulled my cruiser up next to me and told me that back up officers would soon be there. I said to myself, "Thank God," as it seemed that this incident had consumed an eternity. The suspect, however, was not finished. Cadet Barker and I watched in utter disbelief as the suspect sat up, took off his shirt, then stood up and attempted to assault us again! As back up arrived, we were forced to handcuff the suspect to a chain link fence on the side of the road to avoid any threat.

The nightmare was now over! Medical personnel arrived on the scene and transported the suspect to a local hospital where he was pronounced dead. State Police investigators quickly arrived on the scene and the administrative process began while Cadet Barker and myself were transported to the barracks for debriefing. The agency, as well as the investigators involved were supportive and the shooting was ruled justified by the state attorney'

Major Johnny Hughes, and sons Michael and David Hughes, Maryland State Police.

Attorney General Edwin Meese III at the National Troopers Coalition Conference, May 1988. John Hughes, NTC Legislative Director with Mr. Meese.

ffice. As for my weapon, it was examined by oth agency and Smith & Wesson armorers ho decided that the malfunction might have sulted from anything ranging from faulty mmunition to defective internal parts.

As Mother's Day rolls around every year, adet Barker and I do not forget to thank our eavenly Father for his presence that night nd for his protection throughout the ordeal.

Conspiracy to Kill a Trooper
aryland State Police

A significant case that was decided be- re the United States Supreme Court on Feb- ary 19, 1997 arose out of a traffic stop made y Maryland State Trooper David Hughes.

On June 8, 1994, Trooper Hughes ob- rved a paper tag on the rear of a rental ve- icle southbound on I-95. During the traffic op, Hughes noticed that the three occupants the vehicle were nervous and behaving sus- iciously. Hughes ordered the front seat pas- nger, Jerry Lee Wilson, out of the vehicle, which time $7,000 worth of crack cocaine ll to the ground. Wilson was arrested and arged with possession of cocaine with in- nt to distribute. Before trial, passenger Wil- n moved to suppress the evidence, arguing at Hughes' ordering him out of the vehicle nstituted an unreasonable seizure under the ourth Amendment. The Circuit Court for altimore County agreed and granted

respondent's motion to suppress. On appeal, the Court of Special Appeals of Maryland af- firmed. Maryland Attorney General J. Joseph Curran appealed the case to the United States Supreme Court. The case was argued before the Supreme Court on December 11, 1996 by Maryland Attorney General Curran and United States Attorney General Janet Reno. This was Attorney General Reno's first case to be ar- gued before the Supreme Court. Attorney Gen- eral Reno stated before the court that, traffic stops present special dangers to police offic- ers; police officers "are vulnerable to attack, not just from the driver but from the passen- ger... It's the person seated in the vehicle that creates the danger." Maryland Attorney Gen- eral Curran stated, "The risk is real, officer safety is an issue ... every time a police of- ficer stops a vehicle the potential for danger exists."

On February 19, 1997, the Untied States Supreme Court ruled that it made no differ- ence whether anyone in the car had done any- thing illegal or suspicious or posed any threat during the traffic stop. National Troopers Coa- lition Chairman James A. Rhinebarger stated, "This is a great day for police officers across the United States. The ability to order a pas- senger out of a vehicle for the protection of the officer will result in fewer deaths and as- saults on this nation's police officers."

Trooper Michael Hughes also experi- enced the dangers of drug interdiction. On

May 3, 1996, he observed a red Chevrolet trav- eling south on Interstate 95 in excess of the posted speed limit. As a result of the vehicle stop, Annetta Evans and Joanne Jordan of Bal- timore, Maryland were arrested for transport- ing 519 grams of heroin. Trooper Hughes de- termined that the heroin was destined for de- livery to Dwayne Clark of Baltimore, Mary- land. Clark is a known violent heroin distribu- tor who was the subject of a DEA/FBI joint investigation. Trooper Hughes coordinated the arrest with the Washington/Baltimore High Intensity Drug Trafficking Area (HIDTA) DEA and Baltimore City Police Mass Trans- portation Initiative. A controlled delivery was made and Dwayne Clark was arrested and $108,385 in cash was seized.

On the evening of August 27, 1996, Trooper Michael Hughes narrowly escaped death as he was eastbound on Long Bar Har- bor Road when he noticed a suspicious red sports utility vehicle stopped off the road near the intersection of US Rte. 40 and Long Bar Harbor Road. As Trooper Hughes slowed to check the vehicle, a black male stepped from a line of trees and bushes on the right side of Long Bar Harbor Road, firing multiple shots from a 9 mm handgun, striking Trooper Hughes in the upper left arm and shattering the humerus bone. Trooper Hughes' police cruiser was struck eight times. Although wounded, Trooper Hughes was able to accel- erate and drive 400 feet to his residence.

Abingdon Volunteer Fire Department Paramedics and Maryland State Police Flight Paramedics were summoned and Trooper Hughes was transported to University of Maryland Shock Trauma by Maryland State Police helicopter. Maryland State Police and Harford County Sheriff's Deputies immediately responded to the shooting scene and began an intensive search for the suspects.

A week prior to the shooting of Trooper Michael Hughes, on August 20, 1996 at approximately 3:00 a.m., suspects had broken into the home of Trooper Michael Hughes. The suspects entered the second story of the home which was occupied by Johnny Hughes, retired Maryland State Police Major, and his wife, Earlene Hughes. The suspects directed a flashlight beam at Johnny Hughes who was in bed. Johnny Hughes rolled out of bed, grabbing a handgun on his way through the house in pursuit of the intruders. The suspects ran through the house, down the hall to the stair landing leading to a hallway to Michael Hughes' bedroom, and exited the residence through a laundry room door.

As a result of the attempted murder of Trooper Michael Hughes, an intensive investigation was instituted by Maryland State Police Superintendent David Mitchell. The investigative team was led and directed by Detective Sergeant Thomas Coppinger, a relentless, topnotch and renowned Maryland State Police investigator. The investigation focused on the many drug interdiction suspects both Troopers Michael and David Hughes had arrested, particularly on the 1-95 corridor. Since Trooper David Hughes and his wife had recently moved out of his parents' residence and Trooper Michael Hughes had recently sold his home and moved back into the downstairs residence, both troopers became the focus of the investigation. The investigation became far reaching, involving many different police departments. Detective Sergeant Coppinger put together a team of experienced law enforcement professionals. A massive and extensive effort was launched. Trooper Michael Hughes was released from University of Maryland Shock Trauma Hospital a week after the attempted murder and started rehabilitation therapy in January 1997. He and his brother, Trooper David Hughes, and David's wife were placed in a safe house. A $50,000 reward was offered for information leading to the arrest and conviction of the shooter(s).

While the investigation continued, the Fox Network's highly acclaimed national television show, "America's Most Wanted," hosted by John Walsh, produced a reenactment of the attempted murder on January 18, 19 and 20, 1997, and aired the segment on April 19, 1997.

During October 1996, individuals attempted to break into the Hughes' residence again through a downstairs laundry room door. The residence was now equipped with an elaborate alarm system and the perpetrators could not gain entry. As information developed, it was learned that Trooper David Hughes was the target of the shooting and that the shooters had mistaken Michael for David.

On December 11, 1995, Trooper David Hughes had arrested Gregory Allen McCorkle for speeding southbound on 1-95. McCorkle was driving a 1996 Nissan Altima with Virginia temporary tags that were registered to Sergio Barrios. McCorkle displayed an Illinois driver's license. A kilogram of cocaine was found in a black bag under the driver's seat. On February 28, 1996, McCorkle was indicted by a Cecil County, Maryland grand jury on four counts of drug smuggling, possession with intent to distribute, and two traffic offenses. McCorkle posted a $50,000 bond on March 1, 1996.

It was learned that McCorkle believed Trooper David Hughes resided at Long Bar Harbor Road, Abingdon, Maryland and had hired accomplices to help him surveil the residence in an attempt to assassinate David. Information was found that McCorkle would pay the assassins $25,000 to kill David Hughes. It should be noted that McCorkle's original trial date in Cecil County, Maryland was September 3, 1996, a week after Michael Hughes was shot. During the trial, it was learned that McCorkle sent hired hit men to the Hughes residence in June and July 1996 in an attempt to assassinate David Hughes. After the shooting of Michael, in October and December 1996 and during March 1997, McCorkle also sent hired assassins to the Hughes residence to attempt to locate and kill David Hughes. Fortunately, these individuals could not locate David. Informants stated that McCorkle considered hiring a private detective to locate David Hughes' residence, but did not follow through for fear of an information leak. Both before and after the shooting of Michael, McCorkle had individuals go to the Hughes' residence approximately 25 times, attempting to kill David Hughes.

McCorkle then hired an individual to make a bomb and the device was made and delivered to McCorkle. Informants stated that McCorkle and his accomplices attempted to place the bomb on Trooper David Hughes' police cruiser in March 1997 in the vicinity of the Cecil County State's Attorney's Offices; however, heavy pedestrian traffic and other activity made it impossible to deliver. McCorkle also attempted to purchase a military rocket launcher and other heavy military weapons to kill Trooper Hughes.

During May 1997, Gregory McCorkle, Sergio Barrios, and two co-defendants were arrested. To date, 14 other co-defendants were arrested, bringing the total to 18 arrests. The charges vary from attempted murder, conspiracy to commit murder, and drugs and weapons charges in the shooting of Trooper Michael Hughes and the attempted murder of

Trooper David Hughes, in addition to the original arrest and four counts against McCorkle of drug smuggling possession and intent to distribute.

In August 1997, a Virginia grand jury returned a 21-count indictment naming Gregory McCorkle, Sergio Barrios, Norfleet Person, Vernon Bryant, Rachid Zamani, William Potts and Kevin Tinsley. They were charged with conspiracy, continuing criminal enterprise, violent crime in aid of racketeering activity, interstate murder for hire, use of a firearm with drug trafficking, distribution of cocaine, money laundering conspiracy, and attempted murder of a witness.

The trial of McCorkle, Barrios and Tinsley began on October 22, 1997 at the U.S. Courthouse in Alexandria, Virginia. On October 29, 1997, the jury returned verdicts of guilty against all three defendants. The penalty range for McCorkle and Barrios is 105 years and Tinsley's exposure is 55 years. It should be noted that under the U.S. Sentencing Guidelines, 85 percent of the sentence must be served, which is unlike state systems where parole and probation are significant. Sentencing dates are pending for the other co-conspirators, who have already pleaded guilty. Rachid Zamani is the only person arrested to date who has not either pleaded guilty or been convicted. His trial date has not been set. The investigation is continuing toward identifying the actual shooter and in prosecuting McCorkle's sources of supply. Due to the nature and extent of his injuries, Trooper Michael Hughes will be retiring from the Maryland State Police.

Making A Difference
by Trooper David Paine, Massachusetts State Police

A hundred years from now it will not matter what kind of car you drove, how much money you had in the bank, or the type of house you lived in, but that the world may be better because you were important in the life of a child." I have no idea who wrote this little phrase. I'm sure many of you have read it somewhere before. I have a copy tacked up in my little work area at the barracks. It serves as a reminder for me as to why I am on this job and what is truly important.

When I earned the title of "trooper" on that cold December evening in 1986, it was one of the proudest moments of my life. My father pinned the silver badge to my uniform that night. I came onto the job feeling I could make a difference in my state, my town and my community. Dealing with the "underbelly" of our society can test a trooper's values, wit and spirit. There is no denying that we "see it all" out there and then some! Some lose sight of our original mission and end up just as negative, condescending and intolerant, as most of the general public we have to deal with. Many troopers walk the fence every day trying maintain a positive outlook while being bombarded with the discontent and suffering of others daily. Many succumb to this and lose whatever inner spirit they had beforehand. Some build a wall around themselves to block it all out. I found myself slowly changing in this way a couple of years after I got on the job. The compassion was fading and being conscious of other's needs was non-existent. I cared about nothing more than writing many motor vehicle violations, trying to make a daily pinch, getting my accident reports in on time, and finding new places to observe traffic going northbound. The incident which turned the tide for me, so to speak, happened during the first part of this decade.

I was working a typical day shift out of the Foxboro barracks. It was a sunny day in autumn and I had the Route 95 patrol from Route 495 in Mansfield, Massachusetts down to the Rhode Island line. I had written several citations, a couple of warnings, and had booked a minor accident during rush hour. It was just before noon time when I was called to check on a youth walking on the highway northbound in the breakdown lane. Now mind you, this was a weekday and during school hours. So I'm thinking, "Man, it's probably some kid who is truant and ran away from school again". I'm driving to the scene rationalizing to myself, "Well, it won't be much of a pinch, but truancy is truancy and the "twelve or more arrests club" for the month is looking better each moment." (I was also hoping I would I be able to run in my crisp new knee high field boots and breeches if the little devil started to "book" on me!) I arrive at the reported location and, sure enough, there he was walking past the rest area. But he didn't fit the mold of the "truant troublemaker" I had envisioned. He was around 11 or 12, clean cut and neatly dressed. He looked like your typical middle to upper middle-class kid. I pulled up to him, exited the cruiser and walked his way. He stopped and stood silent with his head down and the most dejected took on his face. I took a few moments to talk to him and find out why he was out in the middle of a major interstate. I'm glad I did. The "problem child" turned out to be nothing more than a scared and sad young man. He had never skipped school before in his life. He told me he was "running away" from home. Apparently his parents had recently split. He was having trouble dealing with the fact that the close family he loved so much would be no more. He told me he was the oldest and his little siblings were having a tough time also. I placed my arm around him, tried to ease his fears, and had him get into the cruiser. I then radioed in and transported him to the barracks. We called his father to come pick him up. I sat with him, we talked, and eventually he came around and felt better. Later on, his dad walked into the lobby of the barracks with tears in his eyes, hugged his son and told him everything

would be okay. The boy was in tears also and kept repeating that he wanted his dad and mom to be together again. I had to fight hard not to let my emotions get the best of me. They spoke for a while, hugged and I heard the young man's father tell him he loved him. The father thanked me and said that he would take the boy home. I maintained my professional demeanor throughout and they eventually left. Case closed, or so I thought. Perhaps if I had been completely controlled by the "dark side of the force" I would have shrugged the incident off and forgotten all about it. But afterwards I found myself still thinking about the incident. I wondered if I could have done more for him. I started kicking myself thinking that I should have given him the barracks address, or the phone number so that if he needed help or was feeling bad he could contact me. Some laughed and told me I was letting myself get too involved. For a moment I almost agreed. Then one day it hit me that "getting involved" was the point! Is it wrong to get involved and make even a small difference in a person's life? From that point onward I never looked back. The spirit which was fading returned with vigor and I now look to each day with hope that I'll make a difference somehow. Once in a while I find myself thinking about that young man walking up Route 95. He would be about 17 or 18 now. It may sound corny, but I hope he is okay. I hope everything worked out for his family. And if not, I hope he weathered the rough times successfully. To this day, whenever I see the Norman Rockwell painting of "The Runaway" with the Massachusetts State Trooper, I think of that young boy.

Being a trooper brings with it many responsibilities besides generating "activity" and "stats." Yes, the numbers and the enforcement are important - VERY important. But being a positive influence on the lives of people is also essential. We are leaders, not followers. We must set the standards of values, work ethic, pride and integrity that others can only hope to attain. And to achieve this we must hold on to that inner spirit and those good intentions which led us to our calling as troopers. Continue to march.

Long Cold Road
by Trooper David Paine, Massachusetts State Police

The cracked, salt stained, field boots creaked as the trooper's body swayed to and fro. The pavement was so cold that he felt as though he were standing on a piece of frozen steel. Chills ran through his extremities and deep within his heart. His body shivering in an attempt to ignite that which could not be warmed. An icy, harsh wind whipped at his face and cried to him. He resisted the gale's pressure ever so slightly. He stood unyielding, silent and alone. Behemoths of metal and glass rapidly passed leaving behind clouds of soot and filth in their wake. Their terrestrial

occupants curiously gazing the trooper's way. He felt their repugnance along with their reverence. His frozen lips splitting as the irony of this gave him reason to smile. And smile he did.

As the mind became his only friend and bandit of time. Dancing reflections of blistering fires sparking and cracking, the elation felt when the children ran to him and cheered as he entered the door, the pride on his parents faces the night he first donned the French and electric blue, the spiritual presence of his grandparents which comforted him to no end, hoping to provide food on the table in a home full of love and good cheer. These musings calmed and reassured the trooper. His mind soon carried him back to his wintry reality. Tears began to roll down his cheeks as the frost ripped into his eyes. The hint of an icicle forming on the brim of his garrison cover. He knew many questioned his motives for being there. Was he self serving? Were his reasons laced with greed? He knew for certain they were not. The intervals he spent on the dark, tar-filled, trail were moments away from the bliss of his sanctuary. As the frost laden wind howled, he endured and remained vigilant. Afterwards, when his mind continued its voyage, the trooper envisioned family, friends and the aroma of baking bread awaiting him at the end of the long cold road.

NOTE: This essay was first contained in the Constabulary, an annual booklet for the State Police Association of Massachusetts' golf tournament. (1997)

He's Just A Trooper
by David Paine, Massachusetts State Police

He loves his family and wishes he could spend more time with them.

He misses out on opportunities to work details to be at every one of his sons' baseball games. He has to check his little black book for family obligations before he commits to extra duties. When he stands tall on a detail he can't escape the thoughts that he is taking time away from his wife, children and home.

He's just a trooper.

He doesn't own a summer home, a boat, gold rings, a Jaguar, or a Mercedes Benz.

He wishes he could take his family on more vacations.

His wife doesn't wear diamonds, gold or fluffy fur coats.

For years he was forced to sacrifice many of life's pleasures in order to buy a decent home for his loved ones.

He's just a trooper.

He just smiles while refusing to take a gift from a citizen after helping them.

He doesn't mind sweating all over his uniform when helping an elderly man change a tire.

He loves that look of shock on the face of the drive-through teller when he hands 'them' a gift after they try to charge him half price.

He still corresponds with some of the people he has assisted and the children he has befriended over the years.

He's just a trooper.

He wears field boots laced with cracks yet can still see his reflection in the battered leather.

He faces adversity yet still continues to march while others around him have given up hope.

He projects an image of professionalism despite being demeaned by media and political types.

He still feels pride when donning the coveted ensemble colored French and electric blue.

He's just a trooper.

He thinks about his departed loved ones and wonders if they are watching over him.

He prays the spirit of his grandfather will give him the wisdom to endure the hard times.

He is excited at the prospect of his children coming of age.

He is still learning, maturing, and looking to the future while aging gracefully.

He's just a trooper.

He is a support system standing beside you, ready to lend a hand.

He is someone you can depend on to give of himself to benefit others.

He can be just the man down the street, or the man of the hour.

He is the reflection in the mirror every morning - he might be you.

He's just a trooper.

Things Troopers Don't Talk About
by Dave Paine, Massachusetts State Police

It's a sunny Saturday afternoon in late March. The ground softens as the long winter frost is finally broken. You're on the day shift patrol covering over 24 miles of interstate highway. Your "bluebird" is fairly new with low mileage. You're thinking how "cool" it is to be driving one of these sleds. The uniform you wear is one of the hardest to earn. It's colors are French and electric blue. You feel pride as others look upon you with admiration.

Members of the same sex envy your title while members of the opposite sex look you over and smile. As you cruise along the road, vigilant and ready for anything, you realize that life is good.

A short time later a car passes by in the opposite direction. From across the median you clock the vehicle at 85 mph with "moving" radar. You realize crossing the grassy median is a no-no. But, the next turnaround is several miles away, so you go for it! You crisply turn into the median strip and make your way down the grass laden valley. All of a sudden "IT" happens. As you try to accelerate up the other side the tires start to whirl. Then the cruiser stops dead and you observe mud and grass being kicked up when you look in the side mirror. You try to "gun it" forward, then reverse, to no avail. Reality starts creeping in. You're stuck in the mud up to your axles! How embarrassing. You can now only sit, stew and think about how to get out of this mess with as little disgrace and humiliation as possible. You would think the motoring public would be sympathetic towards you. NOT! They drive by and taunt you by honking their horns and staring. You meekly call the barracks and request a tow for a Ford LTD ...uh... make that a red Toyota Celica ... yeah that's the ticket. You advise them you'll get the plate number later hoping no one at the barracks finds out. Yeah right! Life is good.

Troopers have to eat just like everyone else. So, you stop by your usual dining establishment. After ordering the two cheeseburgers, large fries, and Coca-Cola "value meal" you quickly look for the abandoned rear of a large shopping plaza. It is here that you may eat in peace. You do not need some member of the public "gawking" at you because they wanted to "see how a trooper consumes mass quantities of burnt animal flesh." Spilling food and drink in a MSP cruiser is not fun. After cleaning up the mess all over the seat and floor you exit your cruiser. This is the best time to briskly brush the sesame seeds off of the soft blue velveteen seats and MSP issue breeches. Life is good.

Your uniform is very distinct and recognizable. The campaign cover and field boots alone could set the image of a trooper. And what of those breeches you might ask? Just think about this. You are at an accident scene laying out flares on a clear but cold afternoon. It is January and there are still small patches of ice on the roadway leftover from a previous storm. You certainly didn't realize you were slipping until it was too late. Man! You execute a spin followed by a split that would make any gymnast proud. You quickly regain your composure and stand tall once again. It is not until you are lighting another flare when you feel the breeze. The cool air rushes swiftly up your French and electric blue trousers. You look down to find that the seam in your

breeches has let go in a major way! Your leg is exposed from just below your knee all the way up to your upper thigh. Oh the humanity! What can you do? You do the only thing possible. You continue to march wearing your "pumpkin" colored, long raincoat on a sunny day. Life is good.

Notice to all troopers! There is an ungodly type of fungus in our midst. It is oily, rotten, dirty and leaves a flaky white-like appearance. No I'm not talking about some new chemical substance not covered in the local drug laws! I'm talking about that gross stuff that seems to form on the collars of a trooper's patrol jacket! What is that all about ?!? I know troopers who, after shaving, will lotion themselves up, spread various creams, use bleach and gasoline, and are as clean as a whistle. It just doesn't matter! That flaky 'stuff still mutates onto the patrol jacket collar! Even sandpaper covered with nuclear waste can't clean this junk off. You'd think the state could match our jacket color with the color of the various skin droppings and gross stuff that we encounter! Ahh... life is good.

Hey, it's been fun all. It never ends - troopers getting locked out of their cruisers, the sight of a demented trooper running down the road chasing his campaign cover that was blown off, and on and on. How about walking into the barracks only to find one of those "homemade personalized gags" hanging on the wall about you? And the kicker is - IT'S ALL TRUE! Yes, life is good. And remember, never take yourself too seriously - especially if you're a trooper.

NOTE: This article appeared in the Trooper newspaper, a publication of the State Police Association of Massachusetts.

In High Water
by Senior Trooper Charlie Trader, West Virginia

Occasionally amid the scads of paperwork and frustration in dealing with the court system and the many demands of the job, you get a chance to make a difference. I had that chance on September 6, 1996.

It happened when I was stationed at the Franklin Detachment, located in a mountainous area of the state. For more than two days, heavy rains continued and flooding conditions just got worse. As much as you always try to alert the residents living in particularly bad areas, it seems you are likely to run into people who get themselves in trouble while in high water. During this afternoon, my sergeant, J.R Bean, and I heard through the Pendleton County Fire Department frequency that a man was stranded in his vehicle and surrounded in water.

Sergeant Bean and I drove as close to the scene as we could get. By this time, we saw a civilian pass by in a four-wheel drive pickup who agreed to give us a ride closer to the scene. We rode in the truck for less than a quarter of a mile before coming upon the raging water. From that vantage point, I could see a man walking on a mountain near a truck and I attempted to forge the creek and make my way around the mountainside toward the vehicle.

As I got closer, I could see that a man was stranded in his vehicle with all of the windows rolled up and fogged over. He looked extremely distraught. The gentleman's pickup truck was stuck in the deep waters of Thorn Creek, a tributary of the South Branch of the Potomac River. He and his vehicle were about 25 feet from the shoreline and dry land.

Then, another civilian came to our assistance by bringing us a large section of rope. I took the rope and asked the man to go back and get assistance from Sergeant Bean. I then waded the thigh-high water to get closer to the vehicle and get the man's attention. Once I got his attention, I got directly across from the victim and tied a piece of wood to one end of the rope and threw it to the victim. I told him to tie it around his waist and make sure that it was tight and secure. I then took the other end and tied it to a nearby tree. I had originally planned to get the victim to tie the rope to his truck and use it to hold on to as he made his way back.

While this was happening, the water was splashing over the hood of the truck and the vehicle was bouncing and slowly inching its way down the creek. Sergeant Bean had then made his way up to where I was standing and I told him of my original plan. We quickly decided that there just wasn't enough time.

As the rope was secure, we yelled to the man and told him to step out and that we would pull him in, assuring him that we would pull him in safely. Sergeant Bean, citizen Barry Propst and I took out the excess slack of the rope. The victim immediately went under and downstream when he stepped out of the vehicle. I thought we might lose him, it was really frightening because the water was very fast and very cold and it seems as though he was down under for a while. Then, seconds seemed more like minutes. Just then, the man came to the top of the water and I jumped into the water and pulled him into safety. He was not injured.

It was a very gratifying moment - knowing that we made a difference in his life was really something. He was really grateful and thankful. It was a really rewarding day for me and it happened so quickly. Often, you don't feel like you are getting a great deal out of your work because of all of the paperwork and the court system and then something like this happens.

Life And Death In Seconds
by First Sergeant Rick Gillespie, West Virginia

On Sunday, May 25, 1980, I had been in the field 11 months since graduation from the academy. I was stationed in Franklin, Pendleton County and was one of three troopers assigned to provide law enforcement over a 700 square mile area.

At about 3:00 a.m., I was dispatched to a single vehicle accident, involving an overturned pickup with no one around it. Upon arrival, I couldn't find anyone at the scene. An NCIC check on the vehicle came back negative and it was registered to a resident of an adjoining county in Virginia.

I began conducting the normal accident investigation and requested a tow truck. The tow truck arrived a short while later, having traveled a different route than the one I had traveled. In conversation, the tow truck operator advised me that he had seen two people running along that road.

I decided to check on these people and drove in that direction to see what I could find. After traveling approximately seven miles, I found more than I had bargained for. As I rounded a curve, I saw motion to my left. As I slowed the cruiser I could see something moving along the shoulder and it looked to be 10 feet tall!

As I came to a stop, I could see one person sitting atop another's shoulders. The person on top scrambled off the other's shoulders and fell to the ground. As I exited the cruiser, the person that had fallen to the ground came running toward me. This person, a lady, cried out, "God, help me; he's going to kill me!" As soon as I cleared the driver's seat, she jumped into the cruiser, over the front seat and into the far corner of the back seat. Efforts to learn any more from her were fruitless, as she was literally "scared stiff."

My attention became focused on the man standing beside my cruiser. He was looking at me with a strange look in his eyes and was reaching under his shirt tail toward his pocket. I ordered him to place his hands on top of the car, as I reached inside the cruiser for the department-issued riot baton.

As I focused on the man's hand traveling toward his pocket, he "sucker punched" me in the face with his other fist. I then began striking him with the riot baton and using tactics still fresh in my mind from the academy; however, this man seemed unstoppable. Nothing I did, to include splitting his head open seemed to faze him; he just kept fighting. Finally, I got him on the ground on his back. As I stood over him, he began kicking me in the chest. At this point, I realized that I needed both hands free if I were going to get the handcuffs on him. At this point, I made a mistake and laid the riot baton on the ground near us.

I grabbed one of his feet and wrenched him over onto his stomach. Then I grabbed his foot and pushed it toward his shoulder blade trying to bring him under control. Suddenly, he lurched forward, shooting out from under me and coming to his feet with my riot baton in his hands.

In a flash, he cracked me up beside the head with the baton. As I felt myself feeling very faint, the next thing I could recall was the sound of gunfire and the smell of gunpowder in the air. My training had kicked in and I had shot the individual in the stomach, bringing the fight to a halt. I requested an ambulance for him and back up for me. During the wait, the female advised me that the man had worked for her on her farm. The man had lost all touch with reality and thought that he was the Son of God. He took her against her will and was traveling to a mountain top to conjure up a flood, so that he and she could repopulate the earth as "Adam and Eve."

While at a hospital in Virginia and suffering severe internal injury, this man managed to run from the examination room and escaped the hospital, dragging IV bags and tubes with him. Local police finally recaptured him, with his IV tubes hung up in a fence along an interstate highway.

All that was in the man's pocket that night was a small pocket knife and some marijuana. He recovered from his wounds and later pled guilty to charges relating to the incident. The female victim told investigators she was sure that he would have killed her that night.

First Sergeant Gillespie serves as First District Commander of Company C, based in Elkins. He has served the state police for 19 years.

How I Got the Stork Pin
by Trooper First Class Rick Holley, West Virginia

I was out working a car wreck sometime after midnight on February 3, 1990, and was already at the Emergency Room with the accident victim at St. Joseph's Hospital in Buckhannon when the members of the Upshur County EMS I was with got a call about an unknown medical problem in a nearby area.

I had served previously as a paramedic and had kept my skills current since becoming a state trooper about five years before this happened.

We arrived at the home at about 1:15 a.m. and then went inside the house along with the EMS staff. It was in the bathroom of the house that we found a rather frightened 19-year-old girl in the process of giving birth to her first child. By this time, she was so far along in the process, that there was no way we could move her. We could see the baby crowning upon the first exam.

Since I had experience in this area, I worked with the other EMT in the birthing process and two EMT trainees helped us with the gathering of materials that we would need. We talked to the young woman as she went through a series of contractions. Her mother seemed more stressed than the young girl. She had no idea the girl was even pregnant. The small-boned young woman had concealed the pregnancy from her family.

About 30 minutes into the process, she gave birth to a little girl. I cut the cord and the EMT secured the clamp. We then used the dressings from a burn kit to wrap the baby before we transported the two to the hospital.

Baby Amy Donnelle Yoakum was 6 pounds, 10 ounces and was perfectly healthy. The two went home from the hospital the next day.

That spring, I received a stork pin at the annual EMS banquet. It was my first and only baby delivery as a state trooper.

TFC Holley is now one of two troopers who oversee the department's Breath Alcohol Testing units, which are funded by the WV Commission on Drunk Driving Prevention.

The Worst 45 Minutes
by Senior Trooper Rob Cunningham, West Virginia

I lived an officer's worst nightmare on January 28, 1994 when I encountered a suspect who actually disarmed me and attempted to kill me with my own weapon. I am happy to say that I could turn the situation around and can actually write about what happened.

The cold, wet and snowy day began when I came on duty in Wayne County, West Virginia, next to Kentucky. I had been serving in the field for little more than a year. A suspect had stolen a car in Kentucky and driven to Fort Gay, West Virginia where he broke into a home. The man had packed up several stolen items into the car and then ran the car promptly into a ditch. He then got out and found the neighbor's car with the keys in the ignition and stole it. The neighbor called in a description of the stolen vehicle that was broadcast via radio.

I drove no more than two or three miles when I passed the vehicle headed north. I turned around and began following the vehicle, which failed to stop, resulting in a pursuit across the state line into Kentucky. The suspect refused to pull over and headed quickly down a curvy road where he wrecked the car into a ditch. The man then jumped out and over a guardrail and leading me on a lengthy foot chase over wet ground and through lots of brush. When I finally caught him, we began to struggle on our feet back and forth. During the struggle he told me that there was no way that he was going back to jail.

As we were fighting, I felt something metal against my stomach. The suspect had taken a gun from the waistband of his pants and pushed it into my mid-section. I was able to pull his arm away and to the left as he fired two shots that hit the ground, narrowly missing my mid-section by about 10 inches to the left. By this time, I was able to get him down to the ground and on top of him. He had the weapon cocked in an attempt to shoot me again. I slipped the webbing of my hand between the hammer and the frame to keep the gun from firing until I was able to wrestle it

free from his hands and throw it into the woods. At that very moment, I felt yet another piece of metal in my side and I recognized it to be my own .357 revolver. I snatched it quickly from his hands and positioned myself to shoot the suspect as he broke free and took off running again. I then chased him and as he ran up the hill, Kentucky State Trooper Bobby Jack Woods confronted him and took him into custody.

By this time, I was exhausted and filthy dirty after a 45-minute ordeal involving lots of running, lots of fighting and two extremely close calls with a gun. We later found out that the man had a real problem with the law and that a police officer was forced to kill his dad. The man was prosecuted in Kentucky for wanton endangerment and attempted murder. He got 20 years and I got a lesson of a lifetime. That experience made me a better officer. I am more cautious and I recognize that I can run into this sort of thing again at any given time.

Senior Trooper Cunningham is a now a member of the Executive Protection detail.

One Wild Night In Mingo County
by 1Lt. P.D. Clemens, West Virginia

I may be living proof that police officers don't get a grace period in their career before a situation forces you to become a player in a high-level incident. I had been a trooper for just two years when I was involved in a gun battle and was shot.

I had been called out from my home on March 17, 1979 to assist in a situation in the very rural Twin Branch Hollow in Mingo County, a southern coal mining county in West Virginia. When I was called to assist, I was already well aware that things had already gone bad between the suspect and other officers and I knew that one of our men had already been shot. Officers had been searching for some time for a man and came upon his vehicle in the afternoon hours. Although he was only 31, he'd served some time at the State Penitentiary and was now wanted for an armed robbery. He had been seen a few places in the Mingo and Wyoming county area over the past week. On this day, sheriffs' deputies spotted a parked vehicle that matched the description of the one he was last seen driving.

The incident began at 3:00 p.m. when deputies observed the parked vehicle with a female walking beyond it. The deputies jumped out of their cruiser when gunfire hit it several times. The deputies called for help from both area detachments of the state police. Trooper Robert McComas responded to the scene and began climbing a hillside near where the incident occurred, when he was shot ambush style in the leg. The perpetrator had apparently positioned himself at the top of the

hillside and had a clear view of every officer who attempted to come in toward him.

I was part of the third round of officers, who were called in, and this time we would attempt to approach by the opposite angle. By now, nightfall had set in and I was alongside Trooper Sam Pinion and Trooper Dave Hamlin. Our group was instructed to meet five other units. Hamlin was already in position on the top of the mountain. As senior officer, he was leading our group. After some time, we strategically moved toward the suspect in a V-shape from the backside of the mountain and I was positioned close to the center of the formation, just next to Trooper Pinion.

As we topped the mountain, the suspect popped up from behind a rock and with his semiautomatic sawed off stock weapon opened fire on all of us. He fired 12 quick shots and both Pinion and I were shot during that round of shots. When I was shot, I hit the ground and rolled, returned fire and kept moving. I was hit in the stomach and Pinion was hit in the ankle. The gunman jumped up at least two more times, firing about eight to 10 shots each time. He pinned us down for about 35 to 40 minutes.

Trooper Hamlin yelled out after the first round to see if we were all okay. I told him that I had been shot and he said "P.D., this is not the time to be kidding around." I advised him that I was serious. Trooper Hamlin then fired several rounds, which we believe finally took the suspect out. The officers focused on getting me down the mountain to receive medical care. At daybreak, a state police helicopter was flown in to assess the situation and the suspect was seen lying near a large rock, the same one he had used for cover during the gun battle. His fatal wounds were to his head and his neck.

The state police helicopter flew me to a large medical center in Charleston, which by road travel was about two hours away. Medical personnel later told me that having the helicopter in my area may have sustained my life. My wound was odd. It looked like a bee sting and it never bled, but the internal injuries were extensive. The shot hit my liver, my spleen and my lungs. My lungs collapsed and I underwent extensive surgery. I lost eight pints of blood before the doctors and nurses could begin to see me turn around and begin to recover. Doctors chose not to remove the bullet, but let it work itself out of my body and through my back about four months later. I still have the suspect's weapon at my home today.

I went back to work after five weeks and continued to serve from that area for eight more years. I later came back in a supervisory role as a detachment commander and later as a district sergeant. It's strange because people always ask me if what happened to me changed me, and I would have to say that it didn't. But, I felt "antsy" while on duty for some time after. One time comes to mind when I was driving along with my partner and a car backfired. I nearly jumped through the roof of the cruiser. It was really quite funny for both of us.

1Lt. Clemens, serves as the executive officer for Company B - headquartered in Dunbar, West Virginia. He has served the state police for more than 21 years.

A Shiny, Black Weapon

by Sgt. Greg Barnett, West Virginia

It was early in the evening in February 1996 and dusk had just set in when we received the call of a breaking and entering in progress at a doctor's office in Teays Valley, a growing community about 15 miles from the capital city of Charleston.

We received the call from bank employees, who were working across the street, and had witnessed someone going inside the building after office hours. Trooper First Class Terry McComas had responded when I did and we split to check the building. At first check, we found that the front doors were secure. I attempted to go around to the rear of the building on the right as TFC McComas went the other way. Right away, I encountered the suspect just as I turned the corner. He apparently was waiting for me as I turned the corner. He was holding a *Physician's Desk Manual* in his hand and we immediately began to struggle. I was able to put him up against the wall of the brick building. However, he quickly spun around and dropped a shiny black object from his long, bulky winter coat and into the clench of his hands.

At this point, I believed it was a handgun and my first instinct was to stay on him, as close as I could get to him. If he had a gun, I knew that at this point I was much too close to have the time to drop back and draw my own weapon, there simply wouldn't be enough time. I tackled him and we both hit the building and he began to hit me in the back of my neck and shoulder area with the heavy object in his hands. As I was being struck, I managed to reverse the struggle and roll him over to the ground and his stomach. By this time, Trooper McComas helped me handcuff him. It was at this time that we were able to identify the object as a tire iron.

When I first thought about it being a gun, I guess I just kept thinking that he would definitely shoot me if I gave him the chance, so I moved closer to him and his arms and tried to lock up his hands. We were dealing in "milliseconds" I didn't really have that much time to think. As we were bringing him around to the front of the building, his wife drove up in a van, which we later tracked down as one stolen out of Florida. She had apparently been waiting in the nearby getaway vehicle and we immediately took her into custody as well.

Through these two initial arrests, we worked to link the couple to about 150 burglaries in the Port St. Lucie area and pinned him and his wife as the prime suspects in the recent murder of a pawn shop owner from the same area. The pawn had apparently been fencing the goods brought in from their large-scale burglary operation. They also linked the couple to the attempted murder of an elderly woman from the area. Our interviews with both subjects and the subsequent investigative work helped the Florida authorities build both their felony cases, which are currently set for trial.

At the time of the incident, Barnett had served the state police for more than 12 years and held the rank of Trooper First Class. He has since been promoted to the rank of sergeant and commands a special patrol unit on the Interstate system.

Yes, I Would Have Gone In

by Senior Trooper Brian Allen, West Virginia

While on a traffic stop on November 5, 1996, I was alerted by a passing city worker that his coworker was in trouble at the nearby waste processing plant. I radioed in for help from the local rescue squad and ambulance service as I headed over to the plant, which was just about one quarter of a mile away.

The worker had followed me down and directed me to the plant. Upon arrival, I was able to see a New Cumberland city worker down in the pit. I walked across the metal scaffolding across the pit to get a better view of him. He was up to his neck in the sludge about 12 feet below me. Both men informed me that the pit was about 20 feet deep. His friend and

co-worker also added that the pit contained large "aeration" suction pumps that went off intermittently that could seriously complicate the situation. He was holding on to the elbow of a pipe with both his arms. The only way he was staying above the water line was by keeping his arms pulled up under his chin as if in a constant chin up. This was really exhausting him, and he told me that he may have injured his hip and couldn't hold on much longer. I remember this day as the first day that we had switched to our long-sleeved winter uniforms and it was pretty chilly. Hughes was freezing from the water and the cold air.

I started thinking about what I could use to throw in that the guy could hold. I ran to my cruiser and got out a tow rope and threw it in to him, but it was too short for him to reach. The look on his face, at that point, expressed even more frustration than I was feeling at the time.

It was then that I knew that I really had no choice but to go in and get him and that there was not a lot of time left that he would be able to hold on. While removing my glasses, radio and my duty belt and placing it on the ground, I stepped off the scaffold long enough to spot a long cable lying on the ground. I picked it up and made a loop and went to the edge of the pit so that I could lower it over his head. He let go of the pipe long enough to place the cable under his arms. By this time New Cumberland officer Jeff McIntyre was on scene and we both pulled him to the side of the pit and helped him up over the railing.

Once we pulled him out, the ambulance arrived and administered care. He stayed in the hospital for a day for observation and didn't sustain any broken bones. I went home and took a shower and changed clothes and didn't think too much about it.

Needless to say, my coworkers had a field day with the number of jokes they made out of the situation. Many people have asked me if I really would have jumped in, and I say, "absolutely." I still see the city worker every now and then, and he waves at me just like he always did.

Trooper Allen still serves from the New Cumberland Detachment.

Patrol vehicle, Eastern Washington.

The first laboratories of what is now called the State Police Forensic Crime Laboratory first began in the basement of the West Virginia State Capitol Building.

Maryland State Police, Motor Unit, TFC Thomas B. Cooper.

Chief with Honor Guard, Washington State Patrol.

Commercial Vehicle Officer.

NTC Endorses George W. Bush for President

Chairman Scott Reinacher, Corresponding Secretary, Dan Kennedy and Director of Government Relations for the NTC, Johnny Hughes, speak with George W. Bush and wife Laura concerning NTC issues prior to endorsement ceremonies.

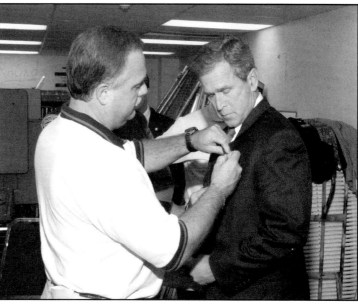

Chairman Scott Reinarcher places NTC pin on George W. Bush, prior to endorsement.

'TC Chairman Scott Reinacher, presents Texas Stetson to then Gov. George W. Bush making him an honorary trooper during endorsement ceremonies in St. Louis MO. On Oct 6, 2000.

UNIFORMS

Alabama

Alaska

Arizona

Colorado

Arkansas

California

Connecticut

Delaware

Georgia

Iowa

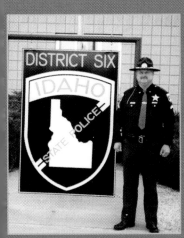

Idaho

Illinois

Indiana

Editors Note: All states were invited to submit photos of their uniforms

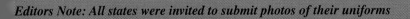

65

Louisiana

Kansas

Kentucky

Maine

Maryland

Massachusetts

Michigan

Missouri

Minnesota

Missisippi

Nebraska

Montana

New Hampshire

New Jersey

North Dakota

New Mexico

Oklahoma

New York

Ohio

South Carolina

Rhode Island

North Carolina

Tennessee

Texas

Vermont

Virginia

Washington

West Virginia

Wisconsin

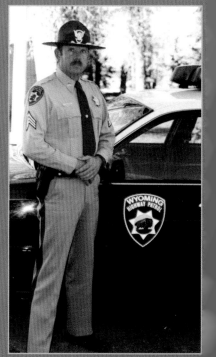

Wyoming

PATCHES

Editors Note: All states were invited to submit photos of their patch

LOUISIANA
UNION JUSTICE CONFIDENCE
STATE POLICE

STATE POLICE
DIRIGO
MAINE

MARYLAND STATE POLICE

MASSACHUSETTS STATE POLICE

MICHIGAN STATE POLICE

MINNESOTA STATE PATROL

MISSISSIPPI HIGHWAY PATROL
VIRTUTE ET ARMIS

MISSOURI STATE
SERVICE AND PROTECTION
HIGHWAY PATROL

MONTANA HIGHWAY PATROL
3-7-77

STATE PATROL
NEBRASKA

NEVADA
BATTLE BORN
HIGHWAY PATROL

STATE POLICE
NEW HAMPSHIRE
DEPARTMENT OF SAFETY

STATE POLICE N.J.

STATE POLICE N.MEX.

NEW YORK
EXCELSIOR
STATE POLICE

NORTH CAROLINA
HIGHWAY PATROL

NORTH DAKOTA HIGHWAY PATROL

STATE HIGHWAY PATROL OHIO

OKLAHOMA HIGHWAY PATROL

RHODE ISLAND 19 25 STATE POLICE

SOUTH CAROLINA SOUTH CAROLINA STATE HIGHWAY PATROL ANIMIS OPIBUS QUE PARATI DUM SPIRO SPERO SPES HIGHWAY PATROL

STATE XVI TENNESSEE COMMERCE TROOPER

DEPARTMENT OF PUBLIC SAFETY HIGHWAY PATROL

UTAH HIGHWAY PATROL

VERMONT STATE POLICE

VIRGINIA SIC SEMPER TYRANNIS VIRGINIA STATE POLICE

WASHINGTON THE SEAL OF THE STATE OF WASHINGTON 1889 STATE PATROL

WEST VIRGINIA STATE POLICE

WISCONSIN STATE PATROL

WYOMING HIGHWAY PATROL

BADGES

Alabama

Alaska

Arizona

Georgia

Illinois

Indiana

Maryland

Michigan

Minnesota

Editors Note: All states were invited to submit photos of their badge

California

Connecticut

Delaware

Iowa

Kentucky

Louisiana

Mississippi

Montana

Nebraska

New Hampshire

New Jersey

North Dakota

Ohio

Oklahoma

Utah

Virginia

Washington

New Mexico

New York

North Carolina

South Carolina

Tennessee

Texas

West Virginia

Wisconsin

Wyoming

CRUISERS

Alabama

Alaska

Arizona

Arkansas

California

Colorado

Connecticut

Delaware

Editors Note: All states were invited to submit photos of their cruisers

Florida

Georgia

Idaho

Illinois

Indiana

Iowa

Kansas

Kentucky

Louisiana

Maine

Maryland

Massachusetts

Michigan

Minnesota

Mississippi

Missouri

Montana

Nebraska

Nevada

New Hampshire

New Jersey

New Mexico

New York

North Carolina

North Dakota

Ohio

Oklahoma

Oregon

Pennsylvania

Rhode Island

South Carolina

Tennessee

Texas

Utah

Vermont

Virginia

Washington

West Virginia

Wisconsin

Wyoming

In Memoriam
Troopers Who Died In The Line Of Duty In The Year 2000

Provided by the National Law Enforcement Officers Memorial in Washington, D.C.

Matthew R. Bond
Date of Death: Jan. 14, 2000
Department: State Police Pennsylvania
Automobile accident. Trooper Bond and Trooper Stuckey were assisting a disabled motorist in a snow storm when his cruiser was struck from behind by a tractor trailer. He was transported to a local hospital where he died the next day. Trooper William Stuckey was the driver of the police unit and he had minor injuries.

Jason Eric Beal
Date of Death: Jan. 15, 2000
Department: State Police Indiana
Trooper Beal was struck by a vehicle while assisting a tow truck driver. He died three days later from his injuries.

Thomas Summer Rettberg
Date of Death: Feb. 11, 2000
Department: Highway Patrol Utah
Aircraft Accident. Lieutenant Rettberg was killed when the helicopter he was piloting crashed during a routine maintenance flight. The mechanic who was onboard was also killed in this accident.

Floyd James Fink Jr.
Date of Death: Feb. 18, 2000
Department: Department of Public Safety, Arizona
Automobile accident. Officer Fink was killed when his cruiser was rear-ended by another vehicle. He was processing a traffic stop on U.S. Highway 60 near Tempe, AZ. Officer Fink was trapped inside his cruiser when it burst into flames.

Brett C. Buckmister
Date of Death: Mar. 21, 2000
Department: Department of Public Safety, Arizona
Automobile accident. Officer Buckmister died after being involved in a two-car accident near Page, AZ. Four others were also killed in this accident. Officer Buckmister was responding to an emergency call when the accident occurred.

David Travis Bailey
Date of Death: April 5, 2000
Department: Highway Patrol, South Carolina
Automobile accident Lance Corporal Bailey was killed in a vehicle accident while attempting to stop a traffic violator for speeding in Greenville County, SC.

Rick Lee Johnson
Date of Death: May 6, 2000
Department: State Police Michigan
Trooper Johnson was killed after being struck by a vehicle during a traffic stop on I-94 in Van Buren County, MI. He was flown to a local hospital where he was pronounced dead.

Robert Perez Jr.
Date of Death: May 15, 2000
Department: Highway Patrol, Ohio
Feloniously killed during traffic stop or pursuit. Trooper Perez was killed after his cruiser was struck from behind while writing a traffic citation on the Ohio Turnpike in Milan, OH. The suspect was high on amphetamines and intentionally struck the back of Trooper Perez's vehicle at a speed of 83 mph. Trooper Perez never regained consciousness and died three days later from his injuries.

Kenneth A. Poormon
Date of Death: May 31, 2000
Department: State Police New York
Trooper Poormon and Trooper Truscott Kelly were killed when their cruiser was struck by a tractor-trailer as they were making a U-turn. The two troopers were patrolling on State Route 28 in Ulster County, New York, when they attempted to stop a traffic violator. Both troopers were killed instantly.

Truscott M. Kelly
Date of Death: May 31, 2000
Department: State Police New York
Trooper Kelly and Trooper Kenneth Poormon were killed when their cruiser was struck by a tractor-trailer as they were making a U-turn. The two troopers were patrolling on State Route 28 in Ulster County, New York, when they attempted to stop a traffic violator. Both troopers were killed instantly.

Lynn McCarthy Ross
Date of Death: July 26, 2000
Department: Department of Safety Tennessee
Trooper Ross was killed when his cruiser was struck by a commercial vehicle while he was working a construction work zone. Although Trooper Ross's cruiser had its emergency lights flashing, the tractor-trailer ran into the back of it and flipped the cruiser over. Trooper Ross was pinned inside the cruiser when it became engulfed in flames.

Randal Wade Vetter
Date of Death: Aug. 7, 2000
Department: Department of Public Safety Texas
Feloniously killed during traffic stop or pursuit. Trooper Vetter was shot and killed by a suspect he had stopped for not wearing his seatbelt. While writing the citation in his patrol cruiser, the suspect exited his car and shot Trooper Vetter several times. He died four days later from his injuries. The suspect was arrested at the scene of the shooting by several other Texas DPS Officers.

Matthew Scott Evans
Date of Death: Aug. 31, 2000
Department: Highway Patrol, Oklahoma
Automobile accident. Trooper Evans was en route to assist another State Trooper in a drug-related traffic stop. On a different call, Oklahoma City Police Officer Jeff Rominger had just begun chasing a vehicle on I-40. During the chase a tractor-trailer topped a hill and collided with the suspect's vehicle. Officer Rominger's vehicle and Trooper Evans vehicle then crashed into the tractor-trailer and the suspect's vehicle. All four vehicles became engulfed in flames. Trooper Evans was trapped inside his cruiser and pronounced dead at the scene. Officer Rominger died en route to the hospital.

Theodore Joseph Foss
Date of Death: Aug. 31, 2000
Department: State Patrol, Minnesota
Struck by vehicle (officer was outside of vehicle when struck) Corporal Foss was struck and killed by a tractor trailer while conducting a traffic stop on I-90 in Rochester, Minnesota.

Sean Alexander Nava
Date of Death: Oct. 28, 2000
Department: Highway Patrol California
Officer Nava responded to a call to an accident on I-5 in the San Diego area. While working the accident scene, Officer Nava was struck and killed by a drunk driver. After striking Officer Nava, the suspect fled the scene. Officer Nava was transported to the local hospital where he died shortly after arrival. The suspect was arrested and charged with DUI, and hit and run, and manslaughter.

Edward M. Toatley
Date of Death: Oct. 30, 2000
Department: State Police, Maryland
Drug-related matters (drug bust, buys, etc.). Trooper Toatley was shot and killed while conducting an undercover narcotics investigation in Northeaset Washington DC. He and several other officers had beer, deputized as federal agents to take part in a Regional Narcotics Task Force for the Maryland and Washington, DC area. While waiting for the suspected drug dealer to deliver a large amount of drugs, Trooper Toatley was shot in the back of the head by the drug dealer. He died several hours later at a local hospital.

Eric Francis Nicholson
Date of Death: May 15, 2000
Department: Highway Patrol, South Carolina
Robbery in progress or pursuing robbery suspects. Trooper Nicholson was shot and killed while attempting to stop a bank robbery suspect. Trooper Nicholson followed the suspect, who was driving a small motorcycle and attempted to stop him. The suspect then produced a small handgun and shot Trooper Nicholson several times before he could exit his patrol car. Trooper Nicholson was flown to a local hospital where he succumbed to his injuries.

Tom Allen Craig
Date of Death: Dec. 14, 2000
Department: State Police Arkansas
Struck by vehicle. Captain Craig was struck and killed while assisting at another accident. Captain Craig was on his way to work, in his cruiser when he stopped to help the driver of another vehicle that overturned during a winter storm. While traveling around the accident scene, another vehicle lost control on the ice and struck Captain Craig. He was killed immediately and pronounced dead at the scene.

Killed in the Line of Duty

Roster of all known troopers killed in the line of duty as provided by the
National Law Enforcement Officers Memorial in Washington, D.C.

Name	Date of *Death RANK*	Department	National Law Enforcement Officers Memorial, Washington D.C. *Panel/Line*
MAURY YOUNG	09/05/1936 State Hwy Patrolman	Dept. of Public Safety, Alabama	25-E: 15
WILLIAM D RAIFORD Sr	10/16/1937 State Hwy Patrolman	Dept. of Public Safety, Alabama	21-E: 12
ARVIL 0 HUDSON	05/20/1952 State Hwy Patrolman	Dept. of Public Safety, Alabama	4-E: 15
HENRY PRESTON BRYANT	12/07/1952 State Hwy Patrolman	Dept. of Public Safety, Alabama	33-E: 1
JULIAN F DRAUGHON	10/03/1953 State Hwy Patrolman	Dept. of Public Safety, Alabama	31-E: 4
HOWARD BROCK	11/08/1957 State Hwy Patrolman	Dept. of Public Safety, Alabama	60-E: 8
JOE F PARTIN	07/25/1960 State Trooper	Dept. of Public Safety, Alabama	42-E: 12
ANTHONY SCOZZARO	12/13/1961 State Hwy Patrolman	Dept. of Public Safety, Alabama	22-E: 4
THOMAS E MAXWELL	10/04/1962 Captain	Dept. of Public Safety, Alabama	19-E: 13
RAYMOND M CARLTON	02/27/1965 Sergeant	Dept. of Public Safety, Alabama	8-W: 9
RANDOLPH G GLOVER	07/19/1967 State Trooper	Dept. of Public Safety, Alabama	43-E: 5
BROOKS D LAWSON	07/31/1969 State Trooper	Dept. of Public Safety, Alabama	37-E: 6
HARLAN B BLAKE	10/10/1970 Trooper Corporal	Dept. of Public Safety, Alabama	45-E: 9
ORMAND FRANKLIN WATKINS	04/11/1971 State Trooper	Dept. of Public Safety, Alabama	36-E: 16
RILEY DELANO SMITH	12/17/1971 State Trooper Crpl	Dept. of Public Safety, Alabama	44-E: 10
JAMES B ROBINSON	12/10/1972 State Trooper	Dept. of Public Safety, Alabama	23-E: 7
BOBBY S GANN	02/21/1974 State Trooper	Dept. of Public Safety, Alabama	23-W: 2
KENYON M LASSITER	04/19/1974 State Trooper	Dept. of Public Safety, Alabama	19-E: 13
JULIAN DOUGLAS STUCKEY	06/27/1974 Trooper Sergeant	Dept. of Public Safety, Alabama	21 W: 21
JOHNNIE EARL BOOKER	11102/1978 State Trooper	Dept. of Public Safety, Alabama	27-E: 9
DAVID E TEMPLE	09/13/1979 State Trooper	Dept. of Public Safety, Alabama	24-E: 8
SIMMIE L JEFFRIES	12/21/1984 State Trooper	Dept. of Public Safety, Alabama	64-W: 8
LARRY D CAWYER	05/25/1985 State Trooper	Dept. of Public Safety, Alabama	20-W: 2
ELIZABETH S COBB	10/11/1987 State Trooper	Dept. of Public Safety, Alabama	39-E: 15
THOMAS 0 GILLILAN	07/0111989 State Trooper Crpl	Dept. of Public Safety, Alabama	24-E: 6
ROBERT WILLIAM JONES	11/03/1991 Trooper	Dept. of Public Safety, Alabama	45-W: 18
WILLIS VON MOORE	02/26/1996 State Trooper	Dept. of Public Safety, Alabama	13-E: 20
DENNIS FINBAR CRONIN	02/18/1974 Trooper	State Troopers, Alaska,	50-W: 11
FRANK STUART RODMAN	12/11/1974 Trooper	State Troopers, Alaska,	42-W: 7
LARRY ROBERT CARR	12/11/1974 Trooper	State Troopers, Alaska,	48-W: 8
ROLAND EDGAR CHEVALIER Jr	04/04/1982 Trooper	State Troopers, Alaska,	31-W: 17
TROY LYNN DUNCAN	05/19/1984 Trooper	State Troopers, Alaska,	32-W: 10
ROBERT LEE BITTICK	10/11/1994 Sergeant	State Troopers, Alaska,	46-E: 19
BRUCE A HECK	01/10/1997 Trooper	State Troopers, Alaska,	30-E: 20
LOUIS 0 COCHRAN	12/22/1958 Patrolman	Dept. of Public Safety, Arizona	35-W: 15
PAUL E MARSTON	06/09/1969 Patrolman	Dept. of Public Safety, Arizona	20-E: 13
GILBERT A DUTHIE	09/05/1970 Patrolman	Dept. of Public Safety, Arizona	36-W: 14
JAMES L KEETON	02/05/1971 Patrolman	Dept. of Public Safety, Arizona	24-W: 17
DONALD A BECKSTEAD	02/07/1971 Patrolman	Dept. of Public Safety, Arizona	11-E: 17
ALAN H HANSEN	07/19/1973 Patrolman	Dept. of Public Safety, Arizona	60-W: 16
GREGORY ALLISON DILEY	12/02/1977 Patrolman	Dept. of Public Safety, Arizona	40-W: 12
NOAH MACK MERRILL Jr	12/11/1978 Patrolman	Dept. of Public Safety, Arizona	30-W: 4
JOHN C WALKER	11/30/1979 Agent	Dept. of Public Safety, Arizona	7-E: 13
WILLIAM H MURIE	11/19/1980 Patrolman	Dept. of Public Safety, Arizona	2-E: 1
THOMAS P McNEFF	10/02/1983 Pilot	Dept. of Public Safety, Arizona	35-W: 9
RICHARD G STRATMAN	10/02/1983 Paramedic	Dept. of Public Safety, Arizona	40-E: 3
BRUCE A PETERSEN	10/27/1987 Officer	Dept. of Public Safety, Arizona	22-W: 21
EDWARD A REBEL	06/28/1988 Officer	Dept. of Public Safety, Arizona	64-W: 16
JOHNNY E GARCIA	10/14/1989 Officer	Dept. of Public Safety, Arizona	26-W: 3
DAVID GEORGE GABRIELLI	08/31/1990 Patrolman	Dept. of Public Safety, Arizona	16-W: 18
JOHN M BLASER	08/31/1990 Sergeant	Dept. of Public Safety, Arizona	15-W: 18
MANUEL HURTADO TAPIA	01108/1991 Sergeant	Dept. of Public Safety, Arizona	39-W: 18
DAVID JON ZESIGER	07/03/1992 Sergeant	Dept. of Public Safety, Arizona	8-W: 19
MARK MAYNARD DRYER	07/03/1993 Reserve Sergeant	Dept. of Public Safety, Arizona	59-W: 19
MICHAEL LYNN CROWE	07/05/1995 Sergeant	Dept. of Public Safety, Arizona	29-W: 20
ROBERT KENNETH MARTIN	08/15/1995 Officer	Dept. of Public Safety, Arizona	26-W: 20
DOUGLAS EDWARD KNUTSON	01/02/1998 Officer	Dept. of Public Safety, Arizona	4-E: 21
JUAN NIEBLAS CRUZ	12/09/1998 Officer	Dept. of Public Safety, Arizona	31 -W: 21
CHAMP CRAWFORD	02/26/1942 Sheriff	State Police, Arkansas	54-W: 20
SIDNEY A PAVATT	09/26/1948 Trooper	State Police, Arkansas	23-W: 9

ERMON BOYCE COX	08/17/1958 Trooper	State Police, Arkansas	43-E: 4
ELMER GLEN BRADSHAW	12/11/1965 Sergeant	State Police, Arkansas	43-E: 15
HARRY F LOCKE	09124/1966 Trooper	State Police, Arkansas	19-W: 5
ALLEN HARVIE BUFFORD	07/27/1969 Trooper	State Police, Arkansas	39-E: 8
WILLIAM RONALD BROOKS	02/27/1975 Trooper	State Police, Arkansas	18-W: 1
KELLY RAY PIGUE	12/08/1978 Sergeant	State Police, Arkansas	41-E: 8
FREDERICK GLEN BAILEY	09/05/1980 Sergeant	State Police, Arkansas	64-E: 9
DALE W WALLIS	04/20/1982 Corporal	State Police, Arkansas	59-E: 11
WILLIAM L ROSE Jr	12/28/1982 Corporal	State Police, Arkansas	2-W: 11
LOUIS P BRYANT	06/30/1984 Trooper	State Police, Arkansas	38-E: 13
ROBERT WHITTINGTON KLEIN	10/15/1984 Corporal	State Police, Arkansas	34-E: 17
PHILLIP GENE OSTERMAN	08/10/1985 Corporal	State Police, Arkansas	28-E: 8
CHARLES MICHAEL BASSING	07/24/1986 Trooper	State Police, Arkansas	I O-W: 6
WILSON A ATKINS Jr	07/03/1988 Trooper	State Police, Arkansas	35-E: 9
CLARK KENT SIMPSON	02/18/1989 Trooper	State Police, Arkansas	55-E: 13
JOHNNY MACK SCARBEROUGH	09/02/1998 Corporal	State Police, Arkansas	27-W: 21
CHARLES MARION ALVITRE	08/26/1923 Officer	Highway Patrol, California	31-E: 6
CLARENCE M PICKETT	11/10/1923 Officer	Highway Patrol, California	12-W: 4
JAMES B POWER	03/25/1925 Captain	Highway Patrol, California	31-E: 16
W R VALENTINE	05/30/1925 Officer	Highway Patrol, California	57-W: 16
JOHN A DERBY	09/27/1925 Captain	Highway Patrol, California	60-E: 6
LUTHER W HOGAN	02/26/1929 Officer	Highway Patrol, California	44-E: 6
HOWARD GARLINGER	10/30/1929 Officer	Highway Patrol, California	15-W: 16
EDGAR J COMBS	09/09/1930 Officer	Highway Patrol, California	19-E: 14
ELBER D WARREN	01/24/1931 Officer	Highway Patrol, California	13-W: 10
BURT REEVES	09/22/1931 Officer	Highway Patrol, California	38-E: 11
J W SHUMAN	03/01/1932 Officer	Highway Patrol, California	6-W: 7
EDWIN B CROOK	07/08/1932 Officer	Highway Patrol, California	23-W: 15
A E HINCK	08/14/1932 Officer	Highway Patrol, California	20-W: 9
FLOYD A RUSSELL	01/15/1933 Officer	Highway Patrol, California	41 -E: 4
THOMAS C BISSETT	01/26/1933 Officer	Highway Patrol, California	18-E: 13
STEPHEN S KENT	03/10/1933 Officer	Highway Patrol, California	53-E: 7
TED DAVIS	03/11/1933 Officer	Highway Patrol, California	30-E: I
JOHN A DAROUX	03/12/1933 Officer	Highway Patrol, California	16-E: 8
JACK E MARKS	04/1111933 Officer	Highway Patrol, California	25-E: 2
OSCAR D McMURRY	03/05/1934 Officer	Highway Patrol, California	61-E: 13
FRANCIS J PERRY	07/07/1934 Officer	Highway Patrol, California	19-E: 7
HUGH C CLINE	08/26/1934 Officer	Highway Patrol, California	37-E: 7
A DONALD HOOVER	08/31/1934 Officer	Highway Patrol, California	31-E: 5
WILLIAM R McDANIEL	10/06/1934 Officer	Highway Patrol, California	22-W: 12
EDWARDILBOND	04/14/1935 Officer	Highway Patrol, California	23-E: 8
IVAN CASSELMAN	08/24/1935 Officer	Highway Patrol, California	32-E: 1
CHARLES H NISSEN	12/17/1935 Officer	Highway Patrol, California	55-E: 13
EARL M AMES	10/1011936 Officer	Highway Patrol, California	22-W: 6
RICHARD H TREMBATH	12/04/1937 Officer	Highway Patrol, California	29-E: 6
E R CARR	01/27/1938 Officer	Highway Patrol, California	64-E: 17
LEONARD NELSON	05/18/1938 Officer	Highway Patrol, California	22-W: 4
E L SHRYVER	07/10/1938 Captain	Highway Patrol, California	31-E: 4
FRED J KOWOLOWSKI	12/26/1938 Officer	Highway Patrol, California	47-E: 12
JOSEPH B MATHEWS	08/10/1939 Officer	Highway Patrol, California	42-E: 2
ERNEST R NELSON	08/29/1939 Officer	Highway Patrol, California	6-E: 12
SAMUEL G COPE	01/16/1940 Officer	Highway Patrol, California	62-W: 18
WILLIAM F MALIN	07/04/1940 Officer	Highway Patrol, California	37-E: 4
MAURICE W OWEN	09/22/1940 Police Officer	Highway Patrol, California	28-E: 21
M PAUL MENGEDOTH	02/07/1941 Officer	Highway Patrol, California	6-W: 16
LESLIE LAUTERWASSER	06/27/1941 Officer	Highway Patrol, California	21-E: 15
ROBERT C HELLER	01/12/1942 Officer	Highway Patrol, California	62-E: 5
SCOTT LEATHERMAN	05/03/1942 Officer	Highway Patrol, California	23-W: 3
ELIOT 0 DALEY	05/17/1942 Officer	Highway Patrol, California	16-E: 15
EMMETT L ELMORE	07/18/1942 Sergeant	Highway Patrol, California	47-E: 4
CLINTON BENJAMIN	08/10/1942 Officer	Highway Patrol, California	20-W: 8
JOSEPH A STUCKER	01/07/1943 Officer	Highway Patrol, California	6-W: 16
WALTER C MAXEY	02/02/1943 Officer	Highway Patrol, California	36-E: 3
FREDERICK WALES	02/07/1943 Officer	Highway Patrol, California	17-W: 15
GEORGE E ELLIS Jr	04/21/1943 Sergeant	Highway Patrol, California	26-E: 11
NELSON S DWELLY	07110/1943 Officer	Highway Patrol, California	14-W: 3
FORREST C GERKEN	02/15/1944 Officer	Highway Patrol, California	19-E: 3
FOREST UNDERWOOD	03/09/1944 Sergeant	Highway Patrol, California	1-W:12
JOHN A REED	05/18/1944 Officer	Highway Patrol, California	64-E: 4
LEWIS GREGG	11/04/1944 Officer	Highway Patrol, California	32-E: 11
DAVID R HENDERSON	12/07/1944 Officer	Highway Patrol, California	12-W: 6
RAYMOND H BERRY	04/08/1945 Officer	Highway Patrol, California	25-E: 4
NORMAN A KESSLER	05/17/1945 Officer	Highway Patrol, California	23-W: 11
JAMES B DALZIEL	06/30/1945 Officer	Highway Patrol, California	49-E: 7
JAMES H VancleWEG	07/12/1945 Officer	Highway Patrol, California	30-E: 9
HAROLD E NICHOLS	09/12/1945 Officer	Highway Patrol, California	11-W: 14
LOREN C ROOSEVELT	06/05/1946 Officer	Highway Patrol, California	16-E: 6
FRANK J MAUS	07/14/1946 Officer	Highway Patrol, California	20-W: 2
STEPHEN W SODEL	09/17/1946 Officer	Highway Patrol, California	64-E: 17
RICHARD L SIMPSON	09/25/1946 Officer	Highway Patrol, California	56-W: 4
WILLIAM L REARDON	10/20/1946 Officer	Highway Patrol, California	28-E: 11
JOHN R WALTERS	11/18/1947 Officer	Highway Patrol, California	53-E: 10
ALVIN FOSS	04/26/1950 Officer	Highway Patrol, California	18-W: 12
WILLIAM C FOOTE	06/23/1952 Officer	Highway Patrol, California	40-E: 8
RALPH A VARGAS	09/30/1952 Officer	Highway Patrol, California	21 -W: 8
JOHN W ARMATOSKI	05/01/1953 Officer	Highway Patrol, California	26-E: I
FRANK M EPPERSON	07/02/1954 Officer	Highway Patrol, California	52-E: 15

WILLIAM M CHANSLER	08/27/1954 Officer	Highway Patrol, California	22-W: 17
JOHN C LaMAR	12/10/1954 Officer	Highway Patrol, California	44-E: 5
JAMES E MARONEY	05/27/1955 Officer	Highway Patrol, California	59-E: 2
CHARLES D GOSS	11/25/1955 Officer	Highway Patrol, California	47-E: 14
GEORGE A WOODSON	12/23/1955 Officer	Highway Patrol, California	27-E: 14
EDWARD A FREY	07/02/1956 Officer	Highway Patrol, California	38-E: 10
RAYMOND A GIEGER	08/10/1956 Officer	Highway Patrol, California	36-E: 10
CHARLES T SMITH	09/09/1956 Officer	Highway Patrol, California	9-W: 7
ELZA P FITZPATRICK Jr	12106/1956 Officer	Highway Patrol, California	53-E: 7
CARL H JESSING	01/09/1957 Officer	Highway Patrol, California	12-W: 11
ROBERT E REED	10/08/1957 Officer	Highway Patrol, California	8-W: 5
CAMILE E MADERE	01/24/1958 Officer	Highway Patrol, California	28-E: 18
ROBERT W SUESS	02/15/1958 Officer	Highway Patrol, California	34-E: 15
JOSEPH F JOHNSTON Jr	10/12/1958 Officer	Highway Patrol, California	21-W: 12
ROBERT B HEBERLIE	11/22/1958 Officer	Highway Patrol, California	4-E: 9
HERBERT F DIMON	02/07/1959 Officer	Highway Patrol, California	57-W: 4
GEORGE E KALLEMEYN	07/21/1959 Officer	Highway Patrol, California	64-E: 5
LEONARD W WINNEY	11/12/1959 Officer	Highway Patrol, California	33-E: 8
RICHARD D DUVALL	02/23/1960 Officer	Highway Patrol, California	1-E: 14
ROBERT D DALE	03/10/1960 Officer	Highway Patrol, California	24-E: 1
WILLIAM E PITOIS	11/04/1960 Officer	Highway Patrol, California	18-W: 16
GARY L GROW	01/18/1962 Officer	Highway Patrol, California	6-W: 14
JERRY E TURRE	04/21/1962 Officer	Highway Patrol, California	41-E: 17
DALE M KRINGS	05/21/1962 Officer	Highway Patrol, California	I-E: 13
RONALD E DAVIS	08/18/1962 Officer	Highway Patrol, California	22-W: 21
CHARLES H SORENSON	03/15/1963 Officer	Highway Patrol, California	41-E: 11
DONALD E BRANDON	04/23/1963 Officer	Highway Patrol, California	62-E: 8
JOHN R ELLIS	11/05/1963 Officer	Highway Patrol, California	31-E: 6
GLENN W CARLSON	11/15/1963 Officer	Highway Patrol, California	36-E: 6
MERLE E DeWITT	12/24/1963 Officer	Highway Patrol, California	31-E: 9
RALPH A MINION	01/06/1964 Officer	Highway Patrol, California	1-E: 13
WILLIAM D HUCKABY	01/12/1964 Sergeant	Highway Patrol, California	56-E: 5
KENNETH L WITKE	01/14/1964 Officer	Highway Patrol, California	23-E: 2
COBURN B JEWELL	02/01/1964 Officer	Highway Patrol, California	15-W: 17
JAMES F STAMBACK	03/23/1964 Officer	Highway Patrol, California	63-E: 12
CHARLES 0 WOODWORTH	08/12/1964 Officer	Highway Patrol, California	62-E: 15
LEONARD L LAYTON	11/08/1964 Officer	Highway Patrol, California	16-E: 4
JERREL H SHOWS	12/23/1964 Officer	Highway Patrol, California	59-E: 1
MERREL L KISSINGER	02/14/1965 Officer	Highway Patrol, California	28-E: 16
MARTIN J TRIPPTREE	12/15/1965 Officer	Highway Patrol, California	63-E: 5
MICHAEL S GRIFFIN	01/13/1966 Officer	IIighway Patrol, California	16-E: 10
WILLIAM C ISAACS	08/2511966 Officer	Highway Patrol, California	16-W: 15
FRANK ARTHUR STORY	07/19/1967 Officer	Highway Patrol, California	22-E: 3
CHARLES R LILLY	10/29/1967 Officer	Highway Patrol, California	32-E: 6
MERLE LEE ANDREWS	12/20/1967 Officer	Highway Patrol, California	37-E: 7
KENNETH E MARSHALL	01/09/1968 Officer	Highway Patrol, California	47-E: 15
WESLEY D JOHNSON	04/15/1969 Officer	Highway Patrol, California	26-E: 1
RICHARD G WOODS	07/16/1969 Officer	Highway Patrol, California	52-E: 13
ROBERT M BLOMO	09/04/1969 Officer	Highway Patrol, California	38-E: 10
AMBERS 0 SHEWMAKER	11/24/1969 Officer	Highway Patrol, California	35-E: 1
WILLIAM R COURT	02/13/1970 Officer	Highway Patrol, California	45-E: 11
RAYMOND R CARPENTER	02/17/1970 Officer	Highway Patrol, California	15-W: 8
JAMES E PENCE Jr	04/06/1970 Officer	Highway Patrol, California	21-W: 1
WALTER C FRAGO	04/06/1970 Officer	Highway Patrol, California	40-E: 11
GEORGE M ALLEYN	04/06/1970 Officer	Highway Patrol, California	15-W: I
ROGER D GORE	04106/1970 Officer	Highway Patrol, California	43-E: 4
NATHAN L SEIDENBERG	10/23/1970 Officer	Highway Patrol, California	8-W: 6
LOREN D SCRUGGS	04/23/1971 Officer	Highway Patrol, California	22-E: 5
ROBERT ANTON MAYER	09/02/1971 Officer	Highway Patrol, California	56-W: 6
DANA EVERETT PALADIN[	07/04/1972 Officer	Highway Patrol, California	60-E: 15
KENNETH GRANT ROEDIGER	08/05/1972 Officer	Highway Patrol, California	62-E: 4
ALFRED G JOHNSON	08/27/1972 Officer	Highway Patrol, California	19-W: 2
WILLIAM D McKIM	02/06/1973 Officer	Highway Patrol, California	32-E: 12
LARRY L WETTERLING	03/09/1973 Officer	Highway Patrol, California	56-W: 9
WILLIAM P SNIFFEN	04/05/1973 Officer	Highway Patrol, California	29-E: 5
ROBERT HAROLD HARRISON Jr	01/11/1974 Officer	Highway Patrol, California	17-E: 3
GERALD N HARRIS	02/27/1974 Officer	Highway Patrol, California	5-W: 10
RALPH D PERCIVAL	06/03/1974 Officer	Highway Patrol, California	31-E: 15
KEITH M GILES	08/25/1974 Officer	Highway Patrol, California	29-E: 11
ROBERT A PHILLIPS	01/06/1975 Officer	Highway Patrol, California	43-E: 4
ADOLFO M HERNANDEZ	06/27/1975 Officer	Highway Patrol, California	58-E: I
FREDERICK W ENRIGHT	06/27/1975 Officer	Highway Patrol, California	17-W: 1
ALFRED RAY TURNER	12/16/1975 Officer	Highway Patrol, California	12-W: 2
GARY LEE HUGHES	05/23/1976 Officer	Highway Patrol, California	40-E: 3
ARTHUR EDWARD DUNN	07/09/1977 Officer	Highway Patrol, California	25-E: 13
GEORGE W REDDING	08/17/1977 Officer	Highway Patrol, California	24-E: 5
WILLIAM BENNO WOLFF	12/30/1977 Officer	Highway Patrol, California	4-E: 1
WILLIAM F LEIPHARDT Jr	05/13/1978 Officer	Highway Patrol, California	33-E: 14
HAROLD E HORINE	05/13/1978 Officer	Highway Patrol, California	61-E: 9
WARD E WASHINGTON	07/10/1978 Officer	Highway Patrol, California	14-W: 11
GAYLE W WOOD Jr	09/01/1978 Officer	Highway Patrol, California	9-E: 15
JAMES E McCABE	09/01/1978 Officer	Highway Patrol, California	10-W: 10
ROY P BLECHER	12/22/1978 Officer	Highway Patrol, California	35-E: 4
WILLIAM M FREEMAN	12/22/1978 Officer	Highway Patrol, California	33-E: 16
DONALD R HOLLOWAY	01/03/1980 Officer	Highway Patrol, California	3-W: 18
ERNEST RAY FELIO	09/07/1980 Officer	Highway Patrol, California	44-E: 9
GERALD ELOIN DORMAIER	12/25/1980 Officer	Highway Patrol, California	11-W: 5

PAUL C JARSKE	02/24/1981 Officer	Highway Patrol, California	23-E: 12
JAMES J SCHUMACHER Jr	06/13/1981 Officer	Highway Patrol, California	59-E: 12
JOHNNY RAMIREZ MARTINEZ	10/02/1981 Officer	Highway Patrol, California	13-W: 2
KENNETH L ARCHER	02/24/1982 Officer	Highway Patrol, California	62-E: 14
GEORGE R CAREY	02/24/1982 Officer	Highway Patrol, California	17-W: 9
DALE E NEWBY	07/17/1982 Officer	Highway Patrol, California	23-E: 7
DAVID W COPELMAN	04/06/1985 Officer	Highway Patrol, California	17-E: 1
RAYMOND E MILLER	08/14/1985 Officer	Highway Patrol, California	6-E: 4
DEAN J ESQUIBEL	08/21/1985 Officer	Highway Patrol, California	36-E: 3
GEORGE FITZMAURICE BUTLER	12108/1986 Officer	Highway Patrol, California	13-W: 1
MICHAEL ALLEN BRANDT	04/06/1987 Officer	Highway Patrol, California	19-W: 14
TERRY WAYNE AUTREY	09/30/1987 Officer	Highway Patrol, California	56-E: 2
MARK THOMAS TAYLOR	11/26/1987 Officer	Highway Patrol, California	17-E: 12
JOHN C HELMICK	02/27/1989 Lieutenant	Highway Patrol, California	16-W: 10
HUGO OLAZAR	09/02/1989 Officer	Highway Patrol, California	29-E: 11
JAMES CHRISTOPHER O'CONNOR	11/15/1990 Officer	Highway Patrol, California	15-W: 11
FIDEL ALEMAN	07/23/1992 Officer	Highway Patrol, California	32-E: 18
JOHN NORBERT McVEIGH Jr	04/17/1993 Officer	Highway Patrol, California	45-W: 19
JOHN LEE STEEL	04/23/1993 Sergeant	Highway Patrol, California	50-W: 19
LARRY JOE JARAMILLO	06/22/1993 Officer	Highway Patrol, California	49-W: 19
RICHARD ALAN MAXWELL	07/11/1994 Officer	Highway Patrol, California	35-E: 19
BRUCE THOMAS HINMAN	10/03/1995 Officer	Highway Patrol, California	42-W: 20
ARTIE J HUBBARD	12/08/1995 Officer	Highway Patrol, California	46-W: 20
DAVID WAYNE MANNING	02/15/1996 Officer	Highway Patrol, California	63-W: 20
DON JOSEPH BURT	07/13/1996 Officer	Highway Patrol, California	18-E: 20
REUBEN FRED RIOS SR	10/27/1996 Officer	Highway Patrol, California	7-E: 20
NOREEN ALLISON VARGAS	11/08/1996 Officer	Highway Patrol, California	28-E: 20
JAMES DOUGLAS SCHULTZ	11/16/1996 Officer	Highway Patrol, California	18-E: 20
SAUL MARTINEZ	05/16/1997 Officer	Highway Patrol, California	48-E: 20
DANIEL JAMES MUEHLHAUSEN	06/01/1997 Officer	Highway Patrol, California	63-E: 20
SCOTT MATTHEW GREENLY	01/07/1998 Officer	Highway Patrol, California	62-W: 21
RICKY BILL STOVALL	02/24/1998 Officer	Highway Patrol, California	53-W: 21
BRITT T IRVINE	02/24/1998 Traffic Officer	Highway Patrol, California	54-W: 21
CHRISTOPHER DAVID LYDON	06/05/1998 Officer	Highway Patrol, California	42-W: 21
ARNOLD B GULZOW	06/26/1941 Captain	State Patrol, Colorado	45-W: 4
WALLACE McCARTY	01/24/1946 Patrolman	State Patrol, Colorado	44-W: 16
HAROLD BECHTELHEIMER	09/1411949 Patrolman	State Patrol, Colorado	29-W: 11
WESLEY ROSETTE	01/31/1951 Sergeant	State Patrol, Colorado	33-W: 9
FLOYD GRESHAM	02/02/1956 Patrolman	State Patrol, Colorado	55-W: 7
MELVIN E PHILLIPS	02/02/1956 Patrolman	State Patrol, Colorado	45-W: 5
RICHARD J CAHALAN	09/28/1957 Patrolman	State Patrol, Colorado	46-E: 7
RICHARD EDSTROM	10/28/1959 Corporal	State Patrol, Colorado	33-W: 4
HIRAM SHORT	07/12/1961 Lieutenant	State Patrol, Colorado	14-E: 9
ALBERT ALCORN	01/23/1966 Sergeant	State Patrol, Colorado	37-W: 1
NICHOLAS CARHART	01/23/1966 Patrolman	State Patrol, Colorado	46-E: I
GERALD WILLIAMS	12116/1967 Patrolman	State Patrol, Colorado	55-W: 9
LARRY BRUCE ENLOE	01/08/1968 Patrolman	State Patrol, Colorado	39-W: 4
THOMAS RAY CARPENTER	12/27/1973 Patrolman	State Patrol, Colorado	55-W: 13
RICHARD P ROSS	07/10/1974 Patrolman	State Patrol, Colorado	43-W: 3
MICHAEL HARDY JAMES	12/18/1975 Patrolman	State Patrol, Colorado	28-W: 13
HUGH PURDY	07/31/1976 Sergeant	State Patrol, Colorado	51 -W: 2
FRANCES I GALVIN	05/24/1979 Trooper	State Patrol, Colorado	51-E: 12
JAMES KEVIN FARRIS	11/29/1980 Patrolman	State Patrol, Colorado	39-W: 16
CHARLES ANDREW FRY	09/26/1987 Patrolman	State Patrol, Colorado	52-W: 16
JOSEPH A YNOSTROZA	12/06/1989 Trooper	State Patrol, Colorado	55-W: 4
LYLE FREDRICK WOHLERS	11/05/1992 Trooper	State Patrol, Colorado	40-E: 18
PEARLE E ROBERTS	11/25/1922 Trooper	State Police, Connecticut	34-W: 8
BARTHOLOMEW M SKELLY	11/14/1925 Trooper	State Police, Connecticut	35-W: 13
IRVING H NELSON	04/06/1928 Trooper	State Police, Connecticut	50-W: 10
LLOYD J EUKERS	07/21/1928 Trooper	State Police, Connecticut	7-E: 4
STANLEY C HELLBERG	06/01/1929 Trooper	State Police, Connecticut	37-E: 6
LEONARD H WATSON	10/22/1932 Trooper	State Police, Connecticut	26-W: 17
CHARLES F HILL	11106/1941 Sergeant	State Police, Connecticut	34-W: 2
EDWARD P JESMONTH	07/20/1943 Trooper	State Police, Connecticut	50-W: 11
KENNETH W STEVENS	06/06/1944 Lieutenant	State Police, Connecticut	5-W: 15
FRANK A STARKEL	07/19/1948 Lieutenant	State Police, Connecticut	61-W: 13
ERNEST J MORSE	02/13/1953 Trooper	State Police, Connecticut	10-E: 1
JAMES W LAMBERT	10/29/1960 Trooper	State Police, Connecticut	24-W: 13
JOSEPH M STOBA Jr	08/06/1962 Trooper	State Police, Connecticut	31 -W: 9
CARL P MOLLER	02/13/1976 Trooper	State Police, Connecticut	59-W: 17
THOMAS F CARNEY	12/06/1982 Lieutenant	State Police, Connecticut	42-W: 2
JAMES H SAVAGE	01/22/1986 Trooper	State Police, Connecticut	42-W: 3
JORGE A AGOSTO	11/22/1989 Trooper	State Police, Connecticut	32-W: 3
RUSSELL A BAGSHAW	06/05/1991 Trooper	State Police, Connecticut	24-W: 18
EDWARD W TRUELOVE	11/13/1992 Aux. Deputy Trooper	State Police, Connecticut	17-W: 19
FRANCIS RYAN	11/02/1922 Officer	State Police, Delaware	14-E: 20
PAUL H SHERMAN	10/16/1945 Trooper	State Police, Delaware	12-E: 16
LEROY L LeKITES	01/13/1950 Corporal	State Police, Delaware	58-W: 13
RAYMOND B WILHELM	05/30/1951 Trooper	State Police, Delaware	34-W: 11
WILLIAM F MAYER	08/08/1955 Trooper	State Police, Delaware	25-W: 8
HAROLD B RUPERT	04/19/1962 Trooper	State Police, Delaware	48-W: 17
ROBERT A PARIS	10/17/1963 Trooper	State Police, Delaware	26-W: 5
WILLIAM C KELLER	01/22/1971 Trooper	State Police, Delaware	2-E: 15
RONALD L CAREY	01/05/1972 Trooper	State Police, Delaware	3-E: 10
DAVID C YARRINGTON	01/06/1972 Trooper	State Police, Delaware	12-E: 2
GEORGE W EMORY	06/03/1972 Trooper	State Police, Delaware	61 -W: 4
DAVID BRUCE PULLING	11/18/1987 Trooper	State Police, Delaware	36-W: 15

Name	Date/Rank	Department	Location
KEVIN J MALLON	03/20/1990 Trooper	State Police, Delaware	15-E: 7
GERARD T DOWD	09/12/1990 Trooper	State Police, Delaware	61-W: 4
ROBERT H BELL	09/07/1993 Corporal	State Police, Delaware	39-W: 20
SANDRA MARIE WAGNER	04/05/1996 Trooper	State Police, Delaware	6-E: 20
LUTHER PAUL DANIELS	12/05/1941 Trooper	Highway Patrol, Florida	16-E: 13
LEROY C BENDER	10/15/1947 Trooper	Highway Patrol, Florida	45-E: 2
HALLEY C STRICKLAND	01/08/1954 Trooper	Highway Patrol, Florida	64-W: 14
EDWIN J GASQUE	10/26/1961 Trooper	Highway Patrol, Florida	23-W: 3
SHERMAN LEE SCOTT Jr	01/03/1965 Trooper	Highway Patrol, Florida	11-W: 15
JOSEPH NEWTON SAWTELL Jr	08/05/1966 Trooper	Highway Patrol, Florida	37-E: 1
JOSEPH PAUL BERTRAND	12/22/1967 Corporal	Highway Patrol, Florida	29-E: 8
JOHN C HAGERTY	03/18/1970 Trooper	Highway Patrol, Florida	30-E: 12
HERMAN T MORRIS	03/16/1972 Trooper	Highway Patrol, Florida	32-E: 7
CHARLES W PARKS	02/06/1973 Trooper	Highway Patrol, Florida	23-E: 3
CLAUDE H BAKER Jr	11/17/1973 Trooper	Highway Patrol, Florida	53-E: 16
RONALD GORDON SMITH	12123/1973 Trooper	Highway Patrol, Florida	24-E: 14
WILBURN A KELLY	03/23/1974 Trooper	Highway Patrol, Florida	21-E: 16
CHARLES EUGENE CAMPBELL	11/16/1974 Trooper	Highway Patrol, Florida	1 O-W: 5
KENNETH E FLYNT	01/01/1976 Trooper	Highway Patrol, Florida	60-E: 14
PHILLIP A BLACK	02/20/1976 Trooper	Highway Patrol, Florida	18-E: 11
RICHARD D HOWELL	08/02/1976 Trooper	Highway Patrol, Florida	29-E: 11
BRADLEY STEVEN GLASCOCK	08/04/1977 Trooper	Highway Patrol, Florida	11-W: 7
ELMER C BARNETT	02/14/1978 Trooper	Highway Patrol, Florida	I-W: 5
ALVIN V KOHLER	09/19/1978 Trooper	Highway Patrol, Florida	39-E: 14
ROBERT P McDERMON Sr	04/11/1981 Trooper	Highway Patrol, Florida	44-E: 5
CLEO L TOMLINSON Jr	07/13/1981 Corporal	Highway Patrol, Florida	38-E: 12
ROBERT L PRUITT	07/13/1981 Trooper	Highway Patrol, Florida	42-E: 13
MERLE J COOK	07/13/1981 Trooper	Highway Patrol, Florida	20-E: 1
FREDERICK L GROVES Jr	09/18/1984 Trooper	Highway Patrol, Florida	21-E: 11
LINDELL J GIBBONS	03/23/1985 Trooper	Highway Patrol, Florida	32-E: 12
JOHN C BAXTER Jr	10/02/1985 Sergeant	Highway Patrol, Florida	23-W: 16
STEPHEN G ROUSE	03/28/1987 Trooper	Highway Patrol, Florida	14-W: 11
JEFFREY DALE YOUNG	08/18/1987 Trooper	Highway Patrol, Florida	1-W: 14
MILAN DEXTER HENDRIX	06/01/1989 Trooper	Highway Patrol, Florida	28-E: 6
BENEDICT JAMES THOMAS	06/09/1989 Lieutenant	Highway Patrol, Florida	29-E: 8
JAMES HERBERT FULFORD Jr	02/01/1992 Trooper	Highway Patrol, Florida	46-E: 18
KIMBERLY ANN HURD	07/16/1992 Trooper	Highway Patrol, Florida	15-W: 19
SAXTON RANDALL JONES	05/01/1995 Major	Highway Patrol, Florida	29-E: 20
DONALD E JENNINGS	06/30/1995 Trooper	Highway Patrol, Florida	28-W: 20
ROBERT G SMITH	07/26/1997 Trooper	Highway Patrol, Florida	33-E: 20
JAMES B CROOKS	05/19/1998 Trooper	Highway Patrol, Florida	54-W: 21
WILLIAM F BLACK Jr	12/2011940 Trooper	State Patrol, Georgia	44-W: 4
JOHN F BASS	02/15/1950 Trooper	State Patrol, Georgia	41-W: 12
CLYDE A WEHUNT	04/20/1951 Trooper	State Patrol, Georgia	53-W: 6
GEORGE W HARRELSON	08/15/1952 Sergeant Major	State Patrol, Georgia	51-E: 12
CHARLES E GRAY	08/16/1961 Sergeant	State Patrol, Georgia	46-W: 11
ROY C MASSEY	08/1611961 Trooper	State Patrol, Georgia	46-E: 10
HARVEY L NICHOLSON	08/18/1961 Trooper	State Patrol, Georgia	38-W: 17
FREDERICK H LOONEY	05/25/1962 Trooper	State Patrol, Georgia	33-W: 5
WILTON L HARRELL	12/23/1964 Trooper	State Patrol, Georgia	53-W: 5
VICTOR H TURPEN	02/23/1965 Trooper	State Patrol, Georgia	52-W: 17
BEN L SENTELL	08/03/1966 Lieutenant	State Patrol, Georgia	63-W: 12
MARK ALLEN PAGE	06/22/1968 Trooper	State Patrol, Georgia	39-W: 3
BILLY A TANNER	04/11/1970 Trooper	State Patrol, Georgia	45-W: 15
EDWARD C TAYLOR	06/26/1971 Trooper	State Patrol, Georgia	37-W: 17
LARRY PAUL COLLINS	11/05/1973 Trooper	State Patrol, Georgia	51-W: 10
JAMES DAVID YOUNG	05/04/1975 Trooper	State Patrol, Georgia	45-W: 16
TYRONE COLLIER DILLARD	02/03/1977 Trooper	State Patrol, Georgia	46-E: 12
WILLIAM G ANDREWS Jr	05/08/1977 Trooper	State Patrol, Georgia	51 -W: 14
KEITH HARLAN SEWELL	01/17/1979 Trooper	State Patrol, Georgia	33-W: 12
JOHN D MORRIS	05/18/1982 Trooper	State Patrol, Georgia	28-W: 8
DONWARD F LANGSTON	07/26/1983 Trooper	State Patrol, Georgia	51 -W: 3
RONALD E O'NEAL	01/10/1984 Trooper	State Patrol, Georgia	46-E: 6
JAMES KEITH STEWART	04/27/1991 Trooper	State Patrol, Georgia	46-W: 18
FONTAINE COOPER	11/25/1935 Policeman	State Police, Idaho	53-W: 13
BENJAMIN T NEWMAN	03/03/1962 Corporal	State Police, Idaho	5-W: 3
WALTER W COX	03/06/1970 Sergeant	State Police, Idaho	28-W: 5
DOUGLAS M DEEN	08/05/1979 Corporal	State Police, Idaho	34-W: 16
LINDA CAROL HUFF	06/17/1998 State Trooper	State Police, Idaho	14-E: 21
ALBERT J HASSON	09/0711924 Trooper	State Police, Illinois	50-E: 6
LORY L PRICE	01/17/1927 Trooper	State Police, Illinois	1-W: 11
PAUL E CLENDENING	02/16/1927 Trooper	State Police, Illinois	44-E: 16
GEORGE E WHEELER	11/22/1927 Trooper	State Police, Illinois	14-W: 15
ROBERT L FISHER	04/24/1929 Trooper	State Police, Illinois	20-E: 8
ROBERT JEFFERSON McDONALD	07/10/1930 Trooper	State Police, Illinois	13-W: 6
ROBERT J CARD	08/12/1930 Trooper	State Police, Illinois	17-W: 7
FRANK M SCHWARTZ	09/11/1930 Trooper	State Police, Illinois	25-E: 11
KENNETH L CHURCH	12/05/1931 Trooper	State Police, Illinois	9-E: 13
GRADY SUTTON	06/30/1932 Trooper	State Police, Illinois	10-W: 15
RICHARD GROJA	05/28/1933 Trooper	State Police, Illinois	53-E: 12
JOHN L McCABE	08/12/1933 Trooper	State Police, Illinois	48-E: 6
JOSEPH MERRITT ELLIOTT	10/20/1933 Trooper	State Police, Illinois	18-E: 4
LEO J LaVELLE	11/24/1934 Trooper	State Police, Illinois	28-E: 11
RAY EMBREE	10/15/1936 Trooper	State Police, Illinois	4-E: 8
FRANK TAMULIS	08/09/1937 Trooper	State Police, Illinois	11-W: 1
ALBERT CECIL BROKMYER	11/19/1939 Trooper	State Police, Illinois	23-E: 14
EUGENE ROBERTS	02/18/1940 Trooper	State Police, Illinois	25-E: 12

ROCCO V GRAGIDO	09/11/1940 Trooper	State Police, Illinois	27-E: 14
RALPH R NEWMAN	08/20/1941 Trooper	State Police, Illinois	6-W: 14
ROBERT R THOMAS	05/15/1942 Trooper	State Police, Illinois	12-W: 13
PHILLIP B GUINTO	08/05/1943 Sergeant	State Police, Illinois	59-E: 2
CHARLES DEANS	08/08/1944 Trooper	State Police, Illinois	16-E: 10
SAM MANGIAMELE	05/25/1945 Trooper	State Police, Illinois	43-E: 6
MARVIN C ARCHER	06/18/1946 Trooper	State Police, Illinois	6-E: 11
FORREST F SPENCER	10/27/1946 Trooper	State Police, Illinois	26-E: 3
GEORGE L FREDRICKSON	09/01/1947 Trooper	State Police, Illinois	59-E: 11
ROY KYLE MOODY	02/28/1949 Trooper	State Police, Illinois	45-E: 13
BEN R SEATON	10/24/1949 Trooper	State Police, Illinois	53-E: 12
ARTHUR PAUL GOETTING	02/04/1951 Trooper	State Police, Illinois	8-W: 12
CORWIN L McCONKEY	03/08/1951 Sergeant	State Police, Illinois	29-E: 2
MILLARD R COURTNEY	04/11/1951 Trooper	State Police, Illinois	56-E: 8
GLENN D GAGNON	12/28/1952 Trooper	State Police, Illinois	63-E: 7
HARRY B BRADLEY	10/24/1957 Trooper	State Police, Illinois	38-E: 7
LEO BURAKOWSKI	09/24/1958 Trooper	State Police, Illinois	22-E: 2
CLARENCE U SWAIN	08/01/1959 Trooper	State Police, Illinois	17-W: 13
MICHAEL T ANGELOS	07/13/1960 Trooper	State Police, Illinois	42-E: 12
DALE A VanVOOREN	12/29/1962 Trooper	State Police, Illinois	42-E: 11
FRANK A DORIS	05/27/1967 Trooper	State Police, Illinois	39-E: 12
WARREN L ALLEN	09/21/1967 Trooper	State Police, Illinois	17-E: 2
FLOYD J FARRAR	12/17/1968 Trooper	State Police, Illinois	21-E: 14
RICHARD G WARNER	04/21/1969 Trooper	State Police, Illinois	64-W: 11
DONALD R BLICKENSDERFER	09/26/1970 Trooper	State Police, Illinois	9-W: 4
FRANK R DUNBAR	05/14/1972 Trooper	State Police, Illinois	33-E: 9
PETE EARL LACKEY	11/27/1972 Special Agent	State Police, Illinois	60-E: 4
LAYTON T DAVIS	03/18/1976 Trooper	State Police, Illinois	1 O-W: 8
GEORGE D CRAGGS	11/06/1976 Corporal	State Police, Illinois	12-W: 18
MICHAEL K McCARTER	04/07/1979 Trooper	State Police, Illinois	19-W: 3
BERNARD D SKEETERS	05/20/1982 Trooper	State Police, Illinois	16-W: 14
JOHN H KUGELMAN	11/10/1986 Trooper	State Police, Illinois	56-E: 14
VIRGIL LEE BENSYL	01/15/1988 Sergeant	State Police, Illinois	29-E: 17
GARY ROBERT DEGELMAN	05/05/1989 Special Agent	State Police, Illinois	39-E: 4
APRIL C STYBURSKI	01/05/1990 Trooper	State Police, Illinois	42-E: 13
CHONG S LIM	06/06/1995 Trooper	State Police, Illinois	18-W: 20
ANTHONY MILLISON	10/27/1997 Trooper	State Police, Illinois	7-W: 21
ERIN MARIE HEHL	10/30/1997 Trooper	State Police, Illinois	35-E: 20
EUGENE TEAGUE	12/20/1933 Trooper	State Police, Indiana	45-E: 15
PAUL MINNEMAN	05/25/1937 Trooper	State Police, Indiana	45-E: 3
RAY DIXON	06/27/1938 Trooper	State Police, Indiana	59-E: 1
GEORGE FORESTER	05/17/1941 Trooper	State Police, Indiana	24-E: 14
RICHARD ENGLAND	04122/1942 Trooper	State Police, Indiana	26-E: 14
HERBERT SMITH	12/05/1946 Trooper	State Police, Indiana	43-E: 2
ROBERT CLEVENGER	09/08/1953 Trooper	State Police, Indiana	12-W: 1
HUBERT ROUSH	01/26/1955 Trooper	State Police, Indiana	45-E: 12
EARL L BROWN	08/31/1955 Trooper	State Police, Indiana	56-E: 3
JOHN R MILLER	09/05/1955 Trooper	State Police, Indiana	16-E: 10
DON R TURNER	01/28/1956 Trooper	State Police, Indiana	58-E: 4
MARVIN E WALTS	03/18/1957 Trooper	State Police, Indiana	50-E: 6
WILLIAM R KELLEMS	09130/1957 Trooper	State Police, Indiana	25-E: 10
JOHN HENRY POWELL	02/27/1959 Trooper	State Police, Indiana	42-E: 10
ROBERT J GARRISON	12/14/1959 Trooper	State Police, Indiana	20-W: 6
ROBERT C GILLESPIE	06/08/1962 Trooper	State Police, Indiana	53-E: 3
WILLIAM F KIESER	03/09/1965 Trooper	State Police, Indiana	51-W: 9
OSCAR MILLS	04/1211966 Trooper	State Police, Indiana	64-E: 15
WILLIAM R RAYNER	12118/1966 Trooper	State Police, Indiana	46-E: 12
RICHARD G BROWN	09/27/1967 Trooper	State Police, Indiana	23-E: 4
ROBERT 0 LIETZAN	03130/1969 Trooper	State Police, Indiana	19-W: 14
GEORGE W CAMPBELL	06/18/1969 Sergeant	State Police, Indiana	64-W: 19
JOHN J STREU	02/20/1971 Trooper	State Police, Indiana	63-W: 7
GLEN R HOSIER	04/2611971 Sergeant	State Police, Indiana	13-W: 11
WILLIAM JOSEPH TREES	06/26/1972 Trooper	State Police, Indiana	44-E: 10
LAWRENCE B MEYER	02/02/1974 Trooper	State Police, Indiana	16-W: 14
LAWRENCE B MYER	02/02/1974 Trooper	State Police, Indiana	21-W: 18
LEWIS EDWARD PHILLIPS	04/16/1975 Trooper	State Police, Indiana	62-E: 2
ROY E JONES	07/03/1979 Trooper	State Police, Indiana	1-E: 17
ROBERT JOHN LATHER II	07/06/1982 Trooper	State Police, Indiana	39-W: 7
STEVEN L BAILEY	12/10/1983 Trooper	State Police, Indiana	35-E: 13
JOHN EDWARD HATFULL	04/13/1987 Sergeant	Statc Policc, Indiana	25-E: 10
MICHAEL EARL GREENE	02/05/1993 Master Trooper	State Police, Indiana	61-W: 19
TODD A BURMAN	07/29/1993 Trooper	State Police, Indiana	51-W: 19
ANDREW PATRICK WINZENREAD	04/25/1997 Trooper	State Police, Indiana	35-E: 20
JAMES PATRICK BARTRAM	03/31/1998 Trooper	State Police, Indiana	7-E: 21
DAVID ANTHONY DEUTER	07/16/1998 Master Trooper	State Police, Indiana	15-E: 21
RICHARD T GASTON	03/04/1999 Trooper	State Police, Indiana	48-E: 21
CORY R ELSON	04/03/1999 Trooper	State Police, Indiana	39-E: 21
ORAN H PAPE	09/29/1936 Patrolman	State Patrol, Iowa	40-W: 15
HAROLD EMMERSON KLINKEFUS	05/18/1949 Patrolman	State Patrol, Iowa	61-W: 12
HAROLD CLARENCE DeGEAR	02/19/1954 Patrolman	State Patrol, Iowa	25-W: 17
RALPH FRANKLIN GARTHWAITE	07/02/1955 Patrolman	State Patrol, Iowa	2-E: 15
MARVIN C VANDERLINDEN	06111/1965 Sergeant	State Patrol, Iowa	15-E: 1
CHARLES GERALD WHITNEY	06/16/1985 Trooper	State Patrol, Iowa	36-W: 8
LANCE G DIETSCH	06/30/1989 Trooper Pilot	State Patrol, Iowa	5-E: 4
STANLEY E GERLING	06/30/1989 Trooper	State Patrol, Iowa	14-E: 5
ALLEN PATRICK NIELAND	10/14/1990 Trooper	State Patrol, Iowa	26-W: 7
MAURICE R PLUMMER	12/16/1944 Trooper	Highway Patrol, Kansas	31-E: 5

JIMMIE D JACOBS	10/06/1959 Trooper	Highway Patrol, Kansas	13-W: 12
JOHN B McMURRAY	12/09/1964 Trooper	Highway Patrol, Kansas	63-E: 5
BERNARD C HILL	05/28/1967 Lieutenant	Highway Patrol, Kansas	60-E: 5
ELDON K MILLER	01/19/1968 Sergeant	Highway Patrol, Kansas	23-W: 2
JAMES DONALD THORNTON	10/02/1973 Trooper	Highway Patrol, Kansas	37-E: 12
CONROY G O'BRIEN	05/24/1978 Trooper	Highway Patrol, Kansas	9-W: 11
FERDINAND F PRIBBENOW	07/11/1981 Trooper	Highway Patrol, Kansas	32-E: 17
LARRY LEE HUFF	11/26/1993 Master Trooper	Highway Patrol, Kansas	60-W: 19
DEAN ALLEN GOODHEART	09/06/1995 Master Trooper	Highway Patrol, Kansas	18-W: 20
JAMES POWELL HAYS	12/21/1935 Patrolman	State Police, Kentucky	52-E: 18
ROBERT ROWLAND	12/22/1935 Patrolman	State Police, Kentucky	19-W: 19
HAROLD J TOLL	11/14/1948 Trooper	State Police, Kentucky	23-E: 16
ROBERT R MILLER	02/14/1951 Trooper	State Police, Kentucky	4-E: 2
LEE T HUFFMAN	05/04/1953 Trooper	State Police, Kentucky	1 O-W: 2
HERBERT C BUSH	10/11/1958 Trooper	State Police, Kentucky	25-E: 9
WILLIAM E TEVIS	05/26/1963 Trooper	State Police, Kentucky	20-W: 17
ELMER MOBLEY	05/28/1964 Trooper	State Police, Kentucky	18-E: 7
CECIL W UZZLE	05/28/1964 Trooper	State Police, Kentucky	64-E: 8
DELANO G POWELL	07/08/1965 Trooper	State Police, Kentucky	29-E: 9
MACK E BRADY	11/09/1966 Trooper	State Police, Kentucky	58-E: 3
WILLIAM H BARRETT	12/19/1971 Trooper	State Police, Kentucky	21-E: 10
JAMES W McNEELY	04/08/1972 Trooper	State Police, Kentucky	38-E: 10
WALTER 0 THURTELL	09/29/1972 Trooper	State Police, Kentucky	56-W: 7
JOE WARD Jr	04/23/1973 Trooper	State Police, Kentucky	13-W: I
WILLIAM C SMITH	04/26/1973 Lieutenant	State Police, Kentucky	17-E: 13
JOHN WAYNE HUTCHINSON	06/04/1975 Trooper	State Police, Kentucky	3-W: 16
BOBBY ALLEN McCOUN Jr	09/01/1975 Trooper	State Police, Kentucky	21 -W: 7
WILLIAM FRANCIS PICKARD	01/21/1976 Trooper	State Police, Kentucky	18-W: 3
WILLIS DURWOOD MARTIN	04/26/1977 Lieutenant	State Police, Kentucky	58-E: 10
CLINTON E CUNNINGHAM	02/11/1979 Trooper	State Police, Kentucky	63-E: 13
EDWARD R HARRIS	11/07/1979 Trooper	State Police, Kentucky	64-W: 7
JEROME S CLIFTON	10/01/1980 Trooper	State Police, Kentucky	21-E: 1
DARRELL V PHELPS	08/07/1981 Detective	State Police, Kentucky	12-W: 2
JOHNNY MONTAGUE EDRINGTON	12/21/1988 Trooper	State Police, Kentucky	53-E: 16
NEILL A YARBOROUGH Sr	02/25/1925 Officer	State Police, Louisiana	6-W: 21
VICTOR A MOSSY	05/13/1936 Trooper	State Police, Louisiana	63-W: 3
JAMES T BROWNFIELD	05/09/1943 Trooper	State Police, Louisiana	39-W: 11
ULIS FLOYD	02/24/1952 Trooper	State Police, Louisiana	45-W: 7
ELI L SMITH	01/29/1956 Sergeant	State Police, Louisiana	46-W: 15
WILMER L MOODY	11/10/1956 Trooper	State Police, Louisiana	52-W: 17
JAMES N POLLARD	11/20/1956 Trooper	State Police, Louisiana	51 W: 8
FRANCIS C ZINNA	03/24/1958 Trooper	State Police, Louisiana	37-W: 12
RUDOLPH H MILLER	09/08/1962 Trooper	State Police, Louisiana	53-W: 8
JOSEPH D FERRIS	02/23/1968 Trooper	State Police, Louisiana	37-W: 15
HUEY P GRACE	10/30/1968 Trooper	State Police, Louisiana	39-W: 14
LAMON WEAVER	04/17/1973 Sergeant	State Police, Louisiana	37-W: 7
WILLIAM C WARRINGTON	07/17/1973 Trooper	State Police, Louisiana	53-W: I
CLARENCE J MILLER Jr	12/04/1975 Sergeant	State Police, Louisiana	52-W: 10
DONALD CHARLES CLEVELAND	07/02/1977 Trooper	State Police, Louisiana	47-W: 4
JEAN CLAUDE CRESCIONNE	04/20/1982 Trooper	State Police, Louisiana	63-W: 1
DAMON L ROBICHAUX	07/21/1982 Trooper	State Police, Louisiana	52-W: 14
WILLIAM MICHAEL KEES	02/05/1983 Trooper	State Police, Louisiana	45-W: 8
STEPHEN H GRAY	05/29/1995 Master Trooper	State Police, Louisiana	10-W: 20
GEORGE DOUGLAS JOHNSTON	11/17/1997 Sergeant	State Police, Louisiana	12-W: 21
HUNG LE	06/30/1998 Trooper	State Police, Louisiana	19-E: 21
EMERY 0 GOOCH	08/09/1924 Patrolman	State Police, Maine	52-W: 6
FRED A FOSTER	08/30/1925 Patrolman	State Police, Maine	29-W: 12
FRANK C WING	08/19/1928 Patrolman	State Police, Maine	51-E: 7
CHARLES CLINTON BLACK	07/09/1964 Trooper	State Police, Maine	27-W: 19
THOMAS J MERRY	07/12/1980 Trooper	State Police, Maine	29-W: 17
MICHAEL R VEILLEUX	06/17/1986 Trooper	State Police, Maine	45-W: 7
GILES R LANDRY	03/31/1989 Detective Trooper	State Police, Maine	47-W: 8
JEFFREY S PAROLA	11/13/1994 Trooper	State Police, Maine	28-E: 19
JAMES A GRIFFITH	04/15/1996 Trooper	State Police, Maine	25-E: 20
JOHN W JEFFREY	09/21/1921 Officer	State Police, Maryland	56-E: 1
WILLIAM G LOCHNER Jr	04/18/1923 Officer	State Police, Maryland	18-W: 4
RAYMOND 0 EICHOLTZ	05/27/1923 Officer	State Police, Maryland	18-E: 12
HUGH K PAINTER	03/30/1924 Officer	State Police, Maryland	60-E: 3
ALBERT E CRAMBLITT	10/01/1925 Officer	State Police, Maryland	34-W: 21
JAMES S NOON	12/15/1927 Officer	State Police, Maryland	33-E: 17
CLINTON R RHODES	01/28/1931 Officer	State Police, Maryland	6-E: 9
THEODORE A MOORE	08/25/1932 Officer	State Police, Maryland	59-E: 4
IMLA DORAN HUBBARD	03/04/1933 Officer	State Police, Maryland	21 -W: 9
JOSEPH E KUHN	04/08/1934 Officer	State Police, Maryland	61-E: 3
CARROLL C CREEGER	12/23/1934 Officer	State Police, Maryland	50-E: 6
WILBERT V HUNTER	02/07/1936 Sergeant	State Police, Maryland	38-E: 12
J F LEO SHAAB	07/22/1937 Officer	State Police, Maryland	34-E: 2
ELLSWORTH D DRYDEN	10/07/1938 Sergeant	State Police, Maryland	15-W: 3
LAUREN M RIDGE	07/14/1950 Trooper	State Police, Maryland	43-E: 2
LEONARD N BROWN	07/07/1958 Lieutenant	State Police, Maryland	18-W: 11
ARTHUR W PLUMMER Jr	04/09/1961 Trooper	State Police, Maryland	17-E: 9
THOMAS ASA NOYLE	10/28/1972 Trooper	State Police, Maryland	6-E: 9
PHILLIP LEE RUSS	10/28/1972 Trooper	State Police, Maryland	63-E: 1
CHARLES STRAINING RATHELL	09/18/1973 Trooper	State Police, Maryland	42-E: 11
DONALD EUGENE PARKERSON Jr	09/18/1973 Trooper	State Police, Maryland	9-W: 14
MILTON VEASILY PURNELL Jr	05/29/1975 Trooper	State Police, Maryland	61-E: 12
MART HUDSON Jr	06/16/1975 Trooper	State Police, Maryland	38-E: 6

WALLACE JOHNSON MOWBRAY	08/10/1975 Sergeant	State Police, Maryland	21-E: 10
GREGG ALEXANDER PRESBURY	12/17/1977	State Police, Maryland	28-E: 16
WILLIAM P MILLS Jr	06/08/1979 Trooper	State Police, Maryland	6-E: 4
GARY L WADE	01/30/1982 Trooper	State Police, Maryland	16-E: 1
GREGORY A MAY	01/19/1986 Corporal	State Police, Maryland	1-E: 15
CAREY S POETZMAN	01/19/1986 Trooper	State Police, Maryland	19-E: 10
JOHN EDWARD SAWA	03/10/1987 Trooper	State Police, Maryland	21-E: 3
LARRY EUGENE SMALL	03/10/1987 Trooper	State Police, Maryland	63-E: 9
ERIC DWIGHT MONK	04/09/1988 Trooper	State Police, Maryland	61-E: 2
THEODORE DENNIS WOLF Sr	03/29/1990 Corporal	State Police, Maryland	20-W: 5
MARK P GRONER	10/01/1992 Trooper	State Police, Maryland	3-W: 19
EDWARD ALLEN PLANK	10/17/1995 Trooper First Class	State Police, Maryland	41-W: 20
JOSEPH THOMAS LANZI	10/28/1995 Trooper First Class	State Police, Maryland	35-W: 20
RAYMOND G ARMSTEAD Jr	03/25/1998 Trooper	State Police, Maryland	26-W: 21
LLEWELLYN A LOWTHER	09/20/1924 Patrolman	State Police, Massachusetts	14-W: 6
GEORGE L PRENTISS	10/01/1927 Patrolman	State Police, Massachusetts	26-W: 6
JOHN E HIGGINS	04/14/1928 Patrolman	State Police, Massachusetts	27-W: 13
CHARLES A BETTER	09/28/1930 Patrolman	State Police, Massachusetts	26-W: 4
CHARLES F McGONAGLE	08/02/1932 Patrolman	State Police, Massachusetts	58-W: 2
EARL W TOBIN	03/30/1934 Patrolman	State Police, Massachusetts	36-W: 12
ROBERT A EDMONDS	12/23/1936 Patrol Officer	State Police, Massachusetts	62-W: 20
JOSEPH W KELLY	07/23/1938 Patrolman	State Police, Massachusetts	14-E: 5
ALBERT T HAYES	02/09/1940 Special Officer	State Police, Massachusetts	40-W: 10
CHARLES J COLLINS	05/20/1942 Patrolman	State Police, Massachusetts	42-W: 1
ALFRED A HEWITT	01/04/1950 Patrolman	State Police, Massachusetts	27-E: 9
DANIEL FURTADO	10/08/1950 Patrolman	State Police, Massachusetts	49-W: 2
ALJE M SAVELA	08/31/1951 Patrolman	State Police, Massachusetts	30-W: 2
WALLACE E MATHEWS	04/23/1953 Patrolman	State Police, Massachusetts	32-W: 7
JAMES H MARSHALL	10/21/1960 Trooper	State Police, Massachusetts	20-E: 18
ROBERT J MacDOUGALL	08/06/1971 Trooper	State Police, Massachusetts	26-W: 8
EDWARD A MAHONEY	11/21/1976 Trooper	State Police, Massachusetts	59-W: 5
PERLEY K JOHNSON Jr	02/13/1978 Trooper	State Police, Massachusetts	7-E: 19
DONALD E SHEA	12/16/1978 Trooper	State Police, Massachusetts	13-E: 11
GEORGE L HANNA	02/26/1983 Trooper	State Police, Massachusetts	25-W: 17
JOSEPH FRANCIS MOYNIHAN Jr	06/19/1990 Trooper	State Police, Massachusetts	33-E: 18
DAVIDSON GOULD WHITING	08/18/1994 Trooper	State Police, Massachusetts	18-E: 19
MARK STEVEN CHARBONNIER	09/02/1994 Trooper	State Police, Massachusetts	34-E: 19
JAMES MATTALIANO	02/22/1995 Trooper	State Police, Massachusetts	21-W: 20
PAUL ANDREW PERRY	02/22/1995 Trooper	State Police, Massachusetts	1 O-W: 20
HARVEY E BOLEN	01/19/1920 Sergeant	State Police, Michigan	13-W: 15
HAROLD ANDERSON	03/12/1921 Trooper	State Police, Michigan	8-W: 16
MILAN PRATT	04/15/1922 Sergeant	State Police, Michigan	56-W: 14
JOHN P CLINTON	01/08/1923 Trooper	State Police, Michigan	23-W: 11
SAM MAPES	05/01/1924 Corporal	State Police, Michigan	39-E: 4
WILLIAM MARTZ	03/12/1925 Trooper	State Police, Michigan	20-W: 17
HOWARD H FUNK	07/08/1926 Trooper	State Police, Michigan	13-W: 14
DELOS A WILLIAMS	06/30/1929 Trooper	State Police, Michigan	38-E: 5
JOHN BURKE	10/13/1930 Trooper	State Police, Michigan	1-E: 3
RICHARD F HAMMOND	01/20/1937 Trooper	State Police, Michigan	35-E: 2
RALPH BROULLIRE	12/18/1937 Trooper	State Police, Michigan	26-E: 2
IRVINE WURM	01/26/1941 Trooper	State Police, Michigan	16-W: 5
JOHN W CAIN	11/26/1941 Trooper	State Police, Michigan	45-E: 3
CHARLES WOOD	04/14/1942 Trooper	State Police, Michigan	18-E: 5
JOHN D RYAN	03/03/1950 Trooper	State Police, Michigan	19-E: 13
GEORGE BRANNY	04/12/1950 Trooper	State Police, Michigan	58-E: 4
PERRY CRITCHELL	03/20/1954 Sergeant	State Police, Michigan	26-E: 4
CALVIN JONES	02/10/1956 Trooper	State Police, Michigan	23-W: 4
GEORGE E LAPPI	11/19/1956 Trooper	State Police, Michigan	24-E: 11
BERT A POZZA	11/19/1956 Trooper	State Police, Michigan	60-E: 1
DUGALD PELLOT	09/30/1957 Trooper	State Police, Michigan	18-W: 1
ALBERT W SOUDEN	09/03/1959 Trooper	State Police, Michigan	17-E: 17
ROBERT RAYMOND GONSER	08108/1968 Detective	State Police, Michigan	24-E: 10
CARL P LINDBERG	05/26/1969 Trooper	State Police, Michigan	60-E: 7
ROGER ADAMS	05/14/1971 Trooper	State Police, Michigan	31-E: 3
CHARLES B STARK	12/31/1971 Trooper	State Police, Michigan	40-E: 14
GARY T RAMPY	12/31/1971 Trooper	State Police, Michigan	15-W: 10
STEVEN B DeVRIES	10/12/1972 Trooper	State Police, Michigan	42-E: 4
DARRYL M RANTANEN	05/27/1974 Trooper	State Police, Michigan	5-W: 10
LARRY LEE FORREIDER	12/05/1974 Trooper	State Police, Michigan	64-W: 1
NORMAN R KILLOUGH	10/07/1978 Trooper	State Police, Michigan	4-E: 5
HARRY A SORENSON	12/05/1978 Detective Sergeant	State Police, Michigan	58-E: 17
DAVID WILLIAM HUBBARD	09/16/1980 Detective Sergeant	State Police, Michigan	I-E: 9
ALLEN PETERSON	08/29/1981 Trooper	State Police, Michigan	32-E: 16
CRAIG A SCOTT	02/09/1982 Trooper	State Police, Michigan	24-E: 9
VICKI MOREAU DeVRIES	07/2211982 Trooper	State Police, Michigan	14-W: 15
TONY L THAMES	06/12/1983 Trooper	State Police, Michigan	16-W: 4
ROBERT J MIHALIK	09/09/1984 Trooper	State Police, Michigan	34-E: 17
PAUL L HUTCHINS	08/30/1985 Trooper	State Police, Michigan	34-E: 15
JAMES E BOLAND	07/26/1987 Trooper	State Police, Michigan	12-W: 13
KERMIT FITZPATRICK	07/07/1991 Trooper	State Police, Michigan	23-E: 18
JAMES R DeLOACH	02/01/1992 Trooper	State Police, Michigan	43-E: 18
STEVEN J NIEWIEK	02/02/1992 Trooper	State Police, Michigan	28-E: 18
BYRON J ERICKSON	07/31/1993 Trooper	State Police, Michigan	62-W: 19
BRYON S EGELSKI	07/11/1994 Trooper	State Police, Michigan	47-E: 19
MANUEL FIELDS	08/27/1994 Trooper	State Police, Michigan	16-E: 19
FREDERICK ANTHONY HARDY	11/06/1999 Trooper	State Police, Michigan	36-E: 21
WILLIAM S KOZLAK	04/25/1934 Trooper	State Patrol, Minnesota	55-W: 5

ROY C LICHTENHELD	10/03/1934 Trooper	State Patrol, Minnesota	52-W: 10
RAY X F KRUEGER	11/20/1959 Trooper	State Patrol, Minnesota	39-W: 10
GLEN A SKALMAN	12/2711964 Trooper	State Patrol, Minnesota	53-W: 6
DONALD BERT ZIESMER	10/15/1973 Trooper	State Patrol, Minnesota	38-W: 17
ROGER CURTIS WILLIAMS	02/22/1978 Trooper	State Patrol, Minnesota	51-E: 2
TIMOTHY JOSEPH BOWE	06/07/1997 Corporal	State Patrol, Minnesota	36-E: 20
ADRIAN COLE	09/13/1940 Trooper	Highway Patrol, Mississippi	I-E: 9
JAMES M BARRY	02/01/1947 Trooper	Highway Patrol, Mississippi	41-E: 11
CYRIL J REICHERT	02/05/1947 Trooper	Highway Patrol, Mississippi	20-W: 13
JAMES H TINGLE	09/07/1950 Trooper	Highway Patrol, Mississippi	50-E: 2
HERBERT E NIXON	04/22/1951 Trooper	Highway Patrol, Mississippi	23-E: 8
CARL M THACH	01/15/1954 Trooper	Highway Patrol, Mississippi	36-E: 12
WALTER W SMITH	09/22/1955 Captain	Highway Patrol, Mississippi	18-W: 7
HURFU L DUCKWORTH	08/19/1959 Trooper	Highway Patrol, Mississippi	56-E: 16
DANIEL E SMITH	11/07/1959 Trooper	Highway Patrol, Mississippi	11-W: 5
JULIAN DAVIS	11/27/1963 Sergeant	Highway Patrol, Mississippi	15-W: 12
MARCUS LaMASTUS	07/17/1965 Trooper	Highway Patrol, Mississippi	16-W: 13
JOSEPH A POL	11/27/1965 Sergeant	Highway Patrol, Mississippi	23-E: 14
TOMMY E KENDALL	05/16/1966 Trooper	Highway Patrol, Mississippi	I-E: 8
WILLIAM KENNY	12/21/1967 Sergeant	Highway Patrol, Mississippi	24-E: 13
WILLIAM 0 SWINDOLL	10/05/1968 Sergeant	Highway Patrol, Mississippi	36-E: 13
JOE CLAY	05/27/1974 Sergeant	Highway Patrol, Mississippi	64-W: 14
BILLY M LANGHAM	12/31/1981 Trooper	Highway Patrol, Mississippi	49-E: 6
GEORGE DANNY NASH Jr	02/04/1983 Trooper	Highway Patrol, Mississippi	20-E: 1
STEVEN K GARDNER	03/23/1984 Trooper	Highway Patrol, Mississippi	18-W: 12
DAVID BRUCE LADNER	04/12/1987 Trooper	Highway Patrol, Mississippi	24-E: 16
RALPH R NEWELL	10/28/1988 Staff Sergeant	Highway Patrol, Mississippi	18-W: 16
TOMMIE EARL OWENS	07/28/1989 Trooper	Highway Patrol, Mississippi	48-E: 6
BOBBY L WELLS Jr	06/27/1995 Trooper	Highway Patrol, Mississippi	17-W: 20
PAUL DENHAM	12/27/1999 Trooper	Highway Patrol, Mississippi	5-W: 22
BENJAMIN OLIVER BOOTH	06/14/1933 Sergeant	Highway Patrol, Missouri	59-W: 9
FRED L WALKER	12/03/1941 Trooper	Highway Patrol, Missouri	42-W: 1
VICTOR 0 DOSING	12/07/1941 Trooper	Highway Patrol, Missouri	26-W: 8
CHARLES P CORBIN	09/15/1943 Trooper	Highway Patrol, Missouri	12-E: 10
ROSSS CREACH	12/12/1943 Trooper	Highway Patrol, Missouri	27-W: 12
JOHN N GREIM	07/13/1945 Trooper	Highway Patrol, Missouri	30-W: 4
WAYNE W ALLMAN	10/27/1955 Trooper	Highway Patrol, Missouri	14-E: 8
JESSE ROGER JENKINS	10/14/1969 Trooper	Highway Patrol, Missouri	2-E: 10
GARY W SNODGRASS	02/21/1970 Trooper	Highway Patrol, Missouri	19-W: 10
WILLIAM R BRANDT	06/12/1970 Trooper	Highway Patrol, Missouri	2-E: 14
DENNIS H MARRIOTT	06/13/1981 Trooper	Highway Patrol, Missouri	40-W: 16
JAMES M FROEMSDORF	03/02/1985 Trooper	Highway Patrol, Missouri	12-E: 15
JIMMIE ELLIOTT LINEGAR	04/15/1985 Trooper	Highway Patrol, Missouri	14-E: 10
RUSSELL W HARPER	02/08/1987 Trooper	Highway Patrol, Missouri	50-W: 5
HENRY C BRUNS	02/16/1987 Corporal	Highway Patrol, Missouri	10-E: 10
ROBERT J KOLILIS	09/21/1988 Trooper	Highway Patrol, Missouri	62-W: 11
MICHAEL E WEBSTER	10/02/1993 Corporal	Highway Patrol, Missouri	43-W: 19
RANDY VINCENT SULLIVAN	02/17/1996 Sergeant	Highway Patrol, Missouri	59-W: 20
DAVID CARGENE MAY	05/17/1999 Sergeant	Highway Patrol, Missouri	59-E: 21
ROBERT G KIMBERLING	10/06/1999 Sergeant	Highway Patrol, Missouri	44-E: 21
ROBERT G STEELE	11/02/1946 Patrolman	Highway Patrol, Montana	10-E: 2
JAMES H ANDERSON	07/24/1954 Patrolman	Highway Patrol, Montana	15-E: 1
RICHARD E HEDSTROM	07/19/1973 Patrolman	Highway Patrol, Montana	48-W: 9
MICHAEL M REN	04/08/1978 Patrolman	Highway Patrol, Montana	32-W: 1
LOYAL M ZINK	06/13/1945 Trooper	State Patrol, Nebraska	44-W: 1
JOHN T MEISTRELL	04/10/1953 Sergeant	State Patrol, Nebraska	46-W: 13
VERNON C ROLFS	05/30/1953 Trooper	State Patrol, Nebraska	46-E: 16
MARVIN L HANSEN	04/08/1954 Trooper	State Patrol, Nebraska	47-W: 5
DUANE F NICHOLS	07/24/1958 Trooper	State Patrol, Nebraska	39-W: 3
RAYMOND M KOERBER	09/18/1961 Trooper	State Patrol, Nebraska	29-W: 1
GEORGE WILLIAM AMOS Jr	04/20/1973 Trooper	State Patrol, Nebraska	53-W: 9
MICHAEL D FARBER	08/24/1980 Trooper	State Patrol, Nebraska	29-W: 9
ROBERT J CHAB	01/06/1984 Trooper	State Patrol, Nebraska	43-W: 17
DONALD MATEJKA	12/23/1989 Trooper	State Patrol, Nebraska	49-E: 9
MARK PAUL WAGNER	03/04/1999 Trooper	State Patrol, Nebraska	43-E: 21
FRANK JOHN McMANUS	04/19/1941 Private	State Police, Nevada	31-E: 19
RAYMOND ELLIOTT	06/01/1947 Trooper	State Police, New Hampshire	51-W: 17
HAROLD B JOHNSON	10/11/1948 Trooper	State Police, New Hampshire	63-W: 10
RICHARD F CHAMPY	02/03/1978 Trooper	State Police, New Hampshire	52-W: 9
GARY P PARKER	11/29/1989 Trooper	State Police, New Hampshire	33-W: 5
JOSEPH EDWARD GEARTY	11/30/1989 Trooper	State Police, New Hampshire	41 -W: 4
JAMES STANWOOD NOYES	10/03/1994 Sergeant	State Police, New Hampshire	36-E: 19
LESLIE GEORGE LORD	08/19/1997 Trooper	State Police, New Hampshire	51-E: 20
SCOTT EDWARD PHILLIPS	08/19/1997 Trooper	State Police, New Hampshire	31-E: 20
WILLIAM H MARSHALL	12/12/1923 Trooper	State Police, New Jersey	30-W: 5
ROBERT E COYLE	12/18/1924 Trooper	State Police, New Jersey	59-W: 10
CHARLES E ULLRICH	02/17/1926 Trooper	State Police, New Jersey	14-E: 12
HERMAN GLOOR	05/09/1926 Trooper	State Police, New Jersey	5-E: 15
WALTER ARROWSMITH	08/05/1926 Trooper	State Police, New Jersey	32-W: 1
JOSEPH A SMITH	08/04/1927 Trooper	State Police, New Jersey	27-W: 6
PETER GLADYS	12/28/1928 Trooper	State Police, New Jersey	60-W: 8
JOHN MADDEN	03/03/1929 Trooper	State Police, New Jersey	7-E: 17
JOHN D DIVERS	05/02/1930 Trooper	State Police, New Jersey	42-W: 9
PETER W IGNATZ	03/04/1931 Trooper	State Police, New Jersey	58-W: 14
LEONARD P McCANDLESS	06/28/1931 Trooper	State Police, New Jersey	7-E: 13
MICHAEL J BEYLON	02/22/1932 Trooper	State Police, New Jersey	25-W: 12
JOHN RESSLER	05/01/1932 Trooper	State Police, New Jersey	11-E: 13

JAMES R HERBERT	07/09/1932 Trooper	State Police, New Jersey	59-W: 9
JAMES SCOTLAND	02/19/1935 Trooper	State Police, New Jersey	26-W: I
WARREN G YENSER	11/09/1935 Trooper	State Police, New Jersey	32-W: 13
JOSEPH PERRY	06/09/1937 Trooper	State Police, New Jersey	58-W: 17
VINCENT C VOSBEIN	06/19/1938 Trooper	State Police, New Jersey	24-W: 8
WALTER B OTTE	01/24/1940 Trooper	State Police, New Jersey	12-E: 7
JOHN I GREGERSON	04/28/1941 Trooper	State Police, New Jersey	58-W: 8
WILLIAM J DOOLAN	10/23/1944 Trooper	State Police, New Jersey	60-W: 10
CORNELIUS A O'DONNELL	07/16/1945 Trooper	State Police, New Jersey	31 -W: 8
CHARLES KOPF	09/27/1948 Trooper	State Police, New Jersey	5-E: 6
WALTER R GAWRYLA	04/21/1950 Trooper	State Police, New Jersey	42-W: 12
EMIL J BOCK	05/26/1951 Trooper	State Police, New Jersey	2-E: 15
STANLEY A CONN	08/27/1951 Trooper	State Police, New Jersey	30-W: 10
JOSEPH D WIRTH	11/25/1951 Trooper	State Police, New Jersey	5-E: 16
JOSEPH C WALTER	09/07/1952 Trooper	State Police, New Jersey	60-W: 4
FRANK A TRAINOR	08/03/1953 Trooper	State Police, New Jersey	32-W: 15
JOHN ANDERSON	11/01/1955 Trooper	State Police, New Jersey	34-W: 7
GEORGE RICHARD DANCY	05/28/1956 Trooper	State Police, New Jersey	30-W: 17
RONALD E GRAY	12/01/1958 Trooper	State Police, New Jersey	10-E: 11
HILARY WELENC	11/20/1959 Trooper	State Police, New Jersey	7-E: 1
JOHN W STAAS	12/0211961 Trooper	State Police, New Jersey	11-E: 10
RAYMOND P FIOLA	02/19/1962 Trooper	State Police, New Jersey	30-W: 11
ARTHUR J ABAGNALE Jr	06/11/1962 Trooper	State Police, New Jersey	35-W: 15
MILAN SIMCAK	06/11/1962 Trooper	State Police, New Jersey	48-W: 9
JOSEPH PAUL DeFRINO	06/11/1962 Trooper	State Police, New Jersey	13-E: 16
ANTHONY LUKIS Jr	05/04/1966 Trooper	State Police, New Jersey	12-E: 5
THOMAS WILLIAM KAVULA	09/19/1968 Trooper	State Police, New Jersey	59-W: 11
ROBERT J PRATO	12/02/1969 Trooper	State Police, New Jersey	49-W: 7
RUSSELL JOHN MOESTA	11/19/1970 Trooper	State Police, New Jersey	15-E: 2
MARIENUS J SEGEREN	07/25/1971 Trooper	State Police, New Jersey	1 I-E: 8
ROBERT JOSEPH MERENDA	11/29/1971 Trooper	State Police, New Jersey	31 -W: 7
WERNER FOERSTER	05/02/1973 Trooper	State Police, New Jersey	31-W: 11
THOMAS ATKINS DAWSON	08/13/1973 Trooper	State Police, New Jersey	59-W: 15
PHILIP JOSEPH LAMONACO	12/21/1981 Trooper	State Police, New Jersey	25-W: 17
JOHN P McCARTHY	09/25/1982 Trooper	State Police, New Jersey	35-W: 14
LESTER AMOS PAGANO	07/19/1983 Lieutenant	State Police, New Jersey	25-W: 8
EDWARD R ERRICKSON	01/25/1984 Trooper	State Police, New Jersey	36-W: 4
CARLOS M NEGRON	05/07/1984 Trooper	State Police, New Jersey	7-E: 5
WILLIAM L CARROLL Jr	07/12/1984 Trooper	State Police, New Jersey	12-E: 6
ALBERT J MALLEN Sr	08/28/1985 Detective	State Police, New Jersey	14-E: 17
THEODORE MOOS	02/27/1987 Sergeant	State Police, New Jersey	49-W: 4
THOMAS J HANRATTY	04/02/1992 Trooper	State Police, New Jersey	6-W: 19
MARVIN R McCLOUD	06/06/1995 Trooper 11	State Police, New Jersey	26-W: 20
FRANCIS BELLARAN	05/23/1996 Trooper 11	State Police, New Jersey	59-W: 20
SCOTT M GONZALEZ	10/24/1997 Trooper	State Police, New Jersey	61-E: 20
LESLIE D BUGG	08121/1946 Patrolman	State Police, New Mexico	54-E: 1
WILLIAM T SPEIGHT	02/24/1949 Patrolman	State Police, New Mexico	49-E: 4
NASH PHILLIP GARCIA	04/11/1952 Patrolman	State Police, New Mexico	49-E: 4
JOHN T RAMSEY	08/05/1953 Sergeant	State Police, New Mexico	54-E: 1
JOE TAYLOR AVEN Jr	08/06/1953 Patrolman	State Police, New Mexico	54-E: I
ROBERT E LEE	08/16/1960 Patrolman	State Police, New Mexico	6-W: 10
JAMES EDWARD CLARK	09/19/1960 Captain	State Police, New Mexico	54-E: 8
BENNIE D WILLIAMS	07/09/1963 Patrolman	State Police, New Mexico	54-E: 8
ANTONIO JARAMILLO	02/0211965 Patrolman	State Police, New Mexico	54-E: 8
ROBERT ROMERO	09/30/1967 Agent	State Police, New Mexico	4-W: 17
ROBERT ROSENBLOOM	11/08/1971 Patrolman	State Police, New Mexico	54-E: I
DAVID L COKER	11/11/1979 Patrolman	State Police, New Mexico	54-E: 8
RICHARD GOMEZ	04/17/1980 Patrolman	State Police, New Mexico	54-E: 8
DAVID M SMITH	08/06/1984 Patrolman	State Police, New Mexico	49-E: 14
LOWELL D HOWARD	08/06/1984 Patrolman	State Police, New Mexico	49-E: 14
MANUEL OLIVAS	02/01/1985 Patrolman	State Police, New Mexico	54-E: 1
SHERMAN L TOLER Jr	03/05/1986 Patrolman	State Police, New Mexico	54-E: 1
WAYNE G ALLISON	02/13/1988 Patrolman	State Police, New Mexico	52-E: 16
GLEN MICHAEL HUBER	01/26/1991 Patrolman	State Police, New Mexico	38-W: 18
JAMES N SKIFF	05/25/1920 Trooper	State Police, New York	14-W: 17
WILLIAM H CURLEY	09/26/1922 Trooper	State Police, New York	9-W: 16
HAROLD C MATTICE	04/28/1923 Corporal	State Police, New York	56-E: 9
ROY A DONIVAN	10/08/1923 Trooper	State Police, New York	57-E: 4
THEODORE A DOBBS	09/29/1924 Trooper	State Police, New York	11-W: 8
ALEXANDER E BOEHM	11/13/1924 Trooper	State Police, New York	38-E: 17
JAMES B LOSCO	07/07/1925 Trooper	State Police, New York	1-E: 15
PHILLIP E GONTERMAN	09/25/1925 Trooper	State Police, New York	59-E: 1
ERNEST F RUDD	10/05/1925 Trooper	State Police, New York	6-W: 12
THOMAS J SCANLON	10/05/1925 Trooper	State Police, New York	22-E: 8
ANDREW J LAWRENCE	09/12/1926 Trooper	State Police, New York	33-E: 1
CHARLES M McGINN	06/20/1927 Trooper	State Police, New York	44-E: 8
HARRY J WHEELER	07/15/1927 Sergeant	State Police, New York	37-E: 11
WALTER CROASDALE	08/22/1927 Lieutenant	State Police, New York	60-E: 4
ARNOLD T RASMUSSEN	09/08/1927 Trooper	State Police, New York	44-E: 5
ROBERT ROY	09/08/1927 Trooper	State Police, New York	8-E: 2
ERNEST M SIMPSON	12/01/1927 Trooper	State Police, New York	23-E: 13
JOHN J LANE	05/13/1928 Trooper	State Police, New York	I-E: 11
EDWARD F DOLPHIN	08/06/1928 Corporal	State Police, New York	21-E: 17
CARL T WILDER	09/07/1928 Trooper	State Police, New York	25-E: 6
JOHN J CAHILL	02/22/1930 Trooper	State Police, New York	44-E: 4
JOHN L FURLONG	03/31/1930 Trooper	State Police, New York	19-W: 8
EDWARD J SWEENEY	05/17/1930 Trooper	State Police, New York	32-E: 10

LEROY J BAKER	08/24/1930 Corporal	State Police, New York	15-W: 14
JAMES M MACLARNON	01/19/1931 Trooper	State Police, New York	64-E: 16
JOHN E FREY	03/18/1931 Sergeant	State Police, New York	1-W: 10
GARLAND BLAIR	10/12/1931 Trooper	State Police, New York	16-E: 8
MARTIN E RYAN	11/25/1931 Corporal	State Police, New York	16-W: 9
THEOPOLIS GAINES	01/15/1932 Corporal	State Police, New York	35-E: 13
TREMAIN M HUGHES	01/15/1932 Lieutenant	State Police, New York	64-W: 11
RAYMOND J CHIPPENDALE	08/12/1932 Trooper	State Police, New York	43-E: 2
VINCENT A DUNN	09/30/1932 Trooper	State Police, New York	20-W: 16
WALTER A PURCELL	03/31/1933 Sergeant	State Police, New York	18-E: 13
HOMER J HARRISON	06/19/1933 Sergeant	State Police, New York	17-E: 8
JEROME B NUGENT	10/13/1933 Trooper	State Police, New York	64-E: 5
RAYMOND A PLUNKETT	01/05/1934 Trooper	State Police, New York	53-E: 1
GEORGE J VAN ANTWERP	08/23/1934 Trooper	State Police, New York	45-E: 15
EDWARD L CUNNINGHAM	10/10/1934 Trooper	State Police, New York	11-W: 13
THOMAS C LYNES	06/03/1935 Trooper	State Police, New York	21-E: 2
JOHN G LORD	07/23/1935 Corporal	State Police, New York	31-E: 10
ANTHONY F LAURENCE	07/27/1935 Trooper	State Police, New York	18-E: 1
CLARK L LEWIS	01/19/1936 Trooper	State Police, New York	39-E: 7
STANLEY C GREENE	02/28/1936 Trooper	State Police, New York	20-W: 1
KENNETH N DEVITT	02/19/1937 Trooper	State Police, New York	37-E: 11
GERARD B KANE	11/15/1937 Trooper	State Police, New York	62-E: 4
ARTHUR A REDDY	11/15/1937 Trooper	State Police, New York	28-E: 4
JOSEPH L FITZPATRICK	11/17/1937 Sergeant	State Police, New York	39-E: 14
WILLIAM T GRAYDON	03/19/1938 Trooper	State Police, New York	31-E: 10
MARTIN J KERINS	08/21/1938 Trooper	State Police, New York	64-W: 13
WILLIAM F DOBBS Jr	08/27/1939 Trooper	State Police, New York	6-E: 3
ROBERT A MOORE	07/3011941 Trooper	State Police, New York	17-W: 15
RICHARD L HEDGES	07/11/1942 Trooper	State Police, New York	29-E: 13
JAMES R GOHERY	12/29/1943 Trooper	State Police, New York	43-E: 4
KENNETH B KNAPP	07/17/1945 Trooper	State Police, New York	9-E: 16
ROBERT V CONKLIN	07/04/1948 Trooper	State Police, New York	53-11: 1
HAROLD F MYERS	12/19/1950 Corporal	State Police, New York	20-W: 6
ARTHUR M DIFFENDALE	06/14/1951 Corporal	State Police, New York	31-E: 12
HARRY ADAMS	09/01/1951 Sergeant	State Police, New York	34-E: 6
PATRICK F O'HARA	02/22/1952 Trooper	State Police, New York	1-E: 15
ARTHUR L LACROIX	07/04/1954 Trooper	State Police, New York	8-E: 4
GERARD THOMAS McHUGH	05/25/1956 Trooper	State Police, New York	9-E: 21
RONALD J DONAHUE	05/23/1959 Trooper	State Police, New York	20-E: 14
DONALD A STRAND	09/28/1960 Trooper	State Police, New York	11-W: 12
JOHN S KELLEY	12/02/1960 Trooper	State Police, New York	16-W: 3
SALVATORE J EMBARRATO	07/06/1961 Trooper	State Police, New York	40-E: 14
STANLEY A BUNNER	06/30/1965 Sergeant	State Police, New York	41-E: 2
CHARLES S DORRIAN	09/19/1965 Trooper	State Police, New York	21-E: 15
JAMES D CONRAD	11/11/1966 Trooper	State Police, New York	59-E: 4
RICHARD A PALLAS Jr	08/31/1967 Sergeant	State Police, New York	39-E: 16
CHARLES WARREN PERKINS	10/26/1967 Trooper	State Police, New York	21 -W: 4
WILLIAM G DOYLE	12/14/1967 Trooper	State Police, New York	59-E: 15
RICHARD T JUNA	02/08/1970 Trooper	State Police, New York	58-E: 17
JOHN G GEORGE	03/01/1970 Trooper	State Police, New York	21-W: 5
RICHARD L WELTZ	03117/1970 Trooper	State Police, New York	22-E: 1
SAMUEL N ROWE	05/01/1970 Captain	State Police, New York	39-E: 11
JOHN F COTTER	11/21/1970 Investigator	State Police, New York	32-E: 7
ROBERT M SEMROV	01/27/1973 Trooper	State Police, New York	6-W: 1
BRUCE B McCULLY	09/30/1973 Investigator	State Police, New York	35-E: 12
LESLIE S GROSSO	05/21/1974 Investigator	State Police, New York	19-W: 6
RAY C DODGE	07/02/1974 Trooper	State Police, New York	5-W: 2
EMERSON J DILLON Jr	10/24/1974 Trooper	State Police, New York	47-E: 3
WILLIAM V McDONAGH	12/14/1975 Trooper	State Police, New York	19-E: 5
GERALD A DEGROOT	06/24/1978 Sergeant	State Police, New York	64-E: 10
ROBERT JOHN GAYLO	05/13/1980 Trooper	State Police, New York	22-E: 7
JAMES A KELLY Jr	08/08/1980 Trooper	State Police, New York	30-E: 14
ROBERT L VAN HALL Jr	12/05/1980 Investigator	State Police, New York	1-W: 7
THOMAS L BUCK	03/19/1981 Investigator	State Police, New York	38-E: 16
THOMAS L PRYME	07/24/1982 Trooper	State Police, New York	28-E: 10
GARY E KUBASIAK	08/30/1982 Trooper	State Police, New York	22-W: 13
BRIAN N ROVNAK	02/02/1983 Trooper	State Police, New York	26-E: 15
DAVID M CORBINE	05/23/1983 Sergeant	State Police, New York	1-E: 2
PAUL ASHBURN	07/26/1983 Trooper	State Police, New York	38-E: 8
RICHARD BENJAMIN SNYDER	09/20/1984 Investigator	State Police, New York	18-W: 7
THOMAS F HUDSON	11/26/1985 Trooper	State Police, New York	24-E: 10
ARTHUR ANTHONY SCARAFILE	05/08/1986 Sergeant	State Police, New York	40-E: 17
ROBERT G DUNNING	06/14/1987 Trooper	State Police, New York	25-E: 18
ALVIN P KURDYS	09/15/1987 Trooper	State Police, New York	18-W: 10
THOMAS J CONSORTE	11/23/1987 Trooper	State Police, New York	44-E: I
JOSEPH THOMAS AVERSA	03105/1990 Investigator	State Police, New York	27-E: 12
RICKY J PARISIAN	05/20/1994 Investigator	State Police, New York	22-E: 19
HOLGER BECK	06/23/1995 Sergeant	State Police, New York	9-E: 20
NATHANIEL BURROUGHS	02/14/1997 Trooper	State Police, New York	1 O-W: 21
GEORGEITHOMPSON	07/02/1929 Patrolman	Highway Patrol, North Carolina	42-E: 10
A J HEDGPATH	10/23/1931 Patrolman	Highway Patrol, North Carolina	61-E: 9
ALBERT STRONG BONEY	11/15/1931 Patrolman	Highway Patrol, North Carolina	43-E: 16
C L FIDLER	03/20/1936 Patrolman	Highway Patrol, North Carolina	57-E: 2
R W ARNOLD	09/17/1936 Patrolman	Highway Patrol, North Carolina	22-E: 14
T MOORE	06/18/1937 Patrolman	Highway Patrol, North Carolina	1-E: 4
GEORGE C PENN	08/22/1937 Patrolman	Highway Patrol, North Carolina	38-E: 13
A B SMART	03/02/1939 Patrolman	Highway Patrol, North Carolina	33-E: 15

H T TIMBERLAKE	12/01/1939 Patrolman	Highway Patrol, North Carolina	9-E: 13
THOMAS B WHATLEY	12/29/1947 Patrolman	Highway Patrol, North Carolina	21-W: 12
W H HOGAN	03/01/1948 Patrolman	Highway Patrol, North Carolina	16-W: 3
J R DAVIS	05/03/1948 Patrolman	Highway Patrol, North Carolina	1-E: 2
C E GALLOWAY	05/03/1948 Patrolman	Highway Patrol, North Carolina	61-E: 13
P W SMITH	05127/1948 Patrolman	Highway Patrol, North Carolina	33-E: 15
R W JACKSON	09/03/1949 Patrolman	Highway Patrol, North Carolina	16-W: 3
C B AVENT	12/12/1949 Patrolman	Highway Patrol, North Carolina	4-E: 9
W L REESE	11/05/1957 Patrolman	Highway Patrol, North Carolina	63-E: 15
JTBROWN	11/05/1957 Patrolman	Highway Patrol, North Carolina	1-E: 10
H T LONG	12118/1959 Patrolman	Highway Patrol, North Carolina	58-E: 17
DAVID B SEARCY	10/15/1960 Patrolman	Highway Patrol, North Carolina	22-W: 7
HENRY A HIGHT	05/31/1962 Patrolman	Highway Patrol, North Carolina	62-E: 14
L E PACE	01/24/1963 Patrolman	Highway Patrol, North Carolina	6-E: 6
WILLIAM T HERBIN	08/31/1964 Patrolman	Highway Patrol, North Carolina	64-E: 13
JAMES H MARSHBURN	09/19/1964 Patrolman	Highway Patrol, North Carolina	44-E: 2
J W WALLIN	04/01/1966 Patrolman	Highway Patrol, North Carolina	15-W: 4
C H HOFFMAN	03/15/1968 Patrolman	Highway Patrol, North Carolina	43-E: 8
PAUL J WILLIAMS	11/08/1970 Patrolman	Highway Patrol, North Carolina	47-E: 17
CLYDE STEPHEN PERRY	07/02/1972 Patrolman	Highway Patrol, North Carolina	21-E: 12
JOSEPH GRIFFIN WRIGHT	09/27/1972 Patrolman	Highway Patrol, North Carolina	47-E: 4
LARRY THOMAS WALTON	12/02/1972 Patrolman	Highway Patrol, North Carolina	34-E: 15
ROBERT RANDALL EAST	12/21/1972 Patrolman	Highway Patrol, North Carolina	31-E: 11
LEONARD MEEKSJr	12/25/1972 Patrolman	Highway Patrol, North Carolina	30-E: 12
W J SMITH Jr	01/11/1974 Patrolman	Highway Patrol, North Carolina	64-W: 17
JOHN S HACKETT Jr	06/19/1974 Sergeant	Highway Patrol, North Carolina	9-W: 8
JAMES A PARKER	06/19/1974 Patrolman	Highway Patrol, North Carolina	19-W: 13
J D TEMPLETON	09/30/1974 Patrolman	Highway Patrol, North Carolina	14-W: 7
WILLIAM DEAN ARLEDGE	10/05/1974 Sergeant	Highway Patrol, North Carolina	58-E: 12
LAWRENCE CANIPE Jr	10/05/1974 Patrolman	Highway Patrol, North Carolina	21-E: 7
GUY THOMAS DAVIS Jr	09/02/1975 Patrolman	Highway Patrol, North Carolina	28-E: 1
HUGH RICHARD GRIFFIN	09/14/1975 Patrolman	Highway Patrol, North Carolina	3-W: 16
ROBERT L PETERSON	05/31/1979 Trooper	Highway Patrol, North Carolina	17-W: 4
GILES ARTHUR HARMON	04/09/1985 Trooper	Highway Patrol, North Carolina	56-W: 14
RAYMOND EARL WORLEY	05/14/1985 Trooper	Highway Patrol, North Carolina	45-E: 16
BOBBY LEE COGGINS	09/14/1985 Trooper	Highway Patrol, North Carolina	64-W: 17
W E BAYLESS 111	02/05/1988 Cadet	Highway Patrol, North Carolina	33-E: 9
MICHAEL L MARTIN	07/22/1988 Trooper	Highway Patrol, North Carolina	14-W: 9
DAMION CORTEZ ROBERTS	08/07/1996 Trooper	Highway Patrol, North Carolina	49-W: 20
LLOYD E LOWRY	09/23/1997 Sergeant	Highway Patrol, North Carolina	17-W: 21
WILLIAM J STARLING	07/20/1998 Trooper	Highway Patrol, North Carolina	50-W: 21
DAVID HAROLD DEES	04/04/1999 Trooper	Highway Patrol, North Carolina	54-E: 21
WILLIAM BRYANT DAVIS	10/21/1999 Trooper	Highway Patrol, North Carolina	47-E: 21
BERYL McLANE	07/30/1954 Patrolman	Highway Patrol, North Dakota	29-E: 7
JOHN F BEST	06/17/1935 Sergeant	Highway Patrol, Ohio	52-W: 17
LEROY S BEDELL	08/20/1935 Patrolman	Highway Patrol, Ohio	39-W: 12
JAMES E IVORY	01/07/1936 Patrolman	Highway Patrol, Ohio	55-W: 4
CHARLES W TIMBERLAKE	08/07/1936 Patrolman	Highway Patrol, Ohio	46-W: 3
KARL E BUSHONG	06/07/1937 Patrolman	Highway Patrol, Ohio	37-W: 10
GEORGE A CONN	09/27/1937 Patrolman	Highway Patrol, Ohio	37-W: 12
CHARLES G CANNON	01/01/1938 Patrolman	Highway Patrol, Ohio	45-W: 13
JOHN G HOUGH	12/03/1940 Patrolman	Highway Patrol, Ohio	39-W: 7
PAUL L McMANIS	09/28/1941 Patrolman	Highway Patrol, Ohio	14-E: 1
JOHN E RUCH	03/04/1942 Corporal	Highway Patrol, Ohio	47-W: 15
VANCE M ANDREWS	11/21/1945 Lieutenant	Highway Patrol, Ohio	52-W: 11
JAMES P GARDNER	02/2811948 Patrolman	Highway Patrol, Ohio	55-W: 1
HARRY D GRIMES	06/08/1952 Patrolman	Highway Patrol, Ohio	55-W: 1
JAMES A FREDERICKA	05/08/1953 Patrolman	Highway Patrol, Ohio	13-E: 12
EARL W CASTERLINE	10/19/1953 Patrolman	Highway Patrol, Ohio	51 -W: 4
FRANK J HOSSLER	09/22/1956 Patrolman	Highway Patrol, Ohio	38-W: 11
ROBERT E KARSMIZKI	03/31/1957 Patrolman	Highway Patrol, Ohio	47-W: 1
ERNEST E COLE	10103/1964 Patrolman	Highway Patrol, Ohio	47-W: 6
JON D BIRCHEM	02/27/1967 Patrolman	Highway Patrol, Ohio	51-E: 13
HAROLD K HANNING	08106/1970 Sergeant	Highway Patrol, Ohio	51-E: 13
JAMES A KIRKENDALL	10/28/1970 Lieutenant	Highway Patrol, Ohio	55-W: 8
JOEL F MILLER	12/06/1971 Patrolman	Highway Patrol, Ohio	44-W: 15
CARLI-THRUSH	02/06/1972 Patrolman	Highway Patrol, Ohio	37-W: 7
WILLIAM J KELLER	10/14/1972 Patrolman	Highway Patrol, Ohio	54-W: 3
DAVID L STERNER	02/25/1973 Patrolman	Highway Patrol, Ohio	33-W: 15
JERRY R NEFF	01/30/1974 Patrolman	Highway Patrol, Ohio	51-W: 17
EDWARD G MOORE	07123/1976 Sergeant	Highway Patrol, Ohio	41-W: 14
CHARLES V VOGEL Jr	01/24/1980 Trooper	Highway Patrol, Ohio	54-W: 8
WILLIAM R BENDER	11/20/1982 Trooper	Highway Patrol, Ohio	46-W: I
JODY S DYE	07/05/1985 Trooper	Highway Patrol, Ohio	39-W: 17
WENDY G EVERETT	08/05/1988 Trooper	Highway Patrol, Ohio	47-W: I
KENNETH A MALONEY	07/28/1990 Trooper	Highway Patrol, Ohio	37-W: 6
JAMES R GROSS	01/19/1996 Trooper	Highway Patrol, Ohio	24-E: 20
SAM R HENDERSON	05/0711941 Trooper	Highway Patrol, Oklahoma	63-W: 3
JAMES A LONG	07/12/1942 Trooper	Highway Patrol, Oklahoma	28-W: 17
THEO COBB	06/24/1951 Trooper	Highway Patrol, Oklahoma	39-W: 4
JOHNNIE WHITTLE	09/14/1953 Trooper	Highway Patrol, Oklahoma	29-W: 14
JOHN RICHARD BARTER	01/29/1959 Trooper	Highway Patrol, Oklahoma	51-W: 14
HOWARD M CRUMLEY	06/28/1970 Trooper	Highway Patrol, Oklahoma	28-W: 5
LARRY BRUCE SMITH	01/2911971 Trooper	Highway Patrol, Oklahoma	47-W: 15
WILLIE JAMES WALKER	02/17/1971 Trooper	Highway Patrol, Oklahoma	53-W: 10
ROBERT EUGENE AKE	09/18/1972 Trooper	Highway Patrol, Oklahoma	47-W: 9
THOMAS F ISBELL	12/20/1972 Trooper	Highway Patrol, Oklahoma	28-W: 17

JOHN C MAGAR	06/29/1975 Trooper	Highway Patrol, Oklahoma	53-W: 11
LARRY VERNE CRABTREE	04/04/1977 Trooper	Highway Patrol, Oklahoma	51-W: 11
CELL C HOWELL	04/27/1977 Lieutenant	Highway Patrol, Oklahoma	28-W: 8
JAMES PAT GRIMES	05/26/1978 Lieutenant	Highway Patrol, Oklahoma	46-W: I
HOUSTON F SUMMERS	05/26/1978 Trooper	Highway Patrol, Oklahoma	43-W: 12
BILLY G YOUNG	05/26/1978 Trooper	Highway Patrol, Oklahoma	52-W: 7
RICHARD D OLDAKER	07/03/1978 Trooper	Highway Patrol, Oklahoma	47-W: 16
RONDAL RAY ALEXANDER	07/03/1978 Trooper	Highway Patrol, Oklahoma	46-W: 8
KENNY LEE OSBORN	07/13/1978 Trooper	Highway Patrol, Oklahoma	38-W: 5
KENNETH DEAN STRANG	03/01/1980 Lieutenant	Highway Patrol, Oklahoma	45-W: 16
EDWARD A ELLIOTT	08/23/1980 Trooper	Highway Patrol, Oklahoma	51-E: 11
TRAVIS LEON BENCH	10/05/1983 Trooper	Highway Patrol, Oklahoma	43-W: 17
GUY DAVID NALLEY	10/27/1984 Trooper	Highway Patrol, Oklahoma	46-W: I
RANDY JOE LITTLEFIELD	01/15/1990 Trooper	Highway Patrol, Oklahoma	43-W: 3
DUANE L GRUNDY	04/11/1990 Trooper	Highway Patrol, Oklahoma	46-E: 17
JOSEPH EARL NICOLLE	07/26/1990 Trooper	Highway Patrol, Oklahoma	44-W: 11
DAVID W EALES	09/24/1999 Trooper	Highway Patrol, Oklahoma	49-E: 21
EARL W PERKINS	11/27/1922 Officer	State Police, Oregon	36-W: 12
AMOS B HELMS	10/18/1931 Officer	State Police, Oregon	58-W: 5
BURRELL MILO BAUCOM	07/01/1933 Officer	State Police, Oregon	62-W: 3
ELMER RAY PYLE	11/07/1937 Officer	State Police, Oregon	24-W: 3
IRA A WARREN	04/07/1938 Officer	State Police, Oregon	60-W: 5
WILLARD A TUBBS	06/21/1939 Officer	State Police, Oregon	35-W: 5
GEORGE R CAMERON	07/05/1944 Officer	State Police, Oregon	48-W: 5
THEODORE R CHAMBERS	04/29/1945 Officer	State Police, Oregon	13-E: 14
DELMOND EDWARD RONDEAU	04/25/1947 Officer	State Police, Oregon	59-W: 15
LEROY H SPICKERMAN	01/17/1948 Officer	State Police, Oregon	35-W: 11
EARL A BURTCH	09/22/1948 Officer	State Police, Oregon	3-E: 17
WILLIAM THOMAS LEVINSON	09/07/1950 Officer	State Police, Oregon	37-E: 11
DALE BENJAMIN COURTNEY	10/01/1950 Officer	State Police, Oregon	32-W: 5
PHILIP B LOWD	06/24/1952 Officer	State Police, Oregon	12-E: 9
RICHARD FRANCIS O'CONNOR	05/08/1956 Officer	State Police, Oregon	14-E: 10
HARLES CURRY SANDERS	02/22/1957 Officer	State Police, Oregon	26-W: 3
FREDERICK CHRISTIAN KEILHORN	09/09/1961 Officer	State Police, Oregon	40-W: 9
RALPH D BATES	11/08/1962 Officer	State Police, Oregon	32-W: 4
WILLIAM M HALL	05/11/1967 Officer	State Police, Oregon	48-W: 6
DONALD TIMOTHY WELP	11/15/1967 Officer	State Police, Oregon	59-W: 15
DANIEL AUSTIN NELSON	07/28/1972 Officer	State Police, Oregon	31-W: 10
HAROLD ROY BERG	05/10/1975 Lieutenant	State Police, Oregon	2-E: 9
HOLLY V HOLCOMB	11/25/1975 Superintendent	State Police, Oregon	31-W: 13
JAMES D SHEPHERD	05/22/1980 Sergeant	State Police, Oregon	10-E: 2
DONALD E SMITH	07/11/1983 Sergeant	State Police, Oregon	6-W: 15
BRET ROBERT CLODFIELTER	09/30/1992 Trooper	State Police, Oregon	60-E: 18
SCOTT ALAN LYONS	09/02/1997 Trooper	State Police, Oregon	19-W: 21
JAMES DALLAS RECTOR	09/02/1997 Sergeant	State Police, Oregon	61-E: 20
RICHARD JAMES SCHUENING	10/02/1997 Sergeant	State Police, Oregon	18-W: 21
JOHN F HENRY	09/02/1906 Private	State Police, Pennsylvania	50-W: 8
FRANCIS A ZEHRINGER	09/02/1906 Private	State Police, Pennsylvania	40-E: 13
TIMOTHY KELLEHER	09/14/1907 Private	State Police, Pennsylvania	36-W: 5
MARK A PRYNN	02/09/1909 Sergeant	State Police, Pennsylvania	31 -W: 7
JOHN GARSCIA	02/21/1909 Private	State Police, Pennsylvania	30-W: 11
JOHN L WILLIAMS	08/22/1909 Private	State Police, Pennsylvania	20-E: 17
JACK C SMITH	08/22/1909 Private	State Police, Pennsylvania	60-W: 7
ROBERT V MYERS	03/28/1913 Private	State Police, Pennsylvania	60-W: 17
ANDREW CZAP	04/28/1918 Private	State Police, Pennsylvania	62-W: 7
JOHN F DARGUS	05/31/1918 Private	State Police, Pennsylvania	42-W: 11
STANLEY W CHRIST	12/01/1919 Private	State Police, Pennsylvania	35-W: 6
BEN F McEVOY	09/21/1923 Corporal	State Police, Pennsylvania	24-W: 5
WILLIAM J OMLOR	10/25/1923 Private	State Police, Pennsylvania	1 O-W: 3
FRANCIS L HALEY	10/14/1924 Private	State Police, Pennsylvania	62-W: 14
EDWIN F HAAS	10/17/1924 Sergeant	State Police, Pennsylvania	34-W: 9
BERNARD S C McELROY	12/21/1924 Private	State Police, Pennsylvania	10-E: 9
BERTRAM BEECH	12/10/1925 Private	State Police, Pennsylvania	42-W: 7
CLAUDE F KEESEY	01/04/1927 Private	State Police, Pennsylvania	26-W: 16
MARTIN A HANAHOE	02/27/1927 Patrolman	Highway Patrol, Pennsylvania	61 -W: 9
THOMAS E LIPKA	04/03/1927 Private	State Police, Pennsylvania	57-E: 15
JOHN M THOMAS	05/08/1927 Sergeant	State Police, Pennsylvania	30-W: 14
JOHN T DOWNEY	08/22/1927 Private	State Police, Pennsylvania	40-W: 14
VINCENT A HASSEN	12/27/1927 Corporal	Highway Patrol, Pennsylvania	12-E: 1
SHARON C WIBLE	02/06/1928 Patrolman	Highway Patrol, Pennsylvania	15-E: 15
ANDREW W MILLER	04/01/1928 Patrolman	Highway Patrol, Pennsylvania	50-W: 9
JAY F PROOF	08/2911928 Patrolman	Highway Patrol, Pennsylvania	14-E: 14
RUSSELL T SWANSON	04/19/1929 Patrolman	Highway Patrol, Pennsylvania	30-W: 6
WELLS C HAMMOND	10/14/1929 Patrolman	Highway Patrol, Pennsylvania	12-E: 12
BRADY C PAUL	12/27/1929 Corporal	Highway Patrol, Pennsylvania	62-W: 13
THOMAS E LAWRY	01/31/1930 Corporal	Highway Patrol, Pennsylvania	11-E: 10
ARTHUR A KOPPENHAVER	07/13/1930 Patrolman	Highway Patrol, Pennsylvania	61-W: 12
CHARLES L STEWART	07/18/1930 Private	State Police, Pennsylvania	30-W: 5
THOMAS B ELDER	03/22/1931 Patrolman	Highway Patrol, Pennsylvania	30-W: 4
TIMOTHY G McCARTHY	05/12/1931 Sergeant	State Police, Pennsylvania	62-W: 16
ORVILLE A MOHRING	12/11/1931 Patrolman	Highway Patrol, Pennsylvania	36-W: 5
JOSEPH A CONRAD	09/06/1932 Patrolman	Highway Patrol, Pennsylvania	30-W: I
CHARLES E HOUSEHOLDER	08/20/1933 Patrolman	Highway Patrol, Pennsylvania	14-E: 2
HERBERT P BRANTLINGER	09/03/1933 Patrolman	Highway Patrol, Pennsylvania	61-W: 5
JAMES A SEEREY	09/10/1934 Sergeant	State Police, Pennsylvania	12-E: 5
FLOYD W MADERIA	12/11/1934 Private	State Police, Pennsylvania	34-W: 14
JOSEPH L FULTON	06/04/1936 Corporal	Highway Patrol, Pennsylvania	58-W: 10

JOE B CHAMPION	07/15/1936 Sergeant	Highway Patrol, Pennsylvania	40-W: 1
J LEE CLARKE	03/01/1937 Patrolman	Highway Patrol, Pennsylvania	49-W: 5
JOHN E FESSLER	04/23/1937 Private	State Police, Pennsylvania	11-E: 15
JOSEPH A HOFFER	04/27/1937 Private	State Police, Pennsylvania	59-W: 10
JOHN J BROSKI	08/14/1937 Private	State Police, Pennsylvania	30-W: 10
JOHN D SIMOSON	12/01/1937 Patrolman	Highway Patrol, Pennsylvania	7-E: 15
CHARLES H CRAVEN	10/11/1938 Private	Highway Patrol, Pennsylvania	35-W: I I
GEORGE D NAUGHTON	01/30/1939 Corporal	State Police, Pennsylvania	40-W: 4
GEORGE J YASHUR	04/01/1940 Private	Highway Patrol, Pennsylvania	42-W: 10
THOMAS P CAREY	06/17/1941 Private	Highway Patrol, Pennsylvania	60-W: 8
JOHN A DITKOSKY	07/24/1950 Private	State Police, Pennsylvania	36-W: 14
FLOYD B CLOUSE	11/02/1953 Private	State Police, Pennsylvania	7-E: 10
JOSEPH F McMILLEN	05/13/1956 Private	State Police, Pennsylvania	6-E: 8
CHARLES S STANSKI	01/23/1958 Trooper	State Police, Pennsylvania	36-W: 17
EDWARD MACKIW	05/31/1958 Trooper	State Police, Pennsylvania	2-E: 4
STEPHEN R GYURKE	08/24/1958 Trooper	State Police, Pennsylvania	32-W: 16
FRANCIS M TESSITORE	08/05/1960 Trooper	State Police, Pennsylvania	26-E: 9
ANTHONY BENSCH	10/03/1961 Trooper	State Police, Pennsylvania	7-E: 16
RICHARD G BARNHART	08/08/1964 Trooper	State Police, Pennsylvania	13-E: 7
GARY R ROSENBERGER	12/12/1970 Trooper	State Police, Pennsylvania	11-E: 2
ROBERT J LOMAS	06/12/1971 Trooper	State Police, Pennsylvania	5-W: 12
JOHN S VALENT	12/09/1971 Corporal	State Police, Pennsylvania	34-W: 11
ROBERT D LAPP Jr	10/16/1972 Trooper	State Police, Pennsylvania	31-W: 11
BRUCE C RANKIN	04/25/1973 Trooper	State Police, Pennsylvania	34-W: 10
ROSS E SNOWDEN	01/17/1974 Trooper	State Police, Pennsylvania	49-W: 13
LEO M KOSCELNICK	08/15/1977 Corporal	State Police, Pennsylvania	2-E: 9
JOSEPH J WELSCH	09/13/1977 Trooper	State Police, Pennsylvania	36-W: 11
WAYNE C EBERT	06/07/1978 Trooper	State Police, Pennsylvania	49-W: 10
ALBERT J IZZO	06/13/1979 Trooper	State Police, Pennsylvania	13-E: 5
DAVID D MONAHAN	04/17/1980 Trooper	State Police, Pennsylvania	60-W: 3
HERBERT A WIRFEL	02/07/1982 Trooper	State Police, Pennsylvania	10-E: 14
WILLIAM R EVANS	01/06/1983 Trooper	State Police, Pennsylvania	11-E: 15
FRANK J BOWEN	10/26/1983 Trooper	State Police, Pennsylvania	9-W: 16
GARY W FISHER	02103/1985 Trooper	State Police, Pennsylvania	49-W: 13
JOHN J BROWN	02/14/1985 Trooper	State Police, Pennsylvania	26-W: 5
ROARK HERBERT ROSS	05/15/1986 Trooper	State Police, Pennsylvania	61 -W: 9
CLINTON WAYNE CRAWFORD	08/17/1987 Trooper	State Police, Pennsylvania	60-W: 4
JOHN A ANDRULEWICZ	05/09/1988 Trooper	State Police, Pennsylvania	61 -W: 8
PAULIALMER	04/12/1989 Corporal	State Police, Pennsylvania	31 -W: 3
WAYNE D BILHEIMER	04/12/1989 Trooper	State Police, Pennsylvania	10-E: 4
ARTHUR L HERSHEY	01/03/1999 Sergeant	State Police, Pennsylvania	6-W: 22
JOHN WEBER	06/17/1925 Trooper	State Police, Rhode Island	42-W: 11
ARTHUR L STAPLES Jr	12/18/1931 Trooper	State Police, Rhode Island	32-W: 2
ARNOLD L POOLE	05/30/1934 Lieutenant	State Police, Rhode Island	50-W: 13
JOSEPH J GALLIVAN	06/22/1937 Trooper	State Police, Rhode Island	5-E: 13
BRADFORD G MOTT	05/06/1941 Trooper	State Police, Rhode Island	5-E: 21
DANIEL L O'BRIEN	08/31/1954 Trooper	State Police, Rhode Island	48-W: 13
WALTER J BURGESS	11/1411959 Sergeant	State Police, Rhode Island	42-W: 1
EDWIN D MILAM	01/01/1934 Patrolman	Highway Patrol, South Carolina	59-E: 10
HANSFORD M REEVES	01/01/1934 Patrolman	Highway Patrol, South Carolina	58-E: 9
ED HENNECY	11/19/1935 Patrolman	Highway Patrol, South Carolina	13-W: 6
LAWSON L RHODES	07/15/1938 Patrolman	Highway Patrol, South Carolina	56-E: 16
WALTER BELL	01/01/1940 Patrolman	Highway Patrol, South Carolina	28-E: 7
GEORGE G BROOME	01/01/1940 Patrolman	Highway Patrol, South Carolina	25-E: 6
ROBERT SMITH	01/01/1940 Patrolman	Highway Patrol, South Carolina	34-E: 4
JOSEPH P MONROE	09/30/1941 Patrolman	Highway Patrol, South Carolina	21-E: 11
NORRIS NETTLES	01/05/1942 Patrolman	Highway Patrol, South Carolina	32-E: 8
ALBERT T SEALY	01/01/1950 Patrolman	Highway Patrol, South Carolina	53-E: 9
ARNOLD R CARTER	01/01/1956 Patrolman	Highway Patrol, South Carolina	28-E: 5
GEORGELLAGROON	01/01/1957 Patrolman	Highway Patrol, South Carolina	18-E: 6
HARRY BOYD RAY	01/01/1958 Patrolman	Highway Patrol, South Carolina	24-E: 9
HENRY C YONCE	01/01/1959 Patrolman	Highway Patrol, South Carolina	20-E: 16
JOHN RAY RIDDLE	01/01/1961 Patrolman	Highway Patrol, South Carolina	26-E: 1
MARION CHARLES STEELE	09/10/1966 Patrolman	Highway Patrol, South Carolina	41-E: 8
RICHARD V WOODS	08/19/1969 Patrolman	Highway Patrol, South Carolina	22-W: 18
ALFRED A THOMASON	01/01/1970 Patrolman	Highway Patrol, South Carolina	57-E: 5
JAMES A TRAYLOR	12/2511970 Patrolman	Highway Patrol, South Carolina	40-E: 14
ROY ODES CAFFEY	10/08/1972 Patrolman	Highway Patrol, South Carolina	19-E: 15
FULTON HOUSE ANTHONY	03/10/1973 Patrolman	Highway Patrol, South Carolina	43-E: 10
BEN WESLEY STRICKLAND	05/31/1974 Patrolman	Highway Patrol, South Carolina	35-E: 12
WILLIE EDWARD PEEPLES	06/29/1979 Patrolman	Highway Patrol, South Carolina	18-W: 16
ROBERT A MOBLEY	07/19/1979 Patrolman	Highway Patrol, South Carolina	6-W: 4
DAVID LEE ALVERSON	11/21/1981 Patrolman	Highway Patrol, South Carolina	21-E: 8
JOHN R CLINTON	05/24/1983 Corporal	Highway Patrol, South Carolina	6-E: 13
BRUCE KENNETH SMALLS	09/27/1985 Trooper	Highway Patrol, South Carolina	5-W: 2
ROBERT PAUL PERRY Jr	04/15/1987 Trooper	Highway Patrol, South Carolina	21 -W: 12
GEORGE TILLMAN RADFORD	10/29/1988 Trooper	Highway Patrol, South Carolina	29-E: 12
HARRY McKINLEY COKER Jr	06/21/1989 Trooper	Highway Patrol, South Carolina	31-E: 6
MARVIN LEROY TITUS	11/21/1991 Trooper	Highway Patrol, South Carolina	8-E: 18
DAVID HUNTER O'BRIEN	12/14/1991 Trooper	Highway Patrol, South Carolina	50-W: 18
HARDY MERLE GODBOLD	02/29/1992 Trooper	Highway Patrol, South Carolina	48-E: 18
MARK HUNTER COATES	11/20/1992 Trooper	Highway Patrol, South Carolina	59-E: 18
RANDALL LAMAR HESTER	04/20/1994 Senior Trooper	Highway Patrol, South Carolina	41-E: 19
MICHAEL ALLEN CHAPPELL	04/17/1995 Lance Corporal	Highway Patrol, South Carolina	7-W: 20
RANDALL SCOTT HEWITT	06/23/1996 Lance Corporal	Highway Patrol, South Carolina	7-E: 20
FRANKIE LEE LINGARD	12/31/1997 First Sergeant	Highway Patrol, South Carolina	20-W: 21
JACOB HAM Jr	02/08/1998 Lance Corporal	Highway Patrol, South Carolina	14-E: 21

BERNARD BENSON	09/17/1941 Trooper	Highway Patrol, South Dakota	49-E: 11
HENRY N RUSSELL	11/19/1958 Trooper	Highway Patrol, South Dakota	49-E: 11
VERLYN LAMONTE METTLER	03/09/1976 Trooper	Highway Patrol, South Dakota	2-W: 13
STEVEN ERIC HOFFMAN	03/12/1980 Trooper	Highway Patrol, South Dakota	49-E: 16
OREN STUART HINDMAN	05/02/1985 Trooper	Highway Patrol, South Dakota	49-E: 11
CHARLES HASH	04/11/1930 Trooper	Dept. of Safety, Tennessee	47-W: 17
WALTER JONES	07/31/1930 Trooper	Dept. of Safety, Tennessee	46-E: 3
LEE LOVELACE	02/03/1934 Trooper	Dept. of Safety, Tennessee	44-W: 7
CLOVIS COLE	05/02/1934 Trooper	Dept. of Safety, Tennessee	52-W: 16
ED KENNEDY	08/22/1934 Trooper	Dept. of Safety, Tennessee	63-W: 6
LINDSAY SMITH	12/17/1934 Trooper	Dept. of Safety, Tennessee	51-E: 15
EARL HICKS	06/17/1936 Trooper	Dept. of Safety, Tennessee	29-W: 9
PAUL SUMMERS	08/08/1936 Trooper	Dept. of Safety, Tennessee	43-W: 10
CARL HICKMAN	09/15/1937 Trooper	Dept. of Safety, Tennessee	63-W: I
LEWIS R BOONE	10/18/1938 Trooper	Dept. of Safety, Tennessee	29-W: 8
CHARLES GEARHISER	11/12/1938 Trooper	Dept. of Safety, Tennessee	55-W: 8
WILLIAM HOWARD JAMES	09/14/1942 Trooper	Dept. of Safety, Tennessee	46-E: 10
JAMES WILLIAMS	01/01/1943 Trooper	Dept. of Safety, Tennessee	46-E: 13
WILLIAM H CRUTCHER	08/03/1944 Trooper	Dept. of Safety, Tennessee	52-W: 4
FRED COLE WALDROP	04/01/1950 Sergeant	Dept. of Safety, Tennessee	53-W: 2
OLIVER D WILLIAMSON	04/06/1952 Sergeant	Dept. of Safety, Tennessee	54-W: 8
OSCAR NEWTON MORRIS	05/09/1956 Trooper	Dept. of Safety, Tennessee	47-W: 6
RAYMOND HENDON	06/03/1957 Trooper	Dept. of Safety, Tennessee	52-W: 2
EDWARD C JOWERS	08/03/1962 Trooper	Dept. of Safety, Tennessee	29-W: 10
JOSEPH EMANUEL DILLARD	09/15/1964 Trooper	Dept. of Safety, Tennessee	46-E: 13
WILLIAM GORDON BARNES	01/22/1966 Trooper	Dept. of Safety, Tennessee	51-W: 7
MICHAEL THEODORE DAFFERNER	04/06/1966 Trooper	Dept. of Safety, Tennessee	51 -W: 2
SAMUAL W GIBBS	08/27/1966 Lieutenant	Dept. of Safety, Tennessee	55-W: 12
EUGENE BRAKEBILL	10/09/1966 Trooper	Dept. of Safety, Tennessee	3-W: 1
ROY ALFORD MYNATT	02/11/1968 Trooper	Dept. of Safety, Tennessee	43-W: 14
C B MARTIN	05/04/1969 Trooper	Dept. of Safety, Tennessee	39-W: 17
SAMUEL F HOLCOMB Jr	03/27/1988 Trooper	Dept. of Safety, Tennessee	44-W: 2
MICHAEL LLOYD RECTOR	05/31/1990 Officer	Dept. of Safety, Tennessee	5-E: 1
DOUGLAS WAYNE TRIPP	05/19/1991 State Trooper	Dept. of Safety, Tennessee	32-W: 18
GEORGE VAN DORSE HOLCOMB	01/26/1992 Trooper	Dept. of Safety, Tennessee	49-E: 18
JAMES DAVID PERRY	10/03/1999 Sergeant	Dept. of Safety, Tennessee	60-E: 21
DOC THOMAS	01/05/1909 Ranger	Dept. of Public Safety, Texas	14-E: 6
QUIRL BAILEY CARNES	07/31/1910 Ranger	Dept. of Public Safety, Texas	14-E: 7
DAN L McDUFFIE	07/07/1931 Ranger	Dept. of Public Safety, Texas	36-W: 2
ARTHUR W FISCHER	01/18/1932 Patrolman	Dept. of Public Safety, Texas	13-E: 4
AUBREY LEE MOORE	04/16/1932 Patrolman	Dept. of Public Safety, Texas	3-E: 6
H D MURPHY	04/01/1934 Patrolman	Dept. of Public Safety, Texas	55-E: 10
EDWARD BRYAN WHEELER	04/01/1934 Patrolman	Dept. of Public Safety, Texas	55-E: 10
JOSEPH N AVARY	05/17/1935 Patrolman	Dept. of Public Safety, Texas	25-W: 14
GUY ALBERT FREESE	07/11/1935 Patrolman	Dept. of Public Safety, Texas	62-W: 6
MART D TARRANT	11/04/1935 Patrolman	Dept. of Public Safety, Texas	26-W: 11
DAVID A McGONAGILL	09/04/1940 Patrolman	Dept. of Public Safety, Texas	49-W: 3
ROGER Q HARRISS	04/05/1942 Patrolman	Dept. of Public Safety, Texas	55-E: 13
FLOYD E LAWSON	04/07/1948 Patrolman	Dept. of Public Safety, Texas	14-E: 2
LOUIS W DICKSON	04/1711949 Patrolman	Dept. of Public Safety, Texas	40-W: 6
BILL J MAHONEY	04/18/1949 Patrolman	Dept. of Public Safety, Texas	5-W: 2
WINFRED 0 HANNA	01/25/1954 Patrolman	Dept. of Public Safety, Texas	36-W: 15
FELIX A MURPHEY	03/04/1954 Patrolman	Dept. of Public Safety, Texas	12-E: 8
ROBERT J CROSBY	11/27/1954 Patrolman	Dept. of Public Safety, Texas	15-W: I
MILTON D BROOKS	01/02/1955 Patrolman	Dept. of Public Safety, Texas	15-E: 3
AUDIE A ISBELL	04/07/1955 Patrolman	Dept. of Public Safety, Texas	36-W: 6
CLARENCE R NORDYKE	07/18/1955 Ranger	Dept. of Public Safety, Texas	30-W: 12
LYNN RAY SMITH	01/25/1957 Patrolman	Dept. of Public Safety, Texas	31-W: 13
BENJAMIN KYLE SMITH	06/23/1958 Patrolman	Dept. of Public Safety, Texas	49-W: 16
HERMAN PAUL MARSHALL	05/17/1960 Patrolman	Dept. of Public Safety, Texas	58-W: 15
OSCAR BOWEN BRETT	12/08/1961 Polygraph Operator	Dept. of Public Safety, Texas	3-E: 13
HOMER A WHITE	12/08/1961 Ranger	Dept. of Public Safety, Texas	21 -W: 4
RICHARD DALE BERENS	03/08/1963 Patrolman	Dept. of Public Safety, Texas	32-W: 8
KENNETH W HARRISON	06/08/1963 Patrolman	Dept. of Public Safety, Texas	50-W: 1
BOBBY LEE MAYNARD	11/30/1964 Patrolman	Dept. of Public Safety, Texas	1 O-E: 7
HARRY LEE MILLS Jr	04/03/1965 Patrolman	Dept. of Public Safety, Texas	27-W: 9
CHARLES AUSTIN PRYOR	04/27/1965 Patrolman	Dept. of Public Safety, Texas	25-W: 6
ROBERT FRANKLIN STINNETT	07/02/1965 Patrolman	Dept. of Public Safety, Texas	14-E: 5
DARVIN K HOGG	04/25/1966 Patrolman	Dept. of Public Safety, Texas	3-E: 7
BILLY RAY WYNN	12/24/1967 Patrolman	Dept. of Public Safety, Texas	40-W: 11
FRED CARLTON BURNS	01/02/1968 Patrolman	Dept. of Public Safety, Texas	10-E: 9
TOM P HOLLAND	04/23/1969 Patrolman	Dept. of Public Safety, Texas	61-W: 16
NORMAN EDWARD ZATOR	10/06/1969 Patrolman	Dept. of Public Safety, Texas	12-E: 12
TRAVIS RABURN LOCKER	11/09/1969 Patrolman	Dept. of Public Safety, Texas	58-W: 5
DOUGLAS HOUSTON THOMPSON	12/07/1969 Patrolman	Dept. of Public Safety, Texas	42-W: 16
GARA OLIVER COOPER	10/02/1970 Sergeant	Dept. of Public Safety, Texas	26-W: 4
BILLY DAN HOWRY	03/18/1972 Patrolman	Dept. of Public Safety, Texas	34-W: 17
GAYLE LAMAR HOLMES	05/19/1972 Patrolman	Dept. of Public Safety, Texas	49-W: 12
MONROE ODiS SCOTT	05/18/1973 Patrolman	Dept. of Public Safety, Texas	60-W: 13
KOBLER C WINN	12/01/1973 Patrolman	Dept. of Public Safety, Texas	35-E: 7
LARRY EUGENE HOBSON	12/01/1973 Patrolman	Dept. of Public Safety, Texas	59-W: 5
ERNEST CLARENCE DOBBS	02/15/1974 Patrolman	Dept. of Public Safety, Texas	40-W: 13
JOHN DAVID OLDHAM	07107/1974 Patrolman	Dept. of Public Safety, Texas	11-E: 17
HAROLD D HAMBRICK	07/07/1974 Patrolman	Dept. of Public Safety, Texas	42-W: 16
HOLLIE LAMAR TULL	09/14/1974 Patrolman	Dept. of Public Safety, Texas	62-W: 14
PATRICK ALLEN RANDEL	10123/1974 Narcotics Agent	Dept. of Public Safety, Texas	34-W: 7
JIMMIE WELDON PARKS	08/10/1975 Patrolman	Dept. of Public Safety, Texas	12-E: 9

MARK ALAN FREDERICK	04104/1976 Patrolman	Dept. of Public Safety, Texas	2-E: 7
TOMIE MICHAEL TUCKER	05/29/1976 Patrolman	Dept. of Public Safety, Texas	24-W: 9
SAMMY CHARLES LONG	11/21/1976 Patrolman	Dept. of Public Safety, Texas	34-W: 3
BOBBY PAUL DOHERTY	02/20/1978 Ranger	Dept. of Public Safety, Texas	60-W: 2
JAMES LEWIS DALRYMPLE Jr	06/05/1978 Sergeant	Dept. of Public Safety, Texas	50-E: 15
JERRY DON DAVIS	10/05/1980 Trooper	Dept. of Public Safety, Texas	34-W: 1
HOLLIS STEPHEN LACY	12/26/1980 Trooper	Dept. of Public Safety, Texas	59-W: 9
HOWARD WAYNE JORDAN	06/02/1981 Trooper	Dept. of Public Safety, Texas	31-W: 4
DAVID IRVINE RUCKER	09/29/1981 Trooper	Dept. of Public Safety, Texas	31 -W: 9
ERNESTO ALANIS	02/27/1983 Trooper	Dept. of Public Safety, Texas	59-W: 8
DANIEL MORRISON HIGDON Jr	03/1311983 Trooper	Dept. of Public Safety, Texas	59-W: 16
MILTON CURTIS ALEXANDER	04/14/1983 Trooper	Dept. of Public Safety, Texas	12-E: 14
ROBERT RAY JONES	09/16/1983 Captain	Dept. of Public Safety, Texas	34-W: 13
RUSSELL LYNN BOYD	10111/1983 Trooper	Dept. of Public Safety, Texas	10-E: 5
WILLIAM PAUL KOHLLEPPEL	04/19/1985 Trooper	Dept. of Public Safety, Texas	7-E: 7
STANLEY KEITH GUFFEY	01/22/1987 Ranger	Dept. of Public Safety, Texas	32-W: 17
RALPH GEORGE ZERDA	05/21/1989 Trooper	Dept. of Public Safety, Texas	32- W: 3
WILLIAM JOHN KUHNLE Jr	05/21/1989 Sergeant	Dept. of Public Safety, Texas	12-E: 10
WILLIE DALE TAYLOR	05/19/1990 Corporal	Dept. of Public Safety, Texas	25-W: 6
MARK JEFFREY PHEBUS	09/17/1990 Trooper	Dept. of Public Safety, Texas	35-W: 2
CARLOS RAY WARREN	03/05/1991 Trooper	Dept. of Public Safety, Texas	25-W: 18
BILL DAVIDSON	04/14/1992 Trooper	Dept. of Public Safety, Texas	9-W: 19
BOBBY STEVE BOOTH	06/16/1993 Trooper 11	Dept. of Public Safety, Texas	35-W: 19
TROY MERLE HOGUE	12/30/1994 Trooper	Dept. of Public Safety, Texas	49-E: 19
TIMOTHY WADE McDERMOTT	05/14/1995 Trooper	Dept. of Public Safety, Texas	2-W: 20
TERRY WAYNE MILLER	10/12/1999 Trooper	Dept. of Public Safety, Texas	6-W: 22
GEORGE VanWAGONEN	05/23/1931 Trooper	Highway Patrol, Utah	12-E: 2
ARMOND A LUKE	12/03/1959 Trooper	Highway Patrol, Utah	50-W: 3
GEORGE DEE REES	07/02/1960 Trooper	Highway Patrol, Utah	26-W: 14
JOHN R WINN	09/22/1971 Trooper	Highway Patrol, Utah	59-W: 3
WILLIAM JOHN ANTONIEWICZ	12/08/1974 Trooper	Highway Patrol, Utah	49-W: 13
ROBERT B HUTCHINGS	07/20/1976 Agent	Highway Patrol, Utah	30-W: 16
RAY LYNN PIERSON	11/07/1978 Trooper	Highway Patrol, Utah	5-E: 4
DANIEL W HARRIS	08/25/1982 Trooper	Highway Patrol, Utah	15-E: 13
JOSEPH SAMUEL BRUMETT	12/1111992 Trooper	Highway Patrol, Utah	62-E: 18
DENNIS LaVELLE LUND	06/16/1993 Trooper	Highway Patrol, Utah	4-E: 19
CHARLES D WARREN	05/16/1994 Trooper	Highway Patrol, Utah	8-E: 21
DOYLE REED THORNE	07/30/1994 Sergeant	Highway Patrol, Utah	25-E: 19
RANDY K INGRAM	10/05/1994 Trooper	Highway Patrol, Utah	48-E: 19
ARTHUR L YEAW	05/13/1983 Sergeant	State Police, Vermont	61-W: 8
WILLIAM J CHENARD	06/14/1987 Sergeant	State Police, Vermont	34-W: 15
GARY ALLEN GABOURY	05/12/1992 Sergeant	State Police, Vermont	47-E: 18
W NEVILLE HATCHER	08/19/1928 Inspector	State Police, Virginia	30-E: 13
PHILLIP C VIA	01/11/1929 Inspector	State Police, Virginia	1-W: 4
CURTIS LEE WOOD	03/11/1929 Inspector	State Police, Virginia	35-E: 14
THOMAS ALLEN BELT	08/18/1930 Inspector	State Police, Virginia	43-E: 6
CHARLES BAZIL BULLOCK	02/15/1934 Trooper	State Police, Virginia	11-E: 18
WILLIAM RAYMOND THOMPSON	09/23/1935 Trooper	State Police, Virginia	45-E: 9
CHARLES WILLIAM PUCKETT	03/28/1938 Sergeant	State Police, Virginia	59-E: 3
CLARENCE LEMUEL MAYNARD	09/09/1939 Sergeant	State Police, Virginia	36-E: 17
URSHELL THOMAS MAYO	02/19/1941 Trooper	State Police, Virginia	20-W: I
WILLIAM STAFFORD TINSLEY	09/05/1942 Trooper	State Police, Virginia	64-W: 1
WILLIAM HAWTHORNE ANDREWS	10/03/1946 Trooper	State Police, Virginia	29-E: 5
ROBERT ELVIN CALDWELL	06/17/1948 Trooper	State Police, Virginia	16-W: 6
ROBERT EDWARD PORTER	06/20/1950 Trooper	State Police, Virginia	32-E: 6
JOSEPH BENJAMIN THOMAS	06/20/1950 Trooper	State Police, Virginia	23-E: 1
WALLACE MONROE SIMPSON	10/23/1951 Investigator	State Police, Virginia	8-E: 16
ROBERT WRIGHT SMITH	11/21/1951 Trooper	State Police, Virginia	62-E: 1
WALTER SINTON PARRISH	10/04/1953 Trooper	State Police, Virginia	38-E: 7
ROBERT LOUIS LODER Jr	01/31/1954 Trooper	State Police, Virginia	33-E: 5
ROBERT FULTON GILES	07/23/1954 Trooper	State Police, Virginia	9-E: 3
HENRY MURRAY BROOKS Jr	06/10/1956 Trooper	State Police, Virginia	16-W: 8
CHARLES EUGENE MORRIS	03/02/1962 Trooper	State Police, Virginia	19-W: 1
GARLAND MATTHEW MILLER	06/13/1963 Trooper	State Police, Virginia	32-E: 13
WARREN YOKELY HAIRLESS	11/18/1968 Trooper	State Police, Virginia	1-E: 15
JACKIE MONROE BUSSARD	05/05/1970 Trooper	State Police, Virginia	41-E: 12
DONALD EDWARD LOVELACE	10/18/1970 Trooper	State Police, Virginia	43-E: 14
RANNIE DeWITT KENNEDY	11/05/1973 Trooper	State Police, Virginia	59-E: 8
JAMES READ HUGHES	06/03/1974 Trooper	State Police, Virginia	63-E: 3
CLAUDE EVERETT SEYMOUR	04/25/1975 Investigator	State Police, Virginia	10-W: 10
BERNARD WALTER WRIGHT	01/17/1976 Trooper	State Police, Virginia	1-E: 3
GARLAND WEST FISHER Jr	11115/1976 Trooper	State Police, Virginia	64-E: 5
ROBERT TINSLEY LOHR	07/22/1978 Trooper	State Police, Virginia	56-E: 11
ROBIN LEE FARMER	09/03/1981 Trooper	State Police, Virginia	11-W: 15
RODNEY DEAN GRIMES	10/09/1983 Special Agent	State Police, Virginia	6-E: 16
JOHNNY RUSH BOWMAN	08/19/1984 Trooper	State Police, Virginia	35-E: 2
JAMES LEROY BIGGS	12/18/1984 Sergeant	State Police, Virginia	25-E: 16
LEO WHITT	04/12/1985 Trooper	State Police, Virginia	18-E: 14
RICKY MARSHALL McCOY	01/03/1986 Trooper	State Police, Virginia	57-E: 3
ALEXANDER McKIE COCHRAN	01/15/1987 Trooper	State Police, Virginia	17-E: 4
HARRY LEE HENDERSON	03/17/1987 Trooper	State Police, Virginia	12-W: 9
JACQUELINE VERNON	08/16/1988 Trooper	State Police, Virginia	23-E: 11
JERRY LYNN HINES	02/20/1989 Trooper	State Police, Virginia	57-E: 5
JOSE MARIA CAVAZOS	02/24/1993 Trooper 11	State Police, Virginia	27-W: 19
HENRYNOELHARMON	02/07/1995 Trooper	State Police, Virginia	3-W: 20
GREGORY PATTON FLEENOR	12/12/1996 Trooper 11	State Police, Virginia	21-E: 20
JESSICA JEAN CHENEY	01/17/1998 Trooper 11	State Police, Virginia	63-W: 21

DANIEL LEE WILLIAMS	12/12/1999 Trooper 11	State Police, Virginia	4-W: 22
VERNON G FORTIN	09/30/1923 Patrolman	State Patrol, Washington	23-E: 17
IRVING M THORSVIG	10/26/1926 Patrolman	State Patrol, Washington	24-E: 6
CONRAD C TOLSON	03/24/1929 Patrolman	State Patrol, Washington	24-E: 8
H DOUGLAS COSSMAN	10/09/1929 Patrolman	State Patrol, Washington	6-W: 5
WILLIAM H PAUTZKE	05/08/1930 Patrolman	State Patrol, Washington	18-E: 8
LOREN G RAY	12/16/1934 Captain	State Patrol, Washington	23-W: 11
ALLEN E LUDDEN	03/15/1938 Patrolman	State Patrol, Washington	64-W: 9
JOHN H GULDEN	12/23/1942 Patrolman	State Patrol, Washington	38-E: 12
THOMAS J HANLIN	05/26/1945 Patrolman	State Patrol, Washington	50-E: 15
PAUL H JOHNSON	12/1211949 Patrolman	State Patrol, Washington	24-E: 8
IVAN BELKA	08/18/1951 Patrolman	State Patrol, Washington	24-E: 4
DON R CAMPBELL	12/21/1951 Patrolman	State Patrol, Washington	61-E: 2
JOHN F WRIGHT	06/28/1953 Patrolman	State Patrol, Washington	20-E: 8
EUGENE A BOLSTAD	09/03/1957 Patrolman	State Patrol, Washington	62-E: 12
ERNEST E EICHHORN	09/16/1958 Patrolman	State Patrol, Washington	I-W:6
WESLEY H WHITTENBERG	12/29/1960 Patrolman	State Patrol, Washington	20-E: 19
CLARENCE C JOHNSON	09/08/1968 Trooper	State Patrol, Washington	44-E: 15
CHARLES FRANK NOBLE	02/05/1972 Trooper	State Patrol, Washington	36-E: 5
JOSEPH A MODLIN	08/15/1974 Control Officer	State Patrol, Washington	15-W: 7
THOMAS L HENDRICKSON	11/17/1974 Trooper	State Patrol, Washington	31-E: 12
GLENDA D THOMAS	05/24/1985 Trooper	State Patrol, Washington	12-W: 10
JAMES S GAIN	03/02/1987 Trooper	State Patrol, Washington	8-W: 9
CLIFFORD R HANSELL	07/22/1987 Trooper	State Patrol, Washington	63-E: 2
RAYMOND L HAWN	01/17/1990 Trooper	State Patrol, Washington	56-E: 5
STEVEN LEE FRINK	03/22/1993 Trooper	State Patrol, Washington	45-W: 19
JAMES E SAUNDERS	10/07/1999 Trooper	State Patrol, Washington	34-E: 21
ERNEST LEE RIPLEY	11/18/1920 Private	State Police, West Virginia	24-W: 8
CHARLES KACKLEY	05/25/1921 Private	State Police, West Virginia	3-E: 3
WILLIAM L McMILLION	06/28/1921 Private	State Police, West Virginia	11-E: 9
GEORGE A DULING	08/28/1921 Private	State Police, West Virginia	24-W: 14
HOWARD A DEEM	06/03/1922 Private	State Police, West Virginia	59-W: 12
JAMES B SHREWSBURY	07/12/1923 Private	State Police, West Virginia	14-E: 10
ULRIC C CRAWFORD	06/2011924 Private	State Police, West Virginia	14-E: 8
THEODORE ROOSEVELT MEADOWS	04/17/1926 Private	State Police, West Virginia	42-W: 13
JAMES LEWIS LOWE	06/2611926 Private	State Police, West Virginia	30-W: 14
BLAKE ALLISON MICHAEL	05/01/1927 Private	State Police, West Virginia	60-W: 5
ARZA A ALLEN	11/01/1928 Private	State Police, West Virginia	48-W: 10
WILLIAM HALL	10/19/1930 Sergeant	State Police, West Virginia	40-W: 11
FARLEY K LITTON	11/08/1935 Trooper	State Police, West Virginia	36-W: 13
FRANKLIN DEWEY PATRICK	08/27/1937 Trooper	State Police, West Virginia	13-E: 10
ALLEN HENRY BENNETT JEFFREYS	07/16/1939 Trooper	State Police, West Virginia	61-W: 11
NEWTON TRESSEL SITES	08/31/1942 Sergeant	State Police, West Virginia	9-E: 7
BURR WHITE HARRISON	12/03/1945 Trooper	State Police, West Virginia	34-W: 7
JOSEPH PIERCE HORNE	09/09/1946 Sergeant	State Police, West Virginia	58-W: 13
ARTHUR MARTIN HURST	06/17/1949 Corporal	State Police, West Virginia	35-W: 5
ROBERT FRANK RULONG	02/1011958 Trooper	State Police, West Virginia	50-W: 6
HARRY EDSEL ROBINSON	11/27/1962 Corporal	State Police, West Virginia	3-E: 15
WILLIAM JOSEPH SHREWSBURY	09/28/1963 Corporal	State Police, West Virginia	25-E: 7
ROBERT BALL NOECHEL	11/01/1965 Trooper	State Police, West Virginia	10-E: 9
HUGH DONALD SWARTZ	10/05/1970 Trooper	State Police, West Virginia	40-W: 2
THOMAS DEAN HERCULES	01/12/1977 Trooper	State Police, West Virginia	35-W: 7
CHARLES HENRY JOHNSON	01/12/1977 Trooper	State Police, West Virginia	5-E: 8
BRUCE THOMPSON BROWN	10/14/1977 Trooper	State Police, West Virginia	12-E: 14
DEWEY C SHREWSBURY	10/25/1978 Corporal	State Police, West Virginia	40-W: 6
PHILIP STEVEN KESNER	11/07/1979 Trooper	State Police, West Virginia	35-W: 6
CARLEN BILL STONE	12/16/1982 Corporal	State Police, West Virginia	35-W: 4
HARRY GLENN LUCAS Jr	09/12/1984 Trooper	State Police, West Virginia	45-E: 18
JONATHAN DAVID HARRIS	07/11/1985 Trooper	State Police, West Virginia	34-W: 4
WILLIAM HOWARD PHILLIPS	07/30/1987 Trooper	State Police, West Virginia	7-E: 9
JAMES THOMAS BRAMMER	04/15/1989 Trooper	State Police, West Virginia	48-W: 14
LARRY GENE HACKER	04/09/1993 Senior Trooper	State Police, West Virginia	34-W: 19
CHARLES MATTHEW TURNER	04/04/1996 Lieutenant	State Police, West Virginia	19-E: 20
DOUGLAS WAYNE BLAND	01/19/1999 Senior Trooper	State Police, West Virginia	52-E: 21
DONALD C PEDERSON	08/26/1972 Trooper	State Patrol, Wisconsin	47-W: 10
GARY G POWLESS	05/18/1980 Trooper	State Patrol, Wisconsin	45-W: 15
DEBORAH M McMENAMIN	10/26/1989 Trooper	State Patrol, Wisconsin	46-W: 14
WILLIAM SCHOENBERGER	04/22/1993 Trooper I I I	State Patrol, Wisconsin	39-W: 19
PETER VISSER	10/12/1981 Patrolman	Highway Patrol, Wyoming	13-E: 10
CHRIS S LOGSDON	10113/1998 Patrolman	Highway Patrol, Wyoming	10-E: 21

Count of Officers: 1435

NTC Conference at State House in Maryland.

To Jim Rhinebarger
With appreciation,

State Histories

Cadets at the Louisiana State Police Training Academy in Baton Rouge.

Editors Note: All states were invited to submit material. In some cases, only a limited amount of material was provided.

Alabama Highway Patrol

"Gentlemen, if I have made a mistake, I'll soon correct that," were the words spoken by Governor Bibb Graves when he introduced the Alabama Highway Patrol to the citizens of Alabama. Governor Graves officially established the Highway Patrol on December 5, 1935. There were 75 officers constituting the nucleus of the Highway Patrol which has grown over the past 62 years into an enforcement unit in excess of 725 officers.

From the original 75 officers, Governor Bibb Graves appointed Walter K. McAdory to serve as the first chief of the newly established Highway Patrol. The state was divided into two districts, one being the North Alabama District and the other, the South Alabama District. A captain was assigned to each district as the district commander. The officers selected to constitute the first Highway Patrol were interviewed and hired by Chief McAdory and the two captains. They were selected for their ability, intellect, reputation, and physical size. Training for the charter members consisted of 10 days, learning highway and criminal laws, first aid, the rules of the road, and developing their driving skills, especially the art of riding motorcycles. In those early days there was no radio communication, and the motorcycles were the constant companions of the Highway Patrol officers.

The Highway Patrol had to prove itself worthy to those it served, and they were intent on demonstrating to the public that their officers were more than strong-armed cops, that they were to protect, to serve, and to make the public proud. Funding to support the Highway Patrol came from a 50 cents license fee. The revenue was earmarked to pay for Highway Patrol equipment and salaries.

The new Highway Patrol officers began their missions in early 1936, after receiving their assignments throughout the state. By the end of the first nine months, the officers had logged 615,335 miles patrolling on motorcycles and 583,756 miles in automobiles.

Throughout the 1930s, the Highway Patrol continued its growth. Three years after its formation, it employed 135 officers who patrolled nearly three million miles. The Highway Patrol began a tradition of law enforcement expansion and evolution in response to the changing needs among Alabamians.

The Highway Patrol faced its first major reorganizational change in 1939, under Governor Frank M. Dixon and Chief T. Weller Smith. Governor Dixon approved a bill on March 8, 1939, redesignating the patrol as the Alabama Department of Public Safety and giving Chief Smith the title of Director of Public Safety. The new department had four divisions: Highway Patrol, Drivers License, Accident Prevention Bureau and Mechanical and Equipment. In addition to separating specific services of the department by divisions, the act prompted several significant changes.

Director Smith began a new program of organizing, training, and equipping the Highway Patrol Division. The most visible result of this program was the issuance of new cars to patrol officers instead of the customary motorcycles. In addition, the uniforms took on a new appearance, blue and gray. A further change, also of noticeable effect, was the awarding of statewide arrest powers to all officers. With the formation of the new department its members, like other state employees, came under Alabama's merit system. In keeping with Chief Smith's modernization of the department, officers were issued new weapons including 12-gauge, 7-shot, semi-automatic, sawed-off shotguns; Thompson submachine guns; and .351 high-speed, long-range automatic rifles. All new recruits were trained thoroughly in handling the new weapons.

Governor Dixon and Chief Smith turned their attention to driver licensing. They believed that testing applicants before licensing would promote traffic safety and help in accident prevention. They believed that before letting the public use the roads with a machine that could kill somebody, they must be tested. The test was designed to determine an applicant's fitness to drive, knowledge of the rules of the road, and attitude toward law and highway safety. The two-year driver's license was introduced and cumulative files on each licensed driver were established. The filing system created a central repository for all driving offenses to provide guidance in the suspension and revocation decisions.

Public Safety entered the 1940s with its reputation clearly established with the public. The news media indicated that favorable comments about the Highway Patrol were uniform and that of appreciation, of recognition for a job well done, and of service clearly rendered. In 1939, for example, officers made 2,000 fewer traffic arrests than the previous year, which indicated to many that safety measures had been effective.

In 1942 the war's supply needs were so pressing that the country could not spare, even for law enforcement purposes, the radio parts necessary for establishing a two-way radio system. It would be two years later, under Governor Chauncey Sparks and Director Van-Buren Gilbert, that the long awaited two-way radio system would become fully operational. The radio system, for the first time, allowed continuous contact between patrol cars and their stations. The impact of this was immediate. Officers saved miles of travel and were able to respond more promptly to accidents and other incidents. The radios gave officers the capability of immediately checking out suspected stolen vehicles, escaped prisoners and other law violators. The new radio system required special training and personnel. To facilitate its operation, the department employed and trained as operators, 13 men and 12 women.

In 1943, by executive order, all existing ranks within the Highway Patrol were abolished and replaced with two new classifications: senior highway patrolman and principal highway patrolman.

Further changes in 1943 required all drivers involved in motor vehicle accidents to submit written reports to Public Safety's director. The Accident Records Unit became responsible for seeing that requirements of the law were carried out.

In 1945 the Department of Public Safety entered into the business of alcohol control. By June 1946, arrests made by the Alcoholic Beverage Law Enforcement Division averaged 400 a month.

In the 1940s, the uniform of the Highway Patrol changed since most of the officers performed their duties in automobiles, and few still used motorcycles in patrolling the state's

Alabama Troopers involved in traffic control at the Talladega Motor Speedway.

highways. The old boots and breeches, part of the standard uniform since 1935, had outlived their usefulness. This was changed to straight legged trousers and regulation black shoes. Boots and boot breeches remained as special uniforms for those few officers still assigned to motorcycle duty. The color of the patrol cars was also changed from solid white to blue and gray.

Director of Public Safety L.B. Sullivan turned his attention to Alabama's speed limit, believing that raising the speed limit on the highways would reduce traffic fatalities. Due to his and others efforts, a bill was passed increasing the speed limit from 45 to 60 mph on Alabama highways. Department salaries were also increased the first year of his term. As a result, the Highway Patrol chief made $400 to $500 a month and patrolmen made $250 to $326 a month. Salary increases were now to be granted on an annual basis by steps, except in cases of meritorious service awards.

One of the most important functions of the department, then as now, was effective training of its personnel. In December 1953, the Alabama Police Academy opened to receive its first class. This class was made up of municipal officers from throughout the state, arriving at Gunter Air Force Base to hear Chief Kimbrough's words: "The purpose for establishing the Alabama Police Academy is to make training available to all law enforcement officers throughout the state. The objective is to upgrade law enforcement at the municipal, county and state levels." During the days to come, the class learned from an impressive faculty drawn from the Federal Bureau of Investigation, Treasury Department, state toxicologist, attorneys, judges, National Automobile Theft Bureau, Department of Revenue and the state's Fire Marshal's Office. A driving force behind establishing the academy was the Alabama League of Municipalities, which sought to improve the caliber of officers statewide.

By the mid-1950s Public Safety faced a monumental task in patrolling more than 62,000 miles of highways and monitoring more than 900,000 registered vehicles. In 1955 Alabama had one million licensed drivers, traveling an estimated 13 billion miles annually. That year, Highway Patrol officers traveled six million miles and investigated 7,435 motor vehicle accidents. They made 38,636 traffic arrests, assisted 9,000 motorists, checked more than 400,000 driver licenses and issued 29,964 warnings. Highway Patrol "courtesy checks" were initiated in every county during the Fourth of July and Labor Day holidays. Officers stopped vehicles for a moment to give each driver a friendly safety message from the governor. More than 300,000 pieces of safety-related literature were distributed to the motoring public during the two holidays.

In the late 1950s, the Alabama Police Law

Nation's largest traffic accident involving 193 vehicles on March 20, 1995, attributing to one fatality and 71 injuries.

Overhead bridge collapses on to I-65.

Enforcement Training Committee was established. This committee was composed of local, state, and federal law enforcement officers. This committee was to plan and supervise the academic activities of the Police Academy. Through the recommendation of this group and with the full support of the governor and the members of the legislature, the academy was moved from Gunter Air Force Base into a new $300,000 facility at Federal Drive and Coliseum Boulevard.

Then a cadet program was established to recruit prospective patrol officers just below the minimum age and train them to become patrolmen. The cadets were assigned to duties that would expose them to their future jobs and were given a solid, hands-on education in the operations of the department.

In 1963 the Alabama Highway Patrol officers became known as State Troopers. The new designation, ordered by Colonel Lingo

and approved by Governor Wallace, was meant to effect a better public understanding of the department and its varied duties. The officers had long since assumed the diverse duties of law enforcement, of which patrolling the state's highways was but one assignment.

It was felt that year that the equipment, weapons, and training materials of the troopers were in poor condition and in short supply. However, the department's budget, depleted by the expense of responding to many civil disorders, could not support the purchase of new equipment and supplies. By the prompting of Governor Wallace, the 1963 Legislature took steps to remedy the situation by raising the cost of driver's licenses and earmarking those funds for Public Safety. All dangerous, obsolete, or worn out vehicles were replaced systematically on the basis of need and availability. In those instances where ve-

Alabama troopers distribute trooper teddy bears to children hopitalized during the Christmas holidays and when children are involved in automobile crashes.

hicles were not needed for full-time emergency services, a rebuilt machine was placed into service. Vehicles were rebuilt in the department's shops, and all new vehicles were equipped with safety belts, new sirens, and emergency equipment.

The communication system was improved by the end of 1963 with the replacement of obsolete radios, the erection of additional relay stations, and the modernization of several old relay stations. A welcome change for uniformed officers was the issuance of short-sleeved, open-collared, light-weight shirts as the summer uniform. Weapons were standardized and replaced as necessary. Reserves of other weapons, gas, and other supplies were brought up to standard. All posts were surveyed and needed repairs made.

In early February 1964, the department moved into the former Highway Building, 500 Dexter Avenue, in Montgomery. During that fiscal year, four new Highway Patrol offices were built, in Eufaula, Gadsden, Decatur, and Mobile. A fifth office later was built in Grove Hill. Also of major importance was the installation of a new interstate teletype system linking post and district offices with the state headquarters.

The late 1960s and 1970s were years of rapid evolution for the Department of Public Safety. Working conditions for troopers improved in the mid-1960s when new patrol cars were equipped with air conditioning, and December 29, 1965, brought about a five-day work week, giving each trooper two days off each week.

In 1966 four disaster control groups were organized. Each group consisted of 50 specially trained and equipped officers, ready to respond whenever a highly mobile, special force unit was needed. A new Highway Patrol District was created in Huntsville

in 1969, bringing the number of districts to 10.

In 1969 and 1970, electronically operated driver license testing machines were installed in six of the states larger metropolitan areas. This innovation improved the efficiency of the state's larger examining stations and decreased both time and personnel in testing prospective drivers. This change was followed in 1972 by the employment of driver license technicians. The effect was to release trained arresting officers for patrol duty, while maintaining the high level of driver licensing services.

During the 1970s the Selma Highway Patrol District was created to relieve the Montgomery District of three counties and the Tuscaloosa District of four counties, and the construction of the department's first firing range, a large, modern facility located near Mt. Meigs took place.

Federal grants received in 1973 allowed Public Safety to equip all patrol cars with protective shields, roll bars, spotlights, electronic sirens, and public address systems. A separate grant, awarded through the Office of Highway and Traffic Safety, was used to purchase 54 Speed Gun II radar units used to enforce the 55 mph speed limit effective nationwide that year. As a result, arrests for speeding violations increased 18 percent. Federal grants led to the formation of the Planning and Research Unit in 1973 to work with the governor's office of Highway and Traffic Safety and the Law Enforcement Planning Agency. In 1975, the Department's Aviation Unit was formed in response to the increasing need for aerial law enforcement capabilities.

Height and weight standards for state trooper applicants were abolished as the result of a suit alleging that the requirements discriminated against women, and the standards were eliminated as part of the screening pro-

cess for prospective state troopers in June 1976. No preferential treatment for female applicants or recruits was ordered by the court.

Public Safety, in 1977, issued the state's first picture driver license. Instead of the old central issue license card mailed to applicants, the new license was a photo card issued locally at the time of application. Public Safety continued its fight against drunken driving, adding to its arsenal two breath alcohol testing vans, familiarly known as "batmobiles." Also that year, the Department formed its Public Information Unit within the Service Division. The unit was created to serve as a central means of disseminating information about public safety to the news media and Alabama's citizens. It also was responsible for department publications.

In 1977 Public Safety's Alabama Criminal Justice Training Center found a home at Craig Field in Selma. After months of negotiations, the property at Craig, valued at $18 million, was transferred to the department at no cost on December 28. At that time, all training activities began to move to Selma, where they are still located. Following the academy's move to Craig Air Force Base in Selma, the training facility in Montgomery continued its usefulness to the department as the site for the Montgomery District Office.

In the late 1970s, the department strengthened its commitment to drug enforcement operations, and by the end of March 1978, it had destroyed $1.6 million in illegal drugs confiscated by the Narcotics Unit.

The year 1979 saw a new class of state trooper recruits in training at the Selma Academy, a class distinguished by the department's first female trooper.

In 1979, the Department initiated a radar certification program to train and certify officers in the use of radar. This was necessary because the increased use of radar in traffic enforcement was accompanied by an increase in court challenges of radar equipment and the operators.

In 1983 Governor George Wallace began an unprecedented fourth term as governor, and two new units were formed within the department in 1985 to better serve and protect the public. The Hazardous Materials Response Team was formed to handle incidents involving explosives and other hazardous materials. The second unit established was the Missing Children Bureau, to respond to the growing need for a central information and investigative unit to serve missing children and adults.

In January 1987, Alabama's first Republican governor since reconstruction, Governor Guy Hunt, was inaugurated governor. Governor Hunt appointed Colonel Tom Wells as his Director of Public Safety. Colonel Wells sought to resolve the 15-year-old Paradise federal court case regarding hiring and the promotion of sworn officers. Following comprehensive hearings and deliberation, U.S. District Judge Myron Thompson approved the proposed settlement on February 1, 1988. An immediate result of the consent decree was the promotion of 50 troopers to the rank of corporal. Promotions to other ranks were soon to follow. Colonel Wells explored the possibility of acquiring an automated fingerprint identification system, known as AFIS. In 1988 Governor Hunt gave his approval to the purchase of AFIS to be housed in the ABI Division of Public Safety and used by law enforcement agencies throughout the state.

A second major new program implemented in the Highway Patrol Division was an enhanced DUI training and enforcement initiative. In addition, the department received another weapon for its DUI fighting arsenal,

24 video cameras donated by the Aetna Insurance Company as part of its "Eye on DUI" program.

Early in 1990, the department's Motor Carrier Safety Unit made advances into the computer age with the installation of mobile data computer terminals in 25 of its vehicles. The system allowed troopers to check driver licenses and vehicle tags from a roadside inspection site in a matter of seconds.

The first trooper class in four years reported to the Training Center in September 1993. This class was unique in that it was the first class for which the age limitation was dropped. In February 1994, Lieutenant Colonel Robert Patterson, assistant director, administered the oath of office to 54 new state

troopers, marking the first time in five years that the trooper ranks grew rather than diminished.

The Highway Patrol celebrated its 65th anniversary on December 5, 2000. The Department of Public Safety has grown and prospered, always in response to the changing needs of law enforcement. It has evolved from a fledgling force of 75 motorcycle-mounted Highway Patrol officers to a multi-faceted, comprehensive, statewide law enforcement agency.

(The Alabama State Trooper Association appreciates the assistance of the Department of Public Safety in providing certain information for this article.)

Alabama Trooper Honor Guard participates in the Governor's Inauguration and at funerals of fellow troopers.

Alaska State Troopers

The Division of Alaska State Troopers is charged with enforcement of all criminal and traffic laws of the State of Alaska. Identification and apprehension of violators and the prevention of crimes and traffic violations are their main tasks. The identification and apprehension of violators throughout Alaska, with an emphasis in areas not covered by a local police unit, is the first step in the justice process. Other responsibilities include the management of the Village Public Safety Officer Program, serving of warrants, transportation of prisoners, and search-and-rescue missions. The Search-and-Rescue Fund is used by the director to reimburse local search-and-rescue operation expenditures.

Law enforcement is a difficult job anywhere, but the Alaska State Troopers face challenges not encountered by other law enforcement agencies in the US. One fifth the size of the continental US, Alaska consists of 586,412 square miles of diverse territory that experiences extreme weather conditions. State troopers cope with blizzards, hundreds of inches of snowfall, avalanches, winds in excess of 100 mph, subzero temperatures, and heavy rainfall. The state is filled with rugged mountains, massive glaciers, tundra, forests, more than 3,000 rivers, more than 3 million lakes and a coastline of 6,640 miles. The vast expanses of the state, combined with the terrain and weather, create a significant challenge for troopers.

The evolution of law enforcement in Alaska began in the mid 1800s with the United States Army and Navy being the sole law enforcement authority throughout the vast region. Later, United States marshals were appointed but were far too few in number. It was the tumult of the gold rush period, both at Skagway and Nome, which first brought to focus the need for an additional law enforcement organization to supplement the US Marshal's Office, which would continue to bear the responsibility for law enforcement in Alaska for the next forty years.

In 1941 the 15th Territorial Legislature established the Territory of Alaska Highway Patrol for the purpose of enforcing the traffic code, but did not provide the new organization with police authority. In 1945, as lawlessness continued to thrive outside the jurisdiction of local police departments, the members of the Alaska Highway Patrol were deputized as special deputy US marshals. In 1948 the Highway Patrol was given the full authority of peace officers to enforce the laws of the territory.

By the early 1950s, the federal Department of Justice recognized the increasing law enforcement needs of the territory, particularly in the bush areas of Alaska. The Territorial Legislature responded in 1953 by establishing the Alaska Territorial Police to provide law enforcement services for the entire territory. Total strength: 36 officers. The Alaska Highway Patrol had already gained a reputation as an elite corps, and formal training became a hallmark of the new Territorial Police. As the officers began to serve in remote posts, they gained a reputation for integrity and capability, a reputation which has been carried forward to the present day.

With the advent of statehood in 1959, the name of Alaska's law enforcement agency was changed to the Alaska State Police and the organization became a division of the Department of Public Safety. The new State Police added 13 former US marshals and 10 new recruits to their ranks, increasing their number to 78 commissioned officers. During this time, the State Police would provide "contract officers" for communities willing to pay for trained law enforcement. Kotzebue, Kenai-Soldotna, Seward, Palmer, and Bethel were among the communities to pay for a "contract officer" from the State Police.

During Governor Wally Hickel's first administration in 1967, the name was changed to the Alaska State Troopers. Under Commissioner Mel Personett, the troopers focused their work in areas of Alaska not being served by community police, and began to offer more sophisticated services to law enforcement organizations statewide. Also in 1967 the Public Safety Training Academy saw its first year of operation.

Today, the Alaska State Troopers number approximately 240 commissioned and 190 civilian personnel. The troopers' major components are five Detachments and a Criminal Investigation Bureau (founded in 1971). The detachments are headquartered in Ketchikan, Palmer, Anchorage, Fairbanks, and Soldotna.

The Department of Public Safety (DPS) is Alaska's primary law enforcement agency whose responsibilities encompass the enforcement of federal, state, and local laws. The mandate of the department is to prevent loss of life and property as a result of illegal or unsafe acts. The department enforces criminal laws, traffic laws, and state fish and game regulations. It provides public protection programs for fire and traffic safety. The DPS has two law enforcement divisions, the Alaska State Troopers (AST), with approximately 260 commissioned officers, and Fish and Wildlife Protection (FWP), with approximately 90 commissioned officers. State troopers are posted throughout the state, many in remote areas.

The main responsibility of AST is the enforcement of all criminal and traffic laws, identification and apprehension of violators, and the prevention of crime and traffic violations. Specialized functions include white collar crime, criminal investigations, narcotics, serving of warrants, prisoner transport, and search and rescue missions.

FWP's main responsibility is to protect Alaska's fish and wildlife resources through enforcement of laws and regulations governing use of natural resources within Alaska and its adjacent waters, as well as through increasing the knowledge of, and respect for, fish and wildlife laws and regulations. FWP also participates in the overall mission of the DPS through enforcement of criminal laws and participation in search and rescue operations.

Sgt. Don Bowman, F./Sgt. Randy Crawford, Pilot. Dogs belong to Dee Dee Jonrowe. Mr. Jonrowe was dog handler.

Patrol vehicles, 1992 Chevy - 1951 Hudson. Front, L to R: Inv. Rosemary Decker, Sgt. Al Cain, Lt. Patrick Kasnick.

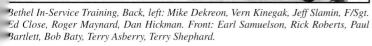

Bethel In-Service Training, Back, left: Mike Dekreon, Vern Kinegak, Jeff Slamin, F/Sgt. Ed Close, Roger Maynard, Dan Hickman. Front: Earl Samuelson, Rick Roberts, Paul Bartlett, Bob Baty, Terry Asberry, Terry Shephard.

Arizona Highway Patrol

"Blaze forth a new star in the galaxy of the states," was the slogan of the Arizona Territory, which was hungry for statehood. After application, only Hawaii and New Mexico waited longer for statehood than Arizona. Arizona's star would not blaze forth on Old Glory until 1912. Even then, Arizona was little more than a territory without roads.

The first statewide law enforcement in the Arizona Territory was known as the Arizona Rangers, established by the 21st Legislative Assembly on March 13, 1901. The "Ranger Bill" created a 14 man force: one captain, one sergeant and 12 privates.

On February 12, 1912, United States President Taft signed the bill granting Arizona statehood. Arizona officially became a state on February 14, 1912. Since the time of statehood Arizona had many names, from the Baby State, to the Land of the Three Cs (Campaigns, Competition and Consequences), to the Grand Canyon State. George W.P. Hunt became Arizona's first governor.

As more and more roads were built, more and more automobiles crowded Arizona's roadways. Governor Hunt, with his chauffeured automobile and his campaign prophecy on the need for improved roads, would find a way to capitalize on the future growth of the automobile industry. He knew that cars moved people and that climate motivated the drivers. Hunt and his successors would all recognize that climate would become an important Arizona commodity. Under Governor Hunt's administration, the Arizona State Highway Department was formed and the Legislature would create, revise and amend the highway code. It was during Hunt's administration that the Highway Patrol, a division of the State Highway Department, would be formed.

In the spring of 1931 the Highway Department, a large and growing arm of state government, was preparing for the addition of a major new division. On June 13, the law enacted by the 10th Legislature creating the Arizona Highway Patrol would go into effect. Two problems had to be solved. The first was finding the right men for the job. The second was finding the money to pay them. The money wouldn't find its way to the patrol until July because the new fiscal year funding wasn't available until that time. But the law is the law, so on June 13, 1931, seven men, who were Highway Department motor vehicle inspectors, became the state's first patrolmen.

They began the work those 16 men, who were chosen and trained during July, who would carry on when they and their patrol cars

hit the streets on August 3. After a brief time, the original seven men returned to work as motor vehicle inspectors. But like the Arizona Rangers, they were forerunners of the patrol.

The men recruited weren't youngsters fresh out of school, "wet behind the ears." They held responsible jobs as sheriffs, postmasters, Southern Pacific railroaders and independent businessmen. Patrolmen were selected on the basis of population in each county. The original recruit list consisted of 19 men. When the training was over, 16 would actually wear the uniform, badge and the gun. Fourteen, one for each 8,000 motor vehicles, would be appointed highway patrolmen; one would become superintendent and one would be chief clerk.

The first superintendent of the Arizona Highway Patrol was James Hall. Hall's first order of business was issuing a distinctive form of dress. The uniform requirements were approved by the state engineer and gained the consent of the Highway Commission. The men purchased their own uniforms and equipment. Whatever the cost of those breeches and shirts, it must have seemed small compared to the honor of being one of Arizona's first patrolmen.

Patrolmen, driving standard gray cars bearing a silver, blue and gold insignia, cracked down on motorists who ignored the

licensing laws. To impress the driver with the seriousness of the action, patrolmen gave out large red tickets as their calling cards. They were hard to ignore. This collection effort worked. During the 18 months of Hall's administration, the patrol paid for itself and contributed to the state at the same time.

From 1931-48 the patrol went through numerous changes, all of which were caused by politics:

•1931-33: During the Depression most people were poor, many were jobless. Businesses were tightening their belts. Only the reasonably affluent could afford cars. The state needed money; automobile and truck drivers appeared to be good sources of revenue. Vehicles were now required to be taxed and licensed. The 14 highway patrolmen trained by Inspector Yoder from California, jumped in their patrol cars and began collecting money from drivers. Gasoline bootlegging began; the patrol cracked down and revenues went up. Election time rolled around.

•1933-37: Tourist travel became important to Arizona. Cars were owned by one out of every six adults and driven by children of all ages. Trucks rolled across the highways between the Mississippi and the Pacific. Truckers were stopped and licenses were purchased to travel Arizona's roads. Road signs went up as traffic fatalities increased.

The DPS Flag made its first official appearance on January 26, 1994, during the agency's 25th anniversary celebration at DPS headquarters in Phoenix. The field of blue reflects boldness and the Department's desire to serve. A golden horizon depicts DPS' broad scope of expertise and the agencies promising future. The saguaro cactus & pine tree symbolize DPS mission as a statewide law enforcement agency with responsibilities extending from the state's vast deserts to its highest mountains. The DPS breast badge demonstrates pride in ourselves, our agency and our accomplishments. The agency's motto "Courteous Vigilance" provides DPS officers with guidance and foundation. The flag black border serves as a memorial for DPS officers killed in the line of duty.

Bell Jet Ranger helicopter currently utilized by the Emergency Medical Services Division at the Arizona Department of Public Safety.

Kawaski "Police 1000" motorcycle currently utilized by the Uniform Division of the Arizona Department of Public Safety.

A Safety Council was called in to aid in protecting the public and a statewide safety campaign was launched. The Legislature expanded the patrol by adding 18 more officers.

•1937-39: People and automobiles from everywhere filled Arizona's roadways. Trucks were scrutinized and couldn't enter the state unless they bought a plate, and passenger vehicles also had to pay fees.

Vehicle seizure was begun when fees were not paid. Drivers were put afoot until they paid. The tactics worked; the criticism followed. Criticism of the state, the patrol, politics, bug inspections and the searching of baggage came pouring in from newspapers in Chicago, from the *Christian Science Monitor* and from the California Automobile Association. Chambers of Commerce within the state asked that something be done about the tourist and bug inspection problem. Newspapers published the stories.

•1939-41: Conservation of resources became paramount due to World War II and the help America provided its allies. Bob Jones defeated Sidney Osborn. The title of captain was changed to assistant superintendent and the salary increased $50 a month.

The copper paint and door decals for patrol cars became items of the past. Black paint went on and decals were put on the back. Smokey Bear hats became part of the tan uniform. Short-wave radio systems operated from the Sheriffs' offices and the patrolman's lonely isolation started to go away. The Legislature made the Highway Patrol a direct agent of the Corporation Commission for all trucking rules and regulations. The patrol started investigating violations and referred them to the county attorneys. One patrolman for every 3,500 vehicles was approved by the Legislature.

Jim Hall was the first to ask for a radio network and heard a resounding "No." But, the Highway Commission approved Allen's request for a statewide radio network and set aside $9,800, even though the patrol was $2,100 in the red. The plan called for four stations, a guaranteed maintenance contribution from the counties, and strong receiving sets at each port of entry. The FCC approved the plan. When completed, the state could be sealed off in the event a convict attempted to enter or escape.

•1941-46: World War II continued. Dealing with the conservation of resources was a job for law enforcement and much of it fell on the patrol's shoulders. The speed limit fell from 60 mph to 35 mph. Gasoline was in short supply and rubber was a necessary war material. Food to feed the fighting forces became paramount. Severe drought conditions existed across the rangeland and cattle weren't fatten-ing the way they should. The drought also caused severe fire conditions. The patrol met this problem through a three-pronged approach: crackdowns on the commercial carriers to reduce the illegal hauling of black market beef; lending manpower to the US Grazing Service to relay fire hazard information, and setting up communications stations to assist the U.S. Forest Service and fight fires when they did start.

A new KNGG, 1,000 watt radio station was built, in part through a federal grant. The patrol officer could now be directed to a needy Arizonan, a stranded visitor, or to the aid of a fellow officer caught in the midst of trouble. About half of the 40 patrolmen had receiving capability in their vehicles; others had both receiving and transmitting capability. For an organization that traveled 1,290,106 miles in 1942, the radio replaced the border station and made patrol work a reality.

The nation's interest was vital. Men of all walks of life joined in service to their country, patrol officers were no exception. Four women, three of them patrol wives, took the rigorous Federal Communications Commission examinations and became the patrol's dispatchers.

•1946-49: Many veterans who had been stationed in Arizona began relocating to the state. Arizona's economy improved and for the next two decades outpaced every other state in the Union. The growth of the Highway Patrol from the 1950s on has been phenomenal.

After 1950, four extremely difficult law enforcement problems occurred: the prison riot of 1953, the Community of Short Creek, the rising death rate from automobile slaughter, the prison riot of 1958. Each of these problems was unique, trying and difficult. Each required the ability to plan, organize, implement and face the consequences. Each situation involved many complex issues. All required action, but even more than action, they required wisdom. Arizona was fortunate that her three governors and her superintendent had the courage to use both discretion and wisdom during that decade. The patrol's superintendent during this decade, Greg O. Hathaway, was the only superintendent to have served under five different governors.

On July 1, 1969, the Highway Patrol became the Uniform Division of the Arizona Department of Public Safety. This new state agency brought together three existing police agencies at the state level: the Arizona Highway Patrol, the Enforcement Division of the Department of Liquor Licenses and Control and the Narcotics Division from the Department of Law. Also incorporated into DPS was the State Crime Laboratory, the responsibility for law enforcement training and the Criminal Identification Section.

John Conlan reported, "The Department of Public Safety was formed to attack the whole criminal operation in Arizona. At the time, we were faced with campus riots, the Vietnam agitation and civil insurrection.

"The state needed a statewide police authority without creating a police state.

"The new department was created because of the belief in the need for federalism at the closest local level. It was not designed to become a monolithic state police system. Its intent was to provide support. Logic indicated this needed to be done, but no one was taking the initiative to do it. The bill was written so that the Highway Patrol would be the main division within the department.

"There was no crime lab available. Across the state, law enforcement officers were going to local druggist and doctors. Our ability to analyze fingerprints, chemicals, weapons or ballistics was impaired.

"Every law enforcement group operated autonomously. Training for these officers was minimal. There simply wasn't enough money available to justify cop trainers to ensure that each county and municipal law enforcement agency had total know-how. Even if the money had been there, there weren't enough people qualified in this area to work in this capacity throughout the state.

"We assessed the state as having three major law enforcement needs. The first was the criminal operation in its entirety. Second was the need for traffic law enforcement. Third was the need for skills in crowd and riot control that could contain mounting civil insurrection.

"Two other states with situations similar to Arizona's were California and Texas. There was a general admiration for what they had done on a larger scale. By relying on the existing strengths of the Highway Patrol, coupled with the concept of the Department of Public Safety Support System objective, we felt we had the answer to giving our law enforcement personnel the tools they needed to do the job. We wanted them to have the tools. It was imperative.

"Fortunately, the Department of Public Safety gave us tools we needed without removing the fraternal, helpful spirit that exists among Arizona's law enforcement people. Finally, they all had a place to turn for the resources we so desperately lacked."

The motto of the Arizona Highway Patrol, "Courteous Vigilance," was adopted and became the official motto of the Arizona Department of Public Safety.

Arkansas State Police

By Dorothy Watters

"The perfect man is needed but cannot be found. The nearest approach thereto should be made. . ." So, Governor J. M. Futrell instructed the three state police commissioners to search for the 13 original state rangers in March, 1935.

Established to combat a burgeoning "moonshine" trade; the state police took the place of the state road patrol, a division of the Highway Department. The newly formed department was given full police power, but was specifically assigned the responsibility of "enforcing the laws of the state of Arkansas against the unlawful manufacture or sale of intoxicating liquors." It was funded by a 25 cent driver's license fee.

A. G. Albright was appointed first superintendent and Robert LaFollette became assistant superintendent on April 1, 1935. The first rangers were hired on April 30, 1935, and four more were hired on May 7, 1935. An identification bureau was established on June 20, 1935 and a "plain clothes investigator" was hired September 13, 1935, completing the full 13 approved positions.

The first rangers were given no formal training by the state police. They relied on good sense, excellent physical condition, courage and whatever training they had received from other police departments. Each ranger covered eight to twelve counties and was away from home many days at a time. To help defray expenses of a life on the road, rangers received $1.50 per day for meals and $2.00 per day for lodging. They stayed in touch with headquarters by telephone and telegraph. "Headquarters" was three rooms in the Old State House in Little Rock.

In 1937, the success of the state police encouraged Governor Carl Bailey to increase the size of the department from 13 to 50 men and to find a permanent home for the State Police in the walls of the Old Penitentiary Building on Roosevelt Road in Little Rock. Criminal investigation, motor vehicle inspection and parole supervision were added to the department's duties as was traffic control. The rangers became officially known as "state policemen."

An 1,000 watt radio station, KASP, went on the air in October of that year, and receiving sets were installed in all patrol vehicles. A 75 mile receiving radius was average during daylight hours, but statewide coverage was expected at night.

By 1941, with World War II hanging darkly on the horizon, patrolmen of the Arkansas State Police had established themselves as a force to be respected and feared. The patrolman was often the only law available in many rural counties. Recognizing this, the legislature authorized the installation of one portable transmitter and 14 two-way radios. The State Police Commission also authorized headquarters buildings in Hope, Warren, Clarksville and Forrest City.

Many patrolmen took leaves of absence for military duty when war broke out in December 1941. Others resigned, and the department simply coped until the end of the war in 1945. Albright resigned in 1944, under pressure, and was replaced by C.T. Atkinson, who in turn was replaced by Jack Porter during a political upheaval of the first order. These problems led the Legislature of 1945 to abolish the Arkansas State Police Department and to establish the Department of the Arkansas State Police (ASP).

Porter then became the first director of the Arkansas State Police. Also, in 1945, every car in the department was equipped with two-way radios.

By 1948, the department was functioning with an authorized 99 man force and state patrolmen became known as "troopers." Death, which had waited 13 years, was ready to claim one of these members. On September 25, 1948, Trooper A.S. Pavatt was shot by Kenneth Speegle, a 28year-old AWOL burglary suspect, in Marion County. Pavatt died in a Harrison hospital. Speegle was captured in Oklahoma and spent the next 20 years in prison before being paroled by Governor Winthrop Rockefeller.

In 1949, the appointment of Director Herman Lindsey was made. That year also brought a second tragedy to the Arkansas State Police. Trooper Bill Gordon was permanently paralyzed during a routine traffic stop in Crittenden County. W.A. Price, of Memphis, Tennessee, shot Gordon point blank, injuring his spinal cord. Gordon later transferred to Little Rock and served as ordinance officer until 1976. Price, injured while trying to escape, was apprehended.

The polygraph was first used by the Arkansas State Police in 1949. Assistant Director Carl Miller and Lieutenant Allen Templeton became the first persons in the state certified to use it.

Lindsey Hatchett took over as director in December, 1953. Hatchett drastically rearranged the structure of the department, cutting its strength to 116 men. The Weight Division, which had been under the Highway Department, was returned as a separate division of the ASP. In that year, the total appropriation for the state police exceeded $1 million for the first time.

Under Governor Orville Faubus, Herman Lindsey replaced Hatchett in 1955 and immediately took steps to try to restore the Arkansas State Police to its previous strength. The Fire Marshal's Office was abolished and was replaced by the Division of Fire Prevention.

In 1957, the legislature finally recognized the need for a strong state police and authorized an increase of 93 commissioned officers. The Driver's License Section was established for the first time, becoming operational in January 1958.

On August 17, 1958, Trooper Ermon B. Cox, of Osceola, and his 9-year-old son, Benny, were in their personal car when Cox spotted a suspected DWI and gave chase. William Luke Young fled to his home, armed himself and shot Cox, who was still in his car.

Benny ran for help. Young was arrested two hours later and executed October 2, 1959, in the electric chair at Tucker Prison Farm.

The Arkansas Law Enforcement Training Academy was established in 1961 at Petit Jean Mountain. Also, director was given the new title of "colonel," corresponding to military rank.

In 1963, the department had very little money. Troopers were required to "double-up" in their cars and drastic mileage restrictions were imposed. The legislature provided some relief in time for the opening of the new freeway system around Little Rock in September, 1963.

By 1966, the financial problems had been solved and the department had once again been reorganized. Trooper Harry Locke was killed in a one-vehicle accident east of Camden when his car failed to negotiate a curve.

In 1967, new Governor Winthrop Rockefeller reestablished the Motor Vehicle Inspection Division and purchased the Arkansas State Police's first airplane for traffic control. Lynn Davis succeeded Colonel Lindsey, who retired after 16 years as director. Davis resigned after 6 months and was replaced by Carl Miller.

Marion Taylor, Jr. became the first black state trooper in 1967. In February, 1968, Governor Rockefeller appointed Ralph Scott, of Camden, to take the place of Colonel Miller, who retired after 31 years with the State Police.

July 27, 1969, was another tragic date in the history of the department. Trooper Allen Bufford was shot by Jessie Ring, a passenger in a car Bufford stopped near Batesville. Ring, who was on parole for murder at the time of the shooting, was sentenced to life imprisonment.

In 1970, the districts of the ASP were given alphabetical designations, replacing the numerical system previously used. At that time, there were 10 districts in the state. The year ended with 389 officers and 122 civilians on the payroll. The annual budget was $5 million.

In 1971, the Arkansas State Police, under newly elected Governor Dale Bumpers, went under the Arkansas Department of Public Safety as the Police Services Division. Colonel Ralph Scott resigned and was replaced by W.C. "Bill" Miller. Colonel Miller reestablished the Criminal Investigation Division as a separate entity of the state police.

David Pryor became governor in 1975. Colonel Miller decided to retire and Douglas Harp was appointed to head the ASP. In that same year, Barbara Cart became the first female trooper, ending a 40-year "men only" tradition.

Trooper Ron Brooks died on February 27, 1975, while attempting to capture three escapees at Clarendon. Larry Hutcheson, of Truman, fired pointblank as Brooks was trying to cuff him. Hutcheson was sentenced to life in prison.

In 1976, Colonel Harp expanded the Fire Marshal's Office and the Drug Enforcement Section, giving them new importance.

Troop "L", in Springdale, was created in 1977, bringing the troops in the state to their present number of 12.

Sergeant Kelly Pigue was killed December 8, 1977, in a two-vehicle accident west of Wynne. A tractor-trailer rig went out of control in a driving rain and crossed into the path of Sergeant Pigue's car.

Another tradition fell by the wayside in 1978, when the Department scrapped the white and blue patrol cars, introducing the solid white vehicle which is used today.

On September 19, 1980, Sergeant Glen Bailey was pursuing a speeding vehicle near

West Memphis. Bailey called for roadblocks and Clay Anthony Ford of Memphis, Tennessee was stopped. Ford jumped from his car and shot Bailey, then fled the scene. Ford was captured a short time later. Bailey died in surgery in West Memphis. Ford, a convicted felon and an escapee, is currently on appeal from a death sentence.

Frank White was elected governor over incumbent Bill Clinton in 1980. In 1981, White assumed office. The economy in general, and the ASP in particular, were in deep financial trouble. The first of what were to become severe economic curtailments occurred when the legislature reduced the strength of the department by 25 people. The Department of Public Safety was abolished in 1981 and Douglas Harp resigned as colonel.

Thomas "Tommy" L. Goodwin, who had retired in 1977 after 22 years service, returned to the state police as colonel. Colonel Goodwin arrived in time to occupy the newly completed headquarters building which was dedicated that year in Little Rock.

Mileage restrictions were imposed in 1982 as a result of the ever-growing financial problems. They were not lifted until June 1983, when a supplemental appropriation eased the situation a bit.

Everyone knows the horror of 1984. What began as a normal year quickly turned into a nightmare that left nine police officers dead. One of those was Trooper Louis Bryant, who died June 30, 1984, near DeQueen. Bryant had apparently stopped a van driven by Richard Snell, a self-proclaimed survivalist, for a routine traffic violation.

Snell jumped from the van and shot Bryant twice before fleeing into Oklahoma where he was captured. Bryant died during surgery in DeQueen. Snell was shot 5 times during his capture.

On October 15, 1984, the nightmare continued when Trooper R.W. "Robbie" Klein was ambushed by two escapees he was trying to apprehend near Wrightsville. Klein died instantly from a shotgun blast to the face.

Arkansas State Police will always be in danger. Some will die. The fluctuations and expediencies of politics and the economy will bring financial problems. Good times will bring surges in growth. Governors, directors and troopers will come and go. It's all been done before, and it will be done again. One thing that remains constant is the dedication and pride that the words "Arkansas State Police" bring to mind.

California Highway Patrol

On August 4, 1929, the California Highway Patrol was created through an act of the Legislature. The new law gave statewide authority to the Highway Patrol to enforce traffic laws on country and state highways, a responsibility which remains in effect today, along with many additional functions undreamed of in 1929.

The primary mission of the California Highway Patrol is "the management and regulation of traffic to achieve safe, lawful, and efficient use of the highway transportation system." As a major statewide law enforcement agency, the secondary mission of the department is to assist in emergencies exceeding local capabilities. The CHP also provides disaster and lifesaving assistance.

During its first 10 years, the patrol successfully grew into a highly respected, effective traffic safety force of 730 uniformed personnel. After World War II, the Legislature decided to consolidate and reorganize the patrol's enforcement and administrative responsibilities. In October 1947, the Department of the California Highway Patrol was established and the position of commissioner was created to head the new department.

The span of enforcement responsibility has expanded dramatically and the CHP has continued to grow and change. Today's respon-

sibilities include truck and bus inspections, air operations (both airplanes and helicopters) and vehicle theft investigation and prevention. The 1995 merger with the California State Police also increased the areas of responsibility to include protection of state property and employees, the governor and other dignitaries.

In addition to its enforcement responsibilities, the department has taken a leadership role in educating the public concerning driver safety issues. The CHP has received state and national recognition for its innovative public awareness campaigns promoting use of safety belts, a designated driver when drinking, securing small children in safety seats and wearing motorcycle and bicycle helmets.

For many years, the concept of consolidating the California State Police (CSP) with the California Highway Patrol (CHP) had been discussed and then shelved. In recent years, reductions in state fiscal resources and a focused effort to streamline government agencies and operations prompted a revival of the CSP/CHP consolidation concept.

In March 1994 Governor Pete Wilson directed Dean R. Dunphy, Secretary of Business, Transportation, and Housing Agency (BT&H), to officially evaluate the feasibility of consolidation. A preliminary fiscal analysis was prepared by the CHP to determine if merging the

two departments could achieve an increased level of public safety and service without higher costs. The analysis proved favorable and a formal consolidation proposal was prepared for Governor Wilson, including an additional report for the governor to present to the Milton Marks Commission on California State Government Organization and Economy (Little Hoover Commission). Preliminary indicators also showed bipartisan support in the Legislature for CSP/CHP consolidation.

CHP's Executive Staff directed the Offices of Primary Interest (OPIs) to establish a liaison with their respective counterparts in the CSP. Initial contacts were conducted with the understanding that consolidation might not take place, but to establish an information base in the event the plan was approved by the Legislature. State police management also began preliminary preparations for a possible merger, including developing a "transition manual," with a detailed overview of CSP activities, administration, responsibilities, and organizational structure. Governor Wilson wanted an economic and structural reorganization that would establish an entity capable of providing the highest levels of law enforcement service for the public, state employees, and state facilities. His goal was to gain legislative approval and complete the consolidation process by July 1, 1995. The CHP immediately formed a CSP/CHP "transition team" to concentrate on achieving the governor's objective and target date. A key element for consideration was maintenance of the current public safety services performed by the CSP while incorporating those services into the existing structure of the CHP.

The Little Hoover Commission held a public hearing on March 16, 1995, and the consolidation proposal was unanimously approved after testimony from BT&H Secretary Dean R. Dunphy, CHP Commissioner Maury Hannigan, and then Deputy Commissioner Dwight "Spike" Helmick, with additional presentations made by CSP Chief Duane Lowe and representatives of the Department of General Services, CSP Association and the California Union of Safety Employees.

The CHP's Office of Special Representative formalized the written language of the governor's reorganization plan to modify sections of the government code and other codes required by the consolidation. Final legislative action came in the form of an assembly resolution in support of the merger.

On July 12, 1995, 271 uniformed officers of the State Police became part of the 5,713

Harley-Davidson FXRP

BMW RIIOORT

CHP Officer and Canine partner.

sworn officers of the Highway Patrol. The 68 non-uniformed employees of the CSP transferred to existing civil service classifications, with the exception of CSP's Communication Operators who were assimilated into the CHP's Communications Operator II classification. The 269 uniformed personnel changed from California State Police classifications to new CHP classifications established specifically for the consolidation. In order to complete this transition of former CSP personnel into CHP classifications, a comprehensive three-phase training program was developed. This training was designed to provide CSP personnel with the tools necessary to successfully perform the full range of the new duties for CHP classifications. Mandatory courses ranging from four days to three weeks were implemented for both uniformed and non-uniformed staff, including field orientation periods for specified classifications. Almost all CSP personnel successfully transitioned into CHP's corresponding rank structure and now receive the same pay and benefits. The merger did not increase CHP's uniformed personnel strength beyond the addition of the authorized CSP staffing level. As a result, the CHP assumed responsibility only for those services which were provided by the CSP at the time of consolidation. In June 1995, all state agencies/departments were provided with details about the merger and the enforcement responsibilities assumed by the CHP. Local police departments and sheriff's offices were also contacted to discuss procedures for responding to calls on state facilities located in their jurisdictions. The CHP continued several contracts for expanded services, including the following state facilities:

•Department of Motor Vehicles, patrol services on a full-time basis for the Hope Street office in Los Angeles; security services at hearings.

•Employment Development Department, patrol services on a full-time basis at unemployment offices in Los Angeles and the Bay Area; security services at hearings.

•Board of Equalization, serving tax seizure and arrest warrants; Franchise Tax Board serving tax seizure and arrest warrants.

•California Courts of Appeal, providing security services at hearings.

•Department of Water Resources, maintaining six field offices dedicated the State Water Project including both ground and air surveillance services. Contract expired December 1995.

•Department of Consumer Affairs, providing security services at hearings.

•Department of Transportation, providing police services at the Transbay Transit Terminal located in San Francisco.

The CHP will also provide dignitary protection services for the following agencies: Secretary of State, State Treasurer's Office, State Controller's Office, State Superintendent of Public Instruction and Department of Insurance.

The CHP is also currently in the process of cataloging every state-owned building and facility in California to provide a resource for dispatching officers to service calls.

One of the key benefits of the CSP/CHP consolidation was efficiencies in governmental expenditures and operations. Preliminary fiscal analysis, however, indicated that there would be both costs and savings associated with the merger although it was originally anticipated that most of the savings would be immediate while many of the costs would be spread over several years.

The fiscal profile initially developed showed costs/savings in two main categories: (1) personnel services and (2) operating expenses and equipment. During the fiscal planning for the merger, the CHP estimated it could

realize substantial savings in equipment and operating expenses; however, fiscal problems developed in three primary areas:

1) Communications: Unanticipated costs were incurred to update and repair CSP telecommunications equipment to ensure its compatibility with existing CHP equipment. Unplanned costs also resulted with the re-establishment of CSR radio communications operations in TIP Dispatch Centers. Originally, plans called for consolidation of the CSR/TIP Dispatch Centers after the first year; however, due to operational issues the centers were consolidated as soon as feasible.

2) Facilities: Savings in the rental of facilities did not occur at the same rate as initially anticipated, although all but four facilities were vacated and operations assimilated into TIP facilities. The department was required to continue rental payments for a longer period of time than expected after vacating some buildings owned and controlled by the Department of General Services.

3) Equipment: The CHP anticipated that CSP vehicles owned by the Department of General Services would be transferred during the merger at no additional cost to the department, however, the CHP was required to purchase the vehicles from DGS to maintain the existing level of service. The consolidation, however, has resulted in undetermined savings by reducing redundancies, including vacating 12 leased facilities, eliminating duplicate contracts for services, and streamlining contracts for law enforcement services. The primary focus of the Highway Patrol has always been California's freeways and the highways in the unincorporated areas of our state, but the merger with the CSP has changed and broadened the scope of the department. The CHP now assumes the responsibilities of protecting the governor and other constitutional officers, as well as everyone who works in or visits a

state building. To accomplish this new mission, the CHP has absorbed and integrated the following CSP units into its organizational structure:

Office of Dignitary Protection (ODP): The reorganization merely placed ODP under the CHP but its role did not change. ODP provides protection to state constitutional officers and other dignitaries as appropriate or provided for under contractual agreements. ODP is also responsible for the department's Explosive Ordinance Unit and dignitary threat assessments/investigations.

Office of Capitol Services (OCAPS): OCAPS, formerly known as the CSP Capitol Corps, is responsible for providing security and protection on the grounds of the State Capitol, including the Legislative Office Building adjacent to the Capitol. The department's Equestrian and Bicycle Units are assigned to OCAPS as well. Additionally, OCAPS is responsible for coordinating security efforts with the Senate and Assembly Sergeants-at-Arms for security of the Legislature.

Office of Court Services (OCS): OCS consolidates reimbursable court security services provided throughout the state under one command. Pending final contractual approvals, OCS will be responsible for providing security services to the Supreme and Appellate Courts at various locations in California although it will be headquartered at the Supreme Court in San Francisco. On July 12, 1995, when the Highway Patrol assumed the authority and responsibilities formerly held by the state police, a "changing-of-the-guard" ceremony was held at the CHP Academy in West Sacramento to commemorate an organization that had provided 108 years of service to the state of California. The CSP/CHP merger offers advantages to the citizens of California through better service, greater protection and reduced expenditures. In the same way that the CHP has always trained its officers to consider no traffic stop as "routine," the responsibility for the security of people working in state buildings will never be taken lightly. With the increased resources of the CHP behind them, state employees and facilities will be safer than ever before. Most states have one governmental law enforcement agency and now California joins this group. The CHP confidently accepts this expanded role because the Highway Patrol will now be able to provide a level of service even beyond that which has always been defined for the department - the emphasis is unchanged; the one constant is how well the CHP will serve the public.

Aerospatiale 350 BA.

Cessna 185 Skywagon.

Bell 206 L3 Long Ranger.

Colorado Highway Patrol

The first administrator or "Chief" of the Colorado State Highway Courtesy Patrol was Joseph J. Marsh. Chief Marsh directed the Colorado Courtesy Patrol in its first years until the advent of World War II. In 1942, he served his country in the uniform of the United States Army, leaving the direction of the patrol to Vernon Drain. Returning in 1946, Marsh served as Chief of the patrol until May 1, 1947, when he retired. Chief Marsh died from a heart attack in 1972.

During the World War II absence of Chief Administrator Joseph Marsh, Captain Vernon Drain was appointed as Acting Chief of the Colorado State Highway Courtesy Patrol. Drain, one of the original members of the Colorado State Highway Courtesy Patrol, attained the rank of Captain while serving as the driver for Governor Ralph Carr, and was appointed to fill this vacancy until 1946 when Chief Marsh returned, assuming control. Drain who left the department in 1946 died March 12, 1951 at the age of 40.

In August of 1935, efforts were underway to select thirty-five men out of 6,000 applicants for the State Highway Courtesy Patrol. The Patrol Board was composed of E. E. Wheeler, chairman of the State Public Utilities Commission, Charles D. Vail, Chief Engineer of the State Highway Department, and James H. Carr, Secretary of State. Carr advocated that 55 men be selected and paid $100 for a month of training at the rifle range near Golden, during which twenty of the men could be weeded out, leaving only those with proper qualifications being retained to constitute the patrol.

About the time the Act was to go into effect, and plans were being formulated for the patrol, a controversy arose between two factions with some believing that the courtesy patrolmen should be armed just as any policing body was expected to be. Another segment believed just as strongly that the new Courtesy Patrol should not be armed, and additionally, should not be issued automobiles but should be limited to motorcycles only. The latter group had a powerful leader in the person of the Governor of Colorado, Ed C. Johnson who made it clear, when by official decree, he announced that as long as he was in office, the patrolmen would go about their duties unarmed and would ride motorcycles, not the automobiles requested by the board. The Governor turned down requests for appropriations for the 19 automobiles and Sam Browne belts and side arms, all of which were submitted by the patrol board.

During the month of September, 1935, plans for establishing a training camp for the State Highway Courtesy Patrol were made by the patrol board, and Joseph Marsh, supervisor of the patrol. The board also agreed upon patrol stations at Greenley, Pueblo, Alamosa, and Grand Junction, with the central station to be located at 1308 Lincoln Street in Denver. The patrol, mounted on motorcycles and attired in horizon blue and gray uniforms, was expected to appear on the highways in 30 days. The question of whether the men should be armed was still debated among state officials with Governor Ed C. Johnson saying that he saw no reason why the men should be armed. Other state officials adopted the opposite view.

Despite opposition from Governor Johnson, the State Highway Courtesy Patrol Board obtained sufficient authorization to order 19 automobiles for the use of the patrol. For a short time, only two members of the executive council had agreed to sign the requisition to equip the patrol with revolvers. Three signatures were required, and another signature was finally obtained. The revolvers were then issued.

The original headquarters for the patrol were located at 1308 Lincoln Street, Denver. In a short time, the patrol moved its headquarters to 1244 Broadway in Denver, providing more room for the department to expand.

The uniform worn by the first class was designed to represent the State of Colorado as much as possible. The uniform consisted of sky blue cap, shirt and blouse to match Colorado skies, silver-gray slacks for the silver industry; gold badge, cap ornament, blouse buttons, and belt buckle for the gold industry; and black trouser stripe, boots, Sam Browne belt and holster for the coal industry. At first, the Sam Browne belt was white when reversed for wear at night for easier visibility, but the

white segment was eliminated after a short trial period. Since the blouse was worn at all times while on duty, there was no need for a shoulder patch on the uniform shirt.

By 1946, through various acts of the legislature, the patrol had a personnel complement of a chief, deputy chief, nine captains, 10 sergeants, and 100 patrolmen. This included the State Auto Theft Division, and the Inspection Division. This decade saw a number of changes as the military brought home the troops following the war. Factories switched back to making cars and trucks instead of jeeps and tanks. Police communications improved as military technology became more available and affordable to Law Enforcement Agencies.

Colorado State Patrol's third chief, Gilbert R. Carrel, was a member of the original Colorado State Courtesy Patrol. Carrel joined the patrol on September 23, 1935, serving the first year of his patrol career in Denver. In February 1936, he moved to Grand Junction as captain in charge of the area, and returned to Denver in 1938 as deputy chief.

During World War II, Carrel entered the military and was in a Seabee unit. Following his return from the war in February, 1946, Carrel returned to his Patrol job as Deputy Chief. On May 15, 1947, he was appointed Chief of the Colorado State Patrol. Chief Carrel retired from the Colorado State Patrol on July 29, 1972, at the age of 66, serving the department for 36 years. Carrel died February 7, 1988.

Deputy Chief James Cole became undersheriff of Arapahoe County Sheriff's Office in 1926, and held this position until 1936, when he applied for the newly formed Colorado State Courtesy Patrol, and was accepted on May 1, 1936. Cole was promoted to Deputy Chief of the Colorado State Patrol on May 15, 1947, and retired on July 31, 1966. Deputy

1960 Ford and Patrolman Goudy.

Chief Cole died October 1, 1969, at the age of 71.

In 1954, Governor Ed C. Johnson returned for another term as governor of Colorado. Since Johnson was governor in 1935, and helped with the start up of the Colorado State Patrol, he took a close interest in its future. By an act of law in 1945, the name of the Colorado State Highway Courtesy Patrol was changed to Colorado State Highway Patrol. Johnson wanted to change the name of the patrol back to its original name, but his plan failed to get the necessary support, and the idea was dropped.

The 1955 legislature increased the patrol strength to 200 patrolmen, 12 corporals, 13 sergeants, 10 captains, a deputy chief, and a chief. At this time, the legislature also transferred the Port-of-Entry Division to the Department of Revenue, thereby releasing 12 port officers for patrol duty.

The specific duties of the state patrol (as described in 1949) were to promote safety, protect human life, and to preserve the highways of the State of Colorado. Investigating traffic accidents, providing first aid, enforcing motor vehicle laws and stopping to assist motorist were the most well known tasks a patrolmen performed. However, numerous other jobs have been performed over the years as well.

On March 17, 1950, Mary Ellen Sposato became the first woman hired by the Colorado State Patrol when she started as a telephone operator. Since this was the beginning of the Korean War, Mrs. Bonnie Wright became the second woman when she was hired in 1951.

In 1947, the familiar seven-pointed gold star, replica of the badge of office, was

placed on the doors of the patrol cars. In 1948, black was dropped from the color scheme, and the cars became the familiar white now in use. A single torpedo type overhead red light with siren mounted on the roof was quite effective except when the siren froze during wet and cold weather.

Around 1949, the current shoulder patch was placed on the uniform shirt. Before this time, wearing the bloused jacket had been mandatory. When it became optional, the leather jacket appeared and the need for a patch on the uniform shirt was necessary. During the same year, the wearing of the tie changed from outside the shirt to tucking in the tie. This provided increased officer safety, as a violator couldn't use the tie to attempt to control the officer.

On March 29, 1950, the Colorado State Patrol Headquarters moved to 1950 31st Street. The new building provided considerably more space, and the automotive shop was also expanded to include a front end alignment machine, thus allowing the shop to begin doing most major automotive repairs. This location served until 1954, when it became obvious that the patrol headquarters again needed to expand. The Highway Department made plans for construction of a new complex at 4201 East Arkansas, and the patrol moved into its new quarters in September 1955.

Growth and technology symbolized the third decade of the patrol. In 1959, Governor McNichols signed a bill increasing the Colorado Highway Patrol by 100 men to a total strength of 335. This large increase in the patrol's complement translated to additional duties and the need for more training. Patrol cars were better equipped; radar units were used in unmarked cars; communications equipment was upgraded; and the patrol moved forward with this new technology.

In 1956, patrol vehicles consisted of various makes of cars with the majority being Ford Interceptors. There were 156 passenger cars and 20 motorcycles being used for highway patrolling. In addition, the patrol had nine pickups, one panel car, one power wagon, five snow cats with trailers, one welding equipment trailer, one power plant trailer, and one Cessna Apache airplane.

With the exception of a few pieces of unmarked equipment, all patrol vehicles were painted white, and were identified by a large gold replica of the patrol badge on each side of the cardoors.

In 1960, the Colorado State Patrol adopted the present door emblem, a replica of the hat ornament, a motorcycle tire with the winged design. This "Flying Wheel" door emblem was designed by Captain Hockey. In 1965, the patrol received 123 Plymouth Furys which were constructed to patrol specifications.

During this decade, the uniform consisted of a blue cap with a black and white cord, replacing the sky-blue cap that was worn in previous years. A black waist length leather jacket was also worn, along with Army pink slacks trimmed with a one and one-quarter inch black stripe. In addition, officers used a gold wheel and wings cap ornament, a yellow rain slicker, and a white cap cover. In 1956, members began wearing collar brass on the uniform shirt, and in 1959, service bars and stars became part of the uniform, indicating years of service with the patrol. The name plate was added in 1960.

Several legislative changes occurred in the fourth decade that affected the operation of the patrol in that decade, and are still in effect today. In 1966, Deputy Chief Cole retired, and Richard Schippers was promoted to deputy chief. Born in Portland Oregon, Schippers came to Colorado in 1937, and applied for the Colorado State Courtesy Patrol. He was accepted in 1938, and his first assignment was with the Ports of Welcome. Enlisting in the Army in 1941, Schippers was discharged in 1945, returned to the patrol, and was stationed in Grand Junction. He was later assigned to Las Animas, promoted to Corporal, and then transferred to Trinidad. Upon the retirement of Deputy Chief James Cole on June 1, 1966, Richard Schippers was named as Deputy Chief of the Colorado State Patrol, a position which he held until his retirement on July 22, 1975.

Colorado State Patrol's fourth Chief, C. Wayne Keith, was born in Grand Junction. After completing school, Keith worked for an oil company in California until the advent of World War II. Following completion of his military obligation, Keith applied for the Colorado State Highway Patrol, and was accepted. He began his service with the patrol in 1946 at the Port of Entry in Limon, remaining there until mid summer. He was then assigned to Patrol duty in Steamboat Springs, and after a year, was transferred to Montrose. The long hours and rugged duty took a toll on Patrolman Keith's health. Medical tests revealed that he had contacted a form of tuberculosis through his wartime duties. Keith took

a three year medical leave from the patrol, and after a slow recuperation period was reinstated with the highway patrol. Following Chief Carrel's announcement of his retirement, numerous officers applied for the position. After testing, Keith was appointed chief of the Colorado State Patrol in May of 1972, serving in this position until his retirement on March 1, 1983.

The fifth decade was a busy and exciting time for the patrol. The year 1976 brought the celebration of America's 200th birthday, and the 100th anniversary of the State of Colorado. Uniformed personnel wore their ties outside instead of the usual tucked-in look and donned a Centennial-Bicentennial tie pin. This decade was also a time of major changes, as Chief Keith retired, and John Dempsey became the new Chief. The Colorado State Patrol even transferred from the Department of Highways to the newly created Department of Public Safety.

The fifth person to serve as the chief of the Colorado State Patrol, John N. Dempsey, joined the Colorado State Patrol on May 19, 1965. After his initial training, Dempsey was stationed as a patrolman in Grand Junction, where he remained until October 1, 1972, at which time he was promoted to sergeant and transferred to Broomfield. Following the retirement of Chief C. Wayne Keith, Dempsey was promoted to chief of the Colorado State Patrol on March 21, 1983.

In 1984, there was a change of administrative departments for the Colorado State Patrol. The patrol was moved from the Colorado Department of Highways to the Colorado Department of Public Safety, leaving a void in the leadership of the Colorado Bureau of Investigation, which was also an agency of the Department of Public Safety. The Director of the Department of Public Safety appointed Chief Dempsey temporarily as Director of the Colorado Bureau of Investigation. Dempsey held this position until a permanent CBI director was named. In July of 1986, Governor Lamm appointed John Dempsey as acting director for the Colorado Department of Corrections. Dempsey served in this position for seven months.

Officer safety is a major concern for Chief Dempsey, and he makes sure that all officers have the best possible training. He continues to purchase state-of-the-art equipment for both the safety of his officers and efficiency of the patrol.

Throughout the years, many programs were initiated by the patrol. Of all these programs, the one attracting the most attention by opposing group was REDDI, which was started in 1980. REDDI stands for "Report Every Drunken Driver Immediately," and was implemented to get drunk drivers off the roadways.

In the first three years, over 23,000 REDDI calls were received, and 5,000 stops were made with the arrest of over 2,800 drivers charged with driving while intoxicated. This program proved to be very effective in bringing the drunk driving issue into the public's eyes, and greatly increasing the odds of arrest for an intoxicated driver.

Specialization is a term that best symbolizes the sixth decade. Patrol members today have specialized areas of expertise. Some of these areas include hazardous materials enforcement and response, criminal interdiction, auto theft, and felony accident investigation. Members remains proficient because they are provided with on-going training and state-of-the-art equipment.

A new retirement bill, HB 1057, was signed into law on April 6, 1989 by Governor Roy Romer. The unusual thing about HB 1057 (the Reduced Penalty Retirement for Colorado State Troopers) was that as it wound its way through the legislative system, there were no amendments. The sponsors and PPA's lobbyist were able to get the bill to Governor Romer for his signature without any changes. In addition, HB 1057 received overwhelming support by the General Assembly, with a final vote count of 95 in favor, three opposed, and two absent.

In 1987, Colorado was one of only two states outside California selected to pilot the Drug Recognition Expert (DRE) program. This proven program enabled specially trained officers to identify suspects under the influence of drugs other than alcohol. Programs in many states began with training provided by instructors from the Colorado State Patrol.

In May 1992, the rank of lieutenant colonel was established. The lieutenant's rank was abolished. Lieutenants became captains, captains became majors, and majors became lieutenant colonels.

In July 1994, Lora Thomas was the first woman to be sworn in as a troop commander. She was assigned as captain for the Limon troop.

Changes in the patrol uniform during this decade included the earing of the commando style sweater, authorized for use in the late 1980s. On March 23, 1990, a change in policy stated that the long sleeve shirt and tie were no longer required during the winter months. The use of the "soft uniform" by the HAZMAT and MCSAP teams was authorized in the spring of 1993.

Prior to 1991, the Colorado State Patrol was using the Smith & Wesson Model 686 revolver. In January, 1991, the patrol sold all existing pistols in their inventory, and replaced them with the Smith & Wesson Model 5906 and Model 3913 semiautomatic pistols, which use a 9MM Luger cartridge. Some Smith & Wesson Model 422 semiautomatic pistols chambered for the .22 Long Rifle cartridge were also purchased for training purposes.

In 1991, the patrol acquired a state of the art vehicle designed and built to provide a Mobile Emergency Communication Center. Costing nearly $300,000, the van was purchased with drug money seized by the State Patrol, Eagle County Sheriff's Office, and the Drug Enforcement Administration. The van, capable of transmitting and receiving 120 radio channels, in addition to Red Cross, local government, CB, Aircraft, and Amateur radio frequencies, is completely self contained, and can function as a central command post.

In May of 1994, the patrol adopted a new hiring process; allowing people to apply for trooper positions anytime during the year rather than waiting for announcements twice a year. The applicant has more flexibility since he or she is responsible for setting appointments for the testing and interviews.

The CLETA (Colorado Law Enforcement Training Academy) was dissolved in April of 1992, and the name was changed to the Colorado State Patrol Training Academy which became a branch of the patrol. An intensive 21 week training course is given to all cadets at the patrol academy.

Connecticut State Police

Connecticut State Police will mark their 100th anniversary on July 1, 2003. As the oldest state police department in the country, the Connecticut State Police have established a proud and enviable record in law enforcement. Conceived during Connecticut's "horse and buggy" days, the department has grown into a modern public safety organization. In recognition of the skill and integrity of the men and women of the Connecticut State Police, governors and state legislators have repeatedly expanded the duties of the department and have called upon its members to "protect and serve" in many new and challenging ways. The list of today's responsibilities goes far beyond anything envisioned in the earliest days.

The simplest measures of state police success comes from the citizens of Connecticut. The department has become so much a part of Connecticut life that the people of Connecticut expect, and often demand, state police involvement in often diverse matters of safety and well-being. The willingness of the people to include state police in so much of their lives is a fair indicator of a job well done. Connecticut trusts its state police for services as urgent as searching for a lost child, and as progressive as providing the latest in law enforcement technology.

The reputation enjoyed by Connecticut State Police has been earned each day during a long, proud history. Traditions passed from generation to generation have remained constant with pride and integrity leading the list. These simple ideals come before all concerns and serve as a guide for the future. All change is measured against the traditions of our past. This is not to say the state police have not been open to new ideas. The history of the department reflects a growth and progress based on the willingness to change. Connecticut State Police have adopted policies, techniques and technologies that are often well ahead of the rest of the law enforcement community.

In 1903 Connecticut was far different from the Connecticut now approaching the 21st century. The population was slightly more than 900,000 and the people lived simpler lives centered around farming in mostly rural communities. Terms such as Interstate highway, forensic science, and gang violence would not become part of the everyday language for at least 50 years.

Today's urban sprawl and super highways make Connecticut life at the start of the century seem idyllic, if not perfect. However, every generation needs to contend with crimes of its era. Concerns about the illegal sale of alcohol and all the related social problems were as real to the Connecticut Yankee of 1903 as gang violence is to today's Nutmegger. Just as modern Connecticut struggles for solutions to present lawlessness, people at the turn of the century sought answers to their crime problems.

The solution put forth in 1903 was legislation creating a state police. The idea was not entirely new, but as an idea, it had been put into practice. Massachusetts had appointed a number of constables having statewide jurisdiction as early as 1865 and the Texas Rangers acted as a quasi-military unit while Texas was an independent Republic in 1835.

The State Treasury provided $13,737.59 in funding to cover all Department expenses during the first fiscal year ending June 30, 1904. The commissioners of the state police voted that the state policemen would be required to provide themselves with a uniform for wear during formal state occasions. The uniform would consist of blue clothes with brass buttons. However, most of the work was done in plain clothes. Nonetheless, buttons, badges, and handcuffs represented the single largest non-salary expense that year; $138 was spent on these items. Running a close second, office supplies amounted to $129.

Before any direct instruction from the Legislature, state police would begin an ac-

Last pictures of Comissioner Hickey before his death. Seated is Gov. John Lodge signing 20 year pension bill which Comissioner Hickey worked hard in passing. July 1953. Three senior troopers look on.

The first FM two-way radio was invented and used in Connecticut. Fred Link, refers to the gift he gave Connecticut as "his baby". His friend retired CSP Trooper Dean Hammond stands with him.

1954 Trooper Richard Chapman, Troop B.

The restored 1941 Ford. Sgt. James Rodgers (Ret) wearing 1941 uniform.

tivity destined to play a major role in the life of every trooper from every generation thereafter. An unknown state policeman made the first arrest for a "violation of highway law" in Chester in 1908. The automobile's popularity had begun to grow and, to the Connecticut Yankee of 1908, traffic was becoming a problem. The 1,500 or so registered cars of the day would pale in comparison to the typical slowdown at today's highway construction sites, but for the fortunate few of 1908 who owned cars, motor vehicle laws were to be obeyed.

State police seem to have had an affinity for motor vehicle law from the onset. The often touted state police "crackdown" was under way for three years before the Legislature mandated department involvement. With speed limits approaching an outrageous eight miles per hour, state police bought four Henderson motorcycles to pursue would be violators. Model "T" Fords followed shortly after. Visibility has always been considered a

factor in motor vehicle enforcement, and, following the complaint of the Legislature that no one ever saw a state policeman, the order was given to remove the canvas tops from department cars. Thereafter, state policemen could be seen making their rounds in snow and rain in the Model "T" version of a convertible.

The 1921 Legislature increased the department's authorized strength from 15 to 50 officers, "all of whom should be uniformed and provided with firearms and motor vehicles." On January 4, 1922, the first complete state police uniforms were issued and the original badges were replaced with a badge style that is the same as today. Many of the original badges issued in 1922 were still being worn by troopers in 1998.

The first training academy was assembled at the Boxwood Manor Inn in Old Lyme on November 7, 1921. Following a three-week course, the graduates were equipped with uniforms, a firearm, and a motor vehicle. Making it through the academy was only half the test; the new state policemen were "placed on probation to test their fitness for police work." The hardships of the early state police must have appealed to few and only the most uncommon of men were attracted to the service. As a newspaper reported in 1935 in an article about recruit training, "Some of them may find they do not like police work as it is carried on by the state police who are on call 24 hours a day, who must live in barracks most of the time with little opportunity for family life, and who maintain lonely patrols in all kinds of weather."

By the year 1927, the department had 108 motorcycles along with 89 Ford cars and 15 larger cars.

The uniformed state policeman on a motorcycle had been a regular sight in many towns, and signs would be hung from roadside poles to tell him the station needed to speak with him. There was no such thing as a "secure line" because all calls of the day were made on party lines. In 1928 the first state police private line telephone typewriter system was installed to connect all stations with Headquarters. Other departments and states were later added and the National Police Communications Network was established.

One-way AM radio systems were in use by city police departments by the late 1920s, but the system was not workable for patrolmen in outlying regions. The department was not satisfied with the limitations of the AM system and sought technological help from the University of Connecticut. Once the first three-way mobile statewide system in the world came along, communications from station to car, car to station, and car to car were possible. A plaque commemorating this milestone in two-way radio technology was rededicated at the new Connecticut State Police Headquarters in Middleton in May 1997.

In 50 years the department had grown from "not less than five nor more than 10 members" to an organization of more than 500 dedicated sworn and civilian personnel. Floods, traffic safety programs, and Supreme Court cases would keep the department in the limelight throughout the 50s. One single event would change department life thereafter. On Jan. 1, 1958, the Connecticut Turnpike was opened to motorists. To meet the anticipated increase in traffic, another 100 state police were added. Responsibility for the "big road" would require new barracks, Westbrook.

The onset of the '60s offered no clues as to what would become the most turbulent decade of the century. In June 1961 the first Black American was appointed as a state policeman. Albert Washington Jr. was a 30-year-old Branford police officer and had placed second among 800 applicants competing for appointment. The first Black state policewoman, Louise Smith, took the oath of office in November 1968.

Working conditions continued to improve during the 60s. In May 1963 troopers were working an average of 63 hours per week. A bill introduced at the Legislature cut the work week to 50 hours. Beginning in August 1966,

state police were paid overtime for work in excess 10 hours a day.

The original state police effort into forensics began in 1935 when the Bureau of Identification was created. Throughout the years state police emphasis on forensics would intensify. In 1979 the Crime Laboratory was renamed the Connecticut State Forensic Laboratory, and Doctor Henry C. Lee was appointed as the first Connecticut State Criminalist.

On June 22, 1977, the General Assembly passed a law that would create the Department of Public Safety on January 1, 1979. State police were designated the lynch pin in this consolidation of the Office of Civil Preparedness, the Military Department, the Municipal Police Training Council, and Board of Firearms Examiners. Many state policemen feared the department was going to be overwhelmed by public safety, but those fears were unfounded.

On December 1994 State Police Headquarters moved from 100 Washington Street, Hartford, to a new home to be called "Midpoint," off I-91 in Middletown.

Connecticut, in 1982, was the first State Police Department to issue 9mm Berettas to its troopers, a decision which would result in the saving of several troopers' lives over the

next 14 years. While far superior to previous firearms, it was determined in more recent years that "the 9mm caliber bullet had not performed as well as expected in several recent shooting situations." In order to give troopers "the best possible state-of-the-art equipment available..." the department, under Commissioner Kirschner, replaced the Berettas with .40 caliber SIG Model P229 pistols. New Mossley Model 500 shotguns replaced the Remmington Model 11-87 semi-automatics used since the 1980s. Also, distinguishing them in August of 1995, Connecticut Troopers were awarded top honors for "best dressed in the nation," for the second time in 10 years.

Ninety-four years of history have focused on the handful of men that have reached the top, and several as the focal point during each era. Each man's appointment to commissioner represents a great personal accomplishment, but their contributions to a certain degree are insignificant when compared to even the newest trooper. The reputation of the Connecticut State Police has been, and will always be, built on the day-in and day-out working of the individual trooper. Every man and woman that has ever worn the badge has made history where it counts: with the citizens of the state of Connecticut.

1927 Station #2, North Canaan, Connecticut. Office & living quarters were located on second floor above telephone office. Operators would take calls and leave messages at business places throughout the area. Troopers Hugh Meade, Steven Stanton, Leonard Watson and Fred Mignerey. Sgt. Fred Brandt, Station Commander, is on far right.

Delaware State Police

The roaring 20s gave birth to the Delaware State Police. Cars speeding at 35 miles per hour, roving bands of troublemakers and bootleggers provided the impetus. The result of these factors led to the beginning, in 1923, of a state police force in Delaware.

Thoughts on the topic of forming a state police organization for the first state had been recorded as early as 1906. Although interest existed, little, if any, positive steps were taken until the State Highway Commission was formed in 1917. As construction of paved highways was begun and registered motor vehicles began to rise, a need to regulate and maintain safety soon became apparent.

The first traffic law enforcement officers were given the auspicious title of "Highway Traffic Police." Started in 1919, the HTP consisted of one officer whose sole function was to patrol the Philadelphia Pike near Wilmington. In the following year the force was increased to three men and three motorcycles. From 1920 to 1923, these men served directly under the State Highway Commission. However, the winds of change were on the near horizon.

Governor William Denney addressed the General Assembly on January 3, 1923, and during his message stated, "In my judgment the Police Force of the Highway Department is not adequate... I desire to suggest that a state police force be organized..." On April 23, 1923, the General Assembly, at the request of the State Highway Department, enacted two laws that created the Delaware State Police. This date marks the official organization of the present law enforcement organization.

The first state police station was located on the southbound side of the Philadelphia Pike at Bellevue. It was an old construction shack that served both as the station and as headquarters. This building housed 14 men who worked 12-hour shifts, seven days a week. From this single location the officers policed the entire state. One day each week an officer was assigned to make what was known as the State Patrol. His tour would start at Claymont, Delaware, the northernmost postal area where the postmaster would stamp his daily sheet. He would then travel south through all three counties, stopping at all the post offices in route. Upon reaching the southern Delaware-Maryland line, he would make a return trip.

A major step in reducing the time for communication of the needs of the public to the police occurred in July 1924, with the adoption of a flag system. Forty-two service (gas) stations were selected throughout the state and their telephone numbers published in the *Wilmington Evening Journal*. Anyone wishing to see a police officer could call the nearest store or station or store attendant who would display a red flag in front of his business. The officer on patrol, seeing the flag, would stop to determine the nature of the complaint. In this manner the public received prompt service (prompt meaning from 1-12 hours).

Officers remained on the road year-round, regardless of rain, snow, or freezing temperatures. Several lost their legs in accidents before the economy permitted the purchase of patrol cars. During 1924-25, the state police facilities were expanded to encompass five locations spanning the length of the state. Police stations were located at the following points: Penny Hill, Station 1; State Road, Station 2; Dover, Station 3; Georgetown, Station 4; Bridgeville, Station 5.

In 1925 the Division realized an increase in manpower and the inauguration of 24-hour service to provide increased protection and better service to the public. In the same year, the Canine Unit was first established to respond to an increase in prowler complaints.

From its inception, the Delaware State Police has attempted to be at the leading edge of innovation. The establishment of a Canine Unit in 1925 is but one in a multitudinal list of accomplishments to provide the best service and protection to the citizens of the state of Delaware. A scanning of the decades provides an indication of how the state police have attempted to be innovative throughout its history.

•**1930-39:** In 1931 the name of the organization, by act of the General Assembly, was officially changed from "state highway police" to "state police." The year 1934 saw the first teletype service that linked the state police with similar agencies in eight states. This was the first outlet with outside agencies other than by mail or telephone. The Bureau of Identification was established at Penny Hill in 1935 as a means of both identification and assistance in criminal investigations. In 1939 the Bureau was moved to Dover and was the foundation for today's State Bureau of Identification.

To reduce the time between receipt of a complaint and arrival of the officer, the first radio communications were established in 1936. Though communications were strictly one-way, the officer received the complaint in a more timely manner. The year 1938 brought an end for the use of motorcycle patrol work. Sidecars had been available to a few officers who had been fortunate to patrol "in style." Twenty-four men joined the force in that same year, thus doubling the size of the organization. In response to the agency's growth and the increase in criminal activity, the division was divided into two sections, Traffic and Criminal.

•**1940-49:** In 1940 the Bureau of Accident Prevention and Traffic Control was established. This unit was responsible for making a thorough study of all accidents and recommending steps to prevent them. In 1941 the Traffic Division acquired a key punch machine that increased the Division's ability to analyze traffic data. To relieve the shortage of manpower caused by World War II, seven women were hired in 1943 to assist with clerical duties. Civilian employees, since this point, have played an integral role in the development of the state police. During the years 1942-43, the Division expanded its communications capabilities. It initiated high frequency communications that enabled two-way radio transmission and reception.

On November 1, 1945, the state police established a system of coding messages. This was the grandfather of the 1973 Public Safety (Ten Code) Code. Also in 1945, a new type of recording device was purchased for use by the Criminal Investigation Division. This instru-

Delaware State Police.

Delaware State Police.

ment recorded sound on film for use with microphones, the telephone, and radio conversations. The year 1946 saw the state police secure an Emergency Field Unit capable of responding to a variety of situations encountered by field officers. Additionally, in 1946, the state police initiated a Drivers Education Program through its new Safety Education Unit.

The year 1947 witnessed a landmark in the investigation of driving under the influence in the state. All members of the Division of State Police received instruction on the use of the intoximeter, a chemical test to determine the degree of alcohol in a person's blood through breath. As a final chapter in the decade of the 40s, the Delaware Association of Chiefs of Police, in conjunction with the state police, began construction of a summer youth camp near the Little Assawoman Bay. This camp, today, is known as Camp Barnes in honor of Colonel Herbert Barnes who played a major role in its development.

•**1950-59:** In 1951 the state police acquired their first polygraph machine. With the training of two officers at the Keeler Polygraph Institute, the Division brought into use a new tool to combat the criminal element. Using radar for the first time, troopers arrested nine motorists on March 13, 1952. Initial units were cumbersome and brought immediate reaction from the public and the political arena. The year 1952 also saw the beginning of a program of underwater divers, today's Scuba Unit.

On May 15, 1953, a new seven-station statewide teletype system went into operation. With this innovation, teletype messages could be received from 14 states outside Delaware as well as between the stations and headquarters. May 30, 1955, as reported by the newspapers, became another landmark day for speed enforcement in Delaware. This was the first "air-to-ground" traffic arrest using an airplane to check the speed of holiday travelers. On July 17, 1957, an event of significant im-

portance to the Delaware State Police occurred. It was on this day that the cornerstone was laid at the new headquarters in Dover. Though not opened until 1959, the building was the centerpiece of the present complex and home of the Delaware State Police. The year 1957 witnessed improvement of the radar traffic enforcement system. On October 31, radar units were placed in the trunks of patrol vehicles to assist with maintaining speed limits.

Another milestone was reached on May 29, 1957 with the first expansion of state police facilities since 1925. On this date Troop 4A, now Troop 7, was opened to give better protection to the citizens of the beach areas. Also in 1957, inaugurated a new unit to assist in deterring juvenile delinquency. The Youth Division of the Delaware State Police began operating on September 19. As a final note to the 50s, a unit that had initially begun in 1925 was reinstituted. The Canine Unit, which had fallen on hard times, was re-established and has remained a functioning unit since.

•**1960-69:** During the latter part of 1960, the state police acquired its first fixed-wing aircraft for traffic and criminal investigations. This plane would provide the foundation for the Aviation Unit. The summer of 1961 witnessed the showing off of the state police's new Education Field Unit. The unveiling took place at the Delaware State Fair. Headlines of the *Delaware State News* boldly asked the question: "Car 21453 where are you?" The car, belonging to the state police, had a large speedometer mounted on its roof. The vehicle was not intended to catch speeders but rather to assist motorists in checking their own speedometers.

The year 1963 saw the initiation of 24-hour patrols of the Delaware Turnpike. In an effort to better serve the public, the state police opened a new State Police Substation, Troop 2A, (now Troop 6) at 3803 Kirkwood Highway in 1964.

In 1965 the state police acquired, from federal surplus, a weasel (a tracked vehicle) to better serve the beach going public. Also in 1965, Camp Barnes, for the first time, accepted physically and mentally challenged campers. Eighty children from the Stockley Center attended Camp Barnes after Labor Day. October 10, 1968, saw the opening of a full-time troop at the Delaware Turnpike when Troop 8 became a fully functional facility. The year 1969 saw a change in the numbering system for state police barracks in the state. Henceforth, the existing troops would have their own designators. Troop 2A became Troop 6 and Troop 4A, Troop 7.

The year 1969 also saw a self-imposed code of ethics by the Delaware State Police. It was the first for any agency in Delaware. The state police, in 1969, joined NCIC. All complaints, crimes, warrants, wanted or missing persons were now on computer for instant reference in a system called CLUES. The year 1969 ended with the establishment of NEWCOM, the central reporting center for New Castle County.

•**1970-79:** On January 22, 1970, the state police established a full-time Drug Unit to combat the influx of drugs into the community. October 15 marked the start of the use of VASCAR by the Delaware State Police.

VASCAR, an acronym for Visual Average Speed Computer and Recorder units were operated by the Traffic Division statewide. The year 1971 saw the expansion of the Delaware State Police Aviation Unit. On February 18, the state police accepted delivery of its first Bell Ranger helicopter.

In June the state police reported progress in attracting black and Spanish speaking recruits. A major goal set by the state police is the hiring of six minority recruits in the next class. The state police, in January 1973, announced plans for the construction of a Police Officers Memorial at the headquarters' complex. This was in conjunction with the celebration of the Division's 50th Anniversary, April 28, 1973. The year 1974 saw the formation of a statewide drug strike force with the state police providing the majority of the manpower. The year 1974 also saw the adoption of a new policy aimed at attracting female applicants to the force.

In 1975 the Division formed a Special Weapons and Tactics unit. The following year, 1976, saw the closing of Troop 8 that has housed criminal and traffic patrols for the southern end of the Delaware Turnpike for eight years. Troop 2 was closed in 1977 for major renovations. It was reopened the following year as the consolidated Criminal Troop for New Castle County. State police initiated the TeleServe Complaint Processing System, for which minor complaints not requiring the presence of a police officer could be handled over the telephone.

•**1980-89:** In 1981 the state police initiated a pilot program in New Castle County for the investigation of fatal accidents. The program that uses the acronym FAIR (Fatal Accident Investigation and Reconstruction). The Division, the same year, was awarded an outstanding achievement award in a national competition for its uniform and dress. The year 1982 witnessed the initiation of the use of roadblock checkpoints to curtail driving under the influence. The year of 1983 saw the initiation of the Delaware Crimestoppers Program in an effort to solve difficult crimes.

The year 1987 was marked by the acquisition of an Automated Fingerprint Identification System (AFIS) that would change the course in the apprehension of criminals. This computer, which can scan 650 fingerprints a second, is an extremely valuable crime fighting tool. September 1988 witnessed the formation of a Serial Killer Task Force that was created with the New Castle County Police to apprehend a suspect who had already killed five women in the New Castle County area. This case, the most expensive investigation and manpower exhaustive, led to the arrest and successful prosecution of Steven B. Pennell.

After the successful completion of this investigation, the state police implemented a well-trained, specialized unit to handle homicide investigations. In March 1989, the state police formed a statewide homicide unit. Also in 1989, the Division created a unit to deal with white collar crime. The unit is known as Financial Organized Crime Asset Seizure Team (FORCAST).

•**1990-95:** The 1990s have seen a concerted movement by the Delaware State Police in the direction of Community Police and community directed services. As a full service police agency, the Delaware State Police sees these activities as a natural extension of its role. Units work directly with or in conjunction with the community and include Camp Barnes, DARE, IMPACT, Community Relations, Community Outreach and Rural Community Policing.

As an organization, the state police have attempted to maintain a high standard of excellence within the framework of the current police technology. The Delaware State Police have made a number of great strides in progress since its inception in 1923. The Division of one officer has grown to over 500 and the motorcycle and red flag have been replaced by evermore specialization. Addressing the problems and concerns for public safety continues to remain a priority.

As the Delaware State Police approach the 78th Anniversary, April 28, 2001, the major concern is still with preservation of life and protection of property. The Delaware State Police are proud of the uniform they wear and the services they perform for the citizens of Delaware.

Delaware State Police.

Florida Highway Patrol

The Florida Highway Patrol is determined to provide citizens with the highest level of professional service possible while promoting safety on Florida's highways through enforcement and education.

Mission: To promote in a courteous manner a safe driving environment through aggressive law enforcement, public education, and safety awareness; reduce the number and severity of traffic crashes in Florida, preserve and protect human life, property and the rights of all people in accordance with the constitutions and laws of the United States and the State of Florida; design and implement prevention strategies and aggressively enforce DUI laws and other violations identified as crash causation factors.

Values:

* Courtesy - Treat others fairly and professionally.
* Service - Render aid and assistance to members of the public.
* Protection - Protect life and property.

Goals:

Provide for the overall safety on Florida's highways by reducing the number of traffic crashes resulting in death, injury, and property damage.

Aggressively attempt to reduce criminal activities occurring on Florida's highways through detection, prevention, and enforcement of criminal laws relating to highway violence, transportation of illegal drugs/contraband, auto theft, driver license fraud, and emissions fraud.

Thoroughly investigate crashes resulting in deaths, injuries and property damage with an emphasis on aggressive occupant restraint compliance, DUI prevention, and educational enforcement programs.

Respond to all calls for service in a timely manner.

Operate proactively by being prepared to respond to all natural and man-made disasters.

Lead by example promoting moral, ethical, and professional standards.

The Florida Highway Patrol is subdivided into the following three commands: Field Operations, Law Enforcement Services and Special Operations. Each command is managed by a Deputy Director, holding the rank of lieutenant colonel.

The Florida Highway Patrol was created in 1939 with 60 uniform members. FHP Organizational Structure: Three Field Bureaus, each commanded by a Chief of Field Operations, each responsible for three to four field troops, one Administrative Bureau, handling administrative functions (Personnel, Fleet Property, Communications). Nine field troops are geographically located, and a tenth troop handles turnpike operations; each troop is commanded by a major; 30 district headquarters, each commanded by a captain. Additional Bureaus in headquarters include Investigations, Training, Inspections and Program Planning.

The primary mission of the Florida Highway Patrol is to create a safe driving environment. During the last five years (1992-1998) 19,274 persons have died in motor vehicle crashes in the state of Florida. These crashes have an economic impact to the state in the amount of approximately $800,000 per fatality, for a total of almost $11 billion.

All troopers are trained in standardized field sobriety testing procedures to remove the impaired driver. Troopers made 11,245 DUI related arrests during FY 1998/99. Roadside sobriety checkpoints, DUI "Wolfpacks" and other periodic enforcement and public education campaigns are conducted throughout the state to deter or arrest motorists who drive after consuming alcoholic beverages.

FHP has a zero tolerance policy on occupant restraint use. FHP Public Information Officers presently use four seat belt convincers to demonstrate the effectiveness of safety belts in vehicle crashes. Safety Belt Blitz operations are conducted periodically to increase compliance rates. These blitzes, combined with routine patrol, resulted in 95,138 safety belt arrests during FY 1998/99.

The Florida Highway Patrol has a strict speed enforcement policy. FHP currently has 1,947 state and county owned moving radar units and 431 VASCAR units. Aircraft is routinely used for speed limit enforcement. Speed Measuring Awareness Radar Trailers (SMART) are used as public awareness tools to increase speed limit compliance. During FY 1998/1999 318,040 speed arrests were made, along with 122,788 speed warnings issued.

Absent a statewide motor vehicle inspection law, defective equipment on vehicles requires closer enforcement action by FHP. During FY 1998/99, troopers issued 136,686 notices for correction and 20,750 citations for faulty equipment.

Thirty-seven felony teams, assigned to patrol the interstate system and other major highways throughout the state in order to stop drug trafficking, seized 3.3 pounds of crack cocaine, 101.48 pounds of cocaine, 4,189.45 pounds of marijuana, $1,614,957 million in currency, and made 3,167 drug arrests during FY 1998/99.

In early 1993, the Florida Highway Patrol, by necessity, reacted to a variety of patrol and enforcement issues affecting the safety of the motoring public. Widespread national and international media reports labeled Florida as a dangerous tourist destination. This label evolved as a result of random acts of violence on the interstate highway system and the brutal murders of several tourists traveling on the highway system.

During Fiscal Year 1996/97, a total of 798 incidents of highway violence were reported to FHP. Those incidents included robbery, strong arm robbery, rock throwing and other acts of violence occurring on the highways of the state. Of the 798 incidents, 45 involved the use or threatened use of firearms.

In 1966, the Florida Highway Patrol celebrated the opening of its new training academy, located at 2908 Ridgeway Street, Tallahassee, Florida. The new three story training facility cost over $700,000 and included two classrooms, a gymnasium, an indoor firing range, administrative offices, a cafeteria, and housing accommodations for recruits.

In 1983, an additional building was added adjacent to the existing facility, creating even more room. This allowed the academy to conduct in-service schools as well as recruit schools.

The 24-weeks of training involves over 1200 hours of instruction covering over 120 courses, followed by ten weeks of field training. Training materials are furnished, as well as meals and lodging, at no cost to the recruit. Students receive salary during training.

Subjects studied range from laws of arrest, search and seizure, defensive tactics and arrest techniques, as well as motor vehicle and criminal law, to name a few.

Upon graduation from the FHP Training Academy, troopers are assigned to a field training officer for at least ten weeks, Assignments may be made to any one of Florida's 67 counties within the Patrol's ten field troops. Troopers must be willing to work rotating shifts, weekends and holidays.

Georgia State Patrol

"Wisdom, Justice and Moderation" has been the motto of the Georgia State Patrol since its birth in 1937. The Department of Public Safety turned 60 in 1997 - 60 years of service, intense pride, sacrifice and dedication to the motoring public of the state of Georgia.

It was the motoring public that advocated the creation of the Georgia Department of Public Safety. In the early 1930s, there was much concern for the rising death rate on Georgia highways. This concern, increased crime, and an insufficient number of law enforcement officers at the local and county levels further revealed the need for a new law enforcement agency.

Members of the General Assembly added to this need with the development of a road system. Also involved in this development were more efficient means of transportation, vehicles with increased power, as well as an increase in the number of vehicles on Georgia roads.

The Assembly also proposed that the state raise money to repair roads by taxing the owners of vehicles in the form of license plates, chauffeurs' badges and a gas tax. In addition, the state enacted traffic laws for the protection of the motoring public.

It was the responsibility of the sheriffs, constables, police and Secretary of State to enforce these laws. During this time, the militia acted as the state law enforcement unit in Georgia. However, a larger, more uniformed body of state law enforcement was badly needed.

There were several attempts in the early 1930s to bring about a state patrol. However, year after year in the General Assembly, bills proposing the establishment of a state patrol unit died in the House and Senate.

In 1936 Ed Rivers was elected Governor of Georgia, and one of the planks in his platform was the creation of a state highway patrol. In January of 1937, during a special 10-day session of the General Assembly, two bills were introduced to create a Georgia State Patrol.

House Bill 18, the 220th Act of the General Assembly, was signed into law March 19, 1937. The Act created and established the Department of Public Safety, to be part of the executive branch of Georgia government. The three divisions of the DPS were to include (1) a uniformed division, known as the Georgia State Patrol (2) a division of criminal identification, detection, prevention, and investigation and (3) a division to license drivers.

The State Patrol was to contain one troop of no less than 80 men with provisions to increase to 120 men. Salaries ranged from $1,200 per year for a trooper 2nd class, to $2,400 per year for a captain. The department was to appoint a Commissioner of Public Safety who would hold the rank of major, and all members of the Georgia State Patrol, except the commissioner, were to be reappointed every three years. They were subject to removal or suspension for cause.

For the enlisted members of the Georgia State Patrol, temporary headquarters were set up at a hotel in Atlanta, and recruitment began. The first troopers were to be at least 5'10" and weigh at least 155 lbs. Approximately 3,000 men applied for the job of State Trooper, but only 102 were picked. From those 102, only 80 would become members of the Georgia State Patrol.

The first Trooper School began on Sunday, July 26, 1937 at Georgia Tech. Classes included Georgia motor laws, geography and counties of the state, firearms, police courtesy, court and legal procedures, regulations of highway traffic and care of motor vehicles. The 80 Troopers graduated from Trooper School August 28, 1937, and were given one week of leave.

One week after graduation, the Troopers returned to Atlanta to receive their uniforms and firearms. The uniforms were Confederate gray and the sidearms were Colt revolvers, valued at $27 each. The first vehicles were 1937 Fords with bulletproof windshields. They were gun metal in color with orange letters. The state bought 33 of these vehicles for $710 each.

The 1937 Ford was equipped with an 85 horsepower, V-8 engine. The engine's power was transferred to the wheels by a 3-speed standard shift transmission. Three of the 33 patrol cars were assigned to each patrol post across the state.

The uniformed division was to perform all duties in checking motor vehicles in the state

to see that they were properly licensed and not overloaded, and in enforcing the provisions of the laws of Georgia, including the proper licensing of drivers. The Division was also to enforce the driver's license laws of the state and if a license was ordered suspended, revoked, or canceled, notification was given to the uniformed divisions to recall the license from the holder.

The state was divided into 10 strategic areas with eight or nine men at each station. The stations were: (1) Griffin, (2) Cartersville, (3) Gainesville, (4) Madison, (5) Americus, (6) Moultrie, (7) Perry, (8) Washington, (9) Swainsboro and (10) Waycross. Headquarters for the State Patrol was the Old Confederate Soldiers' Home in Atlanta.

In the first four months of the State Patrol's operation, the troopers recovered nearly 30 stolen vehicles, assisted in breaking up small crime rings, and obtained more than 300 convictions. There was a decline in traffic deaths in the first year of operation, and in the following year, traffic deaths dropped by one-third.

One of the early problems the State Patrol faced was the lack of communication between troopers and their posts. Before the two-way communications system was set up, it was necessary for troopers to go by certain post offices to sign a log book in the presence of the postmaster in order to show their location on certain days at specified times. The only communication the troopers had between each other was a crude "red-flag system" they devised in conjunction with several gas stations. If the troopers were needed on patrol, certain gas stations would hoist a red flag if there was a call or an accident, alerting the trooper to call his post. By the end of the 1930s, the department began to bring experimental A.M. radio stations to patrol posts throughout the state.

The hours were very long for the first troopers of the State Patrol. Troopers worked until their job was completed, and many days that lasted 15 to 18 hours. Patrols would average 500 miles per day. Troopers were given only four days off per month, but the days could only be taken two at a time.

The Department of Public Safety began to expand during the 1940s. The Drivers License Bureau issued licenses by mail, requiring applicants to take tests every two years to renew. Citizens of Georgia could drive on the family plan, costing the head of the house $1, the spouse 50 cents, and minor children (over 5 years of age) 25 cents.

The Georgia Bureau of Investigation was also established in the early 1940s. The GBI was founded to assist all law enforcement officers. The Bureau was also responsible for pro-

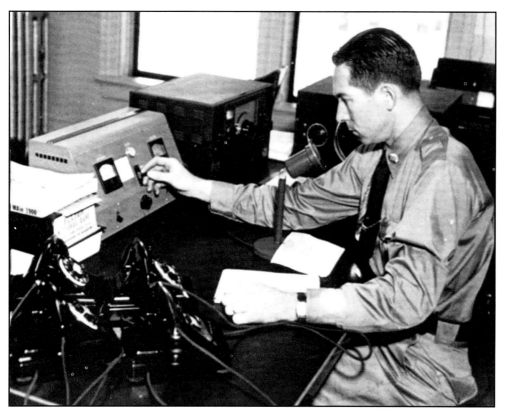

in Atlanta. Renovation of the patrol posts began. However, it would take until 1973 before the new patrol barracks were completed.

The beginning of the 1960s offered new challenges for troopers. The Motor Vehicle Inspection (MVI) Law went into effect in the early part of the decade. The state passed a law which would help troopers remove unsafe and defective vehicles from the roads and highways in the state.

Georgia State Troopers not only witnessed the rise of the Civil Rights Movement during the '60s but were also called upon to assist in protection of the marchers, demonstrators, spectators.

Multi-lane highways were introduced, radar was used as an attempt to stop the tragedy of traffic deaths on the roads. The speed limit was now 70 miles per hour. The job of protecting the roads and the citizens of Georgia grew more challenging and more intense.

In 1966 the Georgia Police Academy opened in Atlanta. This complex served as the new site for training State Troopers. Before this site opened, training was completed at universities and colleges throughout the state, including Georgia Tech and the University of Georgia, and also at the Post in Madison.

More new problems challenged the Georgia State Patrol during the 1970s. Drugs became rampant in the state. New substances were not familiar to the troopers, making it difficult to detect and locate various types of drugs on individuals. These problems forced the State Troopers back into the classroom to learn the improved methods and techniques for dealing with interdiction. Troopers became more aware of drugs and their effects on the Georgia society.

Throughout the decade of the 1980s troopers were faced with problems of drug enforcement, transportation of illegal or foreign substances, changing environments, civil liabilities, court rulings, and federal intervention in the area of hours and wages. However, through educational training and work experience, Georgia State Troopers were able to handle any task with confidence.

In 1983 the Special Patrol Enforcement and Accident Reduction Squad (SPEARS) was created to battle the DUI problem in the Atlanta area. The seven-man unit patrolled the downtown metro area to aid primarily in the DUI problem.

The Democratic National Convention in July 1988 required the presence of 420 troopers for two weeks in July. Their mission was to provide security for the Georgia World Congress Center. Every post in the Georgia State Patrol furnished troopers for the convention detail while simultaneously continuing traffic enforcement throughout the state of Georgia.

cessing fingerprints, handling investigations and collecting other data.

Many of the state's troopers were called to serve when World War II began. Those troopers who were left behind were requested to become military escorts for soldiers and their equipment.

After the war ended, the State Patrol was slow in regaining its strength. By 1946, troopers were called on to help protect various people, offices and state property in the Capitol Building. Postwar reconstruction brought new roads, additional traffic and a higher rate of crime. Within five years, however, the budget of the Georgia State Patrol tripled.

By 1950 the department had begun to expand in all levels. A communications system was put into place and a safety education program was formed. For the first time, the salary of a trooper nearly doubled. The success of the Department of Public Safety and the Georgia State Patrol led to a relocation of its headquarters.

In 1957 the troopers moved out of the Old Confederate Soldiers' Home and into their new Headquarters Building on Confederate Avenue

The 90s have brought many new challenges and opportunities for the Georgia State Patrol. In March 1993, a late winter snow storm, which later would be called the "storm of the century," paralyzed much of north and central Georgia. It was the weekend when troopers were called on to pull stranded motorists to safety as well as the Aviation Unit flying rescue missions to locate people caught by the unexpected storm. In July 1994 many communities of south Georgia were ravaged by torrential rains dropped by Tropical Storm Alberto. The floods of July 1994 will be remembered as the single largest crisis response ever, with more than 400 Department members assisting in the flood relief efforts. Troopers from all parts of Georgia were placed on detail in the flood-ravaged areas and performed admirably. Governor Zell Miller praised the Troopers' efforts during graduation ceremonies for the 68th Trooper School.

"These past two weeks, I have seen the Georgia State Patrol in its finest hour. Everywhere I've been, the troopers have been there doing more than their part," Gov. Miller commented. "I am pleased and proud."

Nearly 200 members of the department participated in the security detail for the 1994 Super Bowl between the Dallas Cowboys and the Buffalo Bills at the Georgia Dome. Members performed duties ranging from monitoring protest groups, crowd control and traffic control, to team escorts and VIP protection.

During the 1996 Olympic Torch Relay, the Georgia State Patrol provided a security escort for the Olympic Flame in the United States from Los Angeles to the opening ceremonies in Atlanta. Troopers served as escorts for the Flame and Torch Runners in both marked cars and by foot alongside the Flame. In the U.S. the Flame traveled by land, air and water on a variety of conveyances.

Beginning April 27, 1996, the Flame traveled over 15,280 miles in 84 days, visiting 43 states and over 355 cities. The DPS's oversight and coordination for the Olympic Torch Relay was necessary to ensure a safe and expeditious journey for this special event.

Once the Olympic Flame reached Atlanta and the Centennial Olympic Games were underway, many months of planning came together for the largest security detail ever in Georgia. Troopers from every post in the state were called on to provide personnel for security at the various state-owned venue sites, transportation and general traffic enforcement, as well as dignitary protection and escorts. One of the additional responsibilities for troopers was the safe transportation of athletes from dormitories to practice sites to the venues.

For the last five decades, the Georgia State Patrol has progressed, not only with troopers patrolling in vehicles, but also in aircraft and helicopters. Through modern technology troopers were introduced to rescue operations, manhunts, air tactics and bird's eye views on traffic accidents. Troopers were also trained to detect and destroy illegal, foreign and domestic substances with the help of aviation.

Today, the Georgia Department of Public Safety employs approximately 858 troopers, 246 radio operators, 334 license examiners, and 530 civilian employees. The Patrol has come a long way from the first 80 troopers selected in 1937.

The Georgia State Patrol has 48 patrol posts, each assigned several counties in the state. It also has 63 Drivers License Examination Stations, along with satellite Drivers License Renewal Stations located inside Kroger Grocery stores.

Through the accomplishments in the last 64 years, the Department of Public Safety and the Georgia State Patrol have proudly lived up to their theme: "Wisdom, Justice and Moderation."

Hawaii Department of Public Safety

Through its Law Enforcement Division, the Hawaii Department of Public Safety preserves the peace and protects the public in designated areas by providing security for state property and facilities; enforcing specified laws and rules for the prevention and control of crime; and serving process in civil and criminal proceedings.

Mission: To ensure the safety of the public through the administration of correctional facilities and services, the protection of the public and state personnel, and security of designated state facilities, lands, and waters by enforcing laws and preserving the peace.

Department of Corrections Mission: To provide public protection by operating humane and secure facilities in a safe working environment, where the health and well-being of the committed are sustained, and opportunities are available for the committed to address issues related to their reintegration back into the community.

Law Enforcement Mission: To provide for the security of designated state facilities, lands and waters. State law enforcement will protect the public and state personnel within its purview by preserving the public peace, enforcing laws, preventing and detecting crimes, and apprehending offenders.

Idaho State Police

Administrative reorganization of Idaho's executive branch of government in 1919 provided for a Department Law Enforcement. Shortly after the new department commenced to function, a Bureau of Constabulary was organized on May 18, 1919.

Statutory duties assigned to the new agency included general state law enforcement. In addition to "detecting and investigating crime," the new constabulary was to "order abatement of public nuisances and to enforce such orders by appropriate court action, to suppress riots, prevent affrays and to prevent wrongs to children and dumb animals," that are inhibited by law." The state constabulary was also charged with the proper organization of various state, county and municipal peace officers.

Two special problems in law enforcement, prohibition and automobile licensing, provided most of the offenses for which the state constabulary made arrests. Enforcement of temperance and moral legislation, in fact, was one of the special statutory charges of the new state police force.

An even more serious problem than prohibition, however, was enforcement of the 1917 Syndicalism Law passed during the war and strengthened in 1919. Idaho had led the nation in adopting such legislation. The Syndicalism Statute had been directed primarily against the Industrial Workers of the World (IWW). Also known by the nickname "The Wobblies," the IWW had become a strong labor organization in the North Idaho lumber and mining camps just before the war. By 1919 the superintendent of the Bureau of Constabulary regarded the IWW as the "most serious problem facing the peace officers of the state" and stationed more than half the force in North Idaho in an effort to drive them out by procuring evidence by which such members might be prosecuted under the Syndicalism Law. That task was a difficult one, since IWW had pointedly advocated avoiding sabotage once such advocacy was outlawed by the syndicalism act. Much effort went into the compilation of a roster of IWW members in Idaho and the northwest, and a number of members were arrested for possessing membership cards before the news of the drive got out and members began to tear up their cards. But by 1920 the Constabulary had the IWW situation well in hand," so that most of the syndicalism arrests resulted in conviction.

Aside from these major classes of activity, the Constabulary caught some robbers, arrested kidnappers, recovered a few stolen vehicles, protected animals from cruelty, and searched for several lost hunters in the winter. More important was a state convention of peace officers, February 6, 1920 sponsored by the new agency. The convention recommended that the state constabulary be authorized to establish a fingerprint record of criminals, and the next Legislature complied, enacting a law which enabled the listing (with fingerprints and photographs) of all "well known" criminals in the United States - whether their offenses were state or federal.

Highway improvement to the point that automobiles could begin to operate at something approaching "high speed" led to a decidedly increased accident rate by 1928. With the advent of hard-surfaced roads came the organization of the State Traffic Patrol. On March 3, 1929, funds were secured by a special legislative appropriation that made the new patrol possible. The actual authority for establishing the state police force went back to the State Constabulary Law that had been left in effect but dormant. Members of the Traffic Patrol actually were commissioned as special deputies under the old statute.

By 1930 a 15 man force had plenty to do: they collected auto license fees, set up light and brake testing stations, enforced spring highway load restrictions, suppressed gasoline bootleggers, kept irrigation water from eroding the highways and enforced all aircraft regulations as well! But their main task was to reduce the accident rate by patrolling the highways. At the end of 1930, they were warning more than 2,000 motorists a month and were going so far as to arrest the most flagrant violators.

The biennial reports for the Department of Law Enforcement for the years 1935 and 1936 indicate that the Highway Patrol had a compliment of 21 trained officers. They performed numerous tasks in the enforcement of the statutes of the state. These included checking cosmeticians' licenses, scouting of anglers' permits, returning lost children and "capturing maniacs." The patrol traveled over one million miles policing traffic in the 21 patrol districts of the state and made over 12,000 arrests during the two-year period. Traffic enforcement was needed even more greatly by 1938 with the completion of the "North-South Highway," what is now known as US 95.

The Idaho State Police Act created by the Legislature of 1939 and signed by Governor C.A. Bottolfsen, set forth duties and authority of the new state enforcement agency. This was the beginning of the present Idaho State Police organization. The act also provided for the installation of short-wave radio stations and to establish fingerprint files. Due to the insufficient appropriation, the radio and fingerprint system were not purchased. On July 15, 1939, a general order was issued by the Bureau to all state police officers advising them of a system of weekly reports by each officer. This was the beginning of regular field activity reports to the Boise office.

During the World War II period the duties of the state police increased quite a lot. Besides its regular function of supervising traffic, the state police personnel were called upon to convoy troops, investigate reports of sabotage and espionage and investigate the character and records of applicants for the armed forces.

The state police increased from 22 to 40 officers in 1947. During July of that year, the department received 40 new Chevrolet coupes with large diagonal stripes down both sides.

In August 1947, the winter uniform ("Ike jacket") was adopted. The officers ordered their uniforms from private sources and paid for them on delivery. The department furnished gunbelts, holsters, and badges. A curious thing is that the first uniform items supplied, other than the above, were the English-style jodhpur boots, which started in 1949.

The fall of 1948 saw the installation of a new statewide state police short wave radio system. This was the beginning of an effective communications system for the law enforcement officers of Idaho. Prior to this time, passing motorists and telephones were used to notify ambulances and wreckers of serious accidents. The frequency listed on the old FCC license is 42.54 mc.

Summer uniforms were adopted in the spring of 1949. The light tan shirt and gabardine trousers had a matching "Ike" jacket and were topped off with a wine colored tie and light brown western style hat. Police style caps and campaign hats had been the official headgear up to this time. The officers had to buy this new uniform and the department started furnishing the blue winter uniform on an "as needed" basis.

The biennial report of 1952 was the first one to mention the state police merit system. Prior to this time, the personnel had been selected on a political party affiliation system. This was a department devised system which needed statutory authority to be worthwhile.

However, department policy prevented the firing of personnel because of party affiliation, as long as they were not actively engaged in politics. The personnel changed every time the politics of the Statehouse changed prior to this time.

The State Police "Port of Entry" program was authorized by the Legislature of 1949 and was in full operation by 1952, with five fixed ports and three roving stations. The State Police provided 10 men from the patrol and hired 10 new men to fill the personnel needs of the ports of entry. This was the start of strict enforcement of truck registration, weight, and equipment laws. The Port of Entry personnel requirements left a total of 25 patrol officers to cover the 44 counties of the state.

In January of 1954 the old "Primea Facia" speed law was replaced with an enforceable recommended speed limit of 60 mph in the daytime and 55 mph at night on all primary U.S. and state highways. Also in 1954, the ISP purchased six radar sets to aid in controlling speeding motorists. These were dubbed the "electronic cops" by the news media of the state. Many publicity ads appeared in newspapers stating, "Take your foot off the gas driver, or a state police radar gadget will get you!"

The Legislature of 1955 enacted a State Police Merit System Law whereby personnel were selected on ability and promoted on personal efficiency ratings. By law, a dismissed officer could request a hearing and get it for

131

the first time in history. With the advent of the Merit System Law, many ISP officers started thinking about a career as a state policeman.

The Legislature of 1955 authorized the addition of 16 men for the State Police. These men were selected from 310 applications and were given two weeks of training prior to assuming the duties of state policeman. This brought the patrol's strength to 44 men. The light brown summer uniforms became the Port of Entry uniform for year-round wear. The blue winter uniform became the constant uniform of the patrolman, topped off with a western style grey Stetson hat.

The State Police became a separate division of the Department of Law Enforcement with acts of the Legislature of 1955. The administration, management and control were vested in the superintendent, who was appointed by the governor.

The Legislature of 1957 authorized the addition of 10 patrolmen and one training lieutenant, bringing the total department strength to 55 men. The department strength was again raised by the 1959 Legislature, when an additional 15 men were promoted to the patrolmen ranks from the Port of Entry. This brought the total strength up to 71 officers. Meanwhile, the Port of Entry programs had grown to include six fixed ports and nine roving ports manned by 45 officers.

The Identification Division files had grown immensely, with over 17,000 fingerprint cards and 50,000 names on file.

A big year for the ISP was 1961 when 30 men were added to the force. At this time the department adopted a new merit system. This provided a rating system for personnel and annual salary increases.

Career minded personnel received added assurance of adequate pensions with the enactment of the retirement law by the 1964 Legislature. This added to the Social Security Program already in effect and made a career in state law enforcement much more attractive.

The State Police left the merit system on January 1, 1967 to go under the new State Personnel Commission which was enacted by the Legislature for all state departments. This was another milestone in the department's history.

A major increase in state police personnel was authorized in 1972, with the addition of 10 patrolmen, 20 radio communications officers, and 26 officers assigned to the federally-funded Alcohol Safety Action Program (ASAP).

During May of 1972, the state police instituted a major reorganization to centralize administrative functions and provide uniformity of law enforcement policy throughout the state. The six district captains were transferred to the Boise office and assigned areas of command. The lieutenants in each district became the district commanders. At the close of 1972 the department strength was the highest in history, with 211 employees.

In 1974 growing concerns over fuel supplies were being heard. President Jimmy Carter ordered a nationwide speed limit of 55 mph as a fuel conservation measure. The ISP had long enforced a speed limit (previously 70 mph on the interstates) but for many the "Double Nickel" became a major social issue.

Idaho's worst disaster to date struck in June of 1976 when the 310 foot earth-fill Teton Dam collapsed, sending a wall of water through several towns north of Idaho Falls. Eleven persons died and thousands were forced to flee. The State Police played a major role in everything from early warning and evacuation to traffic control and area security.

In 1978, hats changed from the previous sheriff's style to the present dark blue flat-brimmed Montana peak style. A new uniform shoulder patch and hat badge were adopted, both items. New stainless steel revolvers and speed loaders were issued. New leather replaced the time-worn and varied belts and holsters. The first of a new breed of patrol cars was delivered with a return to the black and white design with diagonal white striping. (Cars had changed to a blue and white scheme during the period from 1965 to 1978.) New light bars replaced the antiquated "bubble style" lights.

One of the biggest changes for the state police occurred in July of 1982. Earlier that year, the Legislature was convinced by the Department of Transportation that a move of the Port of Entry and Motor Vehicle Divisions from the Department of Law Enforcement to ITD would improve the performance of those areas.

Technology in the form of desktop computers came into the offices of the Department of Law Enforcement in 1983. The Datapoint System was viewed by some with apprehension, but those that "made friends" with the electronic marvel rarely used their typewriters again. Other data processing equipment crept into offices through the department and revolutionized the way many jobs were handled.

In the fall of 1983 the ISP announced, "The Boss was Back," as they took delivery of 12 high performance Mustang patrol cars. With 5.0 liter engines, special handling packages, and 4-speed manual transmissions, these 140 mph pursuit vehicles required the 12 officers receiving them to undergo special driving instruction. The cars were an immediate hit with the public. Parking one in front of the local coffee shop always generated several questions from the public generally regarding, "How fast will she go?"

August 28, 1983 the first (and only) ISP "Sobriety Checkpoint" was held near Hailey. Although no persons were arrested, the press coverage of the controversial enforcement technique was extensive. After evaluation, however, it was decided a better alternative was "DUI Emphasis Patrols." The technique saw numerous drunk drivers arrested and let the

public know the ISP was serious about dealing with this problem.

Idaho being a large state geographically, it's a rare occasion when all state police officers and staff gather in one location. 1985 brought such an occasion - the National Governors' Association Conference held August 3-6 in Boise. The ISP joined with other Department of Law Enforcement agencies in coordinating security for the event.

On May 4, 1987 the much debated 55 mph speed limit was repealed on rural interstates within Idaho. Of the 608 miles of interstate highway in the state, 570 went back to the 65 mph limit.

In 1988, two new programs within the Motor Carrier Safety Assistance Program (MCSAP) were developed. A federal grant was obtained to fund six new truck accident reconstructionists and the Legislature authorized a Hazardous Materials Specialist.

On February 20, 1989, the Idaho State Police Division celebrated the 50th Anniversary of its existence. A ceremony was held in the governor's office and Governor Andrus signed a proclamation proclaiming "Idaho State Police Week." The superintendent, Colonel Rich Humpherys, presented the governor with 50th Anniversary commemorative pistol that was manufactured by commission with the Smith and Wesson Company.

A statewide search for a 50th Anniversary logo was held in all junior and senior high schools within the state. This would be placed on all correspondence during the year and a special pin would be made to wear on the uniform of all officers to commemorate the anniversary.

The winner of the contest was a 16-year-old student at Twin Falls Senior High School, Phomma Keopanya, a Laotian immigrant, who consequently won a $100 savings bond and a chance to come to Boise in a state police vehicle and participate in the Proclamation Ceremonies at the governor's office.

In June of 1989 the Idaho State Police was notified that their patrol vehicle entry won third place in the first annual *Law & Order Magazine* best police vehicle contest. Idaho's entry of one of our famous "skunk" cars took honors for unique design and for being readily identifiable as a state police vehicle.

In reflecting on the ISP's history, the tendency is to remember the major events. Yet it is often the routine, unrecognized duties of each officer or civilian employee that combined, make this the kind of agency that it is. There are certainly events and persons that have gone unmentioned in this publication. That does not lessen their importance. Let each employee derive the simple satisfaction that comes from knowing a job is well done and let the pride of serving with the Idaho State Police motivate them to even greater accomplishments for the future.

Illinois State Police

On June 24, 1921, the 52nd General Assembly of the State of Illinois authorized the Department of Public Works and Buildings to hire a "sufficient number of State Highway Patrol Officers to enforce the provisions of the Motor Vehicle Laws." The Illinois State Police was officially created in 1922 and today, comprised of sworn personnel and civilians totaling more than 3,000, is one of the most modern and efficient police organizations in the country.

Over the years, the Illinois State Police has continually changed in size and organizational structure to provide an increased number of services in the most efficient manner to the people of Illinois. These services are implemented by the Office of the Director through the Divisions of Operations, Forensic Services, Internal Investigation and Administration.

Since its inception, the Illinois State Police has fostered and served with a reputation for integrity, service and pride. Illinois State Police functions include protecting life and property, enforcing both criminal laws and motor vehicle safety laws, responding to emergencies and disasters and providing a myriad of diverse specialized services to both the public and the criminal justice community.

Additionally, each division within the Illinois State Police provides specific services. The Division of Operations' services entail: aircraft support for enforcement and public assistance; vehicle investigations; underwater search and recovery operations; K-9 support for tracking and drug detection; presentations to the public on traffic safety and crime prevention; criminal investigations to detect and suppress the traffic of illicit drugs; develop strategic and tactical criminal intelligence data; investigate serious offenses; and apprehend fugitives. Operations also provides support to many county, municipal and federal law enforcement agencies.

The efforts of both state and municipal police officers are supplemented by the Division of Forensic Services, providing crime scene services, polygraph services, background checks requisite to the purchase of firearms and strategically located crime laboratories. The Division of Internal Investigation specializes in investigating alleged misconduct, corruption, conflict of interest and malfeasance within any agency under the jurisdiction of the governor. The Division of Administration is responsible for administrative support required by all department entities and the operation of the Illinois State Police Academy. This division centralizes the department's vast communications network, data processing, fiscal, logistical, personnel and research

and development functions and provides state-of-art automated fingerprinting identification. The Illinois State Police Academy provides training to cadets, in-service education to troopers and a basic curriculum to state, county and municipal agencies. The shoulder patch worn by the Illinois State Police is symbolic of the integrity, service and pride of the organization. We trust it will be displayed with dignity and honor in remembrance of the dedication of those officers who have served the citizens of Illinois.

The year 1997 marked the 75th Anniversary of the Illinois State Police. There are roughly 3,500 personnel in five divisions (Administra-

tion, Forensic Services, Human Resources, Internal Investigation and Operations).

•**1917**: The Illinois General Assembly approved the biggest road building program in the country; $60 million to build 4,800 miles linking all principal cities and passing through every county. (The only good Illinois paved road in existence at the time was from Peoria to St. Louis.)

•**1921**: As part of taking "Illinois out of the mud," legislative action authorized the Director of the Department of Public Works and Buildings to appoint a "sufficient number" of

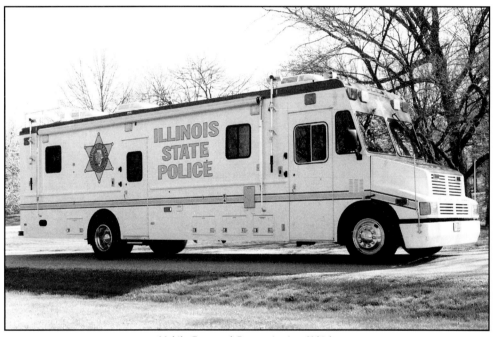
Mobile Command Communications Vehicle.

Chrysler coupes. A few motorcycles were kept in the department until 1956 on a stand-by basis for use in parades and special assignments. Officers in the State Highway Maintenance Police force now totaled 159.

•**1927**: On January 17 Trooper Lory L. Price and his wife were abducted and killed by the Charlie Berger Gang. Lory's body was found in a cornfield and his wife's body was found in a mine shaft. Lory was appointed to the ISP November 6, 1923 and had no children. The skillful investigation and follow-up arrests (and execution of Charlie Berger) helped the ISP overcome much of the strong resistance to their creation and expansion.

•**1927**: Illinois was the first state on the Route 66 path to have its entire length paved. Route 66 was a prime focus of the ISP. Not until 1938 was the entire stretch of Route 66 from Chicago to Los Angeles paved.

•**1928**: A formal traffic accident reporting system (suggested by the National Safety Council) was initiated by the ISP, but use of the forms was not mandatory for other agencies.

•**1930**: One hundred Model A Fords replaced the sergeant's Chrysler squad cars.

•**1931**: The Illinois Bureau of Identification and Investigation began its operation under the Department of Public Welfare (without any funds). The primary purpose of the Bureau was maintenance and indexing of identification information (photographs, measurements, descriptions, finger prints and more) on persons charged with crimes.

The first ISP radio system was authorized, but it did not start operation until 1935. Short wave radio sets were prohibited in automobiles, except those of peace officers, without first obtaining permission from a sheriff.

•**1932**: In 1932-33 a state police unit was assigned to assist Chicago Police and some other agencies to combat kidnappings.

•**June 1934:** The first ISP Weapons Training Section was established. Weapons practice for many years thereafter was held each month at Camp Lincoln in Springfield and other ranges with annual or multiple yearly qualification shoots.

•**1935**: The Bureau of Mines trained two ISP officers as First Aid instructors, who were then certified by the American Red Cross to train and certify other officers in the field. Three more instructors were certified in 1937

•**1936**: The first ISP radio base station at Springfield went on the air dispatching one-

State Highway Maintenance Police to enforce the provisions of the Motor Vehicle Act of 1919. These officers were given limited police authority to enforce the "Motor Vehicle Law" and were equipped with weighing devices for the weighing of motor vehicles and trucks. The original act did not specify any particular number of officers, nor did it provide for any type of compensation.

•**April 1, 1922:** The first eight Highway Patrol officers and Superintendent John H. Stack began their duties. The primary duties of the officers were "protection of the roads" from damage by overweight vehicles. The officers had no uniforms but were provided with a star and identification cards.

•**1923**: Senate Bill No. 311 was enacted on June 29 creating an "Illinois State High-

way Maintenance Police" and provided that the number of officers would not exceed 100 men with their stipulation to be no more than $150 per month. These officers were given whatever equipment deemed necessary, including a uniform, badge and motor bikes (the World War I bikes were equipped with acetylene gas headlights, meaning they had to be lit with matches for night driving). The newly appointed officers received three days of training to build morale and cohesiveness and consistency in activities.

•**1925**: There were 95 State Highway Maintenance Police officers in Illinois with an annual department budget of $227,000.

•**1927**: The first squad cars were purchased and issued to sergeants only who were, in effect, district commanders. The cars were way only to squad cars in that area. By the end of 1937 all stations were in operation, 250 squad cars and 350 motorcycles were equipped to receive police broadcasts.

The ISP joined other states in an interstate communications network using CW transmissions with messages in Morse Code.

•**1937**: New ranks of lieutenant and captain in the Illinois State Highway Maintenance Police were created with lieutenants now commanding each district.

•**1938**: Ten commanding officers of the Illinois State Highway Maintenance Police had 50 watt mobile transmitters, constructed at the State Police Radio Laboratory, installed in their squad cars. These home-made units did a fair job, but they were dependent upon favorable atmospheric conditions.

The State Police administered driver's license examinations under newly enacted law with 60,049 applicants handled the first year by 55 examiners.

•**1939**: The first Illinois State Highway Maintenance Police "battalion" supervisors (five captains) were appointed.

•**1940**: The first tailor was employed, by what would become the quartermaster, to serve 356 sworn officers out of a total of 560 departmental personnel in the Illinois State Highway Maintenance Police.

•**1941**: The 62nd General Assembly established a new Department of Public Safety. A mobile crime laboratory, the first of its kind by a police agency, was dedicated. A special Traffic Safety Section was created to assist with educating and informing the public about safe driving.

•**July 17, 1941:** The first formal State Highway Maintenance Police Academy Class began in the Emmerson Building on the State Fairgrounds with 98 men.

•**August 7, 1941** Superintendent Leo E. Carr issued a "no mustache" order following conclusion of the first State Highway Maintenance Police Training School. The decree also applied to sideburns and similar abnormal extensions of the hairline. He said the new order will make for a "trim looking force."

•**1942**: This year saw the state police radio network increased from nine base stations to 14. All state police cars were equipped with FM transmitters to achieve car to station communication without static in bad weather.

•**1943**: Despite the production of vital war materials, several manufacturers were producing a satisfactory FM mobile transmitter and, as a consequence, all Illinois State Highway

Maintenance Police cars were equipped with this type of unit, enabling them to receive and transmit within a 40 or 50 mile radius of their station.

•**1945**: The manpower cap for the State Highway Maintenance Police was raised from 35O to 500 men with the requirement that the 150 men to be added to the force had to be honorably discharged World War II veterans.

•**1947**: Salaries for Illinois State Highway Maintenance Police officers ranged from $225 per month for starting patrolmen to $345 per month for captains.

•**1948**: Motorcycles were no longer used for patrol duties by the Illinois State Highway Maintenance Police. The Illinois State Police Auxiliary, originally formed under the Civil Defense, was absorbed by the ISP.

•**1949**: A statute totally prohibiting solicitation or receipt of any contribution from a state police officer for any political party or candidate and prohibiting any state police officer from participating in political activities or campaigns became law.

•**1951:** At this time, the word "maintenance" was dropped from the title of the force and the official name became "Illinois State Highway Police." Black and white squad cars became the visual symbol of the Illinois State Highway Police.

•**1953**: State police driver's license personnel and their functions were transferred to the Secretary of State's Office.

•**1954**: Radar speed detection devices were tested and implemented for the first time by the ISP.

•**April 1, 1954:** The Illinois State Highway Police first started wearing the broad brimmed, Montana peak hats and a heavy reefer jacket was issued in place of the long overcoat.

•**1956**: The Legislature granted an increase of 100 men to the force, bringing its authorized total strength to 600.

•**1957**: The 70th General Assembly voted another increase in

personnel of the Illinois State Police, raising the number from 600 to 1,100 men. A Division of Narcotic Control was created in the Department of Public Safety (predecessor of the Illinois Bureau of Investigation - IBI).

•**July 1, 1957**: A formal ISP enforcement policy on the newly enacted speed limits (the old limit had been "reasonable and proper") advised that passenger car violators would be issued warning tickets (except for flagrant violations), but there would be no warning period or tolerance for drivers of 2nd Division vehicles.

•**September 1958**: ISP officers now required to complete seven practice firearm shoots and three firearm qualification shoots per year.

A Bureau of Special Investigations was formed (officially separating some investigative functions from the patrol functions), but it was initially involved in investigations only on requests for assistance from local agencies.

The word "Highway" was removed from the official name of the state police effective in 1961.

•**1959**: The Olympic Silhouette targets replaced the Colt Silhouette targets for firearms training.

•**October 1, 1959**: The Air Arm of the Illinois State Police was officially commissioned with one single engine Cessna 175. Shortly after, two other aircraft of the same type were added and by 1960 the unit was fully operational.

So that the patrol cars could be easily identified from the air, large letters were painted on the car roofs. When a speeder was observed and duly clocked from the air, it became simple for the plane crew to dispatch a patrol car to the chase. In addition to speed checking, the planes have proven invaluable for many other uses. On numerous occasions they have been used on man hunts; to spot "walk-aways" from rest homes and mental institutions; to control traffic, particularly at football games and the State Fair; to aid at prison breaks; and to assist in rescue work at floods and other disaster scenes.

•**January 1, 1961:** A program of formal recognition for outstanding police work performed by officers of the Illinois State Highway Police was instituted: Governor's Award of Valor, Director's Certificate of Merit and the Superintendent's Commendation.

•**June 11, 1961**: For the first time, ISP officers are allowed to remove their uniform tie during the summer (the tie must be available in case of special detail and no part of a tee-shirt or undershirt may be visible).

•**August 28, 1961**: Effective immediately, the ISP Bureau of Special Investigation will be known as the Detective Section. In 1962 it was re-named the Crime Section.

•**February 28, 1962**: "Black-jacks" (or "saps") were no longer required equipment and were not to be carried by any ISP officer.

•**March 1963**: A K-9 Corps of troopers and sentry dogs was established with the trainer working for both the ISP and the Department of Corrections. One dog and handler was assigned to each district. Training of the dog and handler took six to eight weeks. A few years later, after much public criticism of the use of dogs by police officers in several parts of the country in civil rights disturbances, the K-9 Corps was discontinued.

•**1964:** Computer systems were being designed to handle the criminal history information, wanted person and property files, accident records and administrative records.

•**1967:** The black and white squad cars (color adopted in 1951) were replaced with beige colored cars (at a lower cost per car).

The ISP adopted the Model 39, Smith and Wesson semi-automatic pistol as its official service weapon.

A computer terminal in ISP Headquarters at D-9 was connected with the FBI National Crime Information Center (NCIC), allowing entries and inquiries into the federal wanted files.

•**1968:** The first Academy building belonging to the state police was completed at a cost of $1,000,000 near District 9 and the Quartermaster Depot.

The first, formal Chemical TestProgram to identify the drinking driver was initiated as a result of a federally funded project between the Illinois State Police and the National Highway Safety Administration.

On July 1, the Firearm Owners Identification law went into effect requiring residents of Illinois to register with the ISP if they owned a firearm.

•**1970:** The Illinois State Police Emergency Radio Network (ISPERN), setting a single frequency for use in emergencies by all law enforcement personnel and stations in Illinois, was being prepared.

•**March 17, 1972:** Governor Richard B. Ogilvie broke ground for the expansion to the ISP Academy, nearly doubling it in size.

•**1974**: During the mid-east fuel crisis ISP officers were expected to have their squad cars sitting for a total of one hour per shift with the motor off. Gasoline consumption dropped $500,000 and citations issued increased 10% from the previous year. (The speed limit had been reduced to 55 mph on all roads, including the interstates.)

•**1977**: Reorganization of the department left it with five divisions (State Police, Criminal Investigation, Internal Investigation, Support Services and Administration) and about 3,000 employees.

•**1985**: The ISP assumed responsibility for patrol duties on the Chicago expressways.

•**1986**: At the request of East St. Louis citizens gravely concerned about the incidence of gang violence, the ISP agreed to patrol within the city. On October 6, the ISP started boat patrol on Lake Michigan to reduce the flow of illegal drugs and fight boat theft. (The marine patrol was discontinued in 1991.)

•**1988**: The Division of Forensic Services and Identification implemented an Automated Fingerprint Identification System providing computer comparisons of fingerprints from 10 print cards and latent prints from crime scenes to the 2.6 million ten print cards in the master database.

•**June 22, 1989:** The Chaplain's program was implemented.

•**June 30, 1994:** Legislative Audit Commission Report on the Illinois State Police for the two years ending this date, had 13 findings including a strong criticism of the department for the manner in which "Inspectors" are appointed.

•**1994** The August Illinois State Fair saw Illinois State Police officers in uniform sporting shorts, gym shoes and pith helmets while riding in-line skates and bicycles for the first time. The ISP spent $700 each for four mountain bikes for the fair. Reaction to uniform shorts and officers on skates was mixed at best.

•**July 1996**: The Chicago Police Department Crime Laboratory was merged in to the Illinois State Police Forensic Science Laboratory system with the building of a new 85,000 sq. ft., four story, laboratory at Roosevelt and Damen in Chicago.

Indiana State Police

by Marilyn Olsen

The sounds of gunfire and squealing tires were all too familiar in Indiana six decades ago. Although the Indiana General Assembly had created a state department of Motor Vehicle Police July 15, 1921, it had only 16 officers and its sole mission was to apprehend car thieves. In 1925, the force was finally granted some police powers, but even these powers were limited. An officer couldn't arrest even a known criminal unless he was also a traffic violator.

In 1927, the legislature created an accident reporting and recording system as well as an independent agency to conduct criminal investigations, but these bureaus operated separately.

Late in 1928 the department acquired motorcycles and began to replace its automobiles with them. By 1930, the force had now grown to 60. Because there was no formal training, each officer enforced the law as he saw fit.

According to a later department publication, *The Indiana State Police, 1933-83,* "The trooper had to buy his own gun and uniform out of his pocket or out of his munificent salary. The uniform was blue gray, included two pairs of trousers, two shirts, a cap, a jacket and high boots which had to be laced up. The men rode motorcycles which were either Indian or Harley Davidson (because they) were faster and more mobile than police cars. The trooper was to find himself covering some 100,000 miles a year over two unpredictable Indiana roads, most of them unpaved and often worked 16-hour days. Riding a motorcycle through an Indiana winter required inconceivable fortitude and, because the motorcycles had no windshields, the troopers often had to insulate their uniforms with folded newspapers."

In 1931, a state senate bill provided for an increase in personnel and the creation of a barracks system and sub stations.

In 1933, a Division of Public Safety was created under the executive department of state government. The Detective Bureau, the Criminal Investigation Bureau and the Uniform Division became the Indiana State Police Bureau.

Although in 1928 Indiana had become the third police department in the world to be licensed for police radio, in 1934, the Indiana State Police still had no radio equipment and officers were becoming increasingly frustrated by their inability to communicate with one another. Through public subscriptions, the Indiana Banker's Association raised $30,000, the governor's Contingency Fund $20,000, Culver Military Academy donated space and a short wave radio network was created that would link police agencies for the first time. The system signed on the air in April 1935.

While the AM system was a great step forward, the distance between the stations was too great for reliable communications and it was necessary to relay traffic from station to station, resulting in both error in transmission and lost time.

Still, an effort was made to encourage every city police and county sheriff's department to obtain a receiver on the state police operating radio frequency. By 1936, more than 100 agencies had joined the network.

In 1937, a CW (Morse Code Network) was organized which was considerably quicker and cheaper than using commercial telephones.

The state police had no trouble recruiting able bodied young men to fill their ranks. Eighty-one men started the first class at the Indiana State Fairgrounds in hot, muggy weather. Sixty-six young men finished that first class.

On June 10, 1935, the first Indiana State Police Board was appointed.

For the first time, there were specific standards for applicants. Recruits had to be high school graduates, have lived in Indiana for a year, be at least 5'9" tall, be between the ages of 21 and 34, be in good physical and mental health and be "of good moral character." Officers were also prohibited from entering any tavern except in the performance of duty, asked to stay away from persons of questionable character, and banned from seeking free admission on busses, trains or steamboats. Formal charges could be brought against officers who entered a "disorderly house" while not in the performance of duty, smoking in uniform in public while on duty, entering into religious or political arguments with citizens or prisoners or using "third degree methods" in questioning suspects.

In 1937, the force numbered 170 men. Twenty-five plain clothes detectives were assigned state-wide with nine at headquarters and two at each of the eight posts. Twenty-three radio operators and engineers manned the five radio broadcasting outlets. Two handwriting and fingerprint experts and a staff of clerks conducted the activities of the identification bureau. Three clerks were on duty in shifts at headquarters to assure around the clock service.

All officers were assigned to a barracks. Post duty was rotated among the officers with each man subject to call for duty 24 hours a day. The average workday was 12 to 16 hours, but if an officer was working on a case or

Trooper at the capitol building.

Indiana State Police Superintendent Melvin Carraway and Indiana State Trooper Shawn O'Keefe. O'Keefe received a gold star for valor from the Indiana State Police and was named Trooper of the Year by the International Association of Chiefs of Police for rescuing a small child from a flaming wreck.

called to assist another officer in an emergency, a shift often lasted up to 72 hours.

"Our schedule was that we worked seven days and had one day off," said Retired Trooper Dick Wells. "Then every two months when our day off got to be a weekend, we'd get both Saturday and Sunday, except when there'd be a crime or an accident and then you'd get called out anyway."

While the very early troopers had had to furnish their own uniforms, by 1935, they were issued by the department. The uniform consisted of a police style cap, blue tunic, gray breeches and black boots. Officers were also issued a .38 caliber revolver, a pair of handcuffs and a 12-gauge gas gun as well as a short blue overcoat and a white raincoat.

One man at each post received fingerprint training, another darkroom techniques and photography and a third, proficiency in the use of the Thompson sub-machine gun. All were taught the basics of field investigation and collection and storage of evidence.

An investigations division had been created in 1927 as part of the Bureau of Criminal Investigation and Identification and until 1933 just two investigators handled all crimes reported to the department. In 1933, however, the bureau became part of the Indiana State Police and detective functions were transferred to a detective division of five men.

Realizing early that solving crimes would depend heavily on the gathering and analysis of evidence, as soon as the ISP was created, the Laboratory Division was established.

Although solving high visibility murder cases comprised a portion of the ISP's work, the force was still predominantly a highway patrol and, following the repeal of prohibition, drunk drivers were becoming an increasing menace. Although there were laws on the books regarding drunk driving, proof was pretty much limited to the police officer's word against the driver or, in some cases, the driver's ability to blow up a balloon. In 1939 this all changed when Indiana scientist, Dr. Rola Harger, invented the "Drunkometer" and Indiana became the first state to authorize the use of chemical tests to determine the specific level of intoxication. (In 1955 Indiana would again claim a first, this time in the use of the Breathalyzer, invented by ISP Captain Robert F. Borkenstein and still used widely by police agencies around the world.)

By 1940, just as the Indiana State Police had become a stable and well organized police organization, World War II broke out and yet more responsibilities were given to the department. In addition to police duties, the ISP was now called upon to train civilian Civil Defense volunteers, provide security for war production plants and be prepared to defend the state against enemy attack.

The motorcycles were gone, replaced by 6-cylinder cars. Troopers drove their cars 80,000 miles, took them back to the garage where they were overhauled, then drove them an additional 40,000 miles before they were retired.

In 1946 the ISP borrowed a plane used to help control the crowds flocking to the Indianapolis 500. It didn't take long to see how valuable aircraft could be to the department for this and a variety of other functions. The next year, the Aviation Section was created.

Before 1950, Indiana law enforcement officers could impose fines for traffic offenses, but other than that, they had little authority over what came into or was driven through the state by trucks. In 1951 the General Assembly provided for the hiring of 25 full-time police employees and gave them the responsibility of enforcing laws relating to height, width, length and gross weight of vehicles moving on the public highways of the state. The Motor Carrier Division was created.

Eight new posts, which looked surprisingly like the thousands of prefabricated residential homes being constructed to meet the demands of the parents of the first baby boomers, were constructed between 1955 and 1957.

After years of being able to receive radio transmissions, but having to find a farmhouse or business with a phone to send messages back to the post or to other officers, the ISP finally acquired two-way mobile radios and, in 1947, switched to the FM band.

In 1957 the microwave system was installed in Indianapolis and Pendleton. By December 1960, all state police districts and General Headquarters were interconnected by the microwave system which provided both telephone and teletype communications.

In the mid-50s, uniforms were also modified. Light weight, short sleeved, open collared uniform shirts replaced the heavier wintertime shirts and light weight uniform slacks replaced boots and breeches. A fur trimmed winter hat was provided for cold weather.

A narcotics enforcement section was established in 1954 as part of the Investigation Division and two investigators were assigned full time to coordinate department anti-narcotics functions.

In 1957 Indiana became the first state to use color mug shots. In 1969, in response to the increased frequency of campus bombings, the ISP developed an Explosive Ordnance Disposal Unit for interested personnel. At the same time, The Law Enforcement Assistance Agency was developing a three-week school for police personnel in Huntsville, Alabama at the Redstone Arsenal and nine ISP officers were sent.

A statewide computerized filing system, Indiana Data and Communications System (IDACS) was also brought on-line in 1970 and seven years later the portable/mobile radio repeater system and mutual aid communications network, the Indiana Law Enforcement Emergency Network (ILEEN) were added. As a result of the blizzard of 1978, the Indiana Council or Emergency Response Teams (INCERT) was created and with it a communications network developed between the state police and Amateur and Citizens Band (CB) radio organizations.

In 1970 the air section moved to its present location at the Indianapolis International Airport and in 1972, the department became the second state police agency in the nation to have an FAA approved repair station.

That same year, in one of the department's more unusual transactions, the section also acquired two DC3 aircraft, the thought being that these larger planes could provide convenient transportation for state officials back and forth from Indianapolis to Washington, DC. It soon became obvious, however, that the necessary maintenance of such a large craft would be prohibitive and they were sold six months later.

The Indiana State Police today, like many state police agencies, is headed by a superintendent appointed by the governor. The superintendent has an executive staff consisting of an assistant superintendent (with a rank of colonel), three deputy superintendents (with the rank, lieutenant colonel), and, in the current administration, at least, a civilian special counsel. The Internal Investigations and Equal Employment Opportunity sections report directly to the superintendent as does the Chaplain.

The next level of organization are the Bureaus, all of which are headed by a colonel or lieutendant colonel. The Fiscal and Human Resources and Training Divisions make up the Bureau of Financial Management and Human Resources The Communications, Logistics, Records and Information Technology Divisions report to the Deputy Superintendent of Support Services.

The Bureau of Criminal Investigation, formed in 1998, is composed of three divisions: Criminal Investigation, Laboratory and Gaming. The criminal Investigation Division is composed of three sections: Major Drug, Special Investigations and the Criminal Intelligence Section.

In 1998, the Investigation, Laboratory and newly created Gaming Divisions were combined to form the Bureau of Criminal Investigation headed by the assistant superintendent. The Field Enforcement and Commercial Vehicle Enforcement Divisions report to the Deputy Superintendent of Field Operations. The Division of Research Development and Planning has recently been redesignated as

Professional Standards and become a part of the Fiscal Division.

The Special Investigations Section, headed by a lieutenant, consists of four squads each headed by a squad leader. These squads specialize in three areas: white collar crime, vehicle crimes and crimes against children.

The White Collar Crime Unit concentrates on 10 major types of crime: frauds involving welfare, insurance, Medicaid or Medicare, securities, real estate, credit cards, bank transactions, computers, investment scams and tax evasion.

The Criminal Intelligence Section, also headed by a lieutenant, concentrates in three areas: crime analysis, violent crime and administrative support.

Beginning in 1994, the ISP labs acquired the technology and scientists necessary to staff a section devoted specifically to DNA analysis and since that time have been able to successfully prosecute and convict more than 50 criminals. With the passage of Senate Bill 454 in 1995, they are now collecting DNA samples from the 13,000 incarcerated offenders in Indiana to establish a Convicted Offender Data Base Program.

The Indiana Data and Communications System (IDACS) serves as the department's link from the Records Division into national computer systems which verifies criminal histories, searches arrest records and obtains statistical information.

In many ways, the Field Enforcement Division is where the action is. It has responsibility for the department's three specialty teams: Emergency Response, Explosive Ordnance Disposal and Underwater Search and Recovery.

The Aviation Section is also part of the Field Enforcement Division. Currently the section maintains a fleet of 11 aircraft (two airplanes and a helicopter at its hangar at the Indianapolis International Airport and helicopters and planes in both North and South Field Operation).

In operation since 1939, the Logistics Division of the Indiana State Police continues to do what it has always done - make everyone else's job possible. The Quartermaster Section orders and supplies all uniforms and equipment to the department's 1,100 police officers and 167 motor carrier officers, including basic uniforms and weapons and gear for specialty teams. Located down the hall from the Quar-

In 1933, Indiana Governor Paul McNutt consolidated existing police agencies into The Indiana State Police.

termaster is the area responsible for equipping, repairing and maintaining everything that has to do with police cars. The Logistics Division also maintains vehicles that have been seized in drug forfeitures. The Logistics Division is responsible for all of the supplies and equipment for each individual post and the headquarters staff.

The Commercial Vehicle Enforcement Division, composed of both sworn and civilian personnel, is responsible for enforcing the state's laws that apply to commercial motor vehicles. In addition to staffing the state's weigh stations, motor carrier officers inspect Indiana school busses, monitor hazardous materials transportation and conduct post-crash investigations of commercial vehicles.

Although the staff is small, just 15, the Human Resources Division's role is vitally important to the 1,200 or so police officers and more than 600 civilian employees of the ISP.

For most of the history of the department, public and media relations were handled by district-level sergeants (one in most posts, two in the two largest districts). In July 1998, in an effort to involve more of the ISP's field personnel, the public information function was reorganized into seven sections statewide.

Like Human Resources and Logistics, the Records Division is primarily a civilian operation. Its 90 employees have the responsibility of making sure the paperwork of law enforcement is accurate, accessible and available to those who need it 24 hours a day, 365 days a year. The division also maintains the department's Automated Fingerprint Identification System (AFIS) which now has more than 700,000 prints on file. Nearly 4,500 fingerprints now come into the section each month for matching.

The Indiana State Police administration vows that decisions that are made must benefit the trooper on the road, the clerk in the office, the dispatcher, the motor carrier and the mechanic who support and strengthen the Indiana State Police.

In 1933, Indiana State Police Detective Art Keller fired several shots into John Dillinger's car on a wild chase in Chicago. Unfortunately, Dillinger escaped the shoot-out.

In 1939 Indiana Scientist Dr. Rola Harger inventd the Drunkometer and Indiana became the first state in the nation to authorize the use of chemical tests to determine the specific level of intoxication.

Iowa State Patrol

by Scott M. Fisher

In 1933 Iowa's first woman Secretary of State, Ola Babcock Miller, sent out 15 men to patrol Iowa's roads. These "motor vehicle inspectors" were part of an experiment which would eventually lead to the formation of a full-fledged Highway Patrol. Her directive to the men: "Save lives first - money afterwards."

The creation of a uniformed State Patrol had been the topic of hot political debate for many years. Everyone agreed that the automobile had drastically changed both rural and urban lifestyles. Both law abiding citizens and criminals now had lives of greater mobility. Laws had been passed to regulate the operation of vehicles and encourage safety, but cars got bigger, faster, and more affordable each year. Road conditions improved so much that the previous speed limit of 40 mph was changed to any speed that is safe and reasonable." Highway deaths nearly doubled. Despite many attempts, the Legislature could never agree on specific issues regarding the establishment of a state police force and several such bills died in committee. In the meantime, automobile sales, traffic speed, and highway deaths kept going up.

In one year Iowa's road fatalities dropped 15 percent while the rest of the country experienced an increase of 17 percent. Iowa lawmakers received a huge amount of mail praising the inspectors and the work they were doing. Clearly, public demand for a full-fledged patrol was growing.

In 1935, a bill was proposed that would establish a patrol of 53 men, provide a training school, and give these officers general police powers. After much debate, an amendment was added that stipulated that no more than 60 percent of the officers could belong to one political party. The bill passed both the State House and Senate. It became law with Governor Clyde Herring's signature on May 7, 1935.

John Hattery, a popular Story County sheriff, was appointed the first chief of the Iowa Highway Safety Patrol. His monthly salary, was $200.

With the Depression in full swing, over 3,000 men applied for the 50 patrol positions. The requirements included that all applicants be at least 25 years of age, at least 5'10" and residents of Iowa. They were also to be of "good moral character" and, while no college education was required, it was considered an advantage, and former college athletes had a definite edge. Emphasis was placed on each candidate's personal interview.

Approximately 100 men were selected to attend training at Camp Dodge, an abandoned World War I Army Base near Des Moines. The recruits were paid $40 for their seven-week training session. One of their first assignments was to clear a 10-acre area at the camp which was full of tall weeds. The men also had to completely clean their living quarters - three old, abandoned barracks.

A staff of experienced men instructed the men in such things as court procedures, first aid, physical culture, auto mechanics, motor vehicle laws, statutory law, public relations, jujitsu, small arms, and accident investigation. They also spent time in close order drilling, physical conditioning, and motorcycle riding. Above all, the importance of courtesy to the public was stressed to each man. During their training period, the men were not allowed to leave camp except to attend Sunday church services. By the end of July, the final selection of the "Class of '35" members or "First Fifty" had been made.

On July 29, 1935, 50 officers using 37 cars and 12 motorcycles began patrolling the Iowa highways. They were provided uniforms, accessories, equipment, and vehicles. The officers did not have guns on their first day of patrol, but they were provided Colt .38 Special revolvers later in 1935. Their badge numbers, 25 through 75, were assigned in order according to each man's height. The original black and gold shoulder patch was a unique design which survives to this day. It was designed personally by Chief Hattery and Lew Wallace in the shape of a kernel of corn. Some say the

Iowa Highway Patrolman Traverse Grimm on a model 74 Indian motorcycle, circa 1937.

Iowa Highway Patrolman in front of the 1936 Pontiac squad car.

Iowa Highway Patrolman talking with a violator in 1935. The Patrolman is wearing his summer uniform.

two men had been influenced by a medallion they had seen commemorating the Louisiana Purchase. The patrolmen's summer uniforms were khaki shirts, jodhpur breeches, knee-high boots, and Sam Brown belts with holsters on the right side. Their monthly pay was $100.

The state had been divided into 10 districts. Each officer worked 12-hour shifts, six days a week, with no weekends or holidays off. Although each patrolman was on 24-hour call, there was no overtime pay. Their cars were mostly Ford V-8s, with some Pontiacs and Chevrolets. Some of the men were assigned to ride motorcycles - Indian Model 74s. Each vehicle carried a radio receiver, but no transmitter. Broadcasts giving information about stolen cars, wanted criminals, etc., were made at prearranged times every day so an officer could be sure to be in an area where his receiver would be able to pick up the signal. The men were often out of range. They patrolled alone during the day, and then teamed up in pairs for night duty.

Then, as now, if a patrolman stopped to assist a stranded motorist or pursued a suspicious vehicle, he had no way of knowing what he would encounter. Most often he would find a law-abiding citizen, but there was always the chance that he would come face-to-face with a criminal. With no radio transmitter, he was truly on his own.

In the spring of 1937, the Iowa Legislature authorized an increase of patrol manpower by 75 men. A second training camp was planned and 10 of the original 50 class were promoted to sergeant and each put in charge of new district offices in Des Moines, Oakland, Denison, Cherokee, Fort Dodge, Mason City, Cedar Falls, Cedar Rapids, West Liberty, and Ottumwa.

The patrol also took over all duties involving driver's license testing and issuance. Some of the graduates of the training academy were assigned duties as driver's license examiners rather than as road patrolmen. Also in 1937, the holster for the service revolver was moved to a cross-draw position on the left side.

There were new uniforms with the new decade of 1940. The tall boots and breeches were replaced by oxfords and gray trousers. Khaki blouses were replaced by chocolate brown shirts and caps. A white raincoat was also added. School buses, though routinely inspected in various areas of the state, now came under a statewide program of inspection.

World War II created new problems and responsibilities for the patrol. Although the officers were exempt from serving in the military, over 75 men left the patrol for the duration of the war to serve in the armed forces. This created a shortage of trained manpower. Patrolmen were kept busy escorting convoys of trucks, delivering ration materials, and supervising blackouts. There were numerous false alarms about saboteurs

Iowa Highway Patrolman displaying their summer uniforms and model 74 Indian motorcycles, circa 1935.

Motor Vehicle Inspector talks with a traffic violator. Photo was taken in 1935 prior to the creation of the Iowa Highway Patrol.

planning to blow up bridges and railroad facilities. Shifts were changed to 10 hours during the week, but the old 12-hour shift remained for weekends.

In 1942 Patrolman Buck Cole proposed the slogan, "Courtesy-Service-Protection," be adopted as the official patrol motto and it remains so to this day. By this time, the last of the patrol motorcycles had been retired from service, with few regrets. By 1943 two-way radios were being installed in the squad cars. Also standard for each patrolman's car was a first aid kit, tow chain, shovel, flares, fire extinguisher and flashlight. By 1944 all cars had two-way radios.

In 1946 with the war over and some of the veteran officers returning, the patrol districts were realigned and four new ones were added, bringing the total to 14. Over 750 men

applied to the new training academy, which would fill 36 positions, bringing the total manpower to 163. Officers were issued Model 12 Winchester 12 gauge shotguns.

The next few years saw some increases in patrol pay and benefits in order to keep some of the experienced men from taking jobs in private industry, which offered better wages.

Also in 1950, the patrol headquarters moved to the Lucas Office Building in Des Moines and the State Police Radio Network was modernized.

Also in 1952, officers began painting the number of current Iowa traffic fatalities on the trunks of their cars. A year later, David Herrick became the new chief of the patrol.

In 1954 the patrol began using some unmarked cars and was named the safest fleet operation of its type in the nation.

It was in 1955 that the patrol purchased five "tape type" speed markers. The tapes were set 10 feet apart and could measure a vehicle's speed by how long it took to cover the distance. The patrol also began using aircraft for traffic control. Patrolmen flew as spotters with National Guard pilots in light planes and helicopters. The following year the patrol purchased two Piper Super Cubs of their own to use on a permanent daily basis. There was also a uniform change in 1956. Ties were discarded, except for formal occasions such as court appearances.

In 1957 the patrol strength was increased to 275. Each district was required to have a supervisor on duty 24 hours a day, and doubling up of officers for night patrols was changed to single-person patrols only. The Iowa Legislature approved a night time speed limit of 60 miles per hour and $50 more per month for all officers.

Five of the new radar units were purchased in 1958. President Eisenhower visited Iowa to see the state's first 10 miles of interstate highway, and a new point system for moving violations was implemented. The following year, the patrol manpower was increased to 300 and the officers escorted Russian Premier Nikita Kruschev on his Iowa visit.

The patrol celebrated its 25th anniversary in 1960 by placing first in the National Pistol Shoot Competition. That same year, identification badges were added to the uniforms and unmarked radar patrol cars made their debut. The patrol also purchased three more aircraft.

The largest single increase in patrol manpower, 100 men, was authorized in 1965. Short sleeved shirts became part of the summer uniform and Sam Brown belts were eliminated except for formal occasions. The patrol increased its inventory of riot equipment, including helmets with rear neck guards and plastic face masks, gas masks, and riot sticks.

In 1967 manpower strength was increased to 4l0. The Safety Education Unit was increased to 15 officers in 1969 and the patrol was given access to the National Crime Information Center computer.

The 1970s began with the patrol taking over the responsibilities of the governor's security detail. It was also the beginning of serious disturbances on college campuses across the country, including the University of Iowa campus in Iowa City. Peaceful demonstrations often deteriorated into violence and the patrol, led by Captain Lyle Dickinson, was relied upon to bring a sense of professionalism and order to the scene. These incidents occurred for the next several years with the patrol consistently showing great diplomacy and courage in avoiding potentially tragic situations on campuses. The officers had to also use their training in crowd control at rock festivals.

Civilians began taking over the supervision of the driver's license exams in 1971. President Nixon visited a dedication at Lake Rathburn with the patrol providing escort. The campaign hat was adopted as part of the regular uniform and accident investigation kits were purchased for each patrol car. The following year established some new designations for organization of the patrol. Area headquarters were changed to "divisions" and districts were now called "posts." In addition, patrolmen were now referred to as "troopers." The official name was changed from Iowa Highway Patrol to Iowa State Patrol.

In 1976, the Vehicle Theft Unit was formed and capitol security was assigned to the patrol. New breast badges were issued to all officers and Smith & Wesson .357 magnum model 66 revolvers became the standard issue sidearm. Also, the Emergency Assistance Radio System (EARS) was implemented.

In 1977 the patrol began issuing bulletproof vests. That same year the patrol began forming tactical teams trained by the FBI. A year later, the *Des Moines Register* conducted a poll asking its readers who they trusted most. The Iowa State Patrol finished second only to God in the poll, finishing higher than doctors, teachers, clergymen and athletes. Also in 1978, each trooper was issued a moving radar unit.

In 1981 the patrol had its hands full with prison riots, such as the one at Fort Madison,

Iowa's first woman Secretary of State Ola Babcock Miller, with Jimmy Green (left), Lew Wallace (right) and the 15 original Motor Vehicle Inspectors. Ms. Miller is credited with starting the Iowa Highway Patrol.

and escaped fugitives like murderer, T-Bone Taylor, who was apprehended by Trooper Marvin Messerschmidt.

A year later, in 1984, the PR-24 and speed loaders were issued to each trooper. Also, the State Patrol Chaplains Program was formed.

The 50th anniversary of the patrol was celebrated in 1985. Many retired officers, including members of the original 1935 Class, and dignitaries were invited to the ceremony at Hotel Fort Des Moines.

The 90s began several new patrol programs. Five officers were selected to implement the DARE (Drug Abuse Resistance Education) Program to provide drug awareness information to school-age children throughout the state. In addition, the Adopt A Teddy Program was started after much success in other states in helping children deal with anxiety during a traumatic event. Also, cameras were issued to all troopers.

In 1991 training of officers was begun in the Patrol Canine Program to be put into full implementation in 1992. That same year, the patrol joined the Motor Carrier Assistance Program (MCSAP).

The installation of video cameras began in troopers' cars and the Smith & Wesson .40 caliber automatic became the standard issue sidearm. Heavy flooding devastated the midwest in the spring and summer creating a 60-county national disaster area in Iowa which caused thousands of residents to evacuate homes and businesses. Troopers and National Guard units redirected traffic, tested road and bridge conditions, and located stranded citizens. The patrol officers also helped supervise food supply distribution and relayed much needed medicine to flood-affected areas in the state.

A year later, in 1994, the patrol adopted several new pieces of equipment. The "Stop Stick," which deflates the tires of vehicles, became standard issue in all patrol cars.

Chief John Hattery was appointed as the first Chief of Iowa Highway Patrol in 1935.

Iowa State Patrol hat badge.

FLIR (Forward Looking Infra Red) - an airborne thermal imaging system - was mounted on patrol aircraft. This unit allows the observation and recording of visual images even through darkness, smoke and other low visual settings.

The year 1994 was also the year of implementation of the Motorist Assistance Program and the historical book, *Courtesy-Service-Protection: The Iowa State Patrol,* was published through a joint effort by the Iowa State Patrol Troopers Association and author, Scott Fisher. The patrol also opened an exhibit at the Iowa Gold Star Museum at Camp Dodge near Des Moines. The display is a comprehensive collection of patrol memorabilia, including uniforms (many displayed on mannequins), patch and badge collections, license plates, ticket books and door shields. There are numerous

photos dating from Iowa's early days of law enforcement to the present day, including photos and biographies of the troopers who have died in the line of duty.

In the fall of 1997, troopers were issued and received training on the ASP expandable baton. It is the latest in the patrol's efforts to keep abreast of new technology and law enforcement techniques in the commitment to making the roads safer for all.

Many years and miles have gone by since the little band of 15 motor vehicle inspectors took to the Iowa roads. But even with the changes in uniforms, communications, and vehicles, the goals are still the same. The men and women of the Iowa State Patrol of today continue their highly respected tradition of Courtesy, Service and Protection.

Kansas Highway Patrol

Early Beginning: The Kansas Highway Patrol as it is known today was organized in 1937, however, it truly began four years earlier on July 1, 1933.

During the late 1920s and 30s, Kansas was a haven for organized crime. Such criminals as Bonnie and Clyde, Pretty Boy Floyd and Alvin Karpis were notorious. When the Kansas crime rate reached its peak in 1933, the Governor of Kansas, Alfred Landon in an attempt to curb the crime situation, contacted Wint Smith, an attorney for the Highway Department. Mr. Smith was asked to stop the robbers in any way possible.

Through an act of the Kansas legislature, a force of ten motor vehicle inspectors was created to work under the Director of Highways and State Highway Commission, their main duty being the inspection of vehicles.

The term "Highway patrol" was first introduced into the statutes in 1935 to identify the vehicle inspectors. One headline of that era read: "HIGHWAY PATROL SCARES BANDITS OUT OF KANSAS".

Reorganization: In 1937, Kansas passed legislation creating the Kansas Highway Patrol as we know it today. At that time, the statute provided for a superintendent, assistant superintendent and forty-five patrolmen.

Restrictions placed upon the new patrol members by statute were that no other commission or office could be held, except in the Kansas National Guard or United States Army Reserve and no other employment, gift, reward or compensation could be accepted, without the written permission of the governor. Although these restrictions are still in force, permission may now be obtained through the superintendent.

Patrol members were given statutory authority, power and authority of police officers in the execution of their duties with full power when working with a sheriff or chief of police within their jurisdictions, under the direction of the superintendent or, in the apprehension of a fugitive committing a felony violation. Today, the Patrol is vested with the power and authority of peace, police and law enforcement officers anywhere in the state - irrespective of county lines.

Uniforms worn by the Patrol in 1937 were much the same as they are today. Shirts and blouses were french blue and dark blue trousers sported a french blue stripe on each side. Boots and boot breeches were worn during the winter, slacks during summer. Headgear consisted of french blue caps and the uniform was completed with black Sam Brown belts and holsters.

Patrol cars in 1937 were silver gray or aluminum on top and the body of the vehicles were black. The words "Kansas Highway Patrol" were displayed on the front and rear of the vehicle and gold shields enhanced each front door. The Patrol's fleet of vehicles consisted of thirty-one automobiles and four motorcycles.

Early day patrolmen were without police radio contact and in the course of patrolling their districts made frequent checks with their sheriffs and police departments to determine if they were needed and to advise these agencies of their intended patrolling routes in the event that contact was necessary. Patrolmen always rode in pairs in the early days and were instructed to listen to WIBW radio in Topeka as information was sometimes passed on by this means.

Growth and Expansion: In 1939, the authorized strength of the Patrol was increased to sixty-five patrolmen with a provision in the statute that ten patrolmen would be assigned

to enforcement of all laws designed to produce revenue for the State Highway Fund.

In 1941, the organizational structure was changed by law to provide for a superintendent, assistant superintendent, two executive captains in the central office, six captains, six lieutenants and six sergeants. This was also the year that the Kansas Civil Service Law was enacted, but it applied to the Kansas Highway Patrol only in selection and appointment procedures.

In 1945, another advancement was made possible when legislation was passed to provide the Patrol with two-way state radio communications. Until this time, the only radio communication possible was via receivers placed in some of the cars to monitor police departments in the area or district.

The structure of the Patrol was again revised in 1947. Statute, for the first time, identified the superintendent as colonel and the assistant superintendent as lieutenant colonel. The rank of major replaced the executive captain as executive assistant. The rank of captain as a division commander was retained, but the ranks of lieutenant and sergeant were dissolved. Patrolmen were designated as troopers. During this time, uniforms changed as well and "Ike" jackets replaced the blouse. These jackets obtained their name from their cut and style made popular by General Eisenhower in World War II.

Before 1949, examination of drivers was done only when a complaint against a driver had been made. The Patrol conducted these examinations upon request of the Motor Vehicle Department. In 1949, the legislature passed the Uniform Operator's and Chauffeur's Act which required that certain drivers or applicants for licenses be examined, and made the Patrol responsible for conducting these examinations. Twenty drivers license examiners were added to the Patrol structure and after undergoing six weeks of schooling, they were assigned to various locations in the state to implement the new examination program.

During the period from 1955 to 1956, the Patrol entered into a contract with the Kansas Turnpike Authority to furnish troopers to police the Turnpike. One major, two lieutenants and twenty troopers were assigned this duty. Turnpike troopers wore the same uniform as other troopers; their vehicles were painted the same; and they received the same benefits. Changes to the uniform during this period consisted of open collared shirts and semi-western gray straw hats worn in summer, and blouses again replaced the jacket. The rank of lieutenant was incorporated back into the structure with one lieutenant assigned to each of the six divisions as an assistant division commander. One lieutenant was designated to be the assistant to the captain of safety.

In 1957, the manpower limitation was again raised from one hundred forty-five officers and troopers to one hundred sixty; this was in addition to twenty examiners and twenty-three turnpike troopers.

In 1963, the Patrol began to utilize aircraft in its enforcement program. A plane was used to detect violators from the air and reports were relayed to ground units for action. Speeding violations were detected by using stopwatches to clock vehicles between premeasured points on the highway and speed was established by the elapsed time between these points.

In 1964, the Patrol obtained authority to purchase patrol cars equipped with air conditioning. Kansas was one of the first states to have this equipment. A change was also made in the summer uniform allowing short sleeved shirts to be worn for the first time.

Probably the most important development for the Patrol in 1965 was the acquisition of a building at the deactivated Schilling Air Force Base in Salina. This building became the Training Center and Division Two Headquarters for the Kansas Highway Patrol. Sleeping accommodations were available for fifty-five and dining facilities seated about sixty. Two classrooms accommodated one-hundred students. Communications were improved in 1965 when Kansas became a member of LETS (Law Enforcement Teletype System).

In 1967, another gain in communications was achieved when on December 8, access to NCIC (National Crime Information Center) became a reality through the Patrol's teletype terminal on the LET System. The major of the Division of Services became the major of Telecommunications and Support Services. To commemorate the 30th anniversary of the Patrol in this year, a 1937 Plymouth was found and restored as an original patrol car. This vehicle was displayed at the State Fair and various other events throughout the state arousing much interest from the public.

Today: Authorized manpower for the Kansas Highway Patrol has substantially increased since 1937 to an approximate authorized strength of one colonel, one lieutenant colonel, four majors, eleven captains, twenty-five lieutenants, sixty sergeants, three hundred fifty-nine troopers, sixteen capital police, twenty-seven capital guards, fourteen motorist assistance technicians and three hundred-twelve support personnel for a grand total of eight hundred thirty.

The Patrol is divided into three "regions" consuming the entire State of Kansas. The "East Region" (encompassing Troops A, B & H), the "Central Region" (Troops C & F) and the "West Region" (Troops D & E). Other areas of the Patrol include General Headquarters (in Topeka), Turnpike (Troop G), Criminal Interdiction/Canine unit, Motor Vehicle Enforcement and Motor Carrier Safety Assistance Program (Troop I), Safety Education and Training (Troop J), Capital Police/(Troop K), and Protective Services (Troop L).

Motor Vehicle Enforcement Program: This program provides for inspections of vehicles being titled in Kansas for the first time, vehicles going from a non-highway to a highway title and for all reconstructed vehicles assembled or restored from parts of other vehicles. The "VIN" program's purpose is to verify that the vehicle identification number (VIN) displayed on the title is genuine and agrees with the identification number on the vehicle.

Motor Carrier Safety Assistance Program: This is a federally funded program which provides detailed inspections of regulated motor carriers.

Safety Education and Training: In 1965, the Kansas Highway Patrol Training Academy was established at Schilling Air Force Base. The academy provides for attendees and recruits by housing them in the dormitory, providing meals and shower facilities.

Capitol Police: The Capitol Police was formally created by the Kansas legislature to enforce state laws on or about any state owned, leased or rented property or building in Shawnee County, Kansas.

Protective Services: Troop L provides for the safety and security of the Kansas Governor by attending events in which the Governor is present, accompanying him/her to various destinations and various other duties as assigned by the Governor.

The responsibilities, duties and authority of the Patrol have remained basically the same since 1937, except that present day troopers have full police powers. There are, however, a number of operations/programs in which the Patrol is presently involved, some of which include: Canine Program, Critical Highway Accident Response Team (CHART), Honor Guard, Motorist Assistance Program (MAP), Patrol Fleet, Enforcement, Uniforms, and Safety, Education and Training Programs (ie: D.A.R.E.)

Kentucky State Police

For most Kentuckians today, the sight of a Kentucky state police trooper working traffic along the highway, or answering a criminal complaint in the community, serves as a comforting reminder that the safety and security of the Commonwealth and its people are in good hands. Since 1948, when the now familiar gray uniform first appeared, the Kentucky State Police has come to symbolize a standard in integrity, courage and dedicated professionalism that has made "The Thin Gray Line" one of the most respected state law enforcement organizations in our nation.

Although Henry Ford could not have known it at the time, his greatest invention was to pave the way for a new breed of law enforcement officer.

The automobile made the horse and buggy obsolete almost overnight. Safety on the road was a new item to consider as well as the opportunities a vehicle could provide the criminal element. The automobile, along with the territorial limitations imposed by law on local police officers, was the answer to a fugitive's prayers.

In 1932, Kentucky started to seriously consider the idea that maybe the time had come to examine the need for supplementing its system of sheriffs and local police with some sort of state law enforcement agency whose powers of patrol, pursuit and arrest would extend beyond the limits of any one city, county or district to which their officers might be assigned. It was a question fraught with controversy, however, for the local sheriffs were certain to object strenuously if the General Assembly started

moving in a direction that might threaten to usurp their traditional authority.

Although the 1934 General Assembly knew the state needed something along the line of a state police force, the political consequences of enacting such a measure might be seen back home as an erosion of local authority. Instead, they established an "active militia" within the state's military department. That same year, legislatures gave Kentucky a new driver licensing law.

As governor A.B. "Happy" Chandler made his way to office in 1936, the Legislature put together a Government Reorganization Act which provided for the creation of the State Highway Department. Within that department was to be a Division of Highway Patrol with broad powers to regulate and enforce the traffic laws of Kentucky. But Governor Chandler also empowered the patrol, through executive order, with the authority to preserve public peace under the direction of the adjutant general.

For the next two years the Highway Patrol went about the business of enforcing both traffic and criminal laws without serious challenge to its authority. But in 1938 that status began changing. For the next 10 years, controversy over the patrol's power was debated by government officials and two legislatures. All the while, the patrols duties were being diminished.

If anyone ever deserved to be called "The Father of the Kentucky State Police" it would have to be Governor Earl C. Clements. It was he who saw the need, conceived the legislation and had the political courage to mobilize

the support required, both in the Kentucky House of Representatives and the Senate, to get it enacted into law.

In 1948 Kentucky was about to become the 38th state to pass a State Police Act. On February 26 of that year, the final reading of House Bill 291 before the House proposed that a new state police force be established with full jurisdiction and powers of arrest anywhere in Kentucky, except cities of the first five population classes (1,000 residents or more). There, the state police might enter only by invitation of local officials, or upon order of the governor. Not until 1976, was that single restriction on the KSP's otherwise border-to-border authority finally lifted.

Although the measure was to clear the House 72–16, it did so only after stormy debate, and the opposition was even more intense in the Senate. It was a severe test of legislative loyalty to Governor Clements. However, his loyalists prevailed and the final Senate vote was 25-11 in favor of the measure. Two weeks later, Governor Clements signed it into law, effective July 1, 1948.

The original legislation creating the Kentucky State Police in 1948 provided that the new agency was to be a separate unit of state government with full departmental status. It also stipulated that the commissioner of the department would be appointed by, serve at the pleasure of and report directly to the governor.

But future governors were to take a stand on where the state police ought to be positioned within the bureaucracy. In fact during its history, the Kentucky State Police has been a department, a division and a bureau.

Three men helped shape the state police in its first years as a department. They were Guthrie F. Crowe (1948-52), a LaGrange attorney who later accepted a federal judgeship in the Panama Canal Zone; Charles C. Oldham (1952-55), a Louisville attorney and former assistant superintendent of the Bureau of Traffic for the Louisville Police Department; and P.A.B. "Pete" Widener (1955-56). Widener was a prominent landowner and businessman from Lexington who had also been a detective and later chief of the old Fayette County Patrol.

In 1956, following his re-election as governor after an absence of about 17 years from the Capitol, A.B. "Happy" Chandler asked the General Assembly for a reorganizational legislation.

Under that act, the Department of Public Safety was established to include four divisions – one was the Division of Kentucky State Po-

Cans of Gasoline are carried by state troopers to assist stranded motorists. Cecil Gammons is surprised but grateful as Trooper James G. Kinser lends him fuel.

lice. Each division, including the state police, was headed by a division director whose immediate responsibility was to the public safety commissioner. For the next few years, the state police remained a part of the Department of Public Safety, which had four different commissioners: Don Sturgill (1956-60); Lovern (1960-67); William O. Newman 1968-73); and Ron L. Johnson (1973). Of all the commissioners, Newman was the only one to come from the ranks of the state police.

The KSP had five different division directors during that same period. They were Colonel Paul Smith (1956-60); Colonel David Espie (1960-64); Colonel James "Ted" Bassett III (1964-67); Colonel Charles Crutchfield (1968-70); Colonel Larry Boucher (1970-73); and Colonel Leslie Pyles (1973-74).

Bassett, a former public safety deputy commissioner under Lovern, was the only director who did not come out of the state police ranks.

A strong believer in the value of public relations in law enforcement, Bassett created the theme "The Thin Gray Line," which was first used to focus public attention on the need for more troopers, but has since become synonymous with the state police's reputation for pride, service and achievement. Bassett also was the driving force behind the creation of Trooper Island, a state

police-operated summer camp for underprivileged boys and girls that handles more than 700 children annually.

In 1974 the next major reorganization of the state police took place. Then Governor Wendell Ford abolished the Department of Public Safety and established in its place a Kentucky Department of Justice. The new department was made up of three bureaus: the Bureau of Corrections, the Bureau of Training and the Bureau of the Kentucky State Police.

Four commissioners headed the state police while it was a bureau: Ron Johnson (1973-75), who was also the last public safety commissioner; Dr. Truett Ricks (1975-76), veteran law enforcement educator from the school of Law Enforcement at Eastern Kentucky University; Kenneth Brandenburgh (1976-80), who had been vice-president for business affairs at Transylvania University; and Marion Campbell (1981-82) a career state police officer.

In 1980 Governor John Y. Brown Jr. issued an executive order placing certain special enforcement and security responsibilities, that had been in other departments, within the state police.

From the Department of Transportation, the state police absorbed both the old divisions of Highway Enforcement (which was re-named the Vehicle Enforcement Section) and Water

Safety. From the Department of Finance, the State Police took over the old Capitol Security Police (re-titled the Facilities Security Section). Horse Park Security was transferred from the Parks Department as were park rangers, but the latter returned to control of the Parks Department in 1981.

In order to house and direct these new operations, a command-level division was formed called the Division of Security and Compliance. In 1981 this division was re-designated the Division of Special Enforcement and expanded to include separate sections for narcotics and auto theft investigations.

In 1982 the Kentucky State Police underwent its most recent major reorganizational change and was reclassified a department. All of the Special Enforcement sections that had transferred to the State Police from other agencies were re-assigned to other departments except for Horse Park Security (which was finally relegated to the Department of Tourism in 1984) and the Facilities Security Section (which the state police still maintains today). There were several other major structural changes made within the state police in the 1980s that are still in effect. In 1984 four divisions: Records & Communications, Support Services, Special Investigation and Professional Standards, were all downgraded to branches.

ROADS PATROLLED
BY UNMARKED
STATE POLICE CARS

A Service Division and an Administrative Division were added to the remaining Operations Division.

1940s—

The Kentucky State Police is established in 1948 and LaGrange lawyer, Guthrie Crowe, is appointed the first commissioner.

Four sections - Field Operations and Traffic, Quartermaster & Communications, Personnel Training and Public Relations and Investigations - are set up within the department.

The state is divided into four geographical divisions (later redesigned troop commands) and subdivided into 12 district stations.

The first pay raise for troopers comes six months after establishment of the department. Pay for troopers goes from $130 to $150 per month.

Qualifications for troopers are adopted and three-week training schools set up. (Prior to 1948 there was no training whatsoever.)

All patrol vehicles are equipped with radios and all officers are issued .38-caliber Smith and Wesson Special revolvers.

The state police purchases its first piece of laboratory equipment - a comparison microscope for $1,200.

On Muldraugh Hill in Hardin County, the KSP holds its first traffic safety roadblock.

A new uniform is designed which basically resembles the present-day attire.

1950s—

Regulation shoes are added to the basic uniform issue.

The State Police Merit System is created and the KSP Personnel Board established.

Commissioner Charles Oldham creates a highway safety program called "Kentucky Highway Lifesavers" which helps reduce fatalities by nearly 12 percent in 1954. In fact, for 96 straight days that year there were no fatalities.

Troop commands increase from four to six with 15 posts under these commands. In 1955 a 16th post at Henderson was established. For a brief time there was a 17th post at Fort Knox.

Major vice raids are initiated to clean up gambling and prostitution in northern Kentucky and in the Henderson County area.

"Incognito squads" patrol the highways in unmarked cars, checking for speeders and cracking down on overweight trucking.

The state police purchases its first aircraft.

Investigative Unit is elevated to full bureau status.

Auto Theft Unit is created.

The Department of Kentucky State Police is abolished and reconstituted as the Division of State Police within the newly created Department of Public Safety.

Record recruiting year in 1957 - 125 cadets are trained in four classes.

State Police Retirement System is created.

Work week is reduced from six 10-hour days to five 8-hour days.

Retirement age lowers from 65 to 55.

Number of sworn officers up to 400 in December 1959.

1960s—

The new academy building is dedicated. It also houses the crime and photography laboratories and the Frankfort Post.

Cars change color from black to metallic gray.

Theme, "The Thin Gray Line," is coined by Kentucky State Police Director Ted Bassett.

Trooper Island, located on Dale Hollow Lake and straddling the Kentucky/Tennessee line, is established and incorporated.

Safety education increases and a popular KSP attraction for children at the Kentucky State Fair, "Safety Town," begins.

First radar equipment purchased in the early '60s. A few years later the KSP begins using VASCAR (Visual Average Speed Computer and Recorder). Bureau of Data Processing & Statistics established.

Number of sworn officers goes from 427 in 1960 to 592 in 1969.

1970s—

State highway fatalities decrease by nearly 30 percent - the biggest drop since the KSP was formed.

A drug unit is created. The number of detectives increases three-fold.

A Criminal Investigative Command is formed.

LINK (Law Information Network of Kentucky) is set up - a computerized communications system providing state, county and local police with instant access to crime information.

A Public Affairs Branch is created and an Organized Crime Unit is established.

Blue and white cruisers are introduced in the mid-70s. Cruisers are equipped with light bars and security screens.

Five new forensic labs are built in addition to the central lab in Frankfort, which had served as the only KSP crime lab since 1951.

The first female KSP officer, Sandra Schonecker, is hired.

The KSP receives a new radio system.

Dispatchers receive a 45 percent pay raise.

Professional Standards is created and a new disciplinary system is implemented.

Number of sworn officers increases from 592 in 1970 to 983 in 1979.

1980s—

Switched to an all-white cruiser in the early '80s, then back to a gray cruiser in 1986.

Honor Guard is re-formed. The Special Response Team (SRT) and Automated Fingerprint Identification System, along with Canine, Missing Persons and Hazardous Devices units are created. The SRT, Canine Unit and Hazardous Devices Unit are all housed under a Special Operations Section.

High-speed pursuit Mustangs are purchased.

Civilian license examiners take over duties from sworn officers.

Marijuana eradication begins. Later "Green/Gray Sweep" program combines efforts of KSP and National Guard in marijuana eradication.

Traffic enforcement and criminal investigation are brought under a single full-service Operations Division. Criminal investigation becomes a priority.

A Special Investigations Division is formed and later replaced by a Drug Enforcement/Special Investigations Branch.

Administrative and Services Divisions are established. The Highway Safety Branch, formerly in the Cabinet of Transportation, becomes part of KSP.

Toll-free hotline is created for citizens to report suspected drunk drivers.

Kentucky has 715 highway fatalities in 1985, the lowest number since 1950.

"D-Day" traffic safety campaign is created - it develops into a national program.

DARE and Drug Interdiction programs begin.

Number of sworn officers decreases in the 80s from 998 in 1980 to 913 in 1989.

1990s—

Agency drug-testing policy implemented.

Governor's Marijuana Strike Task Force is formed to advance efforts of marijuana eradication.

State police begin implementing or integrating "Enhanced 911" systems in local communities.

The KSP acquires limited number of video cameras to install in cruisers.

Transition from .357 Magnum to 10 mm revolver.

KSP kicks off award-winning traffic safety program "Highways or Dieways? .... The Choice is Yours."

Legislature approves substantial changes in entry qualifications for KSP applicants.

Child Sexual Abuse Program is created.

A new state-of-the-art centralized lab is constructed in Frankfort.

In 1990 there were 939 sworn officers; today, including 77 cadets, there are 965.

Louisiana State Police

Louisiana State Police is an organization founded on an incredibly rich tradition. Our motto, "Courtesy, Loyalty, Service," has given us direction and inspiration. As the men and women of this organization prepare for the future, we must reflect on the legacy and heritage left by those who preceded us. When the Louisiana Legislature passed a bill in 1936 creating the state police, few observers could have predicted the esteem this agency enjoys in Louisiana and across the nation. Louisiana State Police has emerged from a highway commission in 1922 with a force of 16 men patrolling the highways on motorcycles to its current status of a state police force of 1,022 men and women responsible for all elements of criminal and highway safety interdiction in the state.

Louisiana's first attempt at law enforcement on a statewide level came in 1922 in response to the arrival of the automobile. Louisiana had 2,700 miles of roadway and an estimated 102,000 vehicles. The Louisiana Highway Commission was created and given the power to appoint inspectors to enforce laws relating to the highways. The Commission operated with the state divided into 10 districts; 16 officers patrolled the entire state. During the two-year period from 1922 to 1924, 114 serious accidents and 18,918 violations of motor vehicle laws were reported.

By 1928 the Law Enforcement Division of the Highway Commission was beginning to function as a true state police force. Structural changes were made, dividing the state into three administrative districts supervised by captains. The force had grown to 70 uniformed officers with expanded duties such as managing traffic at large gatherings of people. The officers were also called on in times of emergency such as the "Flood of 1927." The men were commended for their meritorious service in the evacuation of flood victims and patrolling the Mississippi River levees. At this time an additional branch of law enforcement, the Bureau of Criminal Investigation, was established to deal with criminal activity not related to traffic laws. In 1932 the State Highway Patrol was given the authority to carry firearms.

On July 28, 1932 the two divisions of law enforcement were combined to form a modern, well-equipped and well-trained force known as the Louisiana Department of State Police. The department thrived under the direction of an appointed superintendent, General Louis F. Guerre. His goal was to model state police after J. Edgar Hoover's famed "G-Men." This was accomplished to a great extent with the establishment of a training school and a crime lab. High priority was given to the crackdown on narcotics trafficking. Under Guerre's direction, the state was organized into 11 districts. A total of 146 state police personnel were assigned to the patrol districts, the training school, and the Bureau of Investigation. It was during this era that the state police adopted the slogan, "Courtesy, Loyalty and Service." Guerre also established the State Police Headquarters at the old prison site on Jaybird Lane (now South Foster Drive) in Baton Rouge. This site is still in use today.

In 1940 the State Civil Service System was established offering "protection from political considerations" to state police officers as well as other state employees. This legislation was backed by reform governor, Sam Jones, and was dismantled by Earl Long when he returned to the executive office in 1948. State police would not gain protection under Civil Service again until 1952.

Another major change came about in 1942 when the Louisiana Legislature abolished the Department of State Police and made it a division of the newly created Department of Public Safety. State police accepted new responsibilities in 1946 when the Driver's License Law was enacted requiring every driver to hold a license for operating a motor vehicle. Prior to this time, only the operators of commercial vehicles, trucks, and buses were required to be licensed. Under the leadership of Colonel Francis C. Grevemberg, state police added an air patrol to its ranks. This was the beginning of the use of aircraft to track down fugitives, assist in emergency situations, and monitor speeders on the state's highways. At the same time a stock patrol, officers on horseback, was established to remove stray farm animals which might be grazing or wandering along roadways. This team of officers would later play a major role in providing security at rock concerts and for civil rights' marches. During Colonel Grevemberg's administration Louisiana first experienced gambling raids. This crackdown

focused on major syndicate-owned casinos, prostitution rings, bookmaking operations, and even included church bingo games. However, the campaign against gambling and associated vices did not last long. When Earl Long took control of the Governor's Office once again in 1956, he announced that state police would no longer "harass and intimidate the citizens." This attitude against using state troopers in gambling raids prevailed through the administrations of Governors Jimmy Davis and John McKeithen.

In 1961 the Legislature passed a new law requiring the inspection of all motor vehicles. Then, in 1962 the Legislature enacted a new highway code which established a maximum speed of 65 mph on multi-lane highways and 60 mph on other highways. Together, these were considered steps toward improving highway safety.

State troopers faced what may have been their most challenging assignment when they, along with the Louisiana National Guard, were called to guard and protect civil rights' marchers in Bogalusa. In 1965 and again in 1967, troopers had the task of trying to prevent the violence and bloodshed that had scarred other cities across the nation during the civil rights' struggle. These demonstrations, in addition to others occurring on college campuses across the country, prompted state police to add "Big Bertha" to its armory in 1968. "Big Bertha" was a homemade anti-riot armored vehicle weighing 13 tons and costing $22,000 to construct.

Under the leadership of Colonel Stanley Berthelot, many changes took place in the department, most of which were instituted in 1969. The Louisiana State Troopers was created in an effort to improve the quality of working conditions, to increase salaries, and to serve as a means to address troopers' major concerns. Also at this time state police increased the efficiency of its air patrol. The airplane was augmented by three helicopters, providing more versatility. Colonel Berthelot also added a Tactical Unit to the force at headquarters and each of the 11 troop districts. This was an entirely new concept for state police, allowing the department to respond to emergency situations which were beyond the capacity of local police to handle.

In 1971 the Narcotics Education Unit was established to enlighten young people and their parents about the dangers of drug abuse. The "Festival of Life," which attracted 60,000 concert goers in June of 1971, proved that drug use among young people had become so widespread that it was impossible to arrest every offender.

In 1972 Colonel Donald Thibodeaux was appointed by Governor Edwin Edwards as superintendent of state police. Colonel Thibodeaux led the department through many reforms, most of which are still in effect today. He began the reorganization of the state police structure by adding three regional of-

Trooper Jimmy Thaxton clears an obstacle at the Louisiana State Police training academy in Baton Rouge.

Troopers in front of State Police Memorial at HQ in Baton Rouge.

fices to supervise the 11 troop districts. During Thibodeaux's administration, personnel in the department increased by 235, and in 1976 Louisiana recorded its lowest highway fatality rate in history, 4.1 deaths per one hundred million miles traveled. Among the new sections formed by Colonel Thibodeaux were the Internal Affairs Unit, which investigates any complaints lodged against members of the state police; the Merit Board, which reviews the applications for promotion in the department; and

the Explosives Control Unit, which oversees all matters concerning explosives and investigates incidents involving suspicious devices.

Colonel Grover "Bo" Garrison took office in November 1976 and was reappointed to the position in 1980 by Governor Dave Treen. Garrison was one of only two superintendents of state police to survive a change in administration. Colonel Garrison led state police to its highest staffing level of 960 troopers in 1984. Many factors contributed to this tremendous

growth, including the availability of funding and increased emphasis on narcotics enforcement and countering drug smuggling. Smuggling had become a tremendous problem in Louisiana during the late 70s and early 80s as a result of increased federal patrols along the Florida Coast. This higher concentration of officers in the Florida area caused smugglers to shift their operations to ports along the inner Gulf Coast. State police still focus a great deal of attention to narcotics enforcement today.

After 1984 the economic picture changed dramatically for Louisiana. Oil prices plunged worldwide and South Louisiana saw a tremendous shutdown in oil production. The loss of oil and gas revenues caused state government to begin trimming its budget. Though the Department of Public Safety was affected by the economic crunch, it began to take on added responsibilities. In 1986 the Charitable Gaming Unit was formed to regulate bingo, raffles, and other charitable fund raisers. At the same time, the Racing Investigations Unit was put into place to maintain the integrity of pari-mutual racing in the state. The Motor Carrier Safety Section was given the responsibility of regulating the trucking industry on Louisiana's highways.

Continued budget cuts in 1988 resulted in the closure of Troop H in Leesville and Troop K in Opelousas and the consolidation of the state police structure into three regional commands with three troops in each region. Also, the Criminal Investigation Bureau was reorganized and reduced in size, severely affecting investigations. The three regions were given additional responsibilities as narcotics enforcement was moved from headquarters to the region areas. As the 1980s came to a close, the Louisiana State Police was a much leaner organization. Through budget cuts, the department was able to maintain its many responsibilities with a manpower of 650 troopers patrolling the state's highways.

In 1992 the department took over a new and much more complex responsibility - river boat and video poker gaming. Operating with a small contingency of troopers, the Louisiana State Police began formulating the tough licensing process for all who either wished to own a river boat casino or operate a video poker franchise. Although the task seemed overwhelming, experienced "highway patrolmen" quickly adjusted from law enforcers to regulators. The department began to flourish with new equipment and more manpower as a result of being the chief watchdog of the new gaming industry. With this newly added equipment and manpower, the department was able to take on a different role in law enforcement, that of assisting all law enforcement agencies by using the Automated Fingerprint Identification System (AFIS). AFIS provides law enforcement with a tool that instantly identifies a person through their fingerprints, which are imperative to criminal identification and arrest. Also, a totally updated 800 megahertz radio system was implemented which allows multi-agency or jurisdiction coordination among all law enforcement agencies.

With the successful completion of seven straight academy classes in the past five years, the purchase of state of the art technology such as AFIS, and the growing number of agents allocated in the Bureau of Investigation, the Louisiana State Police has regained the strength lost as a result of the budget cuts of the late 80s. Coupled with its growth is a new and innovative superintendent, Colonel W.R. "Rut" Whittington. In January of 1996 Colonel Whittington began his "tour of duty" and one of his first directives was to eliminate the managerial tool of "quotas" which had been used in several parts of the state. Governing the organization by trusting its members to do the right thing for the right reason, done in the right way, Colonel Whittington emphasizes troopers using their individual decision making skills.

Louisiana's State Police are men and women from the rolling hills of North Louisiana to the bayous of the South who have devoted their lives to the protection and safety of their fellow citizens. This is our history. As we prepare to embark on a new millennium we are preparing for an even brighter future, mindful of the heritage and the legacy of those who came before us.

Trooper Chris Prescott and Sergeant Steve Bauam. Troop "A" Motorcycles.

A graduating cadet class at the LSP Training Academy.

Maine State Police

The Maine State Police began as the Maine State Highway Police in 1921 when inspectors were hired to patrol the state's roads. The inspectors answered to the State Highway Commission. Some of the inspectors were issued motorcycles while others were assigned to offices around the state. They enforced the motor vehicle laws of the state and collected vehicle registration and driver's license fees. The first Maine trooper to die in the line of duty was Emery O. Gooch when he lost control of his motorcycle in 1924.

In 1925 the state Legislature enlarged the powers of the state highway police to enforce all the laws of the state and allowed for the appointment of a chief. The state highway police was separated from the highway commission and became a separate department. Sixty men met in Augusta to be sworn in as state highway police officers. They were each assigned a motorcycle, a pistol, and a law book, and were assigned patrol areas. They were paid $28 a week.

For 10 years, Maine's troopers patrolled 365 days a year with motorcycles. Many troopers wrapped their legs in newspapers for protection from the bitter Maine winters. The troopers had no radios, so headquarters would contact troopers by calling local stores by telephone. The store owners would hang red flags outside to notify the trooper to call in. All points bulletins came to the troopers by way of Western Union telegrams.

Maine lost another trooper in the line of duty in 1925 when Trooper Fred Foster was killed when his motorcycle struck a horse. Foster had been sworn in just a few months before. Maine's third trooper to die in the line of duty was Trooper Frank Wing. Wing was killed in 1928 when his motorcycle hit an oil truck.

In 1935 the complement of sworn officers was increased to 100 and the name was officially changed to the Maine State Police. In 1936 most of the motorcycles were traded in for black sedans. For the first time, troopers were assigned specifically to police commercial motor vehicles. A new State Bureau of Identification was created within the state police to keep all the criminal records for the state.

By the mid-1940s, the Maine State Police had a new headquarters building in Augusta and new barracks in Houlton and Thomaston. The state police had six field troops. Some troopers were assigned to work criminal cases and became the beginnings of the Criminal Investigation Division. Several detectives started specializing in forensics and it wasn't long before they started a rudimentary crime laboratory. In 1942 troopers' schedules changed from seven days a week to one day off in seven.

During the Second World War, many troopers resigned to join the military services, including the chief of the state police, Henry P. Weaver. Troopers who remained drove with headlights half shuttered at night because of the threat on the coast from German submarines. One of their patrol duties was to check for blackout curtains on all buildings facing the sea.

In 1955 the Maine State Police created a new field troop to patrol the newly opened Maine Turnpike. The next few years saw the first blue lights on the cruisers, the first polygraphs, and the first K-9s.

The Maine State Police has continued to grow and evolve. The complement of the Maine State Police is now over 300 sworn officers and it is now a bureau within the Maine Department of Public Safety. The Maine State Police is a full service agency, from daily rural motor vehicle and criminal law enforcement to many highly specialized services available within no other law enforcement agency in the state.

There are eight field troops which are responsible for all law enforcement in areas without municipal police departments. The field troops consist of a lieutenant, three or four sergeants, and troopers. Troop A, based at the Alfred Barracks, covers Maine's southernmost county, York County. Troop B, located at the Gray Barracks, covers Cumberland, Oxford and Androscoggin counties. Troop C covers Franklin, Somerset and northern Kennebec counties, with offices at the Skowhegan Barracks.

Troop D, based in Thomaston, handles southern Kennebec and Sagadahoc, Lincoln, Knox and Waldo counties. Troop E, based in Orono, covers Piscataquis and Penobscot counties. Troop F, based in Houlton, covers Maine's largest county, Aroostook. Troop G, located in South Portland, covers the Maine Turnpike. Troop J covers Hancock and Washington counties, with offices in East Machias.

The Criminal Division investigates all homicides in Maine with the exceptions of those in Maine's two largest cities, Bangor and Portland. State police detectives are also responsible for child abuse investigations and major crimes investigations. The Hostage Negotiations Team is located within the Criminal Investigation branch. The offices of the three branches of the Criminal Division are located in Gray, Augusta and Bangor.

The Maine State Police Crime Laboratory in Augusta examines evidence not only from the state police, but also from all the law enforcement agencies in the state. It is the only full service crime lab in the state. DNA analysis, fingerprints, firearms and criminalistics examinations are all provided. The state police polygraph examiners are also based at the lab.

The State Police Traffic Division, with offices in Gardiner, is home to Troop K, the largest troop in the state police. With troopers located statewide, Troop K is responsible for commercial vehicle enforcement, enforcing both state laws and federal motor carrier safety laws. The Traffic Division is also home to the Inspection section, which enforces Maine's Motor Vehicle Inspection Program and the Schoolbus Safety Inspection Program. The third section in Troop K is the Accident Sec-

tion. All motor vehicle accident records for the state are processed at the Traffic division. The Accident section is also responsible for the Accident Reconstruction, Forensic Mapping and Vehicle Autopsy programs.

The Special Services Unit, located in Gardiner, has detectives assigned to Criminal Intelligence, Beano and Games of Chance, and the licensing of private investigators. Special Services also includes the Executive Protection Unit, which provides security for the governor and the governor's family as well as visiting dignitaries.

Also within the Special Services Unit are the State Police Air Wing, the Tactical Team the Underwater Recovery Team and the K-9 Unit. The services of these specialties are available not only to the state police but also to any

law enforcement agency in the state. Through the New England State Police Assistance Compact, these specialty services are also available to assist other New England State Police agencies.

State police training's new facility is in Vassalboro. State police recruits undergo a rigorous 23-week academy, followed by a field training program. The Training Unit also oversees in-service training and continuous firearms requalifications. The Planning and Research Unit, located at headquarters, is responsible for state police policy, CALEA accreditation, and grants. The Internal Affairs Unit, located in Gardiner, investigates all complaints against members of the state police to ensure the highest accountability of all state police personnel.

Specialist Trooper David C. Alexander and Trooper Diane A. Vance in Maine State Police summer and winter uniforms.

Maryland State Police

This history is a culmination of many sources which includes the 1985 Maryland State Police Yearbook, documentation from the Maryland State Police and state police headquarters. This account was compiled by the Maryland Troopers Association Public Relations Committee-Frank Esposito, Chairman.

In the beginning Maryland's finest had one primary objective - the motorist and the "growing tide of the automotive industry."

During the 1920s, then Governor Albert C. Richie called for the creation of a motorcycle force to patrol state highways. Today, because of the dedication of its troopers, the Maryland State Police has grown and evolved into one of the most professional and respected law enforcement agencies in the United States.

From the early days of combating "organized poultry thefts" to today's war on illicit drugs and campaigns against drunk driving, Maryland State Troopers were there, called upon in times of crisis and dangerous situations. These law enforcement professionals are looking out for the residents, business owners and the visitors of Maryland. And with the evolution and growth of the state has come a new wave of duties, dangers, crime and criminals.

Today, Maryland State Troopers wearing the prized uniform and badge take to the roads and skies daily in all types of weather and in all conditions looking out for the citizens of Maryland.

On April 26, 1920, four masked men entered the bank in the town of Sandy Springs in Montgomery County. Their avowed purpose was, of course, robbery. Their plans seemed to work perfectly. Entering the bank just before closing, they took the entire staff by surprise. They forced the employees into the vault and looted the bank of all the cash on hand and a large number of securities, escaping in an automobile.

And yet, because it happened that one of the bank directors was slightly deaf and did not hear the command "Hands up," he was shot down in cold blood - without provocation.

This crime has been mentioned because its prominence ultimately led to the organization of the Maryland State Police.

In May 1921, a whirlwind three-day tour of the state was made by this newly organized police force. The people of Maryland were so impressed by the new force. It was efficient, fast-thinking and, most of all, fast-acting.

Entire towns were reported to have turned out to catch a glimpse of, and to cheer on, the arrival of this police force.

The first annual report of this police entity was filled with amazing statistics for its scope and size, which seemingly justified the budget expenditure of $77,490.80 for that year.

The next decade brought few changes to this police force.

On June 1, 1935, Chapter 303 of the Acts of 1935 of the Maryland Legislature went into effect and subsequently separated the Motor

Troopers Coalition members meeting with President George Bush at White House, May 1990.

Vehicle Police Force from the Office of the Commissioner of Motor Vehicles by creating a new department known as the Department of Maryland State Police.

Immediately after Governor Harry W. Nice signed the law creating the Department of Maryland State Police, 54 members of the new force were administered the oath of office. The only changes in the uniforms were the new red and yellow triangular cloth arm patches bearing the name of the new force and a new badge.

The increase of motor traffic caused the few remaining horses to become an ineffective method of patrol. The last horses were sold in June 1935.

In August 1941, the MSP established a training school at the National Guard Armory in Pikesville. The Armory had been vacated after the unit had been called to duty. That site continued to be the agency's training facility until the 1950s.

Following World War II, as the troopers were forced to vacate the Armory, a site nearby was selected as MSP Headquarters. The site chosen was the Old United States Arsenal, which had origins dating back to the end of the War of 1812. The arsenal remained a military installation until the 1880s, when it was renovated into the Old Confederate Soldiers' Home. Almost 60 years later it was again renovated, but this time for the Maryland State Police. On Sept. 9, 1950, the new headquarters was dedicated.

The 1950s also marked a new look for Maryland State Troopers. In July 1951, troopers turned in their old triangular patches and taxi driver-style patrol caps for a patch featuring the shield shown in the state seal and the wide-brim Stetson, which are worn by troopers today.

The decade also brought about new technologies for MSP. The use of radar was introduced, and the department took delivery of its first airplane.

Troopers' base pay was $2,950 in 1956. They were paid on a semi-monthly basis and granted 96 days of leave a year, with 15 days of vacation.

In 1960 the State Police saw the formation of the Aviation Division, with the delivery of the agency's first helicopter. This decade also brought about the formation of two additional significant units, a 10-man dive team established in November 1960 and the activation of an Intelligence Unit to work against organized vice rings.

To further enhance communication capabilities and apprehension of criminals, the state police joined the teletypewriter network in 1963. The close of the decade saw the formation and operation of the agency's Automotive Safety Enforcement Division.

Before the end of 1967, the state police joined the National Crime Information Center, also known as NCIC.

White House, August 8, 1994. Johnny Hughes discusses provisions of the Crime Bill with President Bill Clinton.

The dawn of the 1970s saw another reorganization of the Maryland State Police. The year also gave birth to the state's first Med-Evac Program.

When Hurricane Agnes devastated parts of Maryland, troopers throughout the central region of the state worked around the clock to save hundreds of lives as high winds and floodwaters ravaged the countryside.

In a continuing effort to fight crime, a Narcotics Strike Force was formed between 1972-73. This led to identifications and arrests of many drug dealers in Maryland.

The era ended when the state police retired the last black and green-painted patrol cars. Troopers had been using cars painted in the two-tone paint scheme since 1935. This color combination was replaced by a yellow scheme. The change was initiated as an effort to make cruisers more visible and save money.

The decade of 1976-85 continued to reveal the Maryland State Police's commitment to provide quality law enforcement services to the state and its citizens. The year 1978 brought about the implementation of innovative traffic enforcement programs such as *Mother Goose, Operation CARE, and Operation Yellow Jacket.* These programs paid off for Maryland as traffic deaths dropped to a 13-year low. A year later, the agency's move to improve with the implementation of state police's new accident investigation system.

During that same year, and in the wake of an increasing number of hostage barricade incidents occurring throughout Maryland and the country, the state police organized a highly trained group of troopers and formed the Special Tactical Assault Team Element. The State units are still called upon today for high risk warrant services, barricades, narcotics raids and other incidents requiring their expertise.

In the 1980s, the Maryland State Police again made several changes that directly af-

July 29, 1987, at The White House, Maryland Troopers Association President Johnny Hughes and National Troopers Coalition Chairman Thomas J. Iskyzycki and other National Law Enforcement Officials meet with President Ronald Reagan. President Reagan was given an official "Trooper Stetson" and later placed it on his head making him an "Honorary Trooper."

fected troopers working the roadways and highways. These changes also directly benefited the citizens and visitors to the state.

In response to outcries from the public and formation of such organizations like the Mothers Against Drunk Drivers and Students Against Drunk Drivers, the agency cracked down on motorist driving under the influence of alcohol with preliminary breath testing, Sobriety Checkpoints and the use of federally-funded drunk driving patrols.

In 1984 troopers again saw a change in the color scheme of marked cruisers. The yellow patrol car was replaced by tan cruisers featuring a brown and black stripe. Also changed were the emergency lightings on the cruisers.

Aviation Division, Aerospatiale Dauphin II.

Maryland State Police, Patrol and Rescue Vehicles.

Johnny Hughes NTC Legislative Director with former U.S. Attorney General Janet Reno. Hughes presented General Reno with an "official trooper stetson" and "Honorary Trooper" status. She proudly placed the stetson on her head.

The bubble lights were replaced with modern blue and red light bars.

During the decade, the Maryland State Police brought back the use of its Motorcycle Unit following a 35-year absence.

In 1989 the agency experienced significant change with the delivery of the first twin engine Dauphin helicopter. The sleek aircraft had the ability to carry multiple patients and was fitted with the latest in sophisticated navigational equipment. That same year, troopers also took delivery of better firepower, receiving 9 mm Beretta semi-automatic handguns. The semi-automatics replaced .357-caliber revolvers.

The beginning of the 1990s was a time of turmoil for the MSP. In response to the state's troubled fiscal situation in 1991, then Governor William Donald Schaefer, shocked the agency as well as the citizens of Maryland with cuts to the state police. He announced the closure of two barracks, the firing of the state police trooper recruit class in the academy and the threat to terminate more than 100 troopers on the job. The governor's actions were met by staunch criticism from the citizens, the press and police officers from around the state. Nearly 400 troopers, clad in "Class A" uniform, staged a march on the State Capitol Building in Annapolis in protest.

The 1990s also brought an increased effort by troopers, both those in plain clothes and in uniform, in tackling the trafficking of narcotics. The use of drug-sniffing K-9 units became more prevalent, particularly when working with highway interdiction teams.

As the federal government relaxed its restrictions on the state in terms of a maximum speed limit, the state of Maryland followed the trend of most states by increasing the limit to 65 mph on some of its major interstates. With this change, the state police responded by executing a "Zero Tolerance" policy. This task has been made easier with the use of radar, VASCAR Plus and laser as part of the MSP arsenal.

In 1995 and 1996, the MSP saw two more significant changes. First, the agency returned to the traditional black and green colors for its cruisers, which were commonplace until the early 1970s. A year later, troopers began the conversion to the .40-caliber semi-automatic Beretta as the agency's service weapon. While the weapon carries four less rounds, its performance surpasses the 9 mm formerly.

The 1990s also meant several innovative initiatives for the MSP, when the agency opened its Computer Crime Unit and started the first-of-its-kind Community Policing Academy in the country.

The Maryland State Police is committed to creating a diverse, entrepreneurial organizational culture capable of responding to an ever changing environment. This culture will serve to enhance the quality of life for all Maryland citizens by delivering the highest quality of leadership and police services. Leadership and services will focus on areas related to providing safer highways, reducing violent crime, institutionalizing and practicing problem solving community policing, providing high quality training, leading in anti-bombing and anti-terrorism efforts. All aspects of this vision will be performed with integrity, competence and within the highest standards of the law enforcement profession.

The Maryland State Police became the first state police agency to organize a Bicycle Patrol. The idea originated with Corporal Christopher Sasse, who is assigned to MSP's Resident Trooper Program in the Walkersville area of Frederick County. The ability to appear undetected and unexpectantly has made this type of patrol a success. It also helped establish a close personal contact with citizens.

The Maryland State Police have one of the oldest and continuous K-9 programs of any state police agency in the country. The K-9 Unit has a proud tradition dating back to 1961. Currently, there are 36 handlers working 51 dogs at 18 of the state's 23 barracks in Maryland.

The primary mission of the unit is to support the Field Operations Bureau with a variety of canine functions which enhances the overall mission of the department. These canine functions include patrol dogs, CDS detection, explosive detection, gun detection, and cadaver dogs. The Maryland State Police also have seven bloodhounds in use, which is more than any other state police department in the country.

The State Police organized its first STATE Team in 1979 after looking at the civil liabilities being suffered by other police departments and the growing number of subversive groups emerging. Police departments were faced with perpetrators equipped with large amounts of firepower.

The Maryland State Police Aviation Division celebrates over 40 years of providing medical evacuation (Medevac) service to the citizens of Maryland. It is a public safety-oriented organization. Its mission is to protect and improve the quality of life through the airborne delivery of emergency medical, law enforcement, and search and rescue services to the citizens of the state of Maryland and its neighbors 24 hours a day.

In 1970 a single helicopter provided medevac service for the entire state of Maryland. Today, the Aviation Division has grown into eight helicopter sections geographically located throughout the state. Additionally, a fixed wing section provides prisoner extradition, photographic and other law enforcement services; and a headquarters complex containing its own Federal Aviation Administration (FAA) certified repair facility and various other support and administrative services are located at Martin State Airport.

The most important focus of the MSP Aviation Division revolves around its over-riding commitment to safety. The Aviation Division's admirable flight safety record has been continuously recognized over the years

throughout the air medical industry. Since 1989 the Aviation Division has consecutively flown more than 48,000 accident-free flight hours and safely completed over 37,000 Medevac flights. This impressive safety record enables the program to attract and employ the most highly qualified and skilled pilots and flight paramedics in the country.

In order to fulfill the challenge of its multi-mission profile, the MSP Aviation Division staffs its aircraft with a pilot and a flight paramedic. Each flight paramedic is a Maryland State Trooper who is a nationally registered paramedic and each pilot is FAA commercially licensed and instrument rated with a minimum of 2,000 hours of helicopter flight time. The flight crews are supported by MSP command staff, training and risk management sections, as well as maintenance, inventory, avionics, and clerical personnel.

The Aviation Division currently is compromised of a complement of 154 dedicated personnel (51 uniform and civilian pilots, 45 trooper/flight paramedics, and 58 additional support staff).

Maryland State Police K-9 Unit, TFC Christina R. Force and Daisy.

Maryland State Police Resident Trooper, Cpl. Christopher M. Sassie.

Maryland State Police Superintendent, Colonel David B. Mitchell.

25th Anniversary of Maryland State Police Aviation Division Celebration. April 1995. L to R: Former Superintendents Maryland State Police. Red Travers, 1982-1985; George Brosan, 1985-1987; Johnny Hughes, Larry Harmel, Current Superintendent, David Mitchell, 1995-current; Former Superintendent Elmer Tippett 1987-1992.

Massachusetts State Police
The Millennium Visible

An Introductory Essay

Those are large words. But they fall short of the reality. The Millennium is visible. More, its approach seemingly quickens as one contemplates the challenge of writing an opening essay about an enforcement odyssey now on the cusp of the 21st century. So much is out there. So much has happened. Choices, difficult choices, must be made. It is not easy.

To begin, one visualizes an "historical overview." Composed of three distinct eras, it spans the years from 1921 through the 1996 75th anniversary. In reality, these are three "mini histories," each 25 years long: from the 1921 founding until 1946, from 1946 until 1971, and from 1971 until the present.

Each era was unique. Each witnessed significant organizational change. All were profoundly affected by the social and cultural dynamics of the larger society. The latter, especially, is a fascinating perspective of how and why an enforcement odyssey carves out its historical journey. Clearly, it receives much prompting along the way.

Beginnings
1921-1946

The automobile in 1921 created the uniformed "State Police Patrol." There were other factors, but the new mobility changed how people lived, - and how criminals operated. Trips were reduced from days to hours. Population centers were more closely linked. Mobility expanded steadily. Local law enforcement's reach was weakened. A state-wide enforcement capability was the solution. The environment thus spawned the organization.

This volume's early pages describe in detail the 1921 founding and the first cadres of uniformed troopers. It is worth repeating here that these enforcement pioneers embodied an idea more than an enforcement organization. An idea whose time has come is a powerful force, but it is also fragile. It requires commitment and constancy, overtime. Those first troopers supplied both. And then some. Today's modem enforcement organization endures as their legacy. That is a large accomplishment.

Two profound forces shaped the first 25 years, The Great Depression and World War II. The 1920s had witnessed much turnover in the uniformed force as the organization struggled with its identity. By the end of the first decade, however, structural and staffing stability took hold as the enforcement odyssey found its footing. But more ominous threats were about to descend on the organization, the state and the nation.

Some things can be read and understood. One gets the feeling. But others, the truly transformational, must have been lived. The 1930s Great Depression was such an experience. With it, a pall of social and personal gloom descended upon a nation fearful for its future. The state force did not escape. Organizational expansion and personnel improvements were not ascendant in the presence of fears for the Federal Republic's survival, especially for its democratic institutions.

The 1930s Great Depression immobilized the nation. That is putting it mildly. Fear drove out hope. Personnel of the state force did not complain. With unemployment approaching 25%, they, at least, had jobs. But what a job it was.

The complement of the force during that decade hovered around 250. The duty week remained well over 100 hours.

Most troopers traveled long distances to their duty post, - usually by bus. It was not a job, certainly not a profession, but a lifestyle. The organization, with its rigidity and authoritarian principles, was ascendant. The Great Depression had effectively muffled individual aspirations and the natural tendency to improve the working conditions of a maturing enforcement agency.

One example of the depression's direct effect on the state force was seen in the 25th Recruit Troop which began training in Framingham on August 15, 1933. Twenty-four recruits trained in that class. To put it mildly, they were the select few. They had been appointed to the academy from 7,000 applicants! Moreover, a substantial number of the fledglings held baccalaureates. Some had advanced degrees, a startling anomaly that reflected the Great Depression's impact on the professional classes. It was not the best of times. Not by a long shot.

Still, there at the depression's nadir, an enduring tradition was created when on November 4, 1933, the 25th Recruit Training Troop graduated in their brand new French and Electric Blue uniforms. That evening, in Boston's Commonwealth Armory, the 24 recruit troopers were the first academy graduates to wear the distinctive and distinguished two-tone blue colors that, as these words are written, yet instantly identify one of the nations' premier enforcement organizations. That is not an inconsequential legacy to author in the depths of this country's most fearsome domestic era.

Scholars yet argue about why and when the Great Depression ended. President Franklin D. Roosevelt's New Deal had begun to replace fear with hope. Clearly, his administration's bold legislative initiatives were beginning to turn things around. But it was the December 7, 1941, Japanese strike at Pearl Harbor that galvanized the latent patriotism of the American people. A dispirited population, weary from the depression's long siege, almost overnight transformed itself into the "Arsenal of Democracy." The Great Depression ended right then and there. Japan would pay dearly for its historic miscalculation.

World War II froze the Massachusetts State Police in place. For example, there was one recruit troop during the world conflict. Seventeen recruits graduated from the academy on February 24, 1942, just weeks after Pearl Harbor. There was no graduation ceremony. Diplomas were not officially awarded until after the war's close. Things were spare.

Scores of troopers enlisted in the armed forces. Others were drafted, even though law enforcement officers in some cases were granted deferments. Applicants were hired right off the street as temporary "NOWs," Night Office Watch. Their job was to cover the barracks' desk from l0:00 p.m. until 8:00 a.m. It was not the best of times.

Coupled with the Great Depression, the World War II years created a two-decade holding action in the state force. Put differently, salary and staffing levels were capped by the constraints imposed by the organizational environment. One observes how the phenomenon recurs throughout the long history of the Massachusetts State Police. Organizations are constantly influenced by their social and economic surroundings. They strive to remain consonant with the changes imparted by the environment in which they operate. Failure to do this creates conflict. When a law enforcement agency is involved, it is not a pretty sight. Conflict never is.

That was not a serious problem for the state force from 1921 through 1946, the first 25 years. The Great Depression and World War II imposed their influences with vengeance. Individuals and organizations were equally affected. Two values, powerful motivators each, were ascendant, - security and survival. In their presence, organizational growth and enhancement did not lead the policy agenda. First things are always first.

When the *Enola Gay* on August 6, 1945, dropped an atom bomb on Hiroshima, World War II effectively ended. Days later, the United

States accepted Japan's unconditional surrender aboard the USS *Missouri* in Tokyo Bay. The world's bloodiest struggle was over. The human and material losses, more than 50 years later, are yet being calculated. That assessment, sadly, must continue to accommodate newly "discovered" atrocities in the waning days of the world's darkest century.

In retrospect, one perceives that the 1921-1946 era could accurately be described as a time of survival, both for the organization and for the individual. But with that survival, much was accomplished. The experiment with a uniformed, statewide enforcement agency was settled. Uniformed troopers, quartered in barracks, finely trained and highly mobile, had earned the respect of the citizens they served. This was particularly true in the state's rural areas where those enforcement pioneers had strengthened their limited numbers with the skills and values of the local folk. They could hardly have known that their enforcement techniques would reemerge these many years later as the nation's police agencies implemented a 90's innovation dubbed "Community Policing."

Passages-1946-1971

A depleted state force in 1945 began recruiting applicants without examination. These were the "ETSPOs" the Emergency Temporary State Police Officers. Hired right off the street, they were given uniforms and assigned to a "senior man" for several months. No examination. No training. "Boots," in the classic meaning of that word.

But the "ETSPOs" did a job. They delivered under circumstances that broke some of their numbers. Additional temporary personnel joined the force in 1946. All were World War II veterans. Meantime, regular troopers were returning from the world conflict. They, with the "ETSPOs," got the agency through the war's immediate aftermath. There was even a promise of new cruisers. With statewide examinations posted for trooper applicants, the state force was about to enter a new, 25-year era. It is doubtful that anyone then could have imagined what their organization would look like after the dynamics of those years had run their course. The organization's environment was destined for much change in that quarter century. With periodic spates of conflict, the state force's structure, staffing, and policies kept pace. The result, in retrospect, was a remarkable organizational transformation.

Several hundred World War II veterans graduated from the state police academy in the years immediately following the global conflict. Among them were many of the "ETSPOs." They had survived their temporary trials, passed the examination, and graduated from the academy. No one deserved the two-tone blue more than they did.

Left: Trooper Paul R. Landry Right: Trooper Michael Crosby. Note bullet hole in licence plate, during shootout with terrorists.

The post-war enlistees were a remarkable source. Born in the aftermath of World War I, they grew up during the Great Depression, fought World War II. In short, they were old for their years. Confident yet restrained, they would provide the leadership that moved the state force toward policies designed to loosen the authoritarian impulses that long had been ascendant.

Such openings began in the 50's decade. A new administration quietly encouraged initiatives that resulted in modest reductions in the duty week, equally modest salary increases, and upgrading and expansion of staff and field ranks. Taken as a whole, these initiatives created a liberalizing impulse within the organization. Words written here fail adequately to convey the feeling. But the feeling was there.

The 50's initiatives could not have anticipated the turbulence wrought by the 1960s in the larger society. "Camelot," the Kennedy Administration, in November, 1963 ended tragically in Dallas. Reverend Martin Luther King and Senator Robert F. Kennedy in 1968 were murdered only weeks apart. Center cities burned across the country. Violent riots erupted as the Vietnam War split the nation. The Kerner Commission concluded that the country was dividing into two spheres, one black and one white. Uncertainty was ascendant. The national anxiety was palpable.

The Massachusetts State Police was directly impacted by the societal dynamics. The state force was fully committed to riots in Harvard Yard and Harvard Square, and to massive anti-war demonstrations on Boston Common and at the State Capitol.

The state police massively deployed in Harvard Yard?

The 1921 founders would not have believed it. This was urban policing up close and confrontational. With the clarity that hindsight provides, the 1968-1969 Harvard demonstrations are seen as an organizational passage. Where once the rural force was symbolized by a solitary trooper on horseback or astride his motorcycle, now, in response to societal dynamics, troopers in riot gear were drawn into urban unrest. That was new. And it was different. There would not be a turning back. New policing imperatives slowly were taking hold. The odyssey was taking a turn.

Notably, Senator Barry Goldwater in the 1964 presidential campaign had elevated crime to the national political agenda. Predictably, President Johnson responded with the President's Crime Commission. The commission shortly published several volumes of recommendations, some of them quite radical. Moreover, the Office of Law Enforcement Assistance (OLEA) was established in the US Department of Justice. Its mandate: put several hundred million dollars into the state and local criminal justice system to reduce crime and strengthen professional operations. Thirty-five years and several billion dollars later that historic commitment continues apace in the Federal Bureau of Justice Assistance.

In between, there was the ill-fated Law Enforcement Assistance Administration (LEAA) and its centerpiece, the Law Enforcement Education Program (LEEP). LEEAs rocket like early years ended in political flameout when state and local police, with federal funds, assembled an inventory of "law enforcement" equipment that rivaled the armada that had secured Normandy's beaches in 1944.

LEEP was another story entirely. Federal funding of post-secondary education for the nation's police officers succeeded beyond anyone's fondest hopes. That story has not yet been told.

In a word, it is this: the LEEP initiative opened up the nation's police agencies. For the first time, police officers and those they are paid to protect interacted in a neutral, non-threatening atmosphere. New understandings emerged. Old, unfounded perspectives dissolved. Make no mistake, an historic, healthy transformation was energized and continues apace. Its value for some of the Federal Republic's founding principles cannot be overestimated.

On the individual level, the result was more clearly discernible. An example makes the point. The federal government in 1968 offered competitive graduate fellowships to state and local police, with full tuition and a generous stipend. The host department would pay the officer's salary. The central requirement: applicants had to have a bachelor's degree.

The uniformed branch complement at that time was approximately 900. Only two of the officers held the required baccalaureate. Only two out of 900 were eligible for the graduate fellowships. This was not an anomaly. Rather, it was the norm. And it certainly wasn't a negative. It's simply the way it was. The nation's police officers had always come from the working class. The majority were first and second generation Americans. A college education was not then a priority for families only then emerging from the struggle with inherent barriers to upward social mobility.

Things have changed. The changes have been dramatic. Today's Massachusetts State Police may well be a leading example. The modern organization is staffed by men and women with exceptional educational credentials. Advanced and professional degrees abound. Academy recruits have all completed some college work. Many hold the baccalaureate. And they are only beginning their enforcement odyssey.

The police educational story is a clear illustration of how the organizational environment has imposed its dynamics on the state force. There are many others, not as compelling, perhaps more subtle, but clear examples none-the-less. Time and space limit an exposition of all of them, but brief commentary seems merited in this context:

The Promotional Statute

A promotional statute for uniformed personnel was authorized in 1965. Before that, promotions were based on subjective criteria, never a healthy experience for an enforcement organization. The new law was largely energized by reform impulses from outside the department.

Personnel Practices

The 60's decade witnessed gradual, but steady loosening of traditional personnel constraints. These ranged from such mundane (but really important at the time), changes as summer uniforms, to modest reductions in the duty week. These improvements, long advocated on the inside of the organization were measurably advanced by visible pressures from the outside such as the picketing of Boston's general headquarters by state police families.

State Police Association of Massachusetts (SPAM)

SPAM's historic roots, its own odyssey, are fully described elsewhere. Its 1968 founding seems not to have been a coincidence. Police unions were on the rise. Unions, however, were not in the state police tradition. But traditions are not static. They must adjust, stay in tune with emerging changes in the larger society. Modern personnel likely take SPAM for granted, as though it were always there. But it wasn't there until the organizational environment generated political and institutional attitudes supportive of such a radical undertaking. The idea's time had arrived.

Thus, as the state force in the late 1960s neared its fiftieth anniversary, a modernizing impulse was gathering both pace and direction. How the enforcement odyssey unfolded from 1971 through 1996 focuses this essay's following pages.

Modernization 1971-1996

The modern era had most likely begun in 1969 when Governor Francis W. Sargent appointed a career, uniformed officer as head of the Massachusetts State Police. It was a first. Never since the 1921 founding, 50 years past, had a career trooper been selected directly from the uniformed ranks for the state's top enforcement post. That historic appointment, in retrospect, is seen as a particularly appropriate fulcrum for the modernization impulse that yet energizes the state force even while these words are being written.

The odyssey at that juncture, however, faced its most formidable challenge: the "live-in" barracks' system. Uniformed troopers were still working an 84-hour duty week. Other people worked 40 hours. Clearly, the state force had slipped behind the societal curve. A system that had served so well in its time had outlived the social and economic forces that had created it.

Major surgery was the answer. It came quickly. Everyone, it seemed, had been waiting for the department to lead the effort to resolve its priority organizational issue. When in 1970 the state force provided that leadership, the executive and legislative support was total, and enthusiastic. That September, Governor Sargent signed legislation abolishing the live-in barracks' system. Effective May 1, 1971, a trooper's duty week was reduced from 84 to 40 hours, precisely 50 years after the May 1921 founding. There would be no looking back.

The historical importance of the barracks' abolition cannot be overstated. Overnight, the organizational culture, traditions and operations entered a new era. To be sure, much was lost in the transformation. No question about that. The shared experiences imposed by a disciplined, spare system had created an esprit de corps and camaraderie that for 50 years provided the Commonwealth's citizens with public safety services second to none. The live-in barracks' life, and all that it represented, will always be at the center of state police lore. The enforcement odyssey would have long since ended save for that remarkable concept of policing and the personnel who energized its five decades of public service.

Meantime, the federal government's infusion of several billion dollars into state and local justice systems had begun to make a measurable impact. The Law Enforcement Assistance Administration (LEAA), roundly criticized by its adversaries, is yet to receive the credit it is due for the modernization impulses its programs brought to the American police service. Few remember what it did. A whole range of professional opportunities, skills and services, now taken for granted, did not exist prior to LEAA. Current enforcement personnel, at least many of them, assume that these things were always there. But they weren't. Not by a long shot.

Earlier discussion, for example, focused on the Law Enforcement Education Program (LEEP). LEEP in the 1970s was LEEAs Flagship Program. For the first time in history, police officers got the opportunity to attend college. With the 1971 barracks' abolition, troopers joined the thousands of officers striving to get a college degree with federal financial support. When pay incentives for educational achievements were added, a dramatic transformation in the level of education among law enforcement personnel was underway. Make no mistake. The LEEP Program marks a transforming juncture in the state force's odyssey. In a word, federal funding for police education opened up the American law enforcement community. Moreover, it created a criminal justice educational system, almost overnight.

By any measure, the police educational breakthrough has been a truly remarkable achievement. It is not a coincidence that many similar initiatives were launched during the past quarter century. The federal money has pushed law enforcement in new directions, creating a professional momentum that was unknown just a few years ago.

That momentum, and its results, are especially observable in the state force itself. Nowhere has a modernization ethic taken hold more firmly. Professional goals, standards, plans and practices are pervasive. Uniformed personnel are even more impressive. One need only to observe their professional demeanor to appreciate the personal credentials and commitments that have earned them the distinctive two-tone blue. They are proud to wear that uniform. They are proud of themselves. More, they are proud of the organization that offers them personal satisfactions and professional opportunities that were beyond the wildest dreams of their predecessors in French and Electric Blue. They know they are privileged to serve in the modern era, a time that has witnessed steady acceleration in the pace and direction of the enforcement odyssey.

That focus sharpened in the early 1990s. The Weld Administration's strong support for state police modernization initiatives was crucial, and productive. Recasting the policy of the prior state administration for a prison facility in the foothills of the Berkshires, planners committed the Commonwealth and its state force to a new training and educational complex in New Braintree. Actually, the sprawling facilities already existed, having been constructed in the mid- 1960s by a religious community. A major renovation program was launched, and in 1992 the 70th Recruit Troop began training at New Braintree. With that notable historical transition, the conversion of the Framingham training academy to a modern general headquarters complex became a priority.

Meantime, a consolidation of state enforcement agencies, a proposal long debated, finally came to pass. The result was a new Department of State Police that on July 1, 1992, was expanded dramatically by legislation authorizing state police authority and status for enforcement personnel in the Metropolitan District Commission, the Registry of Motor Vehicles and the Capitol Police. The enormous complexity and historical impact of the consolidation leaves one breathless. Its importance, now and in future years, cannot be overstated. Only time's passage will provide the experience and perspective accurately to assess the public policy benefits, or lack thereof, of such profound organizational change.

Clearly, the state force and its odyssey once again had been dramatically affected by the ideas and forces ascendant in the organizational environment. Not unlike the 1921 founding, barracks' abolition and other historical initiatives, a long-developing idea had been energized by a coalition of seemingly divergent interests.

The consolidation added to the urgency of transforming the Framingham training complex into a modern administrative headquarters. In the public mind, Framingham long had been seen as the state force's nerve center. It represented the visible organization, the sprawling complex on busy Route 9, the Worcester Turnpike, with the academy flanked by supply and maintenance operations as well as Troop A headquarters. Few realized that,

since World War II, the organization's leadership and technical services had been housed at 1010 Commonwealth Avenue on the Boston-Brookline line. They called it general headquarters, and for fifty years it was. But the former greeting card factory. with its industrial elevators, was not an especially inspirational edifice. Nevertheless, the building was witness to the most significant junctures in the enforcement odyssey. And, with its demise as general headquarters, itself became a notable historical image in the organizational mosaic.

That mosaic in October 1994, was measurably enhanced with the dedication of the new general headquarters complex at Framingham. The buildings, first dedicated on May 29, 1971, as a modern training academy, had been dramatically transformed by the multi-million dollar modernization program. For the first time in its history, the state force occupied an administrative and technical headquarters the equal of the nation's best. Much credit is due those who helped plan and execute the dramatic transformation. Their contributions will endure long after they depart their chosen careers in French and electric blue.

In retrospect, the 1971-1996 era looms large. While there were difficult times, much that was positive has come to pass. Principal, perhaps, has been the observable strengthening of the department's professional ethos. Grounded in the personal skills and values of uniformed personnel, it is energized by the organization's superior capacities and its commitment to public service goals. That is a huge achievement.

A state police organization competently providing the public services for which it exists earns the public trust and support crucial to its mission. That is a huge achievement. For a statewide enforcement agency, the equitable and timely provision of its public safety services must always be ascendant in the presence of multiple competing interests. That

must be the enduring and visible constant no matter the inexorable changes that a new century will impose on the enforcement odyssey and the dedicated professionals chosen to make that journey.

The Future Visible

More than 16,000 young men and women on February 7. 1998, began their quest for a law enforcement career by taking the department's entrance examination. More than words can convey on this page, their youthful aspirations affirm the strength of public support state police personnel have earned during the nearly eight decades of public service.

These young people are the future visible. The best and brightest will emerge from among their ranks during a disciplined, demanding selection process. Those select few will be appointed to one of the nation's finest law enforcement academies. There, in bucolic New Braintree, they will internalize the values and skills essential to a professional enforcement career in a new century.

When at graduation they wear French and Electric Blue, they will have earned the honor of carrying those distinctive colors deep into the 21st century. There, they will be guardians of one of the most respected law enforcement legacies in the nation, a remarkable public safety ledger authored by those who have preceded them in a lengthening enforcement odyssey.

Michigan State Police Troopers

Proposals for a Michigan Constabulary first surfaced after the bloody 1913-14 Copper Strike in the Keweenaw Peninsula, which resulted in the mobilization of Michigan's entire National Guard. But there was no political support until the Guard's imminent departure for World War I service created anxiety for domestic security. Michigan's was the only wartime constabulary to survive as a permanent state police. (Oregon and Colorado disbanded their constabularies after the war.)

When the United States declared war against Germany in April 1917, Michigan's leaders mobilized the state's manpower and vast industrial resources for the war effort. The Legislature authorized Governor Sleeper, as chairman of a War Preparedness Board of top state officials, to secure a $5 million war loan and create wartime emergency units of Michigan State Troops.

On April 19, 1917, the Michigan State Troops Permanent Force officially was organized. Despite its legal title, the Michigan State Troops Permanent Force soon became more commonly known as the Michigan State Constabulary or State Police. Some even preferred the title of Michigan Cavalry.

Michigan Agricultural College (now Michigan State University) loaned them a level, 90-acre tract (a poultry research station) along the Red Cedar River just north of the present-day East Lansing Headquarters. Army tents provided temporary shelter while the men assembled pre-fabricated wooden barracks and built stables for horses. Their uniforms consisted of khaki military tunics with distinctive red braiding, cavalry breeches with leather "putts" (puttees), and campaign hats or Stetsons. For arms, Vandercook purchased Colt .44/40 revolvers with Sam Brown holsters, .44/40 Winchester lever-action carbines, and riot batons. "Michigan State Troops" was imprinted on their new badges. The first troop of 50 men was ready for action in late July 1917.

On May 1, 1919, Capt. Ira H. Mannon (one of the original State Troops) opened a rustic Bureau of Investigation and Identification in the old wooden barracks at East Lansing. Starting with a shoebox full of fingerprint records kept beneath his cot next to his desk, the department's first full-time detective became a nationally recognized pioneer in scientific methods of criminal detection.

The State Police Division continued to provide general police services and highway patrol, while Marmon's Bureau of Investigation and Identification delved into major cases. The State Police soon also became responsible for transferring prison inmates and apprehending escapees or parole violators.

In 1924 an expanded fleet of Indian and Harley-Davidson motorcycles were introduced for the highway patrol. The use of sidecars, long coats and fur-lined hats extended the motorcycle season. Khaki military uniforms and campaign hats gave way to black, whipcord police uniforms with visored caps. The first shoulder patches appeared on Michigan State Police uniforms in 1925.

In 1925 the Legislature established the Bureau of Identification by statue, and required all Michigan Police agencies to forward the fingerprints of arrested felons to Captain Marmon's office. His bureau was a model for the FBI and other major police agencies. The state police also received funds and authority to conduct regional recruit schools for local police.

Dedicated in early 1929, Mapes Hall became Michigan's first permanent State Police building. Designed to resemble the Pennsylvania State Police barracks in Harrisburg, this brick structure served as the State Police Uniform Division Headquarters Training School and East Lansing Post. The original property along the river to the north was returned to the college, and the old wooden barracks dismantled.

Following a lengthy legal battle with the Federal Communications Commission (FCC), the department began operating Station WRDS, the first state police radio system, in late 1930. Radio-equipped patrol cars could only receive messages through this one-way dispatch system, and the single, enormous tower at East Lansing had limited range.

Black whipcord uniforms gave way to the now familiar blue and gray in 1930. Many troopers felt self-conscious in these "flashy" new colors, but they had often been mistaken for bus or taxi drivers in the old black uniforms.

Construction of the first standardized, brick state police barracks began at Jackson and Rockwood in 1929. Other than the Marquette Barracks and Mapes Hall, all other state police posts were rented houses or offices, often cramped, poorly heated, and sparsely furnished quarters. In 1931 the new Traverse City Post became the model for district headquarters barracks of the future. Courtesy of Henry Ford, the old Wayne Detachment moved from the noisy Wayne County Highway Garage into a spacious new brick barracks in Ypsilanti.

The department soon outgrew both Mapes Hall and the downtown Lansing offices. The Legislature approved funding for expansion which would consolidate all Department of Public Safety operations at East Lansing. A new pistol range was completed in 1931, and the present Administration Building was dedicated in 1932. The Bureau of Identification now had room to expand and become a full-fledged scientific crime laboratory (including a Fingerprint Section, Moulage Unit, Photographic Unit, and Ballistics Section).

Old troopers recall spending two to four days at state-line blockade points. They took

Troopers assigned Midland 1918. Dow Chemical Security.

turns sleeping in the patrol cars, and relied on nearby farmers to bring food. In those days troopers worked day and night, with few days off. After a long day of motorcycle patrol, troopers would return to the post for paperwork and fatigue duties, then go back on the road in cars for night patrol. Leaving the barracks for socializing required the post commander's approval. Troopers were subject to frequent transfers, and severe discipline for minor infractions. Contrary to popular myth, many troopers and command officers sported mustaches; however, they had to be very neatly trimmed.

The State Police came under the protection of State Civil Service, and the commissioner was removed from political pressures; appointed by the governor, he would only be removed for cause by the state Supreme Court. Significantly, the law did not provide for a deputy commissioner. A separate act created the first pension plan for state police officers with 25 years of service.

After the war, troopers returned in droves to state service after attending brief refresher schools once they were discharged from the military. General Douglas MacArthur, serving as military governor of occupied Japan, requested help from the Michigan State Police in reorganizing the Japanese national police as a democratic, civil police force.

In 1947 the Department purchased an airplane; before the war, the State Police had shared a plane with the Conservation and Highway departments. That same year, the State Police made a major uniform change: gray trousers replaced the old breeches and putts; light blue poplin shirts replaced the former white winter shirts and navy blue summer shirts. Safari style pith helmets were part of the summer uniform.

Michigan's Legislature established the state police "Red Squad" in 1950 as part of the McCarthy-era campaign against un-American activities. State police radio call letters changed from WRDS to KQA 258, and the first married men were allowed to join a recruit school, an allowance for the fact that so many veterans had married after World War II service. The rule requiring permission to marry had not been enforced for several years, but many old troopers resented the "lowering" of selection standards to include married men. Recruits continued to study, train, and bunk in the gym behind Mapes Hall.

The addition of several new posts and recruit schools in 1956 brought State Police enlisted strength over 1,000 for the first time, and experimental radar units were tested in patrol cars.

An underwater recovery squad of 16 divers was trained in 1957, and Ford Motor Company produced the updated film, *State Trooper*. The Department purchased .30 caliber M-1 carbines to provide officers more effective firepower during dangerous pursuits.

Trooper on patrol with soldier during 1967, Detroit Riot.

1st marked patrol car, Model A, 1930.

The state began enforcing a new, mandatory retirement age of 56 in January 1958, part of a legislative package to correct a weakness in the original State Police Pension Act. Previously, if an active duty officer with more than 25 years' service died, but not in the line of duty, his widow would receive no pension.

In 1963 new State Civil Service rules changed the troopers' traditional six-day work week to a five-day, 48-hour work week. This change caused administrative turmoil and a major re-evaluation of state police manpower needs, because it instantly reduced the number of available personnel statewide on any given day.

The Michigan State Police Troopers Association (MSPTA) emerged in 1964 as a fraternal organization dedicated to promote troopers' welfare and the dignity of the state police profession.

In 1965, the department was reorganized, and the Michigan Department of State Police became one of 19 state departments (the new State Constitution allowed no more than 20).

Five new functions were added to the state police: the State Safety Commission, the Michigan Law Enforcement Officers Training Council (MLEOTC), the Fire Safety Board, the Civil Defense Advisory Council, and the Private Security Licensing and Regulation Section.

With 200 new trooper positions authorized, the department intensified recruiting efforts and worked with the Civil Service Commission to expand the available pool of candidates. Minimum height standards dropped back to 5'9," age eligibility expanded (from 22-30 to 21-30), and residency requirements were relaxed.

The years 1967-68 also saw the introduction of vehicle safety check lanes, the

South Rockwood Detachment, 1927.

Col. Vandercook.

Mounted Head Quarter Troop, 1921. Col. Roy C. Vandercook (left).

breathalyzer, and "VASCAR" for speed enforcement.

To pursue the fight against illegal drugs, the department expanded coordination of cooperative narcotics concept teams with local police across the state. In 1988 the department became a leader in the National Drug Awareness Resistance Education (DARE) Program in Michigan's elementary schools.

Also in 1988, the Legislature provided funds to replace the traditional .38 caliber service revolvers with the new Sig-Sauer 9 mm semiautomatic pistols. More than two years were required to complete the training and transition process for the 2,000-plus state police enforcement officers across the state. The department had previously replaced the M-1 carbines with Heckler & Koch .223 caliber assault rifles.

The Central Records Division unveiled the technological miracle of the Automated Fingerprint Identification System (AFIS) as a crime-solving tool in 1988. Since then, the Forensic Science Division began using Deoxyribonucleic Acid (DNA) analysis in major criminal cases. In 1991 a modern Hazardous Materials Training Center was also added to the Academy complex with the help of private industry.

The Fire Marshal Division began implementing a legislatively-mandated inspection program for underground gasoline storage tanks in 1989. In 1990 a prototype Resident Trooper Detachment of the Gaylord Post opened in the Township Hall at Lewiston, allowing the department to experiment with a form of community policing in a remote, resort area.

As the department observes 75 years of "Pride in Service" to the people of Michigan, the rich traditions of the past will provide a solid foundation for progress toward the centennial. At this time the Michigan State Police employs over 3,000 enforcement officers and civilian personnel. There are 65 posts, and many teams, detachments, motor carrier scalehouses, satellite crime labs, and criminal investigation offices across the state.

The years since the 75th anniversary have been filled with an almost dizzying array of organizational innovations and technological advances. The Uniform Services Bureau consolidated the traditional system of eight districts into seven in 1992.

State police assisted the U.S. Secret Service during several visits by presidents, candidates and Pope John Paul II during the early and mid-1990s. Troopers have also mobilized for the World Cup Soccer Games and several Ku Klux Klan rallies.

Perhaps most significant has been inauguration of the new digital, 800 Mhz Michigan Public Safety Communications System (MPSCS). Launching Phase I of the project for the First and Second Districts took place in February 1997. Plans call for coverage of the entire state by the new system by the year 2000.

All posts and worksites now use computers for report writing on-line with the department's mainframe computer at East Lansing. Pilot programs have already been launched to test lap-top computers, mobile data terminals, and global positioning devices for patrol cars. Computerization has already made possible the Automated Incident Capturing System (AICS), the State-wide Information System (STATIS), and the Computer-Aided Dispatch (CAD) system. Recently, most worksites went on-line through WAN and LAN networks, allowing access to the Internet and E-mail. The department has even established a home page on the Internet. The challenge is to keep up and forge ahead with the rapid advances in technology.

In recent years, the Michigan State Police has been rated as the most respected law enforcement agency in Michigan, and has won awards as the best-dressed state police agency for its sharp uniforms. The department's files contain hundreds of letters of praise from citizens, business organizations and public officials.

To emphasize the spirit of cooperation and common purpose among Michigan's Criminal Justice agencies, the Michigan State Police Executive Council recently proposed a new vision statement for the department: "To ensure the safety of our citizens through the pursuit of innovations and initiatives which coordinate and improve the collective efforts of the Criminal Justice System."

The Michigan State Police has made vast strides since its rustic origins as a mounted Constabulary in 1917. Dedicated people, and an organizational commitment to professional, efficient police service while fulfilling a leadership and supportive role among other law enforcement agencies has helped win the department the public and political support which was necessary for its very survival. By that continued support, the people of Michigan have validated the department's motto: "A proud tradition of service through excellence, integrity, and courtesy.

Sgt. Jack Cleghorn on motorcycle patrol - 1920.

Corporal Ray Sullivan, safety program for school children.

Minnesota State Patrol

Since 1929 troopers have battled summer tornadoes and thunderstorms, winter's minus 40 degree temperatures, as well as blizzards and spring floods in a state where the climate sometimes changes from one extreme to another in a matter of hours. Despite the weather and indeed because of it, the tradition of the Minnesota State Patrol has always been one of service. This tradition of service, as well as fair and courteous enforcement to the citizens, remains at the heart of the mission of the Minnesota State Patrol.

In the middle 1920s the need for an agency with statewide jurisdiction in traffic enforcement was becoming apparent in Minnesota. In 1929 the state Legislature passed the bill creating the Minnesota State Highway Patrol with an authorized strength of 35 men at a salary of $120 a month. Those first troopers were also required to provide their own motorcycles.

From 1929-69 the State Patrol was under the control of the Minnesota Department of Highways.

In 1931 the state Legislature increased the number of officers to 70 and the second academy was held. The same training regimen was followed continuing the emphasis on courtesy. New officers were assigned to veteran officers for the first field training program following graduation. Early troopers worked 29 days a month, lived in barracks and were expected to work up to 16-hour days. Motorcycles were the primary vehicles used in patrolling from April to November, when officers switched vehicles to the Ford Model A for winter patrolling. Radios were nonexistent. Officers were required to call in to the District Headquarters for messages. A red light on a town watertower, or at a local filling station, told the officer that he was to call headquarters for a message.

Championship, the administration decided that the Highway Patrol uniforms should be of the same colors as the University of Minnesota. Maroon and gold uniforms have remained a State Patrol tradition ever since.

In 1936 the Minnesota State Patrol Highway Patrol Association, later renamed the Minnesota State Patrol Troopers Association, was founded as a response to the need for an organization to protect officers from political firings. It was limited in membership to only active officers and was not affiliated with any other labor or fraternal group.

In 1941 the Patrol compliment was authorized at 126 men. Many officers left for service in World War II. In 1942 the sixth training academy was held at Camp Ripley with 50 men enrolled; however, due to World War II many stations were reduced to one-man compliments. In 1943 the Department of Highways began the establishment of a statewide police radio system with the purchase of two towers. Until that time the patrol had relied on local city police departments and telephones for communication. The first retirement pension for officers passed the Legislature in 1943.

In 1955 the Legislature increased the compliment to 255 men, to include 33 supervisors. For the first time patrol sergeants were appointed. In September the State Patrol was divided into eight districts statewide. Aircraft was added in 1957. The first helicopter was added in 1970. In 1957 authorized strength was again increased to 330 men. Two patrol academies were held in 1957, with 105 officers graduating. Officers were required to contribute seven percent of their monthly salary to their pension with the State Patrol matching that contribution.

In 1969 the Minnesota State Highway Patrol became part of the newly created Department of Public Safety and manpower was

Duluth Harbor Ore Boat.

42nd Class of Minnesota State Patrol.

increased to 458 officers. Capitol Security Division was formed. The following year, 1970, the compliment was increased to 504 officers.

In 1971 Minnesota Highway Patrol Officers were given increased jurisdiction with authority to arrest for crimes committed in their presence anywhere in the state. Prior to that, Highway Patrol authority extended only to crimes committed on state trunk highways.

In 1974 the name of the organization became the Minnesota State Patrol, dropping the word "Highway" from the title. Trooper I and corporal ranks were created in 1974, with the rank of station sergeant created in 1975. The first contract was negotiated and signed in 1974, with the association remaining an independent labor union with working troopers negotiating the contract with the state.

In 1986 the State Patrol started District 4700, a Commercial Vehicle Enforcement Division. The division which includes both troopers and civilian commercial vehicle inspectors serves as the primary Commercial Vehicle Enforcement unit in the state.

The Minnesota State Patrol has a proud history of service. The men and women in the maroon uniforms and squad cars have been responding to the calls for help since 1929.

The 1929 Legislature passed a bill creating a Highway Patrol. The bill placed the organization under the Minnesota Highway Department and authorized the Commissioner of Highways to employ, not exceeding 35 men, with pay not to exceed $150 per month. The first training school was held January 18-April 1, 1930. Fifty men enrolled, including initial nine appointees. Salary was $120 per month. Original uniform consisted of breeches and blouse of oxford gray. Working schedule: 12 hours per day, seven days per week, one day off per month.

Legislature increased the size of the Patrol not to exceed 100 men in 1935.

Minnesota Highway Patrol Officers Association formed.

In 1937, a new pay bill passed by Legislature. Minimums of $150 per month plus $5 per month raise for six years. First time minimum pay mentioned in bill. Supervisors minimum $180 per month with raise of $5 per month per year with maximum not to exceed $200.

In the 1940s, the commissioner given permission to acquire land for radio tower. Radio used for several years but receiving through other police stations. Towers acquired on North Snelling Avenue in St. Paul and Redwood Falls.

Retirement bill passed. Officers contribute 6% of monthly salary not to exceed $15 per month. Highway Commissioner to contribute like amount. 66% of funds formerly contributed to officers to Minnesota State Employees Retirement Fund transferred to new fund (not with complete approval of officers). Under this law a patrolman could retire after 20 years of service and could start drawing an

annuity at age 58. Military service claimed many officers.

The 1950s saw Legislature passed law increasing patrol to 198 men. Increased patrol by one more captain and two more sergeants. Total of 216 men, including chief, assistant chief, two inspectors, six captains and eight sergeants. The Department was reorganized with one new district added, 10 new stations created. Legislature changed Retirement Bill; 20 years service, age 55, pension of $150 per month. Pension increased by $3 per month for every year worked over 20 years. Member required to retire at age 60.

Ninth training school held February 15-April 10, 1954 at Camp Ripley; 25 enrolled - 23 graduated.

Legislature increased salary in 1955 to $305 starting pay. Tenth training school held June 6-August 13 at Rosemount; 46 men graduated and were the first entire group to be immediately assigned.

Legislature increased salary in 1957 to $355 per month starting. Airplanes inaugurated in June. Eleventh training school held February 1-April 25; 53 enrolled - 46 men graduated (11 men immediately assigned). On April 26th the governor signed bill increasing patrol to 330 men; 34 men appointed.

Fifteenth Highway Patrol Officer Candidate School held March 19-May 25, 1962 at the Minnesota Highway Department/Civil Defense Training Center in Arden Hills. 35 candidates - 29 graduated.

Sixteenth Highway Patrol Officer Candidate School held September 23-November 29, 1963 at Arden Hills Training Center. 35 candidates, 29 finished.

One new base radio station was added at St. Cloud in 1965.

In 1968, one new radio base station added at Mankato for a total of nine. Salary increased to $506 per month for starting patrolmen. Legislature increased size of Highway Patrol to 438 officers. Nineteenth training school held March 18-June 7 at the Highway Training Center in Arden Hills with 37 men graduating.

Starting salary increased to $667 per month in 1969. Legislature increased size of Highway Patrol to 458 officers. Also placed the Highway Patrol in the newly organized Department of Public Safety. One new radio base station was added at Duluth for a total of 10. Twentieth training school held April 7-June 27 at Highway Training Center in Arden Hills with 34 men graduating.

In 1970 Legislature increased size of Highway Patrol to 504 officers. The Highway Patrol took over Capitol Complex and Mansion Security. Highway Patrol acquired a helicopter. Twenty-first training school held April 6-June 26 at Highway Training Center in Arden Hills with 30 men graduating. Patrol school salary raised to 70% of starting patrol officer's salary.

In 1974 starting salary increased to $870 per month.

Highway Patrol was reorganized. Region concept was revised in that regional commander reverted to staff position with the exception of an operations major. The name of the organization was changed to Minnesota State Patrol. Trooper I and corporal ranks were created. Twenty-fourth training school held April 1-July 19 at Highway Training Center in Arden Hills with 17 men graduating.

Starting salary increased to $908 per month in 1975 and a new rank of station sergeant created.

1976 starting salary increased to $967 per month. Twenty-fifth training school held May 10-August 27 at the Highway Training Center in Arden Hills with nine men and three women graduating (first time for women).

1977 starting salary increased to $1,075 per month. Twenty-sixth training school held May 23-September 9 at Highway Training Center in Arden Hills with 21 graduating.

1978 starting salary increased to $1,157

per month. Twenty-seventh training school held June 5-September 22 at Highway Training Center in Arden Hills with 19 graduating.

Twenty-ninth training school held September 24, 1979-January 11, 1980, at Highway Training Center in Arden Hills with 18 graduating.

1981 salary increased to $1,362 starting per month. Thirtieth training school held February 23-May 8 at Highway Training Center in Arden Hills with 21 graduating.

The thirty-seventh training school held at Highway Training Center in Arden Hills July 30-October 19, 1990, with 26 graduating - appointment date October 20.

Mississippi Highway Safety Patrol

On April 1, 1938, Senate Bill Number 161 was passed by the Legislature of the state of Mississippi, creating the Mississippi Highway Safety Patrol. The initial act provided patrolmen, and additional personnel (besides the commissioner and chief of patrol) including the Director of Driver License Bureau, Chief Record Clerk, Stenographer, and five assistants allotted to the Driver License Bureau.

From 3,300 applicants, 633 were selected to take competitive physical and mental examinations, from which 97 were selected as recruits to attend school. From this number, 53 were chosen upon graduation as patrolmen and 13 were placed on reserve. All patrolmen were issued uniforms, Sam Browne belts and holsters, and the newly designed Smith & Wesson .357 Magnum revolver. Thirty-five Harley-Davidson motorcycles and 20 automobiles were purchased by the state for use by the department.

Mississippi spared nothing in equipping her troops. For sidearms, they were given the latest of all pistils, the .357 Smith & Wesson Magnum pistol built on a caliber frame. For duty on the highways they used the best obtainable motorcycles and 19 fast patrol cars.

Headquarters were at the old state hospital at Jackson. The troopers themselves were distributed among the state's more than 80 counties. They had a daily average patrol of at least 80 miles to make.

When the original force reported to their scattered runs, Mississippi and the nation were still reeling from the effects of the Depression. Unemployment was high and people were quarrelsome. Individualism was not an anachronism from the past, and patrolmen often had to back up an arrest with proof he was big enough to take an arrested person to jail.

Tales told of these patrol pioneers are legend. Perhaps most are untrue, but one which seems to have remained through the years concerns a patrolman reporting to a new assignment in a town know for its rowdy element. So the story goes, this nameless patrolman rode his motorcycle on Saturday evening into a service station frequented by the "town toughs," braked, carefully removed his gun belt and holster, silently hung the gun belt on the mo-

torcycle handlebars, and then introduced himself. "And," he added, "I am ready to whip every man here, one at a time, because I am here to stay."

He stayed, and so did the patrol. Possibly one of the aforementioned men was the main character in this scene.

The basic principles adopted in the early development of the patrol soon convinced the people of Mississippi it had a definite place in state government and gradual growth over the years from 53 men to an authorized strength of 581 and an increase in the number of district miles is a tribute to those responsible for maintaining high standards of performance.

While the original force was being trained at Camp Shelby, the Old Asylum property (now site of the multi-million dollar University Medical Center) was being renovated as State Headquarters. Several agencies, the WPA, and later patrolmen themselves worked toward making the condemned property at least serviceable. The facility was used continuously by the Highway Patrol until December 1955 when the headquarters was moved to a new facility at 1900 Woodrow Wilson Avenue (which is now the "old" Headquarters Building).

MHP Trooper Alex Hodge seized 5,500 lbs of marijuana during a traffic stop. This is one of the nation's largest highway seizures.

Annual Memorial Services, Remember those who made the ultimate sacrifice.

Missouri State Highway Patrol

The Missouri State Highway Patrol was created in 1931 by an act of the 56th Missouri General Assembly, during the tenure of Governor Henry S. Caulfield. The authorized strength of the patrol was established at 125 officers and patrolmen, however, due to limited appropriations only 55 patrolmen were trained for active duty at the Saint Louis Police Department Academy.

During its first full years of operation, the patrol worked hard to establish a reputation of helpfulness to law abiding citizens while vigorously enforcing the law. In 1932 the small force of patrolmen made over 38,000 arrests, recovered 381 stolen vehicles, arrested 14 persons for bank robberies and solved several murders.

The primary responsibility of the Missouri State Highway Patrol is to enforce the traffic laws of Missouri and to promote safety on its approximately 33,000 miles of state-maintained highways. The state is divided into nine troops, geographically, and each troop is commanded by a captain. Each troop is divided into zones which are each under the supervision of a sergeant. The department now has a force of 825 uniformed officers and approximately 900 support personnel. On July 1, 1974, the Missouri State Highway Patrol became an agency under the Department of Public Safety. This was done in accordance with the Omnibus State Reorganization Act of 1974.

Many special services are offered to the public from each of our nine troops. There are specially selected men known as public information and education officers who conduct safety and education meetings for school groups, church groups and civic and service clubs. These officers also conduct programs in the areas of farm safety, safety for women, defensive driving, school bus driver's workshops and court referral programs to name just a few. They are also involved in driver educa-tion and drug abuse programs for youth groups.

The Missouri State Highway Patrol has been given additional responsibilities since it was organized in 1931. For example, in 1952 the department was given the responsibility for the administration of the state's driver license examination program. Experienced uniformed personnel supervise several hundred civilian employees who conduct the written, vision and road driver license tests. The additional responsibility of administering the State's Motor Vehicle Inspection Law was also given to the patrol in 1969. Another duty of the department is to enforce all laws relating to size, weight and speed of commercial motor vehicles and all laws designed to safeguard state maintained highways. The patrol also cooperates with other state officials in the enforcement of regulations relating to the collecting of revenue derived from highway users, such as license fees and taxes on motor vehicle fuels.

The Missouri State Highway Patrol is very active in the fight against crime in the rural areas of Missouri. This fight against crime is implemented through a cooperative effort on the part of city, county, state and federal agencies. The state law enforcement agency cooperates with and assists other police agencies in the area of criminal investigation, communication and training.

Trained and experienced highway patrol investigators are at the disposal of Missouri law enforcement agencies upon request. These men are specialists in the investigation of auto theft, homicide, organized crime, arson, burglary, forgery, bomb disposal and even cattle theft. A few of the specialists are used on a full time basis as narcotic agents in the fight against the sellers and users of illegal drugs.

The Highway Patrol has one of the most complete criminal laboratories in the midwest located in Jefferson City. It includes a complete laboratory for the analysis of evidence, a section for ballistics analysis, latent print analysis and handwriting analysis for documents. Satellite laboratories are also located in Macon, St. Joseph and Willow Springs. The Patrol Criminal Laboratory facilities are at the disposal of peace officers throughout the state.

Instant and accurate communications among police agencies is a must in today's highly mobile society. The Highway Patrol houses a computerized teleprocessing communications systems known as the Missouri Uniform Law Enforcement System; in short, MULES. MULES is a computer based law enforcement, criminal justice, information system which includes a computer teleprocessing terminal, in city, county, State and federal agencies in Missouri. Those agencies who have terminals in this computer can receive information in seconds on persons, vehicles and property.

Training is available to police officers throughout the state at the Missouri State Highway Patrol Law Enforcement Academy in Jefferson City. Classes at the academy include basic police school and advanced police school and are offered to the officer or his agency.

Recruits for the Missouri State Highway Patrol are selected from applicants nationwide through selective examinations and extensive back ground investigations. Each trainee must complete 23 weeks of rigorous physical and mental training to be eligible for commissioning as a probationary trooper. The probationary training period is for one year under guidance of the field training officer and supervision of his sergeant and troop commander.

The academy training phase includes more than 1,000 hours of classroom and practical exercise instruction by patrol instructors. Firearms training includes instruction in the

use of the Glock Model 22 40 S & W caliber semi-automatic pistol for uniform duty. A recruit class will shoot more than 60,000 rounds of pistol ammunition in 86 hours of firearms training. The issue shotgun for use in patrol cars is the Remington Model 870 Wingmaster Pump Shotgun, 12 gauge, with 20-inch barrel. Over 16 hours of fundamental and combat training is conducted with the shotgun.

The Missouri State Highway Patrol regulations require that each member fire the qualifications courses three times yearly. Special

weapons training includes firing by special anti-sniper teams and SERT teams across the state.

Special civil disturbance control training has been given to all patrol personnel, and each troop has specially assigned personnel on troop "task forces" which are on call for civil disturbances or disasters anywhere in the state. Special assigned weapons personnel are assigned to the headquarters group of each task force for control by the task force commander.

The Missouri State Highway Patrol hosts a Cadet Patrol Academy which is sponsored by the American Legion each summer. The cadets learn by first hand experience, during a one-week session in the training academy, the basic principles and responsibilities of law enforcement. The participation is limited to those who are 16 to 18 years of age, and in the upper 50 percentile of their class. The cadets are introduced to most of the basic subjects of law enforcement, and they are particularly interested in the firearms safety and basic range instruction with police revolvers. An award is presented each year to the high shooter in the Cadet Patrol Academy.

The motto of the Missouri State Highway Patrol is "Service and Protection." Members of this organization have made a sincere effort down through the years to live up to this motto. It is through these efforts that this department has developed a reputation for being one of the finest law enforcement agencies of its kind in the country. The Missouri State Highway Patrol will continue to faithfully carry out its responsibilities and duties so as to better serve and protect the citizens of Missouri.

Montana Highway Patrol

During 1933 and 1934, Montana led the nation with a 74 percent increase in highway fatalities. Montana citizens and legislative representatives recognized the need to create an enforcement agency with the mission to curb needless deaths on Montana's highways. As a result, the Montana Highway Patrol was created in 1935.

Twenty-four candidates were selected for the first Highway Patrol Recruit Academy, from a pool of 1,500 candidates. In May 1935, the first Highway Patrol officers began safeguarding Montana's highways in new Ford coupes and on Harley Davidson motorcycles. The officers were authorized to enforce 11 traffic laws. However, their main focus was to educate and assist the public.

In the first year officers patrolled Montana's highways, the number of fatalities decreased 25 percent. The Highway Patrol's efforts led to an increased demand for continued enforcement and education to reduce fatalities.

In 1943, a Safety and Education Division was created within the Montana Highway Patrol. Uniformed Highway Patrol officers assumed the responsibility of educating all citizens — from toddlers to senior citizens — on highway traffic safety. This responsibility is critical to the Highway Patrol's mission of service to Montana's citizens.

In 1948, the Driver License Bureau was created within the Montana Highway Patrol to administer the written and driving tests necessary to obtain a driver's license.

The historic 3-7-77 was added to the shoulder patch by then-Chief Alex B. Stephenson in 1956. The emblem is a tribute to the Vigilantes, the first law enforcement group in the Montana Territory.

In 1961, Montana Highway Patrol officers assumed the enforcement of gross vehicle weight laws on the motor carrier industry.

During the late 1960s and early 1970s, Montana experienced a dramatic increase in fatalities. In 1972, traffic fatalities reached an all-time high of 395. As a result, the legislature approved additional positions, bringing the number of uniformed Highway Patrol officers to 220. (This number had declined to 202 officers by 1994.) The Montana Highway Patrol was reorganized as a bureau within the Montana Department of Justice in 1972, resulting in the elimination of the Highway Patrol Board.

Highlights during the 1970s included:

— creation of the Accident Prevention Unit in 1973, to provide trafficsafety enforcement to documented problem areas statewide.

— the addition of four females officers in 1978.

— a reorganization that moved the Driver License Bureau from the Highway Patrol to the Motor Vehicle Division in 1979. Civilian employees assumed the testing duties previously performed by Highway Patrol officers.

During the 1980s, the Montana Legislature enacted a mandatory seat belt law that has since been credited with saving numerous lives. Also in the 1980s:

— the Highway Patrol was elevated to division status within the Department of Justice in 1983.

— the Motor Carrier Safety Assistance Program (MCSAP) was created within the Highway Patrol as the Motor Vehicle Inspection Bureau, with Highway Patrol officers performing or assisting Motor Vehicle Inspectors with in-depth motor carrier inspections.

— the Highway Patrol in 1988 became the first state highway patrol in the nation to become nationally accredited. The accreditation

process took three years to complete and was considered a critical element in enhancing the professionalism of the Montana Highway Patrol. The accreditation was a result of the work and dedication of the officers of the Highway Patrol.

In 1995, Congress repealed the federally mandated daytime speed limit. Under a law previously enacted by the Montana Legislature, Montana's speed limit reverted to the so-called "basic rule" that was the only daytime speed limit law in force before the national speed limit was enacted in 1974. That law requires motorists to drive in a manner that is reasonable and prudent for traffic, weather, road and vehicle conditions.

On May 1, 2000, the Patrol celebrated its 65th anniversary. The Patrol has a long and proud tradition of excellence. Although the Montana Highway Patrol's responsibilities have grown, its mission still centers on the basic premise that prompted its creation in 1935 — protecting the lives of those who travel on Montana's highways.

Nebraska State Patrol

The following article was compiled by the Fiftieth Anniversary Committee and has been condensed from the history of the State Patrol.

In recent years, law enforcement, as other areas of government, has undergone modernization and thus, change. Our population has grown with trends moving toward industrialization and urbanization and with tremendous advances in communication and transportation, law enforcement has had to adapt to its occupational environment.

As America's use of motor vehicles increased, so did crime. Law-abiding citizens needed supervision when operating their motor vehicles and local and county law enforcement agencies could not handle all the problems by themselves. The need for state controls became increasingly clear to the people of the State of Nebraska.

As chief executive, the governor was responsible for enforcing the laws of the state. This included enforcement of laws which are related to motor vehicles. In 1933, Governor Bryan realized that county and local police organizations were not doing an adequate job and he added traffic control duties to the responsibilities of the State Sheriff.

Because the State Sheriff's office could not effectively handle the problems of criminal law enforcement in Nebraska, let alone those involving traffic control, it became obvious that the creation of a new department was necessary.

Traffic accidents, coupled with the toll of death and injury caused a negative impact to the social and economic welfare of the public. This resulted in pleas for action even before the Model T touring car gave way to the enclosed body styles introduced during the 'Roaring Twenties'.

Establishment of a patrol system in Nebraska did not occur overnight. There was much talk of a patrol before its creation in 1937.

On February 3, 1937, Legislative Bill 147 was introduced in the Nebraska Legislature. This bill proposed a Division of Highway Safety and Patrol in the Department of Roads and Irrigation and creation of the office of Director of the Nebraska Safety Patrol. It would also allow the Nebraska Safety Patrol to control who obtained and retained licenses to operate motor vehicles.

With the passage of LB 147, the State Safety Patrol began initial operations. The first step was to recruit patrolmen. Of the more than 3,500 men who applied for the position of Patrolman, approximately 850 were found eli-

1996 graduation picture of Troopers and Carrier Enforcement Officers

gible. After minimum requirements were met, 205 men were selected to take a written examination. Of that group, 118 were given personal interviews and of these, 64 received training as recruits at Camp Ashland in May, 1937. The recruits averaged 30 years of age, had approximately one year of college, stood 6 feet tall, weighed 170 pounds, and most were married and had families.

On November 22, 1937, 44 men in trim boots and breeches stood proudly erect for the Oath of Office. The remaining 20 personnel were placed on the reserve list. These 44 men assigned to those areas in Nebraska with the largest volumes of traffic. Their primary goal was to reduce the number of motor vehicle accidents.

During early operations, assignments to personnel from Patrol Headquarters were made by letter, telegram and telephone, since radio communication was non-existent. Officers on patrol were required to telephone their local offices at prescribed intervals from scheduled locations for additional assignments. At other times, they were required to watch for specific signs, such as a red pennant hung outside certain service stations and roadside cafes, as the signal to call their supervisors.

With the passage of Legislative Bill 12, which created the Division of Law Enforcement and Public Safety, the Nebraska Safety Patrol became a state police organization. This bill gave the superintendent of the patrol the powers of the state sheriff which, in turn, caused the abolition of the State Sheriff's Office. No personnel changes were made and both agencies became part of the new organization. The plan was designed to promote better and more cooperative law enforcement in the best

interest of the general public. In accordance with this plan, officers of the Patrol were given special instructions and were commissioned as deputy state sheriffs.

Another important duty (already was performed by the organization) was the assignment of 12 safety patrolmen to the Fort Crook traffic detail. With traffic flow reaching peaks of 1,600 cars per hour, steps were taken to provide safe travel through the immediate area on Highway 75 during the construction of the Martin Bomber Plant.

February 19, 1946, saw the addition of another important tool in law enforcement. On that date, the Patrol began to broadcast from its station with a new three-way, FM, nine-station radio system which was located in Lincoln. Since that date, six other stations have gone into operation.

Experience gained during the initial months confirmed that radio communication was an effective tool in the work of the Patrol. It made possible the speedy apprehension of criminals, recovery of stolen cars, prompt aid to the victims of accidents and (in general) more effective enforcement and protection of life and property.

LB 532, which provided for the inspection of school buses, was passed during the 1947 session of the Legislature. The Patrol made state-wide inspections during the fall of 1947 and the spring and fall of 1948. The inspections included the checking of brakes, lights, windshield and windshield wipers, window glass, tires doors, heaters, steering gear and defrosting equipment.

Due to the high percentage of out-of-state drivers involved in traffic accidents while driving through our state during the tourist season

Patrol K-9 unit.

of 1947, a special effort was made during the tourist season of 1948 to stop a recurrence of this situation. Officers were stationed at Fremont and Ogallala on Highway 30 to aid all tourists, inform them of Nebraska's traffic rules and supply them with a specially prepared leaflet. Information in the leaflet asked the tourists for their assistance in reducing accidents.

The Patrol's activities toward gaining greater obedience to traffic laws, as designed by the Legislature of the safety and protection of Nebraska's motoring public, have steadily increased. On charges filed by the Patrol in court, conviction rates average nearly 98 percent. The reduced traffic death rate and the high rate of convictions on charges filed, are an indication of the worthiness and quality of men serving the public as State Troopers.

As the Patrol continued to grow, it was decided that an improved ratings within the Patrol which would be comparable to ratings held by administrators and division heads of other state patrol organizations, the rating of the superintendent of Law Enforcement and Public Safety was advanced from captain to colonel in June, 1951. In turn, the lieutenants, as division heads and troop area commanders, were made captains and sergeants became lieutenants. Corporals were advanced to sergeants and the corporal rating was discontinued.

The Patrol began to analyze accidents investigated by troopers for the purpose of providing information as a basis for suggesting changes and improvements in highway design, restricted speed zones and the placement of traffic direction and control markers. This also aided the Patrol in concentrating their manpower and activity needs in high-frequency accident areas.

Mid-1954 saw the beginning of the use of aircraft and radar as a means of detecting traffic law violators. Beyond a doubt, aircraft and radar were the most practical approaches in the control of speeding motor vehicles.

Nebraska Safety Patrol officers flipped their lids in December, 1955. Officers doffed their light blue, billed caps and donned new, dark blue, flatbrimmed hats. The reason for the change was to distinguish Safety Patrol officers from other uniformed cap-wearers such as policemen, post men and railway conductors.

On January 1, 1956, the Nebraska Safety Patrol, along with 33 other states, inaugurated the National Police Teletypewriter Network which allowed conveying printed messages over telephone lines.

In July, 1959, motorists were interrupted as troopers launched a hard-hitting traffic control technique in three areas; Omaha, Lincoln and Grand Island. The mass checking proved so successful that it became a regular patrol procedure.

With the opening of the interstate highway in August, 1960, there came a greater need to patrol this long expanse of isolated highway for the protection of citizens who traveled it. This dictated the need fro greater numbers of patrol officers and prudent planning by the Patrol's administrative staff to place manpower in the areas of greatest need. This same situation exists today with the president 500-plus miles of Nebraska interstate highway which must be constantly and adequately patrolled.

In keeping with the present-day trend of color schemes for patrol vehicle replaced the traditional black and white. This color, not as distinctive in traffic since it matches the colors of the motoring public vehicles, was an aid to traffic law enforcement. It also provided greater safety at accident scenes as it could be seen more easily at night.

In 1965, the Legislature authorized the establishment of the rank of major and the restoration of the corporal rating. This resulted in the revision of the organizational chart and the troop area boundaries. It was decided there would be three majors; one as field administrator for the Western portion of the state, another as the field administrator for the eastern portion and the third as assistant to the superintendent in general administration.

In the spring of the 1966, due to growing public interest in the Driver Improvement Program which was developed by the National Safety Council, the Safety Patrol trained troopers in each of the six troop areas to qualify themselves as certified instructors in what is now known as the "Defensive Driving Course".

In October, 1967, the Centennial Class, consisting of 41 officer candidates, was the first to graduate at the Nebraska State Patrol Training Center. The Training Center was leased from the Lincoln Airport Authority and was located at Lincoln Air Park. The facility consisted to two classrooms, a kitchen and dining hall, recreation room, library, dormitory, staff offices and an infirmary.

The Patrol's newest division, the Drug

Control Division, was created by the 1967 Legislature. Four officers received two week training from the Federal Bureau of Narcotics at Washington DC Of these four, two officers were located in Lincoln, one in Omaha and one in Scottsbluff.

With the passage of LB 907, the Patrol's name was changed from "Nebraska Safety Patrol" to "Nebraska State Patrol". Changing the Patrol's name from "Safety" to "State" also resulted in a change of badges.

The Patrol made great progress in 1968 in terms of acquiring the latest in police equipment. VASCAR (Visual Average Speed Computer and Recorder) units were placed in 12 patrol vehicles throughout the state and schools were scheduled to train officers to use this new speed measuring device. The big advantage in using VASCAR was that a moving violator's speed could be accurately clocked from a moving patrol car.

In early 1970, a grant to the Nebraska State Patrol for $500,000 was approved by the Law Enforcement and Criminal Justice and the US Department of Transportation's, National Highway Safety Bureau via Nebraska's Highway Safety Program. The grant allowed the Patrol to purchase a 206A Bell Jet Ranger Helicopter and a computerized message "switcher." The helicopter was primarily used for the research of traffic problems and the surveillance of motor vehicle violators. The computerized message switcher permitted the Patrol to offer the combined Law Enforcement Information Network (CLEIN) which allowed terminals in the Nebraska Law Enforcement Teletype System and the Nebraska Telecommunications System to communicate with each other.

With continued civil unrest throughout the country, and especially within Nebraska, it became important to the Patrol to stay abreast of newly introduced equipment and training for it's personnel. Security of the legislative chambers became the responsibility of the Patrol and plans were formulated to handle this assignment properly. In addition, the Governor's Security Division (prior to 1970) was comprised of only two officers. Originally, all the Nebraska State Patrol did in the connection was to the Governor at certain times. However, since 1970, the Governor's Security Division has acquired additional duties. In addition to providing transportation to the Governor, it is also responsible for providing security to the Governor.

In 1972, 18 Custom MR-7 moving radar units were purchased with funds from Highway Safety. This allowed troopers to detect speed violators without interfering with routine patrol duties.

Throughout 1972, Troop "E" was plagued with incidents of civil disturbance. When the museum at Fort Robinson was seized by members of the American Indian Movement, troopers from Troops "E", "D" and "B" were sent to the Gordon-Rushville area in response to that disturbance.

One of the new developments during 1972 consisted of purchasing and equipping a mobile crime laboratory which was then available at crime scenes for the search and preservation of evidence. The success of this equipment was so overwhelming that additional units were requested to better serve Nebraska. Another unit which was purchased and assembled was a bomb van and a trailer. This unit was available to any agency which was located or found an unexploded device.

June, 1973, saw six troopers fully equipped and patrolling in pre-selected areas of Eastern Lancaster County to apply the concept of the Selective Traffic Enforcement Program. The alertness of team members resulted in a 34 percent reduction in motor vehicle accidents during June, July and August, 1973, as compared to the same period in 1972. It was the opinion of the Patrol that the Special Selective Traffic Enforcement project had been very successful up to this time.

With the worldwide petroleum shortage and rapidly increasing gasoline costs, the federal government asked motorists to comply with a voluntary national speed limit of 55 miles per hour. The voluntary national limit began in the fall of 1973 and lasted until the spring of 1974. The energy savings resulting from the lowered speed limit paved the way for a mandatory national speed limit of 55 miles per hour.

A golden strip embedded in the pavement west of Sidney marks the completion of the interstate highway across Nebraska. The ceremony was held in a west Sidney rest area on October 19, 1974. Construction on the interstate began on October 19, 1955, and took approximately 19 years to complete at a cost of over $300,000,000.

Nebraska joined 44 other states in the Combined Accident Reduction Effort (CARE). The focus of the campaign was to enforce the 55 mile per hour speed limit from coast-to-coast and to be alert to all other violations of state driving laws and safety. CARE was the largest single traffic enforcement effort that has ever taken place in the United States. Nebraska was second in the nation in the percentage of reduced fatalities in 1977 as a result of this effort.

Traffic enforcement efforts received special emphasis through the use of federal funds which made available a third selective traffic enforcement team and a mobile radar unit for each traffic cruiser in the state as well as surveillance and additional crime lab equipment.

In July, 1980, all state vehicles began using gasohol. This was due to worldwide problems of decreasing fuel, increasing costs and the efforts of Governor Throne and the Legislative who had developed a gasohol program as an alternative energy source.

Different uniforms for Troopers and Carrier Enforcement Officers.

Nevada Highway Patrol

The 1949 Nevada Legislature created the Nevada Highway Patrol by consolidating the Nevada State Police, Inspectors from the Nevada Public Service Commission and several Inspectors from the Nevada Department of Taxation. On July 1, 1949, the Nevada Highway Patrol Division was created within the Nevada Public Service Commission. These officers were directed to act as field agents and inspectors in the enforcement of the State laws as they pertained to Nevada highways. But the history of law enforcement on Nevada highways goes back many years before the Nevada Highway Patrol was created.

In 1908 the Nevada State Police was created to provide a state level law enforcement presence as a result of labor strikes in the mining communities. When Henry Ford made ownership of the automobile accessible to the populous of America by mass producing the Model T Ford, the problem of enforcing the laws of the road soon followed. On June 23, 1923, the first Nevada State Highway Patrolman was hired by the Nevada Highway Department under the supervision of the Inspector of the Nevada State Police. This officer and the Inspector of the State Police would travel throughout the State collecting automobile registration fees and enforcing the laws of the highway. Nevada was one of the first western states to have an organized highway patrol function.

By 1934, the highway patrol force had grown to three officers still supervised by the Inspector of the State Police. They were given silver patrol cars with gold stars on the door; red lights and sirens, and told to patrol the roads. One officer was assigned to Reno, one to Carson City and one to Las Vegas.

This sub-unit of the Nevada State Police remained operational until the State Police was reorganized in 1943. At that time, the Nevada State Highway Patrol was absorbed into the State Police who continued highway law enforcement until 1949 when the Nevada Highway Patrol was organized.

In 1957, the Legislature created the Department of Motor Vehicles and transferred the Nevada Highway Patrol to this new department as a division.

In 1985, the name of the Department was changed to the Department of Motor Vehicles and Public Safety to reflect the many new law enforcement agencies that had been added. So today, the Nevada Highway Patrol is a division of the Nevada Department of Motor Vehicles and Public Safety.

Today the Nevada Highway Patrol serves the citizens and visitors of our State with 356 commissioned officers and 177 civilians. The duties of the Patrol range from enforcing the laws on the highways to operating the State's criminal history repository. The headquarters office is located in Carson City with regional offices in Las Vegas, Reno and Elko. The Nevada Highway Patrol is dedicated to ensuring safe, economical, and enjoyable use of the highways: protecting peaceful citizens against violence and disorder and assisting law enforcement agencies throughout our State and the nation.

The philosophy of the Nevada Highway Patrol is as follows:

With unwavering respect for the Constitutional rights of all persons to liberty, equality and justice, it is our fundamental duty to serve the citizens and the highway users of Nevada in a manner which assures their protection, safety and opportunity to conduct their lives in an atmosphere of peace. We will respond promptly and with attentiveness to persons and or other agencies with emergencies or needs of assistance; we will be vigilant in identifying and assuring the prompt mitigation of highway hazards; we will continuously seek opportunities to educate and inform the Nevada community about traffic safety; and we will aggressively enforce the laws of Nevada in a caring manner, with courtesy and impartiality. We will nurture a workplace environment which is free of bias and prejudice and will provide every individual the opportunity for self realization and growth. Through the judicious use of the authority and resources granted us be the people of Nevada, we will safeguard their faith and trust.

Mission:

Enforce the traffic laws of the state, investigate traffic collisions, enforce and regulate motor carriers transporting cargo and hazardous materials, maintain Nevada's central Criminal History Repository, and operate statewide message switcher to process criminal justice information.

To improve the quality of service provided to citizens and visitors using Nevada highways.

To gain voluntary public compliance with traffic laws by providing meaningful traffic safety education to the broadest possible segment of citizens and highway users,

To reduce the frequency and severity of collision events through applied enforcement techniques targeting causative violations,

To reduce commercial vehicle collisions and hazardous material releases through inspections and enforcement, targeting safety defects, driver deficiencies, and unsafe motor carrier fleet practices.

To coordinate, audit, and train criminal justice users and maintain criminal history files, wanted persons files, point-of-sale background checks for firearms sales to state, local and authorized private agencies.

New Hampshire State Police

It is believed that the weather on July 9, 1869 was a typical summer's day in New Hampshire. At 7:00 a.m., Governor Stearns was presented with a hand written piece of legislation which would eventually lead to the formation of the New Hampshire State Police. The legislation entitled, "An Act to Create a State Police in Certain Cases", outlined just what would constitute the proposed State Police.

It was determined that the officer would be called a "Constable of the State". This constable was to be given the authority to appoint deputies in any city or town where, "...in his personal observation or upon application of ten or more legal voters in any city or town in this State that the local authorities fail to enforce any law in this state." They, "...shall have and exercise, throughout the State, all the common law and statutory power of Constables,...and also in all the cities of this State, all the powers given therein to City Marshals, Police Officers, and Watchmen..." The proposed Constables would not have the authority to serve civil processes. As proposed, "It shall be the duty of said Constable and his deputies to see that the laws are enforced and observed in all parts of the State..."

Historians have suggested that one of the primary reasons for such legislation was the result of a petition asking, "...that the legislature enact a law for a State Police to more adequately enforce the laws of the State." Apparently at that time, local law enforcement authorities were slow to act, if at all, enforcing various "anti-drinking laws". In fact, the proposed law explicitly stated that, "...they shall especially use their utmost endeavors to repress and prevent crime by the suppression of liquor shops, gambling places, and houses of ill fancy..." However, limitations were set on this enforcement in that the Constable or his deputies could act only if "... there shall be a failure, neglect, or inability on the part of the local authorities to enforce the laws of the State..."

The proposed legislation failed to achieve the needed backing of two-thirds of the male voters in New Hampshire. Fortunately, interest in the establishment of the New Hampshire State Police did not disappear altogether. During subsequent years, additional, but vain attempts to pass such legislation failed. However, State level law enforcement did exist prior to the actual inception of the New Hampshire State Police.

On May 1, 1915, the New Hampshire Legislature passed Chapter 154, entitled "An Act Creating the Office of Commissioner of Motor Vehicles". It is important to realize that this legislation helped create the uniformed Motor Vehicle Highway Patrolmen. These individuals enforced traffic laws at this time.

According to this law, "The Attorney General...may employ an investigator, to assist him in the apprehension of criminals...". These individuals were described statutorily as, "ex-officio constable(s) through the State and have general powers to enforce all criminal laws of the state, serve criminal processes and make arrests, under proper warrants, in all counties of the State".

In 1931 a State Police Commission appointed by Governor Tobey and the Governor's Council presented a report to the legislature noting that "...today, with the development of a network of improved highways and the universal use of the automobile, a problem of law enforcement and criminal apprehension has been created for which the established system of local protection had proved inadequate." The State Police Commission noted, "It is common knowledge that depredation on fruit growers, cattle raisers and poultry farms and on isolated filling stations and vacant summer homes are becoming increasingly frequent and that in practically every instance the automobile provides a convenient agent for the escape of the criminal...The experience of New Hampshire with its archaic system of policing, its duplication of functions, its conflict of authority and the resultant lack of cooperation between enforcement agencies, both state and local, illustrates the fundamental weakness of the old scheme."

Overall, the Commission plainly recommended, "...that the present Legislature provide for the establishment of a State Force with full police powers, charged with the enforcement of all criminal laws." The Commission went on to recommend that the new agency be a "...separate and independent department..."

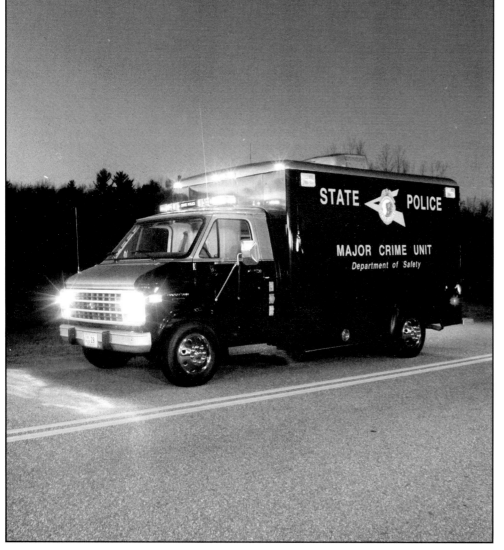

which would encompass as many existing enforcement agencies as possible and be directed by a Superintendent appointed by the Governor and Governor's Council.

After examining State-level enforcement, the State Police Commission also suggested that the consolidation include the twenty-two uniformed Motor Vehicle Department motorcycle officers employed at the time, the three inspectors of the Department of Weights and Measures, and the powers of the [State] Law Enforcement Department (which dealt with liquor laws). It was further suggested that the need for criminal investigators become a reality. Up to that point in time, most State (and Country) criminal investigations were performed by private detective agencies. Therefore, the Commission recommended, "...that the Superintendent of the State Police be authorized...to create a State Detective Bureau, which shall maintain facilities for the detection of crime in the State."

A final recommendation by the State Police Commission was concerned directly with the establishment of a Bureau of Records and Identification within the Department of State Police. In reference to this, criminal statistics, fingerprint taking and other methods of identification would be undertaken. The Bureau would also maintain records of, "...revolver purchases and revolver permits issued within the State."

The Commission suggested that the new Department should be comprised of at least fifty troopers. It was estimated that the starting salary of these men, including equipment and maintenance, should be $3,000.00 a year. After taking into account the salary of the Superintendent, motorcycles, cruisers, training and additional equipment concerns, the cost for the Department of State Police to be $185,000.00.

On February 2, 1937, Mr. F.P. Wadleigh, a legislator from Milford, introduced Bill No. 254 to the New Hampshire House of Representatives. This piece of legislation was part of the natural evolution of a process begun approximately sixty-eight years before. The Bill was entitled, "An Act Creating A Department of State Police".

Bill No. 254 did not easily pass through the legislative process. Numerous committees examined the Bill and it finally was approved by the House and sent to the Senate. Again, Bill No. 254 found itself subjected to many amendments, readings and voting sessions. On June 29, 1937 the New Hampshire State Police was created and subsequently became a statutory reality as Chapter 134 of the Laws of

New Hampshire. According to this statute, the law became effective July 1, 1937.

The New Hampshire State Police became the fifteenth such organization of its type in the United States. In 1961, the legislature enacted Chapter 166, also known as, "An Act to Establish a Department of Safety." It was the intent of the legislature that, "to improve the administration of the state government by providing unified direction of related function in the field of public safety, a single highway patrol, consolidating criminal enforcement functions in the division of state police, and making possible...the integrated administration and

operation of these and other safety functions of the state government."

Thus, the Department of State Police became a Division of State Police within the newly created Department of Safety. The final effective date for the reorganization per Chapter 166:17 was July 1, 1962. Further, Chapter 106-B of the New Hampshire Revised Statutes Annotated was adopted and entitled "The State Police". Today, Chapter 106-B remains in effect and provides the statutory guidelines for the present-day functioning of the New Hampshire State Police.

New Jersey State Police

On July 1, 1921, H. Norman Schwarzkopf, a graduate of the United States Military Academy at West Point, was appointed as the first superintendent of the state police. He subsequently organized the first training class, which was held at Sea Girt in September 1921 and consisted of 116 men. Of this number, 81 officers and troopers completed the rigorous program and were ordered to duty on December 5, 1921. Once the first class completed training, the academy moved to Wilburtha, where training continued from 1922 to 1971.

When the state police began operation in 1921, the force of new officers was divided into two troops. Troop A was headquartered at the Raleigh Hotel in Hammonton and covered south Jersey, with substations in rented quarters at seven locations. Troop B was headquartered at the Imperial Hotel in Netcong and covered north Jersey with five substations. A platoon headquarters was established in Freehold with three substations. This was the forerunner of a third troop, Troop C, which was established in 1928 to patrol central Jersey.

The original transportation system consisted of 61 horses, 26 motorcycles, 18 cars, one truck, and an ambulance. The horse remained the principal means of transportation throughout the 1920s. Toward the end of the decade, cars and motorcycles were added as the demand for increased services in traffic enforcement and the investigative field heralded a change in the basic patrol function. This period also witnessed the emergence of the state police as a service agency for local police departments with the establishment of Fingerprint, Criminal Records and Auto Theft bureaus. By the 1930s, the State Bureau of Identification and a statewide teletype communications system had been established. These facilities marked the initiation of a movement away from the concept of a strictly rural police force toward one which would eventually provide a myriad of special and technical services to law enforcement agencies throughout the state.

During 1946 the graduation of the first peacetime class initiated a continuing expansion of responsibilities and required increases in authorized strength. In 1948 the governor implemented the recommendations of the Constitutional Convention and consolidated many of the executive departments. The Department of State Police became a Division of the Department of Law and Public Safety, which is headed by the attorney general.

The state police continued to increase their personnel as they accepted the responsibilities of Civil Defense and Disaster Control at West Trenton, the Heavy Duty Rescue School at Hammonton, the Municipal Police Training Academy at Sea Girt, and the enforcement of laws pertaining to liquefied petroleum gas and hotel fire safety. Expansion in the Investigation Section occurred as the result of concentration on specialized investigations, narcotic and gambling raids and increased technical services such as laboratory analysis and polygraph examinations.

In 1955 Colonel Joseph D. Rutter assumed command and organized the division into its present five-troop configuration. Troops A, B and C patrol south, north and central Jersey, respectively, while Troop D patrols the Turnpike and Troop E patrols the Garden State Parkway. Division Headquarters and the State Police Academy were located in West Trenton. The consistent pattern of innovation continued with the establishment of the nation's first State Police Underwater Recovery Unit in 1956. Troopers for this unique service were trained by U.S. Navy SCUBA divers at Bayonne Naval Base. The value of this unit was demonstrated by its subsequent record of evidence recovery, coupled with outstanding service at disaster and accident scenes.

Colonel David B. Kelly was appointed superintendent in 1965, during a time of dynamic and tumultuous change for the nation, the state and the state police. The ability to deal with civil and racial disturbances was tested throughout the 1960s. During 1967, state police personnel were charged with riot control in the violence-stricken cities of Newark and Plainfield. Throughout these turbulent times, division personnel were tested both as individuals and as a disciplined unit working as a whole. The fact that the division responded effectively was clearly evidenced in the governor's directive that the state police conduct training in riot control for all police agencies in the state. Thus, "Operation Combine," a training program for command and tactical control of civil disorder, was established. As a result of this program, a statewide response strategy for municipal, county and state agencies and the Alert radio system for inter-agency communication during disasters, was implemented.

During the late 1960s, the division continued to accrue added responsibilities and achieved higher degrees of recognition. The end of the decade witnessed an increased public awareness of the violent and deleterious nature of organized crime. The division again became a pioneer in new investigative efforts. Intelligence and Organized Crime Task Force

Bureaus were created to monitor and interdict both traditional and nontraditional organized criminals. As the legislature originated and enacted new laws governing electronic surveillance, witness immunity, statewide grand jury, gun control and uniform crime reporting codes, the New Jersey State Police was charged with the enforcement of these laws to wage war against organized crime. This time also saw the creation of the Division Traffic Bureau to enforce traffic safety laws and a Tactical Patrol Research and Analysis Unit to identify target areas for selective enforcement and assist local police departments in handling specific traffic problems.

On October 24, 1975, Colonel Clinton L. Pagano was sworn into office as the ninth colonel and superintendent of the New Jersey State Police.

Colonel Pagano's tenure brought with it a sustained period of growth for the division. The many demands for specialized police services dictated a change in the organizational structure to more effectively administer the division's many mandated and assumed responsibilities.

In an effort to remain the most prestigious law enforcement agency, sophisticated criminal investigation efforts were initiated by the new superintendent. Arson investigators, fu-

gitive tracking, and major crime investigations were only some of the functions that became specialized tasks, while basic and extended training for troopers and municipal officers increased proportionately at the State Police Training Academy which moved to Sea Girt in 1971.

The staff organization within the division has kept pace with the growth and diversification of the state police mission. Intelligence gathering procedures were expanded and through Colonel Pagano's efforts, one of the first analytical units in the country was established. Sophisticated intelligence systems were instituted and have been recognized by several government commissions, including the International Association of Chiefs of Police (IACP).

In December 1977, Colonel Pagano authorized the signing of a formal contract with Seton Hall to further professionalize policing. State police recruits are awarded 24 credit hours which are approved by Seton Hall and conform with the Middle Atlantic States Association standards.

In 1978 the state police in cooperation with the College of Medicine and Dentistry of New Jersey, expanded the services of the Helicopter Patrol Bureau to provide the state's first organized Air Rescue Medical Evacua-

tion Program (Med-Evac). This service is designed to expedite the transportation of persons who have sustained life threatening injuries.

During the fall of 1979, the state police embarked on an experimental program to recruit, select and train an all-female class in a concerted effort to increase the number of female state troopers. Thirty females completed the course and were sworn in as troopers in June 1980. This special class, a first in the nation, was a one-time infusion of women into the state police. Since that time, the academy has accepted and graduated several additional female troopers.

Under the leadership of Colonel Pagano, the increased responsibilities have had a tremendous impact upon the profile of the division and have provided the opportunity for the state police to effectively demonstrate its versatility and proficiency. This was demonstrated by the most extensive manhunt in state police history: the search for the killers of Trooper Philip Lamonaco, beginning with his murder on December 21, 1981. Through unmatched determination and sophisticated investigative techniques, suspects Raymond Levasseur, Patricia Gross, Richard Williams, Jaan Laaman, and Barbara Curzi were arrested on November 4, 1984. The search culminated with the April 1985 arrest of Thomas Manning and his wife, Carol. These arrests halted a 10-year reign of career criminals who were members of the Jonathan Jackson-Sam Melville Unit of The United Freedom Front. This terrorist group was responsible for 18 bombings and numerous bank robberies throughout the east coast.

The era of the 90s began with the appointment of Colonel Justin J. Dintino as the tenth superintendent of the New Jersey State Police. Under Colonel Dintino's leadership, major investigative initiatives on the Columbian and Jamaican drug cartels and other organized crime groups were instituted.

Several new technological innovations continue to expand the division's capabilities in providing the finest in crime fighting techniques. The completion of the Automated Fingerprint Identification System (AFIS) provides computer-optic technology with high-speed scanning devices to classify, store and retrieve the 1.1 million criminal fingerprint cards currently in the system. AFIS eliminates the time consuming, labor-intensive manual system of classifying and comparing fingerprints and will enable law enforcement to solve previously unsolved crimes.

A scientific breakthrough in crime detection occurred with the innovative technique of detecting an individual's unique genetic "signature" in blood, semen, or hair roots. With the establishment of a DNA Testing Unit at the South Regional Laboratory, DNA (Deoxyribonucleic Acid) profiling, a genetic tech-

nique that takes over at the point conventional blood grouping begins to leave questions unanswered, moved closer to reality. Since only identical twins have identical DNA characters, the technique will reduce investigative hours and increase the likelihood of successful completion of cases.

Colonel Carl A. Williams, a career law enforcement officer with more than 30 years of distinguished service to the citizens of New Jersey, was sworn-in as the eleventh superintendent of the New Jersey State Police on June 9, 1994 by Governor Christine Todd Whitman.

Throughout his career in the New Jersey State Police, Colonel Williams has served in nearly all aspects of state police operations. Prior to his appointment as superintendent, Colonel Williams supervised the state office of Emergency Management, the section within state police responsible for coordinating statewide emergency operations.

As head of the OEM, Colonel Williams promoted a strong working relationship with the Federal Emergency Management Agency and, as a result, New Jersey's municipalities are better able to benefit from the numerous federal programs geared to assist state, county and local governments in the aftermath of devastating storms and disasters.

One of Colonel Williams' single most significant achievements was the development of the state police "Augmentation Plan," an advanced police training session where more than 800 new troopers received specialized instruction over a two-year period.

The New Jersey State Police has remained in the forefront of creative policy implementation and investigative techniques. It has clearly surpassed the original mandate of a statewide rural police force. Its illustrious history is replete with commendations for innovation and expertise in criminal investigations, traffic enforcement and technical services. From those early years when the mounted trooper brought law and order in his saddlebags, more than 5,000 dedicated men and women have followed in his path. The horse and motorcycle have yielded to the automobile, helicopter and power boat responding to multi-channel bunked radio dispatching. In addition, computers provide instant responses to queries for police information throughout the country, while highly sophisticated criminal investigation and special and technical laboratory services are among the finest in the nation.

Technological innovations have enhanced and expanded the original purpose of the state police; yet there still exists a network of substations that fulfill the initial role of the state police: to provide general police protection to the rural residents of New Jersey.

The current body of more than 2,600 enlisted and 1,200 civilian personnel share one distinction regardless of their rank or designation, they are members of this state's most prestigious law enforcement agency—the New Jersey State Police.

New Mexico State Police

New Mexico remained without a state police force until March 14, 1933, when a bill was passed creating the New Mexico Motor Patrol. A board of supervisors was created to oversee the newly created force. This board consisted of the governor, the attorney general and the highway engineer.

The board of supervisors studied several states and found New Mexico most resembled the Texas Patrol. Texas Patrol Captain Homer Garrison was on loan to head the first school of the New Mexico Motor Patrol at the St. Michael's College in Santa Fe.

As positions for the patrol were advertised, 135 men were examined; 18 were selected to attend the 30-day training school. Of the 18 men only 10 were commissioned at a graduation ceremony on August 5, 1933. Each new patrolman was issued a Harley Davidson motorcycle equipped with siren, red light and other accessories necessary for the operation. The salary for the chief patrolman at the time was $150 a month and $125 a month for a patrolman.

Unlike the uniforms of today, the motor patrol uniforms included brown leather gear and brown cap brim, a dark drab green shirt and trousers for winter wear. In the summer, a tan shirt replaced the green shirt. This was similar to the military color scheme. When in their dress uniform, they wore a white shirt under their green blouse with a black bow tie. Their breast shield and cap badges were of polished brass. Their side arm was a Smith and Wesson .38 revolver. After a few months, the boots, Sam Browne belt, and cap brim were changed from brown to black. The motor patrolmen were allowed $10 a month clothing allowance for maintaining their uniforms.

A bill was introduced and passed in the 12th State Legislature and on February 25, 1935, the New Mexico State Police became a reality. All of the existing motor patrolmen were automatically commissioned as state police officers with a provision made to increase the manpower to 30 officers.

The uniform was black oxford breeches with a wide light gray stripe down the pant legs, a black matching cap, a tan shirt, later to be replaced by a lighter gray shirt with a black bow tie. For dress, a black oxford gray tunic blouse was worn under the Sam Browne belt. The side arm issued was a Colt .45 revolver. The badges were changed to gold plated with the seal of New Mexico in the center, the same style used today. The New Mexico State Police shoulder patch was designed with silver thread and black lettering on the left shoulder.

The shoulder patch was the same design then as now, except for the silver thread being replaced by white thread.

In 1935 the department purchased seven two door Chevrolet sedans to supplement the 10 existing motorcycles. The cars were equipped with a red spotlight and siren. They had no heaters as this was considered a luxury.

A new headquarters building was designed and constructed by WPS on Cerrillos Road in Santa Fe for a cost of $19,000. It was completed in November of 1935 and contained offices for the chief, identification, supply, a five-man dormitory, a large gymnasium and a full basement. This served as headquarters for the state police until the new and present complex was completed in January 1971.

In late 1936 a new uniform shirt was designed of black oxford gray with light gray cuffs, pockets, and epaulets matching the breeches. This same style of shirt is still used today.

In 1937 the application age was raised from 21 to 23. All patrol cars were replaced with motorcycles except one for the chief, one for the investigator and one for general use around headquarters.

In 1938 door shields were placed on the patrol cars—the same style used on patrol cars today. During 1940 additions were built onto headquarters to include an auto shop, larger dormitories, and an indoor pistol range.

In 1946 the two-way radio system went on the air with a radio repeater located on Sandia Crest near Albuquerque. Radios were installed in all 41 patrol cars. The early call letters were KCQA.

In 1956 by a vote of the officers, a new light gray shirt with black oxford gray trim was adopted. This was before the units were equipped with air conditioners and the shirts were being tested for coolness. In subsequent years, however, the shirts reverted back to the original color and design used today. This same year the state police acquired its first aircraft, a Cessna 180, which was on loan from the State Corporation Commission.

With the rising problem of narcotics use and distribution, the state police saw a need to form a Narcotics Section. In late 1960 a patrolman was assigned as a state police narcotics agent. Over the next several years the Narcotics Division would grow into several well-trained agents responsible for making numerous major drug busts.

The transition from white over black patrol cars to all white patrol cars with the single rotating red light on the top began in 1961.

In late 1963 the department created the Special Investigations Division, placing 10 investigators in that division. As protests and riots began increasing around the country and several underground organizations were being established to undermine the government agencies, the state police would send agents of the Intelligence Division into college campuses around the state to document information concerning up-coming criminal events.

During 1967 the Planning and Research Division was created and a planning officer

New Mexico Motor Patrol. August 5, 1933. Graduation Day.

New Mexico State Police Officer, 1938.

New Mexico State Police, 1943.

was assigned to that division. The department also implemented a fleet safety program for grading fleet accidents. Another minor change was made to the uniform when a gold braid was added to the cap bills of captains and above.

The department's budget began to grow as more personnel were added and more equipment was purchased. In 1968 the department's budget exceeded $4,000,000. The dive team had increased to 28 divers assigned to areas adjacent to lakes and rivers around the state. The department also implemented the NCIC system utilizing one model 37 ASR, which was used in the communications office in Santa Fe.

During this year, money was appropriated for a new state police headquarters and State Police Academy. The new complex consisted

of the state police offices and State Police Academy, a new automotive maintenance shop, radio communications building and a driving track for the academy.

In 1969, the department budget increased by $300,000. A Public Relations Office was created with one officer assigned to this position. This office was discontinued within the year. In the latter part of March 1969 the Legal Division was established and one attorney was hired.

The Crime Laboratory was yet to be completed when the first lab technician was hired. The sole responsibility of the technician was to use "seed money" which had been appropriated to order equipment so the laboratory would be in operation upon completion of the building. The Santa Fe District office was completed next to the new headquarters build-

ing during 1970 and the relocation into the new headquarters was completed as of January 1971.

The State Police Aircraft Division received a new twin engine Cessna Skymaster 337 to replace the older Cessna. During this year, the department started phasing out the all-white police car to return to the desired white over black units.

As the department continued to grow, a second pilot was added to the Aircraft Division in 1972. The department's budget was now up to $6,400,000. An automated message switching system was installed at headquarters, which was to serve the criminal justice community statewide. In addition, 25 high speed teletype machines were installed throughout the state. The NCIC system was transferred from the Bureau of Criminal Identification to the Communications Division in June 1972.

The Narcotics Division confiscated $5.9 million in drugs during 1972 and an air detail was added to enhance that division.

In the early part of 1973, the New Mexico State Police Tactical Team was organized. It consisted of a northern and southern team, each supervised by a lieutenant.

The Communications and Records Divisions merged and became the Information Division. In August, the department started its Search and Rescue Team by appointing the department's first coordinators.

In 1976 the new teletype system was added throughout the state that could, among other things, print 150 words per minute. 1976 also saw the beginning of a new era as the predominantly male-oriented department commissioned, for the first time in its history, two female officers.

During 1978 the department started purchasing electronic sirens to replace the manual single toned traditional siren used for years by law enforcement agencies.

The Search and Rescue Team was officially underway during 1979 and the department acquired its first helicopter, and Aerospatiale SA341G.

The department underwent another re-organization where it was placed under the newly created Criminal Justice System along with the Corrections Department. The chief was now responsible to a cabinet secretary over the Criminal Justice Department. This change made the state police a division instead of a department. This status was a little difficult for some of the old timers to accept.

To the relief of the state police, on July 1, 1979, Governor Bruce King signed an Executive Order removing the state police from the Criminal Justice Department, making it once again its own independent agency. During this time frame, the Personnel Management Division became a division of its own, having been separated from the Personnel and Training Division.

During 1980 and 1981, the department purchased a few light bars that extended across the top of the unit in contrast with the more traditional double rotating red lights familiar to state police units. During 1980 the state police started testing slick-top patrol units to patrol interstate highways.

During 1983 the department's authorized strength for commissioned officers was 381. The yearly seizure of cocaine for state police was $239 million, primarily on Interstate 40, The state police also seized $1.6 million in drug related cash.

The New Mexico State Police became a leading agency in the nation of drug interdiction, and as a result of this nationwide publicity, several state police officers traveled the nation training other agencies in profiling the cocaine "mules."

During the mid-1980s, several new federal regulations were instituted relating to law enforcement agencies that would affect the state police, bringing about drastic changes. One change was the Fair Labors Standard Act, which no longer allowed officers to work over eight hours without being compensated either by monetary means or compensatory hour off. Prior to this, the state police had a day and night shift covering 12 hours each. As the federal government required police agencies to compensate overtime, the "general hours" shift was gone forever. The state police paid sergeants and officers overtime for the first time beginning in July 1984.

Another long time state police tradition was broken during this year when short sleeve uniform shirts were approved for summer apparel.

As the State Police Aircraft Division grew, the pilots and planes were used in a diversity of areas. One was an aircraft speed zone. A pilot would fly to a specified district and with the assistance of one of the district officers as an observer, circle the painted speed zoned clocking cars with stopwatches. The pilot would then call the description of the speeding car to ground troops who would then pull the car over and issue citations accordingly.

As the DWI problem was getting worse throughout New Mexico, the department purchased four Pontiac station wagons, fully marked, for the purpose of being used as mobile Bat-Mobiles. Guidelines were also set for the department to implement sobriety checkpoints for the first time. Federally funded overtime projects were also initiated to combat the increase in drunk drivers.

The year 1985 marked 50 years of state police existence, which the department celebrated in grand style.

During this decade, the Department of Public Safety brought under it several former agencies, which included the New Mexico State Police, Department of Alcoholic Beverage Control, Civil Emergency Preparedness

Chief Frank Taylor in foreground.

New Mexico State Police, Tactical Team.

Steve Tingwall, Kevin McPhearson, Grey Toyu, 1996.

Division of the Office of Military Affairs and the New Mexico Law Enforcement Academy. A non-police cabinet secretary was appointed over DPS, as it became known, and the rank of deputy chief was abolished and replaced with the rank of lieutenant colonel.

During the many meetings of the newly formed Department of Public Safety, talk arose of changing the state police badge and possibly the shoulder patch to include the letters "DPS" on them. The transition was not an easy one for the state police. The department started looking at the physical fitness of its officers and initiated a voluntary program where officers could participate if they chose. The test would be done biannually and was comprised of running 1.5 miles, sit-ups and push-ups.

The department ventured away from tradition during the year of 1989 by putting six unmarked units equipped with the new HAWK radar to patrol around strategic locations throughout New Mexico. The stealth units as they became known, were multicolored slick tops with the red lights mounted on the front push bumpers and in the rear window deck. The units proved to be effective in traffic enforcement and in 1990 the department once again deviated from tradition by purchasing six Ford Mustangs.

During 1990 the department elected to transition from the traditional revolver the state police had carried for years to the semi-automatic. This year was also the first time the state police officers were issued hand-held radios to be carried on their uniforms. The new radio was such that radio traffic was transmitted from the hand-held, to the unit, through the repeater, and on to the district being called.

The unmarked patrol program was gradually phased out. This was also true of the Ford Mustang project. The year 1993 saw the last Mustang patrol unit for the state police.

The rank of lieutenant colonel was abolished and again replaced with the rank of deputy chief.

Effective October 1, 1991, the department implemented a mandatory physical fitness program, which was designed to give all officers ample time to meet at least minimum standards. Physical fitness time was also allotted to the officers so they would be able to take one hour at a time during a regular workshift for up to three hours a week.

During the year 1993, the department would change the style of their fatigues from gray trousers and shirts with a black baseball cap to the black military type battle fatigues.

In June 1995, there was a restructuring of communications operations at headquarters and the Santa Fe patrol district. The restructuring moved half of the communications personnel from the headquarters radio room and the radio consoles back to the Santa Fe patrol district. Radio Communications had been moved out of the patrol district several years earlier, leaving Santa Fe district as the only patrol district which did not have its own radio communications operation. The communications operators and supervisor moved back to the Santa Fe district operations were transferred from the Technical and Emergency Support Division to the direction and control of the State Police Division. The remainder of the headquarters communication personnel remained under the Technical and Emergency Support Division to monitor and maintain the computer and switcher operation that supports the district communications operations throughout the state.

The New Mexico State Police has grown tremendously over the past several decades into what is now one of the top law enforcement agencies in the nation. As the state police continues to grow to meet the rising needs of modern law enforcement with updated equipment and training, it strives to preserve the tradition and close camaraderie of each officer as being a member of a family with a proud heritage.

New York State Police

It is perhaps the ultimate irony that the most heinous of crimes, deliberate and cold-blooded murder, was the germinal event that led to the founding of the New York State Police. Sam Howell was confronted by robbers as he delivered a payroll in 1913. When he refused to hand over the payroll, he was shot seven times. Although he escaped with the payroll, Mr. Howell subsequently died of his wounds. Before he died, he was able to identify his attackers, but local law enforcement officials refused to attempt to apprehend the attackers, even though they were holed up in nearby woods. The murderers were never caught. Miss Moyca Newell was so outraged at the escape of the killers that, with the assistance of her friend, Miss Katherine Mayo, she initiated a movement to establish a state force that would provide police protection to rural areas in New York State.

The Wells-Mills Bill, which appropriated $500,000 to establish a Department of State Police, was passed by one vote in the Senate on March 20, 1917. It had an easier time in the Assembly, where it was passed by a vote of 81-60. On April 11, 1917, Governor Whitman signed the bill into law under Chapter 161 of the Laws of 1917.

The first of the original 237 officers and men began training at a National Guard Camp in Manlius, New York. The training was a combination of military drill, horsemanship and legal training provided by two judges and an assistant attorney general.

Realizing that more formal training in law and police procedure was needed, in 1921 the New York State School for Police was organized, which became a standard for police training. It was the first police school in the nation to be certified by a state education board, and was authorized to award its graduates a State Certificate as a "Professional Policeman."

Their training completed in the fall of 1917, the troopers undertook their first assignment policing the New York State Fair. After exemplary duty there, the 232 officers and men assigned to the four troops rode out across the state on horseback to Batavia, Syracuse, Albany and White Plains. Strategically located "substations," generally rooming houses or hotels, were established in a town in each county. From these locations the men fanned out in pairs, riding their horses as far as 150 miles before they turned around and headed back.

Communications were rudimentary in those earliest days. Each patrol was required to report to the troop barracks every evening

Patrols leaving the Troop K Barracks, White Plains.

and notify the troop commander where it was, and where it expected to be 24 and 48 hours hence. If an emergency arose, a call would be placed to the next stop and a message left for when the patrol arrived. Often the local telephone operators, who knew everyone in their district, were able to intercept the troopers by informing everyone on the party lines along the route to flag the patrol down if they saw it and have them call in.

In addition to their law enforcement duties, the troopers quickly became the people that rural New Yorkers turned to whenever they had troubles of any kind. Before the creation of social service agencies, the state police was the only government agency readily available to country dwellers.

Troopers gradually assumed more responsibility for vehicle and traffic safety, taking over all motor vehicle enforcement from the Motor Vehicle Bureau in 1926.

The most important development of the 1930s was the initiation of modern communications systems. In 1931 the division inaugurated its teletypewriter system, the forerunner of the New York Statewide Police Information System the division operates today.

The growing system of good roads and the widespread use of cars significantly impacted criminal law enforcement efforts during the 1930s. With the increasing mobility and sophistication of criminals, a dedicated investigation bureau that could conduct complex investigations was needed so that the uniform force could maintain patrols. A dedicated investigative bureau could also provide investigative expertise and assistance to local departments. Consequently, the Legislature autho-

rized the creation of a Bureau of Investigation in 1935. The same legislation authorized the creation of a Crime Laboratory. In 1936 the Bureau of Investigation became the Bureau of Criminal Investigation and the Crime Laboratory opened in Schenectady.

The outbreak of World War II resulted in a serious drain of division manpower. The division started the war with an authorized strength of 1,000, but 295 were placed on military leave during the war.

Six members made the ultimate sacrifice in the service of their country between 1942 and 1945. Additional war duties added significantly to the workload of members remaining in the under strength division. In 1942 the state police developed evacuation plans for the state and established emergency truck control rerouting stations to divert traffic around New York City in case of sabotage or other emergency. A major commitment was also required for military convoy escorts through the State.

With the end of the World War II, attention was turned toward upgrading equipment and acquiring new technology. Communications were vastly improved during the immediate post-war years. By the end of 1947, the division had instituted a statewide two-way radio system in its stations and cars. It also acquired 42 backpack walkie-talkies and 16 portable transceivers run by generators.

The end of the war and the resurgence of highway traffic tolled the death knell for one of the oldest state police traditions, as well. Mounted patrol miles had declined steadily throughout the 1930s and early 1940s. In 1947 only 2,115 miles were patrolled on horseback, less than 1/100th of the number 30 years before. In 1948, for the first time in its history, the New York State Police did not report any mounted patrols.

Another major change was the opening in 1954 of the New York State Thruway. The New York State Police assumed sole responsibility for policing the Thruway and its authorized strength was increased from 899 to 1,201 members in 1953 in order to provide the additional Thruway patrols. With the increase in vehicle traffic, driving while intoxicated became a major problem.

In 1953 a law was passed that allowed the securing of blood, breath or urine from a driver for analysis to determine blood alcohol content. In 1954 the division made more than 1,000 arrests for DWI for the first time in history. A program to evaluate breath testing devices began in 1953 with a pilot test of the Harger Drunkometer conducted jointly by the Laboratory and Troop G. By the end of the decade, the breathalyzer was in widespread use by the division.

Technology was also applied to speed enforcement. In 1956 the Thruway Detail was the first in the state police to use concealed identity cars and radar for vehicle and traffic enforcement. These innovations were expanded to all six troops the following year. 1956 also saw the first use of helicopters to observe heavy traffic conditions.

In 1957 the New York State Police found concrete proof that a nationwide network of organized crime existed when they uncovered a conference of organized crime leaders in progress in Appalachian, New York. The meeting disbanded when the troopers arrived, but subsequent investigations were the beginning of the war on organized crime. In 1958 the division created its first Criminal Intelligence Unit with 26 members initially assigned. This was the vanguard of what would become an army of law enforcement officers who would be enlisted for the war on organized crime in the coming years.

The 1950s saw the first harbingers of another major crime problem that would confront the state police in future years— illegal drugs. There were sporadic references to illegal drugs in the first four decades, but 1955 is the first year that the state police had a separate section on narcotics in the Annual Report.

The 1960s ushered in a period of unprecedented change in U.S. society. Technological advances in electronics, telecommunications and transportation changed the American lifestyle. The social fabric of the nation was also changing. The first wave of the "baby boom" reached adolescence and young adulthood and many of its members openly rebelled against society and those who represented its authority. Some turned to illegal drugs and rock and roll, culminating in the Aquarian Festival, better known as Woodstock, for many the single event that epitomizes the tenor of

the decade. Others turned to more sinister and violent rebellion.

In 1965 the New York State Police entered the computer age when the Electronic Data Processing Section was created. In 1966 computerized message switching equipment was installed to reduce the transmission time of teletypes and the process of creating a computerized database of stolen property and wanted persons was begun. In 1967 the New York State Police became the first New York State Agency to maintain an on-line, real time computer system when the new Computer Oriented Police System, the forerunner of the New York Statewide Police Information System, was placed in service. Radio improvements also continued.

The state police made great strides in the application of technology to improving highway safety during the 1960s. The use of radar for speed enforcement increased throughout the decade. In 1962, radar accounted for 57.4% of all speeding arrests. In 1968 the first VASCAR units were placed in service to enhance the division's speed enforcement capabilities.

Drunk driving increased dramatically during the 1960s, as did the division's efforts to identify and apprehend drivers operating motor vehicles under the influence of alcohol. The use of breathalyzers was expanded. In 1968 there were breathalyzers available in every Zone Station. In 1969 every station had a breathalyzer and an extensive training program was underway to train every trooper in the use of breathalyzers and court testimony procedures.

The reorganization and modernization that began during the 1960s continued into the early 1970s. In 1970 the New York State Police Academy was finally completed and the first class of 98 recruit troopers was admitted in May. In 1971 the new headquarters for Troop K was completed. More specialized units were established as criminals became more sophisticated. In 1970 the New York City Drug Enforcement Task Force teamed state police personnel with federal drug enforcement agents and New York City Police Department personnel to have a major impact on illegal drug trafficking in the New York City metropolitan area. The rise of organized crime resulted in the formation of an Organized Crime Task Force, with New York State Police investigators assigned to work with the attorney general's office. Special hazardous device units were formed and members trained to deal with bombs and other explosive devices in response to the rise in terrorism and bombings across the state.

A program of laboratory expansion was begun in order to provide better service to the state police members and local law enforcement agencies dependent on the State Police Crime Laboratory for evidence analysis. In 1978 the Mid-Hudson Regional Crime Laboratory opened in Newburgh.

Satellite offices were established in 1977 in order to save fuel and allow troopers to spend more time on patrol by stationing them closer to their posts. The program was initiated with 34 satellite offices. This number increased to 60 by the end of the decade. In 1977 the first recruit class in two years was authorized and 229 recruit troopers were hired.

The use of VASCAR for speed enforcement expanded when 200 units were acquired in 1971. This number was doubled in 1972. In 1975 the state police acquired its first radar units capable of operating while the troop car was in motion.

During the 1980s the New York State Police grew to more than 4,000 sworn members, becoming the largest full service state police in the nation. This growth was essential to meeting as the state police took the lead in law enforcement efforts against the burgeoning crime problems confronting the state: illegal drug trafficking, violent crime, child abuse and exploitation, computer crimes, consumer product tampering and bias motivated crimes.

New responsibilities did not diminish the role of the New York State Police in providing police protection for rural areas and ensuring the safety of travelers on the state's roads and highways. The New York State Police evolved into what is truly a full service law enforcement agency. In rural areas that do not have the resources to provide local police protection, the state police provides primary police coverage, first response to calls for police service and investigative and support services in serious criminal cases. In suburban areas, the state police provides full services in areas not covered by a local department, patrols state roads and interstate highways, supports local police departments and provides sophisticated investigative and technical assistance to departments investigating major crimes. In urban areas, the state police concentrates on drug trafficking, violent crime, money laundering and organized criminal activities that cross jurisdictional boundaries.

The expansion of facilities and services continued in the 1980s. Under legislation that took effect on January 1, 1980, the New York State Police took over responsibility for policing the Long Island Parkway and three shorter parkways upstate. The parkway police who were providing these services were absorbed into the New York State Police. With the addition of the Long Island Parkway to existing state police duties on Long Island, it was impractical to continue supervising state police activities on Long Island from Troop K Headquarters in Poughkeepsie so a new Troop L was formed and became operational January 1, 1980. In 1986 Troop L Headquarters relocated from Islip Terrace to a new headquarters facility in Farmingdale.

Many new programs were initiated to address specific crime problems. One of these was the Special Investigations Unit (SIU) inaugurated in 1983. The creation of the SIU doubled the number of state police personnel dedicated to investigating organized crime. The SIU works closely with the Organized Crime Task Force attached to the attorney general's office.

In 1984 the state police and the Division of Criminal Justice Services began the 12 Most Wanted Program. This program publicized the most violent criminals wanted for crimes committed in New York State and solicited public assistance in locating them so that they could be apprehended by the proper law enforcement authorities. Auto Theft Units were also created to combat organized auto theft rings.

The rising number of hazardous materials spills and accidents on the state's highways prompted the formation of the HAZ-MAT Unit. These specially trained troopers were equipped to respond to incidents involving the release of hazardous materials anywhere in the state. More importantly, they were charged with identifying shippers who used unsafe or inferior equipment, unsafe handling procedures and unqualified drivers.

The greatest challenge facing the state police was the explosion of illegal drug use and trafficking, particularly in cocaine and its malevolent offspring, crack. With the emergence of cocaine and crack as the drugs of choice during the 1980s, a new threat appeared, the vicious criminal cartels that controlled the cocaine trade. Two characteristics that made these cartels particularly dangerous were their propensity to violence and the unprecedented wealth derived from the cocaine trade that allowed them to buy the most so-

Woodstock, 25 yrs. later.

phisticated technology and weapons available in the world.

To meet this threat between 1986 and 1987 the state police added more than 200 members who were assigned full time to narcotics investigations. By the end of the decade, over 300 specially trained narcotics investigators were dedicated to identifying and apprehending criminals involved in illegal drug trade, with an emphasis on mid- and upper-level dealers.

In 1985 the federal government initiated a program to share assets seized from illegal drug traffickers with local law enforcement agencies that cooperated in their seizure. This quickly became one of the most effective tools available in the war against illegal drugs. In the first full year of the program, the state police received $677,000. Superintendent Constantine made pursuit of seized assets a priority and to date, the division has received more than $31,000,000 from seized assets.

Many local police departments, district attorneys, coroners and medical examiners lack access to specialists in forensic sciences. Such experts can be essential to the successful investigation and prosecution of serious crimes and to the identification of bodies following a disaster or an unexplained death or homicide. The New York State Police Forensic Science Unit (now the now the Medicolegal Investigations Unit) was created to address this problem. The leading experts in forensic disciplines are available through the unit to assist law enforcement agencies and coroners and medical examiners. The services of this unit have been invaluable in a number of major criminal investigations across the state.

Troop K Honor Guard at the National Law Enforcement Officer's Memorial.

North Carolina State Highway Patrol

The mission of the North Carolina State Highway Patrol is to ensure safe, efficient transportation on our streets and highways, reduce crime and respond to natural and manmade disasters. This mission will be accomplished, in partnership with all levels of government and the citizens of North Carolina, through quality law enforcement services based upon high ethical, professional and legal standards.

In 1921 there were 13,743 trucks and 136,815 automobiles comprising a total of 150,558 registered vehicles in North Carolina. By 1929, North Carolina registered vehicles had increased to 503,590. Following yearly increases, in 1929 there were 690 motorists killed in motor vehicle crashes—an increase from 673 killed in 1928.

By 1929 the control of vehicular traffic was a matter of grave concern to all North Carolinians. So much so, that the North Carolina General Assembly passed an act authorizing the establishment of a State Highway Patrol. The newly authorized organization was given statutory responsibility to patrol the highways of the state, enforce motor vehicle laws, and assist the motoring public. The organization was designed as a division of the State Highway Commission.

The pioneers of the North Carolina State Highway Patrol consisted of 10 men who were later designated as one captain and nine lieutenants. These men traveled to Pennsylvania to attend the Training School of the Pennsylvania State Police. While in Pennsylvania, the 10 men studied law, first air, headlight adjustments, vehicle operation and law enforcement related subjects to be used in North Carolina's first State Highway Patrol Training School.

The first North Carolina State Highway Patrol Basic School began on May 20, 1929 at Camp Glenn near Forest City, North Carolina. Of the original 400 State Highway Patrol applicants, 67 were selected to report to school. Forty-two men completed the school and 37 members were chosen to receive the "Oath of Of-

fice" in the State Capitol Building in Raleigh, NC. Monthly salaries established for this new state law enforcement agency were established as follows:

Commander	$200.00
Lieutenant	$175.00
Patrolman	$ 87.50

After training, the original members toured North Carolina as a group. The group traveled from the eastern portion of North Carolina in Beaufort, to the western parts of the state near Asheville, and back to the State Capitol in Raleigh.

On July 1, 1929, the 37 patrolmen met in the House Chambers of the State Capitol for the official swearing-in ceremonies. During the ceremony, the Honorable Henry A. Grady, Superior Court Judge, charged the members of the State Highway Patrol to be courageous, professional, impartial, loyal and patient in the performance of their newly identified duties and responsibilities.

Logistically, an office was established in Raleigh to serve as State Highway Patrol Headquarters, and a district office was established in each of the nine districts throughout the state. Statewide, all patrolmen were issued Harley Davidson motorcycles and lieutenants drove Model "A"

Ford Coupes. A Buick automobile was issued to the patrol commander.

The General Assembly increased the State Highway Patrol's complement to 67 in 1931 and reduced the number of lieutenants to six. By 1933 the State Highway Patrol had increased in number to 121 members, who were then responsible for issuing driver licenses and enforcing the new driver license laws.

Since its inception in 1929, many pages of North Carolina State Highway Patrol history have been written. The current patrol commander, Richard W. Holden, is the 21st commander of the now more than 1,400 member organization. Including non-sworn personnel, the North Carolina State Highway Patrol now employs nearly 2,000 people. In contrast to the early days, troopers now use mobile data computers in their new Ford Crown Victoria and Chevrolet Camaro patrol cars, along with dual antenna radars, vascars, and electronic citation capabilities.

The history and rich tradition of the North Carolina State Highway Patrol is engrained and sealed in North Carolina cul-

ture. To date, 52 members of the State Highway Patrol have given their lives in service to the citizens of the great State of North Carolina. The contribution these troopers have made stands as a constant reminder of the dedication and commitment of North Carolina's State Highway Patrol.

Ohio State Highway Patrol

In Ohio, bills to form a state-based police force were introduced on several occasions, beginning in 1917. In 1933, the 90th General Assembly considered the bill, which eventually created the Ohio State Highway Patrol. HB 270 outlined a Highway Patrol which would enforce: state laws relating to registration and licensing of motor vehicles, laws relating to motor vehicle use and operation on the highways and all laws for the protection of highways. Very important to the passage of the bill was a provision prohibiting use of the patrol in labor disputes and strikes. The bill also stipulated that the force would be limited to 60 officers who were between the ages of 24 and 40 years and placed under a $2,500 performance bond. When the Ohio State Highway Patrol was born, it was announced that classes would begin on Tuesday, October 3, 1933, and that the new force would be operational in approximately 30 days. Accounts vary as to how many actually entered training camp, but the most likely figure is 112. Of these, 40 percent were doomed to flunk or drop out. It was decided that patrol substations were to be located in private residences, but even at this late date (slightly more than a week from graduation), the actual homes had not been selected. On November 3, 1933, it was announced that graduation of the new "safety conservators" would be on November 15, 1933, making the actual time spent in camp 37 days.

Among the earliest services provided were traffic checks, stopping and checking for certain mechanical defects. If a defect was noted, the driver was issued a correction slip, which was to be signed by a mechanic and returned to the local sub-post within 48 hours.

As the 1940s opened, the nation was preparing for what appeared to be an inevitable entry into the war raging in Europe. The division had already been delegated a few wartime duties, beginning in 1939 when the Federal Bureau of Investigation requested the patrol's assistance in investigations of un-American activities. In February 1941 the commanding general of the Fifth Corps Area of the U.S. Army called upon the division to coordinate the movement of military and civilian traffic in the state. Ohio was the first state in the nation to complete plans for the rapid mobilization of troops and equipment. In 1941 alone, 154 convoys were moved under the direction of the patrol.

In April 1942, the division hit a peak of 297 patrolmen. From there, the number steadily decreased. By 1945 uniformed officers numbered only 139. Highway travel was strictly regulated during the war to preserve scarce materials. A 35 mph "victory speed" and travel restrictions were imposed requiring close enforcement.

In early 1952 the division purchased "intoximeters" and began training officers in their use. This was the first "scientific" method of determining alcohol presence. At about the same time, the use of aircraft for enforcement finally went beyond the occasional manhunt. On July 4, 1952, patrolmen were observing

Ohio State Highway Patrol. First annual meeting, 1934. The entire force, minus only Col. Black.

traffic conditions from the air and spotted a semi-truck driving recklessly. They radioed its position to an officer patrolling below, who subsequently stopped the vehicle. That same year saw the greatest advance of all - speed measuring devices. In spring 1952, the patrol unveiled several of the devices, conducting highly visible demonstrations to familiarize judges and prosecutors with the new concept. A radar team generally set up on the side of the highway, placing "radar speed control" signs up the highway to avoid the speed trap stigma, the officer radioed the description of violators' vehicles to an "interceptor officer" waiting further down the road.

It was in 1960 that the division obtained its own chemical laboratory and hired a civilian chemist. The new lab enabled the patrol to be more self-reliant in its investigations.

Although the manpower increases were a welcome boost, low pay was a continuing problem. In 1965 turnover of uniformed officers reached 8.6 percent and in 1966 that number soared to an alarming 13.3 percent. While the effort to secure higher pays progressed, other measures were introduced to make patrol life more desirable. In 1966 the transfer and placement policy was modified to permit assignment of officers in their home areas, at their request. This overturned a policy, which existed since 1933, and assisted in retaining officers as well as recruiting new ones.

By July 1968, 27 motor vehicle inspection teams were in operation. Probably the most significant advancement of the era was the approval of a grant request to develop and install a completely automatic law enforcement information retrieval and communications system. Dubbed LEADS (Law Enforcement Automated Data System), the system became operational in 1968, providing officers with instant access to three massive computer files: Ohio vehicle registration listings; Ohio operator license and arrest records; and an "auto alert" file on stolen vehicles, parts and license plates. Another important feature was a hookup with the National Crime Information Center (NCIC) and connection with the Law Enforcement Telecommunications System (LETS). Over 200 LEADS terminals were "on-line" after the first year (including local, county and state agencies). In the mid-1960s, the nation began experiencing a surge in civil demonstrations, Ohio being no exception. Unfortunately, the rash of civil disturbances experienced during this time (63 incidents between September 1967 and May 1970) became a very serious matter. In addition to campus disorders, several prison riots erupted in 1968, including a major siege at the Ohio Penitentiary in Columbus, and smaller ones at London and Lebanon. Speed enforcement took another giant stride during this time with the introduction of moving radar. Officers were able to obtain accurate readings of motorists' speeds while the patrol car was moving in the opposite direction.

Another important piece of legislation was House Bill 600, which authorized the governor to commit State Highway Patrol officers to aid local authorities in civil disturbances at the request of a mayor or sheriff. Communications capabilities were also substantially upgraded in 1973. Forty-six new, four frequency, low band base stations were installed around the state. Mobile Radio Extension Systems (MRES) were also obtained that year, enabling officers to maintain communications with their posts and other patrol cars while out of their cars.

The Ohio State Highway Patrol Retirees' Association was formed in May 1975 as a fraternal, patriotic and historical association devoted to assist all members, widows, widowers and orphans of the Highway Patrol Pension System. After one year of existence it boasted 171 members.

The effort to supply field officers with soft body armor (bulletproof vests) was finalized with the issuance of this equipment during the first week of July 1976. Another policy change took effect the same month allowing officers the choice of carrying their service revolver on the left, rather than on the right side.

Rural fatalities dropped 11.4 percent in 1980 and 12.2 percent in 1981. These successes paved the way for continued reductions throughout the 1980s. In 1979 the troopers were successful in forming own "Troopers Only" FOP (Fraternal Order of Police) Lodges in all nine patrol districts. This provided a forum in which troopers could discuss problems affecting troopers. House Bill 837, became effective March 23, 1981 and gave troopers the same right of search and seizure (within its jurisdiction) as any other police officer. The law also extended full arrest powers anywhere in the state when officers are assigned to a protective detail. The motoring public was brought into the OMVI reduction effort with Project REDDI (Report Every Dangerous Driver Immediately). The program revolved around educating the public in how to spot and report drunk/dangerous drivers to local police agencies. Citizens Band radio usage was stressed as a fast and efficient manner in which to reveal the locations of violators.

The Ohio Troopers Coalition was established in 1984 and the first issue of the *Ohio Trooper* magazine was published. Only personnel in the trooper rank could be members. In 1985 the Ohio Troopers Coalition used a portion of the magazine income to start Ohio Troopers Caring, a charitable organization that took troopers into Ohio's children's hospitals to interact with the children.

The passage of legislation in early 1985 led to the placement of all scale operations, equipment and facilities under patrol management. During the week of July 8-12, 1985 elections were held to determine the bargaining agent for troopers, dispatchers and communications technicians. This followed the passage of Senate Bill 133, Ohio's Collective Bargaining Bill for public employees, which became law October 6, 1983. Of 1,053 eligible votes, 798 were cast (732 for the Ohio Labor Council/Fraternal Order of Police). The first contract vote was conducted in March 1986, with Bargaining Unit 1 employees (troopers, dispatchers, and radio technicians) overwhelming vote in favor of the agreement. However, both houses of the State Legislature rejected the contract. A final meeting between the two sides was required to settle differences and, on April 28, 1986, the first labor agreement in the history of the Ohio State Highway Patrol was officially signed. The key points were the establishment of permanent shifts by seniority bid, the elimination of penalty transfers and double backs, a grievance procedure and a regular pay increase.

In the mid-1980s, the division launched an expansive drive to impede the flow of illegal drugs on Ohio highways. Operation CIN (Confiscate Illegal Narcotics) was initiated in 1986 with the development of a training curriculum designed to assist troopers in detecting illegal drugs during the course of normal traffic stops. In July the Patrol's Fairground Security was upgraded with the transfer of six police officers from the Ohio Expo Commission. The new officers (who received the new rank of police officer) were assigned to the fairgrounds on a permanent basis.

In July 1989, the patrol was granted accreditation at the national CALEA meeting held in Columbus. The first Highway Patrol sobriety checkpoints were held during the busy weekend of July 4, 1989. After that, the program was put on hold until a test case brought before the U.S. Supreme Court in 1990 affirmed the constitutionality of the checkpoints and outlined the guidelines necessary for their use. In 1990 Trooper C.J. Linek was elected president of The Ohio Troopers Coalition, and the Coalition began to supply "Teddy Trooper" teddy bears to each patrol cruiser to be given to children by troopers in traumatic situations. The Coalition replaced bears on an ongoing basis.

The continuing effort against the transportation of illegal drugs was greatly enhanced with the acquisition of six drug detection dogs in mid-1990. Obtained with assets seized in drug arrests, the dogs and six handlers (selected from the ranks) completed several weeks of training in early 1990 and went into action on April 11, 1990. Slightly more than two weeks later, canine "Rex" alerted his handler, Tpr. Robert J. Burns, to over 70 pounds of marijuana concealed in the bed of a truck, recording the first major dog-related drug seizure. To augment the canine drug program, 15 two-officer Traffic and Drug Interdiction Teams (TDITS) were placed into service the following year. The TDIT teams, undertake normal traffic enforcement duties with special emphasis on detecting couriers of illegal narcotics.

The Special Response Team (SRT), took shape in early 1991 as members began regular and rigorous training sessions. The team is cross- trained in weapons and chemical agent use, extraction techniques, and rapid response methods. Regular training sessions and advanced equipment and weaponry ensure the team is prepared to respond at any time.

The Ohio Troopers Coalition instituted a "Bears Against Drugs " program to enable troopers, along with mascot Teddy Trooper to interact with grade school children and warn

of the dangers of drugs, alcohol and tobacco. This program was nominated for the presidential 1000 points of light award. A unit developed to employ advanced crash reconstruction techniques to determine causation in crashes also began providing impressive results. In 1991 alone, the Crash Reconstruction Unit completed 93 cases, 46 of which resulted in guilty verdicts against defendants. With the help of the Troopers Coalition and the Fraternal Order of Police Troopers Lodges, a request for funding for an additional 127 troopers was approved by Legislature in full in mid-1991. This was the first cooperative venture between the division and the Troopers Coalition.

The REDDI program initiated during the 1980s was modernized for the 1990s with the "1-800 GRAB DUI" toll-free number to report intoxicated drivers. To encourage participation, highway signs and license plates for cruisers appeared throughout the state. In just under a year, over 18,000 calls to 1-800-GRAB DUI were recorded. The program was later extended to cellular phone users. With statistics indicating that the majority of DUI arrests represented persons who were multiple DUI offenders, progressive steps were taken to assure those lawbreakers were identified as such at the time of enforcement. The Multiple Offender Program, involving police officers from departments throughout the state, was launched to target multiple DUI offenders, especially those who continue to drive while under suspension for DUI.

The patrol's record has not been obtained without personal sacrifice. Thirty-three patrol officers, two load limit inspectors, one radio operator, and one auxiliary officer lost their lives in the line of duty for the citizens of Ohio. Today, the patrol operates with a complement of over 1,300 uniformed officers and approximately 1,000 support personnel including driver examiners, dispatchers, motor vehicle inspectors, load limit inspectors, motor carrier inspectors, special police officers, technicians and civilian specialists. Dozens of facilities are administered by the patrol including 54 regular patrol posts, four Ohio Turnpike installations, administrative offices in Columbus, Cincinnati, and Cleveland; highway weigh stations and driver examiner stations. The Ohio State Troopers Association now represents Bargaining Units #1 and #15 in contract negotiations. The primary mission of the Ohio State Highway Patrol continues to be attaining the highest level of safety for motorists using Ohio's highways. Through selective enforcement, public education, and cooperative ventures, the traffic fatality rate remains below the national average and maintains Ohio's status as one of the safest of the heavily populated states.

North Dakota State Patrol

In 1985 Larry Remele and Ginger L. Sprunk co-authored "A History of the North Dakota Highway Patrol" in recognition of the 50th anniversary of the Highway Patrol. Much of the information in this article was taken verbatim from that manuscript.

The North Dakota Highway Patrol symbol is a profile of Red Tomahawk, a Teton Dakotah (Sioux) Indian who lived on his land near the Cannonball River on the Standing Rock Indian Reservation near Mandan, North Dakota.

The North Dakota Highway Patrol officially adopted the profile of Red Tomahawk as the patrol vehicle door emblem and department symbol in 1951.

Motto: We treat people as ladies and gentlemen, not necessarily because they are, but because we are.

The North Dakota Highway Patrol is committed to professional public service reflecting recognition of the inherent value of each individual in our society. Our officers strive to earn and maintain trust, respect and confidence by exemplifying the belief that the freedoms, rights and dignity of all citizens must be protected and preserved. To this end we pledge ourselves to the highest standards of morality, fairness, honesty, dedication, professionalism, and courage.

The North Dakota Highway Patrol was created in 1935 by the 24th Legislative Assembly. That assembly gave the state highway commissioner, with the consent of the governor, authority to appoint a state Highway Patrol superintendent.

The Highway Patrol's realm of responsibility was specifically defined as enforcement of motor vehicle laws on state highways.

When the house bill reached conference committee in early March 1935, the two different versions were combined. The result was a Highway Patrol responsible to the state highway commissioner and whose duties were limited strictly to traffic control. The final bill also reduced the authorized manpower to 10 and mandated that the deputy superintendent be a motor patrolman." The North Dakota State Highway Patrol became a part of state government as of July 1, 1935.

The patrolmen initially spent about two weeks in St. Paul, MN to attend the Minnesota State Highway Patrol training program. In addition, a course in emergency medical aid was completed through the American Red Cross in Bismarck. The five patrolmen subsequently traveled to Duluth, MN to drive the 1935 Buick coupes purchased for them back to North Da-

One of the first North Dakota Highway Patrolmaen speaks with a motorist.

kota after shipment on a Great Lakes freighter from Michigan.

Once back in North Dakota, these first highway patrolmen began service on August 22, 1935. Attired in their blue uniforms, these officers set out on their first task, delivering over 100,000 driver's licenses to the clerks of court in each county in the state.

A patrol tradition of assisting motorists in distress developed into an expected part of an officer's job. Such assists included changing flat tires, towing vehicles and furnishing gasoline to stalled motorists. The patrol continued to expand its equipment inventory. The original five Buick coupes were joined by two Fords, a Plymouth, a motorcycle, and a LaFayette. And over 248,000 miles of North Dakota roadways were patrolled in each of the years between 1937 and 1939.

With the demands of the war and the accompanying shortages of gasoline, tires and new automobiles, accidental deaths on state highways, which had been increasing steadily during the 1930s, declined.

The patrol kept up its educational activities in schools and communities and its regular traffic duties. It was also reported to have been periodically assigned to guard significant bridges to protect them from potential sabotage. Existing records from this era are incomplete and very little is known about how the patrol operated during these wartime years.

Following these war years and the end of the Great Depression, new political changes affected the Highway Patrol. A new insurgency, this time from the conservative point of view, resulted in the ascension of the Republican Organizing Committee to power after 1943.

Initially, the growing use of state roads and the concurrent increase in the state highway

death toll concerned state lawmakers. Their response was to enact bills in 1943 that established procedures and criteria for revocation and suspension of driver's licenses.

Four years later, the lawmakers moved toward making the patrol a more professional agency. The age requirement was changed from 25-55 to 25-40 years of age. A nine-month probationary training period was established and procedures for removal and suspension of officers were developed. In 1949 the North Dakota Highway Patrolmen's Retirement System was created by law.

The 1947 Legislature allowed an increase in the force to 42, and set the budget at just over $500,000 for the biennium, an increase more than 10 times the original 1935-37 cost. That session also assigned the responsibility for formal examination of all drivers to the patrol.

Driver's license examinations became the single, most time-consuming patrol duty, and

North Dakota State Patrol Logo.

over time, brought the agency into contact with virtually every North Dakotan at least once. More than any other single activity, the administration of driver's tests between 1947 and 1983 created the image of the patrol in the minds of state residents.

As the structure of the patrol changed, so did its responsibilities. Once limited almost solely to traffic law enforcement, the agency gained responsibility for enforcing closing hours at liquor establishments located outside municipal limits, and for enforcing state law on the grounds of all charitable and penal institutions and the capitol grounds in 1965. The patrol also gained authority to enforce all criminal laws on highway right-of-ways in 1967.

During the 1960s, the demands for better and more professional law enforcement necessitated a larger force. The 1969 Legislative session authorized the construction of the law enforcement training center in Bismarck.

Completed in 1971, the training center offered instruction to all law enforcement agencies in North Dakota. Administered by the patrol, it is still the center for all law enforcement training in North Dakota.

Several events involving the patrol centered on the activities of students during the late 60s and early 70s. In 1969 the small town of Zap, ND became the site for a huge college party.

In May 1970, several thousand students and other protesters demonstrated against the anti-ballistic missile installation under construction near Nekoma. And as early as 1966, protesters picketed test firings of minuteman missiles near Lakota. On May 25, 1973, a 10-hour sit-down strike by prisoners at the North Dakota State Penitentiary was ended when Highway Patrol officers, in riot gear, marched into the prison yard. In each case, Highway Patrol officers were on hand to keep control of the situation.

The patrol entered the 1980s with a new look; the department welcomed its first female officer. While female employees had served the department almost since its creation in 1935, none had served in the field as an officer. Heidi R. Sand became the first in 1979. During this same period, the number of officers increased to 102.

The following four years saw many changes for the patrol. Probably the most significant was the consolidation, in 1983, of the Truck Regulatory Division of the State Highway Department and the Highway Patrol.

In 1982 the patrol hired civilian personnel to administer driver's license examinations. This allowed officers to concentrate their efforts on law enforcement.

Responding to the national concern with the problem of drunk drivers, the familiar RAID (Remove Alcohol Impaired Drivers) program was implemented and showed immediate effectiveness across the state.

Several equipment changes occurred, as well, that allowed the patrol to stay in step with the changing times. The most notable change was the replacement of the all-to-familiar, single top light. It was replaced with new "state-of-the-art" light bars.

In 1985 the department celebrated its 50th anniversary. And, although the patrol had not formally been giving driver's tests since 1982, legislation was enacted in 1987, removing this responsibility from the patrol.

On July 29, 1989, the North Dakota Highway Patrol received national accreditation status from the Commission of Accreditation for law enforcement agencies. The patrol became the first law enforcement agency in the state of North Dakota to become accredited; the eighth state agency and the 109th national agency to receive this status.

In 1992 the department added its first K-9 unit to the patrol force. Shadow, a 1-year-old German Shepherd at the time, is still on duty with the department.

Another important change was the replacement of the familiar revolver sidearm with a more modern .45 cal. semi-automatic pistol. Also in 1992, the department added two capitol security officers to assist with law enforcement on capitol grounds and to provide security for the Supreme Court and the Legislative sessions.

The only thing moving faster than technology was the rate at which it appeared to be catching up with the department. The patrol was faced with the most difficult position of balancing the cost of modernization, the increasing demands and expectations placed on the patrol, and the demands of a more conservative public insisting on a more streamlined and cost-effective state government. In 199_ the department went from an organizational structure consisting of eight districts to five districts and, consequently, reducing the number of district commanders.

A problem facing today's Highway Patrol is the increase of criminal activity on state highways. Utilizing the department's Tactical Response Unit, a criminal highway interdiction program was initiated that, to this date, has proven to be one of the department's most successful programs. Also developed was the "Project One-on-One" to emphasize the department commitment to community policing.

This program was developed to assist juveniles who find themselves in trouble with the law. Working with the juvenile authorities and parents, troopers spend time with young traffic violators who go through the juvenile system. This provides a positive role model and the opportunity for the juvenile to see law enforcement's side of the problem of traffic enforcement.

Currently, the department is in the process of purchasing and installing mobile data terminals in each patrol vehicle. Officers will be able to access driver and vehicle information immediately from a computer terminal mounted in the patrol vehicle.

Today the patrol has an authorized strength of 132 sworn troopers and 68 civilian support staff. And while material changes will occur as time goes on, the goals of the North Dakota Highway Patrol will remain constant: to remain the best and most professional law enforcement agency possible. The means by which we achieve these goals are clearly presented by Colonel Hughes in the mission, values, motto, commitments and theme of the North Dakota Highway Patrol.

Speed enforcement with Laser Radar on I-94 in Fargo, North Dakota.

North Dakota State Police Cruiser in front of the capitol.

North Dakota Highway Patrolmen at a road block.

Oklahoma Highway Patrol

The Oklahoma Highway Patrol (O.H.P.) was created on April 20, 1937 when Governor Ernest W. Marland signed legislation creating the Oklahoma Department of Public Safety (D.P.S.). J. M. Bud Gentry was named as the first Commissioner and H.E. Bailey was selected for the Assistant Commissioner slot. Gentry's first actions were to travel to Pennsylvania, Iowa, Michigan and Maryland to observe how similar agencies were organized and operated. By May 1937 he had the basic framework on paper, and issued a statewide call for recruits to becomes Oklahoma's first highway patrolmen.

About five hundred eager young men answered the call. In the hard times of the depression, the one hundred fifty dollars per month salary was very attractive. The initial one hundred forty cadets were comprised of farm boys, businessmen and others who were personally interviewed and selected by Gentry and his staff.

These men reported to the University of Oklahoma campus in Norman for the first highway patrol academy. Two instructors from Maryland and Michigan were selected to organize and run the academy and train future instructors. Physical fitness and professional courtesy were stressed. As driving and firearms instruction were crucial elements of the training, classroom instruction was by no means ignored. The new lawmen learned the ten rules of the road, accident investigation, arrest procedures, and how to deal with the public in as many situations with the public as possible. Gentry and his staff selected an office building on Northwest Tenth and Broadway in Oklahoma City as the department's first headquarters. To insure the agency's presence would be felt statewide, four district headquarters were established in Perry, Enid, McAlester and Lawton. At these locations base operations were conducted in mobile trailers connected to a telephone system for communications. As these headquarters these headquarters were established, eighty-five cadets received their commissions as trooper and reported for duty. Within thirty days, a second academy began and the maximum legal number of one hundred twenty-five was realized.

The Registration division was organized and Oklahoma's first driver examiners were sent into the field. The Traffic Control Division developed a system for traffic accident and arrest file maintenance. The Department of Public Safety was functioning agency as of July 15, 1937; a remarkable span of just ninety days after Marland signed the legislation. T o d a y , the Oklahoma Highway Patrol currently has a membership of approximately 700 troopers. They are assigned to geographically located Troop headquarters across the state and are identified by alphabetical designators. The Majority of patrolmen possess traffic assignments and work out of thirteen field Troops, A through M and turnpike Troops, X and Y. These field troopers are responsible for patrolling Oklahoma's 111,994 miles of city, county, state and interstate roadways. Field troopers are first responders to emergency situations from traffic collisions to natural disasters and civil disorders. Troopers provide everyday service to the public, whether it be a motorist assist or promoting Oklahoma to a visitor in the state. Troopers are prepared and willing to take the initiative to offer assistance when needed.

To fulfill its ever-expanding role and to comply with legislative mandates, the department has created additional branches within the ranks of its uniformed personnel and given them specialized responsibilities. These divisions are comprised of both sworn and ci-

vilian personnel. Personnel assigned to the patrol's aircraft division provide airborne assistance to OHP ground units in the traffic enforcement, manhunts, search and rescue missions, and intelligence gathering operations. This division also provides transportation for state administrative personnel. The department currently operates with a fleet comprised of nine fixed-wing aircraft. The Executive Security Division carries out the department's statutory mandate to provide protection, security services and transportation for the governor and their immediate family and the lieutenant governor. Several other special service troops which make up the OHP are a full time bomb squad, East and West Tactical Units, a Training division, a Size and Weights Troop and a Criminal Interdiction Troop complete with canines.

Since 1937 the Oklahoma Department of Public Safety has grown in a multi-service safety and law enforcement organization. Department personnel are dedicated to equally and objectively providing service and protection, upholding the laws and Constitutions of the United States and the State of Oklahoma in order to promote a safe and secure environment for the public. The department is staffed by more than 1,300 trained civilian and uniformed employees occupying a wide variety of roles in many geographic locations throughout the state. The departments is responsible for policing all state roads and highways as well several thousand miles of lake and river shore-lines throughout the state. Security and law enforcement activities protecting employees, visitors and property at the state office buildings in Oklahoma City and Tulsa are conducted by department personnel. The department is also responsible for the security of the governor, his family and the Governor's Mansion and its grounds. The DPS is responsible for the licensing of all motor vehicle operators, including the testing of those who apply for the first time, and the renewal of those who currently hold valid licenses due to expire. Maintaining the active driving record of the approximately 2.3 million driver license holders is another responsibility of the department. Administrative activities by the department help reduce the number of unsafe and uninsured drivers on the state's roadways. This is accomplished through enforcement of the provision in the Implied Consent, Bail Bond, Points System, Medical Aspects, and Financial Responsibility statutes. Also, vehicular mechanical safety and hazardous materials transportation is regulated through the Vehicle Inspection and Size and Weights statute. One of the primary responsibilities of troopers assigned to the Size and Weights division is the enforcement of Oklahoma vehicle codes governing commercial motor vehicles. This includes the size, weight and type of the cargo along with the mechanical safety of the vehicle itself. Personnel also enforce federal regulations governing the proper transport of hazardous materials by

commercial carriers. Communications and information access for department members and law enforcement agencies statewide are achieved through the telecommunications system maintained by the department. Several thousand apprehensions and tens of millions of dollars in property are recovered yearly through the system. All traffic collision reports submitted buy Oklahoma's law enforcement agencies are maintained and managed by the department. The federally mandated Highway Safety Office which promotes safety on the state's highways is a branch of the DS. The efforts of state and municipal agencies, along with non-profit organizations, are enhanced by the programs administered through this office. With the department's diverse responsibilities, the goal is to reduce the number and severity of traffic collisions on the highways of the state through the promotion of traffic safety, vigorous enforcement of traffic regulations, and administrating the operation and use of motor vehicles. Since its inception, the OHP has proudly and diligently served the people of the great state of Oklahoma. In the sixty-three years of its existence, twenty-eight troopers have made the ultimate sacrifice. Their memories will be forever etched in our minds.

Oregon State Police

Governor Julius L. Meier had made a survey of the Royal Canadian Mounted Police, the Texas Rangers, the State Police of New Jersey, Pennsylvania, Michigan, and other states that had been highly successful. Governor Meier incorporated the best features of these agencies into the Department of Oregon State Police and appointed a committee to design the State Police.

The organizational committee members were Adjutant General George A. White, Chairman; Brigadier General Thomas E. Rilea of the National Guard; Luke S. May, a Seattle Criminologist; Roy R. Hewitt, Dean of the Willamette University Law School; and A. E. Clark, a Portland attorney. In addition to this committee, Major General Smedley D. Butler, United States Marine Corps, came to Oregon as an advisor to the group.

The Oregon State Police was created on February 25, 1931, when the Senate passed the bill, and the House approved it on March 1, 1931. The new department would begin operations on August 1, 1931.

The new law consolidated under one head the law enforcement activities previously performed by the State Highway Commission, the Secretary of State, the Fish and Game Commission, the State Fire Marshal, and the Prohibition Commissioner. In addition to enforcing the traffic laws, the game and fish codes, the laws relating to arson and fire prevention, and the prohibition and narcotic laws, the State Police were charged with the enforcement of all criminal laws throughout the State of Oregon. The Department was to serve as a rural patrol and to assist local law enforcement agencies, It consisted of 95 sworn police officers.

The first State Police superintendent, Charles P. Pray, was State parole officer and a former Department of Justice agent. His appointment was effective June 7, 1931. Upon creation of the Department of State Police, Mr. Pray, announced its objective to be "dignified and courteous law enforcement service devoted to the needs of the public." This concept has not changed throughout the years.

Captain Harry N. Niles of the Portland Police Department assisted in setting up the new organization, outlining and establishing a standard system of reports and records.

Mr. Harold G. Maison, formerly with the State Traffic Division operating under the Secretary of State, was appointed as chief clerk at general headquarters in Salem. Starting August 1, 1931, and he was charged with setting up and maintaining a system of reports and records.

Charles H. McClees, formerly with the State Game Commission, was appointed as captain and placed in charge of game and commercial fish enforcement. He was stationed at general headquarters, and he held this position until his retirement on July 1, 1947.

The charge of the Bureau of Identification and Investigation at General Headquarters was given to Captain George C. Alexander involving the investigational activities of the department. He was appointed deputy superintendent January 1, 1932, and served in that capacity until December 1, 1938, when he was appointed as Warden of the State Penitentiary.

Mr. Pray organized the field forces by establishing four districts in the state and thirty-one patrol stations. The original district boundaries were designated by rivers and highways and later redesignated by counties.

Mr. Pray's first report to the public was published January 20, 1933, covering the department activities for December, 1931. The report stated that the State Police made 415 arrests, resulting in fines amounting to $16,986.60. Two hundred liquor violations had been detected and 181 traffic citations issued.

Chapter 406, Oregon Laws of 1939, authorized the establishment of a Crime Detection Laboratory in the Department of State Police. It would be located at the University of Oregon Medical School in Portland.

Superintendent Pray, on June 14, 1939, appointed the first director, Dr. Joseph A. Beeman. Since that time, the laboratory has relocated to the Justice Center in Portland, and regional laboratories have been established at Pendleton, Springfield, Medford, Coos Bay, Ontario, and Bend.

On June 1, 1941, Mr. George A. Kanz, a former deputy sheriff and assistant to the superintendent of the Washington State Penitentiary, was appointed director of the State Bureau of Identification and Investigation at general headquarters. In July of that year, all fingerprint records and photographs were transferred from the State Penitentiary to the State Bureau of Identification and Investigation.

The Oregon Legislature approved legislation, in 1993, that included the organizations of the Oregon State Fire Marshal's Office, Oregon Emergency Management, Law Enforcement Data System, and the Oregon Boxing and Wrestling Commission within the Department of State Police which were formerly autonomous.

The purpose of the Patrol Services Division is "to provide a uniform police presence and law enforcement services throughout the state with a primary responsibility for traffic safety and response to emergency calls for service on Oregon's State and Interstate Highways."

Pennsylvania State Police

Pennsylvania's coal fields, iron mills, and timber forests played a vital role in the Industrial Revolution. Pennsylvania changed in the late 1800s from a largely agricultural state into a complex industrial center.

By 1900 the state found itself torn by bitter disputes between managers and the laborers they employed. Violence became common in the new communities that sprang up around the coal fields, iron mills, textile factories and railroad yards. By the turn of the century it was obvious that the town constables, sheriffs and similar local officials, though adequate to keep the peace in more stable times, were unable to manage the new populations and the violent labor troubles of the times.

The turning point came in 1902 with what became known as The Great Anthracite Strike. During the aftermath, it was finally recognized that peace and order should be maintained by regularly appointed and responsible officers employed by the public. This led to the formation of the Pennsylvania State Police.

The department became a model for other state police agencies throughout the nation as the first uniformed police organization of its kind in the United States .

Strong and persistent opposition to the department's creation was evident because of the fear, mostly by organized labor, that the State Police would be used as a private army. Therefore the original complement was limited by law to only 228 men. They were to patrol Pennsylvania's entire 45,000 square miles. The force was divided into four Troops.

The State Police soon proved its worth by controlling mob violence, patrolling farm sections, protecting wildlife and tracking down criminals, establishing a reputation for fairness, thoroughness and honesty.

In January 1908, the superintendent established weekly training programs in each troop, a technique that still exists today. Troop C was moved from Reading to Pottsville and was also designated as a State Police training school on June 1, 1909.

By 1919, the demand for additional State Police units brought about the first increase in the force, authorizing a maximum of 415 men. That same year saw the transfer of State Fire Marshal duties to the State Police.

The State Police was authorized to establish Troop E, the fifth troop, on July 1, 1919. It was established in Lancaster. Also in 1919, the State Police established motorcycle patrols to deal with the growing number of motorists.

In February 1920, a State Police training school was established in Newville, Cumberland County. Also that year, the superintendent created the Bureau of Criminal Identification and the Bureau of Fire Protection. Seventy motorcycles were purchased and 14 were assigned to each of the five troops in April 1920. Patrol zones were established and owners of telephones along the patrol zones were given steel discs or flags to indicate a telephone (flag stop). Motorcycle patrols would interrupt their patrol activity to telephone their station for assignments when they saw a flag stop displayed. Troop commanders' monthly conferences were established that June.

On August 25, 1922, the superintendent issued a special order bestowing the rank of major upon the deputy superintendent. This was the initial use of that rank in constabulary history.

In 1923 the State Highway Patrol was created within the Department of Highways to enforce the vehicle laws of Pennsylvania's burgeoning highway system. The State Police installed the nation's first state wide police radio telegraph system, a system which remained operational until 1947. A State Police Training School was established in Hershey, Dauphin County, on Cocoa Avenue, in 1924, remaining at that site until 1960. The State Highway Patrol secured the use of the Hershey Inn in Hershey, to train Highway Patrol recruits.

The State Police, in 1927, issued a regulation that prohibited any member from marrying without the superintendent's approval and established a public radio station in Harrisburg, WBAK. The year 1930 saw the establishment of a Headquarters Detective Division.

The State Police, in 1932, established a Photographic Section and a small Crime Laboratory Division. That year the first polygraph was purchased and a Criminal Intelligence Section was formed.

With the Highway Patrol's 10th anniversary, a formal inspection at Long-wood Gardens, near Kennett Square, Chester County took place. Original members were presented with a uniform star insignia representing 10 years of service. The practice of issuing service insignias continues today.

On January 1, 1938, a medical unit was established by the commissioner, and the first medical officer was appointed to the rank of major. Additionally, the commissioner established a Communications Division.

In February 1938, the Commissioner ordered 267 passenger cars painted white with black hoods and the lettering, "Pennsylvania Motor Police" on the door. These cars became known as Ghost Cars.

In June 1939, legislation passed that added to the responsibility of the Pennsylvania Motor Police the return of escaped convicts and parole violators. Other responsibilities to the Motor Police included annual school bus inspection and inspection station supervision.

On February 5, 1942, the Executive Service Section was created .

Act 52 of April 28, 1943 changed the name of the organization from the Pennsylvania Motor Police to the Pennsylvania State Police. A new responsibility for enforcing the Uniform Firearms Act that year was added that year as well.

State Police were assigned to assist the Pennsylvania Aeronautics Commission in the investigation of aircraft accidents and aircraft violations in 1945 and continued until 1972.

The first state wide radio telephone system installed and the elimination of 'flag stops' in 1946.

In 1947, new laws authorized the State Police to assist the Department of Revenue in collecting the state's cigarette tax and enforcing the Fuel Use Tax. The Department of Revenue provided the State Police with cruiser type motor launches to patrol the Schuylkill and Delaware Rivers and Lake Erie. A 1949 law authorized the State Police to inspect dry cleaning and dying plants.

The State Police changed the terms 'private second class' and 'private first class' to 'private' in 1953. That rank continued until 1956 when the term was replaced by 'trooper.' The Retired State Police Association was formed during the mid 1950s.

Chrome badges were replaced by gold badges in a leather case in 1959, and washable summer shirts were issued. Straw campaign hats were introduced for summer wear. New officers' caps with gold braid and the 'scrambled eggs' were issued, as were new black and gold patches.

On March 2. 1960, a new State Police Academy in Hershey opened. The academy was officially dedicated on June 13, 1960.

Married men were permitted to apply for the State Police for the first time on October 1, 1963. That same year also saw the commissioner establish a Youth Aid Division.

The radio teletype system was computer-

channels. For the first time, patrol cars had the ability to communicate with local police jurisdictions as 11 channels were allocated to local and municipal police organizations.

The enforcement of Pennsylvania's liquor laws was transferred to the Pennsylvania State Police in July 1987. A Bureau of Liquor Control Enforcement was established as the department welcomed 144 enforcement officers, 81 clerical personnel and 2 attorneys who transferred from the Liquor Control Board.

The Automated Fingerprint Identification System (AFIS) came into existence in 1990 to utilize computer technology in reading, matching, comparing, and storing fingerprint images. Without AFIS, manual search of 1 million fingerprint cards on file would take about 65 years to complete. AFIS can accomplish the same task in about 30 minutes and is available to all law enforcement agencies in Pennsylvania.

In June 1992, two new bureaus were created to better meet community needs and law enforcement challenges. The Bureau of Drug Law Enforcement provided a united and coordinated front in enforcing drug laws. The Bureau of Emergency and Special Operations, consolidated the functions of Aviation, Executive Protection, Special Emergency Response Team, Canines and Underwater Search and Recovery.

On September 22, 1992, the first law enforcement DNA testing laboratory opened in Greensburg , and the State Police's airborne thermal imaging system was opened on Nov. 15, 1993 to bolster State Police search, surveillance, apprehension and rescue capability.

The department purchased 4,500 new semi-automatic weapons in 1993. It had been the more than a decade since the last purchase of new weapons. The 40 Caliber Beretta has more firepower and is expected to improve the safety and effectiveness of State Police officers.

The Pennsylvania State Police became the largest accredited police agency in the world on July 31, 1993. In order to gain accredited status from the Commission on Accreditation for Law Enforcement Agencies, the department had to comply with 733 professional police standards.

KPMG-Peat Marwick LLP (KPMG) was contracted to perform an enterprise-wide evaluation of the Department's business processes and to develop an information technology strategic plan in May of 1995. This meeting launched the Department's Automation Project. On June 30, 1996, KPMG delivered to the State Police and the Executive Information Technology Steering Committee an information technology strategic plan, presented and accepted by the Department. In September of 1996, the Department issued a request for proposal for the implementation of the Enterprise Network, which was the first priority

ized on June 1, 1965. On October 5, 1967, a new law eliminated the two-year enlistment process and provided for one enlistment until discharged or retired. Also in 1967, an 18-month probationary period for cadets and troopers was established.

Six area commands were created in January of 1968. Short sleeve shirts were also issued for the first time. New small chevrons were issued for noncommissioned officers. In November 1968, the State Police Aviation Division was established.

On October 1, 1971, the first female applicant was accepted as a cadet in the Pennsylvania State Police. The academy class, containing the first female Troopers, graduated on July 7, 1972.

On July 1, 1973, the State Police received responsibility for administering the state wide Uniform Crime Report. The following year the State Police received a new radio communications system.

A new State Police Department Headquarters building was dedicated on September 12, 1978. Department Headquarters no longer had to share its facilities with other state agencies.

Operation SPARE (State Police Aerial Reconnaissance and Enforcement) was initiated on October 20, 1978 as troopers clocked motorists with a stopwatch from a State Police helicopter.

A sellout celebration at the Hershey Convention Center marked the Department's 75th Anniversary with more than 1,000 persons in attendance. A memorial, honoring those persons killed in the line of duty, was dedicated at the academy. The monument was paid for by contributions.

In June 1980, department members were issued a new sidearm, the .357 magnum Ruger, a stainless steel, four inch barrel revolver. This was the first major change in State Police issued weaponry in its 75 year history.

In October 1980, the State Police expanded the aviation division with the addition of a federally-funded Cessna 182 Skylane to assist in the State Police Aerial Reconnaissance Enforcement (SPARE) Program.

The Records and Identification Division completed the first phase of computerizing the Master Name Index of the criminal history file on October 16, 1981, thus providing a more efficient response to criminal history record inquiries.

The Department's Laboratory Division added a new lab in Lima, Delaware County in October 1982.

The State Police developed 'Pennsylvania Crime Watch' in an effort to reduce and solve crime in December 1982. In July 1984, Pennsylvania was recognized by the National Crime Prevention Coalition for the best state crime prevention program in the nation.

In 1985, the Office of Professional Responsibility was created to enforce the high standards of conduct among all State Police officers and employees.

A program aimed at the interdiction of drug trafficking along the Commonwealth's highways code-named, "Operation Whiteline" was announced in April 1986. The program was designed to train patrol personnel in the recognition of drug traffickers and their methods of operation.

Also in 1986, Pennsylvania Crime Stoppers was created in the Bureau of Community Services. Crime Stoppers utilizes the news media and citizens to locate criminals who are sought by police. Through Crime Stoppers, rewards are offered for information that helps police locate the criminals.

The need for the State Police to acquire expertly trained officers versed in the most modern concepts available to manage potentially lethal incidents realized, the State Police announced the formation of a Special Emergency Response Team (SERT).

A new radio communication system replaced the department's four-channel mobile radios with a system featuring 32 separate listed in the information technology strategic plan. In July of 1997, a preliminary award was given to IBM Corporation for the implementation of the enterprise network for the Department. On November 29, 1997, the Bureau of Technology Services was formed, from the former Information Systems Division of the Bureau of Records and Information Services, to support the growing technology needs of the Department. On June 11, 1998, a contract was put in place between the Pennsylvania State Police and IBM Corporation for implementation of the Enterprise Network.

In August of 1995, a ceremonial unit to standardize the response and appearance of members at funerals and parades was formed.

In April of 1996, the authorized use of video cameras in patrol cars was begun. The cameras provide additional documentation of patrol stops. The department initially equipped 66 marked patrol cars with the video cameras.

In February 1997, the Department acquired the Integrated Ballistics Identification System (IBIS) through the use of federal grant monies and the assistance of the Bureau of Alcohol, Tobacco, and Firearms.

On May 12, 1997, the 100th Cadet Class graduated 129 new troopers from the academy in Hershey.

In October 1997, 15 specially equipped, all-wheel-drive vans were distributed to the troops. One Forensic Unit van was assigned to each troop to be utilized by the Identification Unit when responding to crime and accident scenes. Each van, equipped with police lightbars, an elevated platform, roof-mounted spotlights, cell phone, storage compartments, and a folding ladder, also carries specialized investigative equipment. Cameras, metal detectors, forensic light sources, electrostatic dust print lifters, fingerprint processing equipment, and evidence vacuums assist at crime scenes.

The Pennsylvania Department of Transportation (PennDOT) assumed responsibility for the administrative supervision of Safety/Emissions Inspection Stations and motor vehicle dealers on January 1, 1998, thus relieving the Department of the responsibility of Official Inspection Station regulatory functions.

Rhode Island State Police

The Rhode Island State Police is the law enforcement agency charged with upholding the laws of the state of Rhode Island and the protection of the citizens of the state from crime. It is comprised of 201 officers.

Major responsiblities include reducing the incidence of crime and highway traffic accidents resulting from unlawful behavior and the criminal use of motor vehicles; reduce the incidence of serious crimes in the state and increase the crime clearance rate through more arrests and successful prosecution; upgrade statewide crime statistics to keep abreast of developing criminal patterns and trends; detection, apprehension and prosecution of organized crime figures; investigation of cases involving missing and exploited children; serve as state control terminal agency for the Rhode Island and National Law Enforcement Telecommunications Systems and the National Crime Information Center of the FBI; record checks of individuals applying for positions in residential facilities or family day care homes; regulation of charitable organizations conducting games of chance.

In Providence, 1925, a department of State Police was formed. The General Assembly had thus authored chapter 588 of the Acts and Resolves on April 2, 1925. It was historic legislation. For the first time this state would have a highly organized, uniformed statewide law enforcement agency.

There seems little question that the structure of the department was modeled basically

Trooper Arthur G. LaVallee with bloodhound "Rookie" assisted by Coventry Rescue personnel on search detail for lost 3 year-old child in 1959. Child located after a 6 hour search in heavy, dense, briar-filled woods. Child in good condition when found.

on the Pennsylvania State Police. The legislative intent was to create a highly disciplined, mobile police organization. The force was designed to deal with new and rapidly expanding enforcement problems, especially those compounded by the automobile.

The founding statute was unique in several ways. A particular feature was the precise manner in which authority and accountability were placed in the office of the superintendent. One is hard pressed to identify another state which authorized the comprehensive administrative authority as that accorded the Superintendent. The General Assembly clearly decided to focus responsibility for the success or failure of the new enforcement concept in that one office. Moreover, the superintendent, then as now reported directly to the office of the governor. Such an administrative channel is found in only a few State Police organizations. The direct line of reporting that the Assembly specified between the governor and the superintendent identified precisely both the authority and the responsibility for the administration of the Department.

The highly competitive enlistment process was absolutely necessary. These men would bear substantial responsibility for carrying out a totally new concept of law enforcement in Rhode Island. The enormity of the responsibility has been obscured by the passage of time. There were no precedents to follow. The people of Rhode Island had never laid eyes on a uniformed State Police officer enforcing the law in their state. It was a totally new concept of law enforcement, one that was to be severely tested on frequent occasions during the early formative years.

State Police headquarters opened on April 14, 1925 in the Marine Corps Armory on Benefit Street in Providence. A special effort was made to use equipment manufactured in this state. The original badges, collar ornaments and other such items were produced by native jewelry makers. Motorcycles would be an important factor in the mobility of the new troopers. Thus the famous Police Indian, manufactured in Springfield, Massachusetts, became part of the early history of the Department. For firearms, the Colt 45 was selected.

Every effort was made to enlist qualified applicants. The general Assembly had authorized an original complement of twenty-three. A selection board composed of five former army officers was organized. Instructions for applying were carried in the major newspapers of the state. Applicants were instructed

to report by the counties in which they lived, beginning on April 20. The men were warned that the mental and physical examinations would be stringent. Again military influence was observed when it was made clear that the physical examination would be the same as that given to officers of the United States Army. Each aspiring trooper was required to present certificates from three citizens as to his fitness and qualifications for State Police responsibilities. Applicants were placed on notice that the amount of power and influence they might have would be of no interest to, nor have any effect on members of the Selection Board. This point was further emphasized when the newspaper advertisement specified that the Department would do without enlisting the original members until qualified applicants were identified.

Approximately six hundred aspirants applied for the twenty-three positions. Unbelievable as it may seem, screening procedures eliminated all but thirty whom were deemed qualified, and placed on the eligible list for appointment. From that highly selective group, twenty-three were appointed.

Early in May the recruit training program got under way in the Benefit Street Armory in Providence. All of the eager appointees had seen service in the Armed Forces. Some had left good jobs to embark on a new and untried adventure as state law enforcement officers. Then as now, the question was asked as to why one chose a career in law enforcement. Opportunities for greater compensation and shorter hours beckoned elsewhere. There has always been something more, however, which has motivated highly qualified individuals to seek such service. Whether perceived as a personal challenge or the fulfillment of personal ambition, the result has always been characterized by a sense of pride in the organization. The reward has been the satisfaction felt by those who have had the opportunity for public service in the State Police.

Training began in earnest on May 11, 1925. By that time, revolvers, riot guns, automobiles and motorcycles had been delivered. The first class of State Police recruits would undergo comprehensive training. Firing practice on the range was conducted each day. Horses were used during training, both with and without saddles. The recruits were required to complete courses in automobile mechanics. It was a reminder that each officer would soon be servicing and repairing his own motor equipment. Classroom instruction was emphasized. Long sessions were held to make

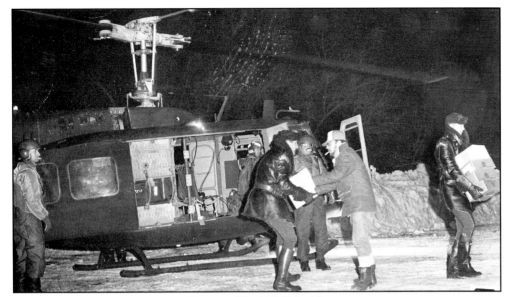
Courtesy of Gerold P. Richard Sr.

Troopers Paul G. McElroy left and Anthony Perare investagate a bad accident with injuries on 07/21/76.

certain that all understood the statutes they would soon be called upon to enforce. The famous Harvard Law School "case system" was used to impart critical elements of the criminal law. Courtroom presentations sharpened requisite skills required of each of the new members.

Wakefield 1925

Following one month of training in the Armory, the entire recruit class and its instructors traveled to a new location in South Kingstown. Further training began there on Friday, June 12, 1925. The facility was a private residence. Rustic and meticulously groomed, it was, in fact, the Chaffee summer home. A large house, stables, a garage and twenty acres of land provided an excellent training site; unique and unexpected, but welcome! All aspects of enforcement situations were stimulated. These responsibilities would soon be faced in actual situations by the fledging officers. The staff and recruits settled into their new quarters, living, working and eating together. Thus barracks life early became a tradition of State Police service in Rhode Island.

A distinguishing feature of today's police training programs is the deployment of recruits while still engaged in a training academy program. The idea is to provide the opportunity for field experience while the recruit is still undergoing basic training in the enforcement sciences and related responsibilities. Ideally, seasoned officers observe the recruit in these actual enforcement situations. This observation then allows for increased training in areas where the recruit officer appears to need further education and refinement. In other words, the police trainee is exposed to both classroom instruction and actual enforcement duties before being certified for graduation from the training academy. This new approach undoubtedly has substantial merit. It is also widely used in the educational programs of many leading universities.

The Rhode Island State Police utilized this procedure from the beginning. For example, On June 27, 1925, the first motorcycle patrols were dispatched to several areas of the state. In addition, patrols were established on Aquidneck Island as early as August. The latter were coordinated from a temporary Barracks in Portsmouth. The Portsmouth location would later become the site of a permanent installation from which enforcement activities would be directed throughout Newport County. After the field experience the recruits returned to training for further development of requisite skills.

On August 6, 1925, the first class successfully completed all required training courses. A suitable ceremony was conducted, attended, no doubt, by both State and local dignitaries. Superintendent Chaffee congratulated each of his new men. He also warned them that they faced a totally new enforcement responsibility.

The men had been issued their first official equipment. It was the best available. Most of it was manufactured in Rhode Island. In addition to their regular uniforms, the troopers were issued the following: slicker, sheep skin coat, leather belt with shoulder strap, and related personal items. Each officer was also issued a Colt 45 revolver with a leather holster and supply of ammunition. Additionally, a riot stick, handcuffs, and flashlight were issued to each man. Two Winchester twelve gauge shotguns and ammunition were assigned to each of the designated patrol commanders.

Motor equipment would be critical to enforcement mobility. That was ensured by the acquisition of the following: one Marmon Touring Car, one Chrysler Roadster, one Buick Roadster, three Ford Touring Cars, and four Ford Runabouts. The trusty motorcycle remained the centerpiece of that first rolling stock. Ten bikes completed the motor equipment as the statewide force began its first field operation in earnest.

Temporary substations were quickly established. One was opened on August 17th on Block Island and other in Arnolds Mills on September 18th. These were temporary sites designed as a response to enforcement needs during the first vacation season. The force was deployed to achieve maximum coverage in spite of its extremely limited personnel strength. It seems incredible to think now that a state force numbering twenty-three could have had any effect at all. The mere presence of troopers, however, had a strong psychological impact on potential law-breakers. The public perception of the Department's capability for swift and even-handed enforcement served to deter criminal acts. Those first troopers went into the field and established respect for the new force.

As noted, the new force had used training techniques which today are presented as innovative ideas.

South Carolina Highway Patrol

By 1930 the need for driver control had become manifest in South Carolina. Lack of such control had caused an untold number of accidents, injuries and deaths. It was in this atmosphere that the Driver Licensing Act of 1930 became a law. This law required persons who operated motor vehicles to have a driver's license, and it was this law that created the Highway Patrol to enforce the laws governing travel on our roads.

The new South Carolina Highway Patrol consisted of 69 men charged with patrolling the 5,991.7 miles of highways that were in South Carolina at that time. The original members of the Highway Patrol were given no formal training. They were simply issued a gun, a badge, a uniform and with a few verbal instructions, they began enforcing the new laws. Patrolmen were given powers equal to those of county sheriffs regarding road matters (arrest without warrants, detention of those apprehended, etc.) and were responsible for enforcing the provisions of the new licensing law and promoting highway safety.

The Highway Patrol's uniforms were inspired by the Pennsylvania State Police, and were designed for comfort and convenience in patrolling on motorcycles. Heavy leather gloves, called gauntlets, and black leather jackets were worn for protection against the elements. Trousers were tailored with a black stripe down the outside seam; they fit closely from the knee to the ankle, like jodhpurs. For a short while leather puttees were used, but these were replaced by black leather knee length boots. Both the trousers and the shirts were made of gray material with a bow tie of black leather snapped on the shirt collar. The uniform was topped by a visored cap of the type still worn by motorcycle police in many of our larger cities. With variations, this uniform was worn until 1949, when dark green trousers and poplin shirts replaced the old uniform. This was later replaced by tan colored uniforms that were used until 1979, when the present gray uniform was adopted. A law was enacted making it unlawful for any other agency to wear uniforms like those worn by the South Carolina Highway Patrol. There have been many additions since this time for the comfort and protection of the trooper.

In 1932, new patrolmen received training for the first time. The first Patrol Training School was held at Camp Jackson, which had been abandoned at the close of World War I. Here the recruits underwent three months of training in all phases of patrol work.

In 1934 the patrol was showing signs of growth. A traffic engineer was appointed and an identification officer was employed. The patrol now consisted of 79 members, 60 of whom were patrolmen.

During the first seven years of its existence, the expansion of the patrol can be categorized as phenomenal. By 1937, the year the Highway Safety Act was made law, the patrol consisted of 90 members, 79 of whom were patrolmen.

Motorcycles had gradually been replaced by automobiles as the patrol grew. Although the license inspectors had automobiles as early as 1928, the big change-over came around 1937. Today, a majority of patrolling is done in patrol cars, but the patrol has re-introduced motorcycles after a 50 year hiatus. The unit currently consists of six Harley Davidson FLHPT and 11 BMW RT1100 motorcycles.

The patrol continued to grow and expand its duties at a rapid rate until 1941, when the United States entered World War II. The war effort claimed many of the patrolmen, and gas rationing brought almost all highway travel, except for vital business purposes, to a halt. Activity of the patrol was curtailed to a virtual

Riot Squad.

South Carolina Troopers.

South Carolina Troopers.

Norwood Bellamy, 1941.

P.W. Gulley.

standstill as major emphasis during the next four years was placed on national defense.

At the close of World War II, the unprecedented growth in vehicle registration and highway travel brought new demands for increased efficiency in traffic law enforcement. In 1947 patrol cars were equipped with two-way radios and later with car to car communication facilities.

The 1960s saw a number of significant innovations in the patrol. Radar was introduced in 1962 as a tool to apprehend speeders, and unmarked patrol cars were first used in 1965. The 70s started off with a ground breaking ceremony for the South Carolina Criminal Justice Academy in Columbia. The academy was completed and opened in 1972, and, since then, the patrol has trained all of its recruits at that location. September 1977 brought yet another change to the Highway Patrol when women were hired for the first time. At this time, seven women, along with 52 men, underwent the 12-

week patrol training course at the Criminal Justice Academy in Columbia.

In 1978 the Legislature passed a law allowing the Highway Patrol to adopt a uniform to be worn exclusively by the patrol. The color of the patrol cars was changed by that same legislation to metallic silver with blue stripes. Uniforms presently worn by the patrol are gray with navy trim and the shoulder insignia has silver letters on a navy background. All troopers are issued both short sleeve summer uniforms and long sleeve winter uniforms. In 1993 the South Carolina Highway Patrol was voted *Law and Order* magazine's "Best Dressed Officers."

The issued side-arm for patrolmen was initially a five inch blue steel Smith and Wesson or Colt .38 special revolver. In the mid-80s, the patrol phased in the Smith and Wesson 4-inch stainless steel model 65 .357 revolver. In 1992, after 62 years of carrying a revolver, the South Carolina Highway Patrol began testing

semi-automatic weapons. After research and evaluation in 1993, the South Carolina Highway Patrol adopted the Glock Model 22 .40 caliber semi-automatic handgun, which is being carried by all Highway Patrol personnel.

In 1980 the South Carolina Highway Patrol celebrated its 50th anniversary and it is proud of its history and its record of accomplishments during this time; however, modern travel has created new and more complex problems placing more and greater responsibilities on the patrol to assure that safe and orderly use of the highways is preserved.

In the late 80s the patrol began participating in the Governor's RAID Team in cooperation with three other state law enforcement agencies. This team includes a drug detecting canine unit. The Forensic Investigation Unit was begun to provide assistance with accident investigations that required more technical expertise. The 80s also saw the name of the rank change from highway patrolman to state trooper.

The high performance Mustang patrol vehicle was added to the patrol fleet in the 1980s. However, in 1994 unmarked Ford Crown Victorias began to replace the Mustang. During the same year, each of the seven patrol districts, in addition to seven dog handlers, were issued a semi-marked 4x4 Ford Explorer as an Emergency Preparedness and Special Enforcement Vehicle. In 1995 the Camaro was introduced as a pursuit vehicle.

In 1993, due to government restructuring, the Highway Patrol became a part of the newly formed Department of Public Safety.

In 1995 the Department of Public Safety and the Highway Patrol established a specialized unit to conduct in-depth investigations of traffic collisions involving fatalities and/or severe injuries. This unit, called the Multi-disciplinary Accident Investigation Team (MAIT) consists of three teams of highly trained state troopers who have specialized skills in accident reconstruction, traffic engineering and automotive engineering. April 1995 also saw the addition of the Division of Support Services to the Highway Patrol. Support Services includes Physical Fitness; the Civil Emergency Response Team (CERT); the Honor Guard; Administrative Enforcement and Polygraph and Recruiting.

Today's Highway Patrol troopers undergo a rigorous 20 week training program at the South Carolina Criminal Justice Academy in Columbia with eight weeks of field training upon graduation. All trainees live under military-type discipline while at the academy and are taught various subjects ranging from traffic law and narcotics investigation to communications and human relations.

Because the Highway Patrol is committed to maintaining their motto of "COURTESY, EFFICIENCY, SERVICE," only a select group of men and women are chosen to join the ranks of South Carolina's finest. Typically, out of more than 1,500 applicants, a Trooper Basic class consists of only 50 men and women. There are seven patrol districts throughout the state in addition to Patrol Headquarters in Columbia, South Carolina.

Despite all the changes over the years, the South Carolina Highway Patrol remains committed to ensuring traveling motorists and the citizens of South Carolina that they will continue to be the great organization in the future that they have been in the past.

The mission of the South Carolina Highway Patrol is to provide equitable service and protection and to uphold the laws and constitutions of the United States and the State of South Carolina in order to promote a safe and secure environment for the public.

South Carolina Troopers.

South Carolina Troopers.

South Dakota Highway Patrol

In 1935, Tom Berry, the governor of South Dakota, recognized the need for an organization to enforce the traffic laws and provide assistance to the motoring public. He appointed ten men that were known as the "Courtesy Patrol." This Courtesy Patrol was tasked with enforcing all the laws in South Dakota and helping to inform the public about the states emerging traffic regulations. Each man was given a car, then called a "milk wagon"; a tow chain; a first aid kit and a gallon of gasoline. The new officers were assigned to patrol the 2,000 miles of hard surfaced roads and 4,000 miles of gravel highways.

The officers were required to work seven days a week, twelve hours a day, and were subject to call twenty-four hours a day. The patrol cars were not equipped with radios for communication, so each officer made occasional telephone calls at filling stations to see if they were needed for an investigation or emergency. They were required by Courtesy Patrol regulations to stop and aid all motorists on the highway. If the motorist was changing a tire, the patrolman stopped to help. He never left a stalled automobile until the driver was safely on his way.

The Courtesy Patrol was disbanded and the new Motor Patrol was founded when the legislature abolished the Department of Justice in 1937. The authority for the Highway Patrol was transferred to the Highway Department. Walter J. Goetz, Chief of Police in Aberdeen, was appointed superintendent and was authorized to hire eight men to serve as South Dakota Motor Patrolmen. Chief Goetz served as superintendent eighteen years and retired in 1956. The number of Motor Patrolmen was increased from eight to forty during his tenure, which is most noted for the acquisition of two-way radios for each patrol car in 1948. Chief Goetz guided the Motor Patrol through manpower shortages during WWII, the flooding of the Missouri River, and Missouri River dam construction. The Patrol was involved in many life-saving efforts during the record blizzard of 1949. The blizzards and floods of 1952 taxed the resources of the Motor Patrol. In 1953, the South Dakota driver's license was ushered in, and 179 people died on South Dakota roads that year.

The role of the motor patrolman as an enforcement officer began to change when a 40

million dollar highway construction project began in 1956. Traffic fatalities were on the rise and the Patrol was given a mandate to reduce fatal accidents. Governor Joe Foss appointed Jasper J. Kibbe as patrol superintendent of the Highway Patrol on August 1, 1956. Kibbe was a former FBI agent and during his tenure he increased the manpower to fifty-two men. Record keeping and activity reporting were improved and colleagues considered Kibbe an excellent administrator.

The Oahe Dam closure completed and a record 240 people died on South Dakota roads in 1958. By executive order, various colored and unmarked patrol vehicles were utilized for a time to help reduce the death toll from traffic accidents. The port of entry system was started on a trial basis.

J. J. Kibbe resigned as superintendent and Captain Don Shepard was appointed acting superintendent until Patrolman Ken Balogh was appointed superintendent by Governor Ralph Herseth on September 1, 1959. Balogh served as head of the Patrol from 1959 to 1961. The Implied Consent Law for drivers and drivers tests were initiated by the legislature during this time. Forest fires threatened the towns of Deadwood and Lead. Severe flooding came to Sioux Falls in 1960. Balough expanded the port of entry inspection stations and installed top mounted police lights on patrol cars. He organized the safety education section of the Patrol and authorized the use of two-tone patrol cars.

Patrolman Cullen P. With was appointed superintendent on January 15, 1961. The Highway Patrol continued to grow to meet the demands caused by natural disasters, traffic and motor carrier enforcement, stopping traffic deaths, and violence from strikes. With initiated the ranks of sergeant and lieutenant, four door patrol cars with air conditioning, created the operations manual, started recruit training and in-service schools, and began a firearms qualification program. He served as the Patrol leader until 1965.

Ted Arndt was appointed superintendent on May 1, 1965. During his term, flash floods in the Black Hills caused a major mobilization of the Patrol to respond to the emergency. A March 1966 blizzard killed ten people and 95,000 head of livestock died. Two hundred and sixty people died in highway related acci-

dents and multiple fatal accidents killed 32.

Captain Delton Schultz took over in 1967. The Motor Vehicle Safety Inspection Program was approved and the state employees retirement system was created. The Patrol became responsible for security for circuit judges following a shooting of a circuit judge in Rapid City. Additional men were added to the force. Over 100 inches of snow blanketed South Dakota in 1969. The Patrol was heavily involved in rescues, relays, and security work during the winter months and during the flooding conditions that followed. Two hundred and ninety-six people died in traffic accidents in 1969. Demonstrations from militants in the Black Hillsbegan in 1970. The Rapid City flood of 1972 killed 260 people and caused millions in property damage. The Indian demonstrations resulted in the Patrol being involved in many tactical operations.

Colonel Dennis Eisnach was appointed superintendent in 1974. Militant groups of the time caused the Patrol to form the Initial Response Unit (now called the ALPHA Team). Then Governor Kneip took a great interest in the activities of the Patrol and authorized 75 more men and women to be hired and trained. The district concept was reorganized under Eisnach and vast improvements were made in the administration of the Patrol.

Jerry Baum was appointed director of the Highway Patrol in 1979 by Governor William J. Janklow. Budget cuts forced a reduction in manpower and the Patrol strength fell to 142 uniformed officers. Despite the reduction in officers, Director Baum set enforcement standards for DUI and drug interdiction. Baum ushered in the age of technology.

Organized in 1982, the South Dakota Highway Patrol's Vehicle Theft Unit consists of three investigators who investigate organized vehicle theft, odometer fraud, and motor vehicle title fraud. Rebuilt vehicles are examined by the unit for the Division of Motor Vehicles. The unit works the Sturgis Rally and the Ports of Entry using pro-active techniques to reduce motorcycle, truck, and trailer thefts.

In 1987, Governor George Mickelson appointed Colonel Jim Jones to head the Highway Patrol. During his term, Jones organized the South Dakota Highway Patrol's 50th Anniversary celebration. Jones recognized the importance of fair and effective law enforcement. The prevention of DUI related fatal and injury accidents were his top priorities. Jones dedicated his energies towards training personnel to meet the demands placed on the troopers.

Governor Janklow appointed Superintendent Gene G. Abdallah in 1995 and he served until 2000. Abdallah personified the "get things done" attitude of the South Dakota Highway Patrol. Always moving forward, Superintendent Abdallah did not look back at what he had accomplished. He looked to the future and the possibilities.

Colonel Tom Dravland received his appointment as superintendent on January 8, 2000 from Governor William Janklow. Colonel Dravland served as major of the South Dakota Highway Patrol for Colonel Jim Jones and Superintendent Gene Abdallah. Colonel Dravland has brought experience and leadership to the Patrol. The mission of the Highway Patrol will continue to be DUI interdiction, drug enforcement and accident prevention.

Under the direction of fourteen governors and twelve superintendents, the men and women of the South Dakota Highway Patrol moved from a reactive organization to a proactive group of men and women who anticipate changes in highway safety and enforcement techniques. The South Dakota Highway Patrol has matured into a professional law enforcement agency prepared to respond to the ever changing needs of the public it serves. Today 157 members of the Highway Patrol wear the uniform and badge with pride and distinction.

Tennessee Highway Patrol

In 1926, a State Police Act was passed, which was patterned after the 1821 law creating the Texas Rangers. The first state policeman was James J. Lester and the first chief was Johnny Burgis. One of the prime functions of this 15 man unit was the collection of fees and taxes. They were not well liked, for the most part, and in an article datelined December 11, 1929, in the Nashville Tennessean, the State Police was described as being "obnoxious, bullying and disgraceful to the state."

The State Police of 1927-29 wore corduroy-like uniforms, then went to police blue. The state furnished two badges, a cap and coat and the officer purchased everything else. The headquarters of the State Police was in the Masonic Lodge Building on 7th Avenue North in Nashville.

After the 1927-29, experience, Tennesseans turned to a new approach for providing themselves with protection. The highway system was growing. An extraordinary session of the 66th General Assembly was called into session on Monday, December 2, 1929, at 12 noon. Item 17 of the agenda called for: "The creation of a State Highway Patrol for the purpose of better enforcing the laws, rules, and regulations relating to traffic on, and use of highways, and the collection of taxes and revenues to the state." On December 14, 1929, Governor Henry Horton signed the law creating the Tennessee Highway Patrol.

The newly formed Tennessee Highway Patrol's main focus would be protection, not prosecution of law-abiding motorists. They were to enforce the traffic and state revenue laws of that time. The patrolmen were 21 years of age or older, received a straight salary, and were required to wear a uniform at all times while they were on duty.

Several hundred applications for employment, on the Patrol, were received. All applicants had a physical examination and filled out forms giving their life's history.

In January 1930, 55 motorcycles and five cars were purchased, the chief of the Patrol and the four district chiefs had cars assigned to them. The remainder of the men rode Harley-Davidson motorcycles just as they came from the factory.

The uniform chosen was very similar to the one still worn by the State Troopers of today. It consisted of forest green trousers, jacket, cap, and a white shirt. As summer approached, and the coat was no longer needed, it was decided that a tan shirt would look better than a white one and was therefore subsequently changed. A shoulder patch, similar to the one now worn, was attached to the left coat sleeve. At that time no patch was worn on the shirt. The initial issue of clothing was two pairs of pants, one blouse, one cap, one Sam Brown belt, a gun, a coat and cap badge, and set of leather puttees. The officer had to purchase his shirts, ties and shoes. The new officers spent one month in the school. They were exposed to traffic, tax and revenue laws, court procedures, first aid, and the operation of a motorcycle.

The patrolmen continued the use of motorcycles almost exclusively until 1936, when the patrol recorded its first death in the line of duty in an automobile accident. The life of a Highway Patrolman involved long hours and bad roads. Often the officers would leave the district office and be gone for three or four weeks.

The Highway Patrol began to investigate the field of radio communications as early as 1934. The method for contacting a patrolman, once he was at work was at best, a hit-or-miss proposition. A phone call to a store or filling station on the route that he was supposed to work would result in a flag or sign being hung out in case he rode by. This was to notify him to stop, and call the headquarters, because he had an assignment.

In 1935, through an agreement with radio station WSM (AM 650) in Nashville, THP engineers ran field tests to determine power output and converge in the Volunteer State. Mr. Jack DeWitt assisted patrol officials and ran signal tests using the WSM transmitter site on Villa Place in Nashville. Once the station had gone off the air at dark, an engineer of WSM under Mr. DeWitt, ran field test patterns for two weeks in early April 1935. From many directions, acknowledgments of receptions of our broadcasts were received including one from Toronto, Canada. This pioneer work in communications paved the way for the radio system that would be built in 1941.

It was business as usual with the Highway Patrol as the world situation began to deteriorate. During 1939, Governor Prentice Cooper directed that a communications division be created for the Highway Patrol. The patrol's units, until this directive, had been sharing a radio system with the Davidson County Sheriffs Office. In 1937, Sheriff Ivey Young had a radio system installed by Percy Griffith, a vice president of Braid Electric Company in Nashville. Under an agreement, the Highway Patrol furnished the dispatches and the sheriff furnished the radio system. Radios were first used in Patrol vehicles in Nashville under this agreement. Mr. Griffith was asked by Governor Cooper to create a radio system specifically for the THP. He was appointed as a full member of the patrol in 1940 and retired as captain of the Communication Division.

In 1942, two cars were equipped with two-way radios on a test basis. These two units were stationed in the maneuver division, headquartered in Lebanon, Tennessee. The range for transmission from the mobile units was approximately 12 miles. The THP also served as the FBI dispatch point and was a part of the Civil Defense warning system.

The world situation dictated a need for the United States to bolster its defense at home and abroad. In June of 1941, extensive maneuvers by the US Army were held in the Middle Tennessee area. Thirty-five patrolmen were assigned in the area to assist with the sudden influx of servicemen, war machines, and their support companies.

It is a little known fact, but during World War II the Highway Patrol escorted numerous submarines and boats through the state. A ship builder in Illinois had a government contract to build submarines for the Navy. When several of these subs were completed, they traveled down the Mississippi River to New Orleans.

Communications continued to be a hindrance. With 98 one-way radios, the dispatcher could only put out a call, three times in a ten minutes period, and hope that the call was received. Fortunately, most of the men didn't want to miss anything, so they stayed close to their radios.

Vehicles were difficult to obtain in the forties. In 1943, the department located nine Ford six-cylinder cars at a dealership in Long Island, NY. Patrolmen were sent to drive them back to Tennessee. The cars were "flat head sixes." Seven more new Fords were found in Philadelphia. These would prove to be the last new cars received by the Patrol until after the war.

The war made many lasting marks on the Patrol. Even the uniform had undergone a dramatic change by war's end. Since the founding of the Patrol, puttees and eventually boots and riding britches were worn. During the war, leather became a scarce commodity and the price of boots became so high that the uniform was changed to "straight-legged pants" and low quarter shoes. Gas, tires, and other parts were difficult to obtain during the war, but Captain Lewis, who was appointed maintenance officer from 1943 until his retirement, went before the Rationing Board and got what was necessary.

Another uniform change occurred in the late forties. A knee length overcoat became the standard issue. It flared out at the bottom and was double breasted, and if it was buttoned, to draw your weapon, you had to draw it through a slit in the pocket. The men hated the coats and called them the "Turkey Gobbler" coats because of the way they fanned out at the bottom resembling the spread feathers of a turkey.

The Patrol has always provided security for visiting presidents and dignitaries. On one occasion, men of the THP provided security for President Franklin D. Roosevelt at the dedication of Warm Springs, Georgia. On June 16, 1947, two officers from Tennessee traveled to Washington, DC, to provide an Honor Guard for President Harry Truman.

The Highway Patrol continued its growth through the fifties. Lasting marks, however, were made upon it by events that transpired in the closing days of the forties. The strength of the Patrol when Commissioner Sam Neal came into office was 168 men. In July of 1949, 76 new appointees joined the ranks bringing the total to 231 sworn personnel. One hundred new troopers were authorized by the 1956 General Assembly, with 50 of them being added in 1957 and the other 50 in 1958.

The Patrol had operated with four basic districts or divisions. In July of 1949, the four districts became eight and Patrol Chief W. T. "Fuzz" Shelton gave names to each patrol sector. Knoxville became the Smoky Division, Chattanooga the Valley Division, Nashville the Bluegrass Division, and Memphis was the River Division. In 1952, Commissioner G. Hilton Butler briefly experimented with only four districts again, but soon discovered that the administrative problems were too great over such a large geographical area, and the eight districts were restored.

In 1951, in cooperation with Ft. Monmouth, NJ, and under the direction of R. R. Turner, the first contact by radio teletype was established. This was a test program conducted with several states, and was the foreigner of the National Crime Information Center (NCIC) and Law Enforcement Teletype System (LETS). On March 14, 195 1, the Tennessee Bureau of Criminal Identification was created.

In the early fifties, in an attempt to standardize the performance of the Patrol, Commissioner Sam Neal issued the Tennessee Patrolman's Manual. The 156-page book contained all phases of activities a patrolman encountered and gave excerpts from Tennessee Law concerning the performance of their duty.

A change was made in the uniform when the cap, reminiscent of the days of the motorcycle officers, gave way to the "sheriff" style hat. The western style hats were worn until 195 9 when the uniform was changed back to the caps. The trooper's badge was changed to the design now worn, and the green pocket flaps and epaulets were added to the tan uniform shirts. On the vehicles, in 1950, the first red roof light was installed. In 1954, the acquisition of eight pieces of equipment changed forever the enforcement activities of the Patrol. Radar became a new word in the Patrol's vocabulary. It was used in posted zones throughout the state.

A marked changed took effect on July 1, 1959, and it was readily apparent to even the casual observer. The Highway Patrolman was changed to State Trooper. Patrol cars, remaining the familiar cream and black, were marked on the trunk lid with the reflective words "State Trooper" and side markings were changed from the long-used oval to a state seal accompanied by the words "Tennessee State Trooper" embossed on an outline of the shape of the state.

The Patrol began to look skyward in 1953 and for a short time experimented with one

Tennessee State Troopers.

Tennessee State Troopers investigating an accident.

fixed wing aircraft. The tests were soon abandoned; however, a new tool was added to the enforcement and assistance arm of the Highway Patrol with the acquisition of a helicopter. In March of 1957, Sergeant Truman Clark and Trooper Bob Searnon traveled to Texas to the Bell Helicopter factory and school, and upon completion of the pilots' school, took delivery of the first THP chopper. The second was delivered in July of '57 and the third arrived in 1958. Tennessee thus became the first police agency in the nation to use helicopters in police work.

The Patrol earned national publicity during the fifties for its imaginative use of massive roadblocks to check for the drunk driver, the unlicensed driver, and generally to make the Patrol's presence felt. Life magazine had a multi-page spread. A Congressional Comnlittee on Traffic Safety, chaired by Rep. J. Committee Loser, Tennessee, on October 7, 1957, observed a I 00-man roadblock on Murfreesboro Road near the Third District Headquarters. The congressman, along with Congressmen Kenneth Roberts of Alabama, Pal F. Schenck of Ohio, and Walter Rogers of Texas, held hearings in the Federal Building in Nashville on how federal legislation might help reduce traffic accidents and deaths.

The constant need for innovative methods of dealing with highway safety brought about the formation of a group known as the "Yellow Jackets". This hand-picked squad was formed in 1958 and lasted some six months. The troopers rode motorcycles emblazoned with a "Yellow Jacket" in addition to the regular Patrol markings. The uniforms were special, including black leather motorcycle boots, black pants with a yellow stripe, a yellow shirt with black pocket flaps and shoulder straps, a black tie or ascot, and a yellow leather jacket with black trim.

The name, interestingly enough, was somewhat of an accident. Years before, two officers stopped to check out a "Goodtime" house at 12th and Charlotte in Nashville. Someone inside spied the officers and sounded a warning to the other patrons. Several comments were made about not caring if the police were there. Then someone spoke up and said, "You better care - that's them yellow jackets!" Years later, when Commissioner G. Hilton Butler was looking for a name for his motorcycle unit, one of the officers originally involved related the incident. The name struck Butler's fancy and the "Yellow Jackets" were born.

The sixties proved to be most memorable for the long periods of unrest and strife that plagued Tennessee and the rest of the nation. However, their vehicles went through a dramatic improvement in 1967. For the first time the Patrol vehicles were purchased equipped with four doors, automatic transmission, power brakes, and air conditioning.

The Highway Patrol faced the new decade with its usual resolve to combat highway

Tennessee State Troopers.

Tennessee State Troopers.

deaths. Additional duties were added to the Patrol's authority when the General Assembly passed "Safe Boating" legislation and in 1963 empowered the Patrol to enforce it. The result eventually was a unit consisting of three boats and six men. These officers traveled throughout the state in the apprehension of violators, the promotion of safety and the recovery of the bodies of water-related fatalities. Some two years later the water safety program was transferred to the Game and Fish Department, now, know as the Tennessee Wildlife Resource Agency.

Civil rights marches became an almost daily occurrence in the 'sixties. Some Tennessee cities were hit by small confrontations in 1967 and in March 1968. The strike in Memphis, by the garbage and sanitation workers, led to the outbreak of violence and on Thursday, March 28, 1968, two hundred fifty officers of the Highway Patrol were ordered to Memphis to assist local authorities in the restoration of law and order.

Things seemingly began to cool down, and on Wednesday, April 3, 1968, most of the TBP units were released to return to their regular duty stations. The next night, April 4, 1968, saw violence explode throughout Tennessee and the nation when Dr. Martin Luther King, Jr. was assassinated, as he talked with aides on the balcony of the Lorraine Motel in Memphis. Once again Patrol units were activated and dispatched to Memphis and Nashville. Trouble erupted on Friday night, the 5th of April, at the campus of Tennessee State University in Nashville. This involved numerous exchanges of gunfire, the shooting out of streetlights by the police and the subsequent searching of a dormitory on the TSU campus for those responsible for sniper fire. On Sunday, the 7th of April, authorities resumed to the TSU campus when arsonists burned the building housing the ROTC units. As the strife subsided, it was mutually agreed that a miracle had taken place when neither rioters, police nor guardsmen had lost their lives.

In the fifty-year history of the Patrol, the 10 years most characterized by technological advances and improvement of hardware is the decade of the seventies. Spin-offs from the technology of Vietnam and the Space Program provided manufacturers with the miniaturization. Computer chips and transistors came into their own and their usage was immediately implemented in development and manufacture of police equipment from the moving radar set to the compact two-way radios used by police agencies.

A change that drastically altered the physical appearance of the Patrol was instituted in early 1971. The familiar cap, that had been a part of the uniform for most of the Patrol's life, was replaced by the Montana Peak or Smokey Bear hat. At the same time a straw version for summer was introduced along with the winter felt model, as were cross-draw holster and three-inch wide belt. The leather goods, along with a cartridge and handcuff case, were coated with Pattina-Tiara, a high gloss finish. A one inch black stripe was added to the trouser legs, rounding out the uniform change.

The Patrol was destined to see organizational growth and refinement. A Planning and Research Division was organized in August of 1971 and immediately assigned the task of working out a five day work week schedule, and a manpower allocation formula for use in all 95 counties. The five-day workweek became reality on October 1, 1971, and the manpower allocation formula was placed into use shortly thereafter.

February 1, 1972, saw the creation of a mobile strike force, consisting of eight troopers, a sergeant and a lieutenant. The unit was called the "Tact Squad" and has played a vital role in the day to day operation of the Patrol as well as responding to emergency calls of all descriptions at all hours of the day and night and throughout the state. The squad is well armed with various types of weapons, including automatic weapons, tear gas generators, and anti-sniper weapons. Each member is trained as an Emergency Medical Technician and Explosive Ordinance Disposal Technician. The first vehicles were five station wagons. The large amount of equipment soon necessitated going to the carry-all type trucks, and later to vans. A semi-trailer was also equipped to outfit 100 officers for emergency duty in civil disorder or natural disasters.

A federal grant to the Department of Safety in June of 1976 provided for the purchase of a vehicle to be used in bomb disposal situations. A one-ton van, bomb disposal trailer, portable x-ray, bomb sled, cryogenic devices and other related equipment was purchased and assigned to the Tactical Squad. It has been used on many occasions, particularly in the disposal of old dynamite often found abandoned for one reason or another.

The Tactical Squad furthered its ability to serve by the acquisition of two canines, who have made numerous responses in the search for fleeing criminals, lost children, or elderly citizens, and in the control of unruly crowds at public gatherings. Also trained in explosive detection, they provide the Patrol with yet another tool in the law enforcement arsenal.

The Aviation Section of the Patrol received a sizable boost in the latter half of 1976 when the department received two UH-IB (Huey) Bell helicopters. The state office of Civil Defense through the surplus property program made this acquisition possible. These two aircraft have served the people of Tennessee in many unusual ways. In the floods of 1979 the Tact Squad used the Hueys to rescue more than fifty people trapped in the Mill Creek area of Nashville. In a one month period of October 1979, over $12,000,000 worth of marijuana was spotted from the air and subsequently destroyed.

The Tennessee Highway Patrol is an equal opportunity employer as witnessed by the fact that on July 17, 1973, Billie Jo Meeks became the first female trooper in the Patrol's history. She was assigned to interstate duty out of the Jackson District. Two other females were employed by the Patrol, Terri C. Seabrook, the first female black trooper, was stationed in the Knoxville District, and Robbie L. Hancock who was the first female member of the Patrol to be assigned to the Governor's Security Force.

The uniform of the Highway Patrol underwent another modification in May of 1976. This change has provided for the summer comfort of the troops almost as much as air conditioning the patrol cars. Short sleeved shirts with an open collar became standard issue and are worn from May to October.

Good communications have always been a high priority with the Highway Patrol. In August of 1975 the Patrol took delivery of a communications trailer, designed by members of the department for the specific needs of this organization. There are two dispatch stations included, the ability to transmit and receive on all THP frequencies and mutual aid frequencies as well, and the capability to monitor other emergency channels. It can operate off a power drop but is fully self contained with two 15 kw generators on board. The first assignment for the communication trailer was at the Tennessee State Fair in September 1975.

The concept of the Patrol as "Servants, Not Lords" was magnified on December 15, 1977, with the inauguration of the Assistance to Interstate Drivers, or AID program. Each AID Unit contained a full complement of equipment to assist stranded motorists on the interstate highways and provided assistance of all kinds, in any situation. On December 15, one hundred sparkling new 1978 Plymouth Patrol cars lined up side by side in front of the Air National Guard hanger at Berry Field, Nashville. The newly trained officers left in convoy with blue lights flashing. The sight of 100 Troopers created chaos as the units hit 1-40 and split for the trips east and west.

February 1978, saw the realization of another longtime goal. The one-man one car concept was instituted, providing each officer with a vehicle assigned personally to him. At the same time it provided for the additional visual presence of the Patrol on the highway, made call out responses much faster and cut drastically the maintenance costs brought about by "pool" vehicles.

In January 1979, the Underwater Search and Recovery Unit was organized. This unit was a part of the "Tact Squad" and recovered bodies, numerous assorted weapons, a stolen safe, stolen cars, and three cases of dynamite. It continues today to respond throughout the state at the request of local law enforcement officials.

Two programs were initiated in 1979, which proved very successful. The STEP (Selected Traffic Enforcement Program) and Operation CARE (Combined Accident Reduction Effort). The STEP program targets the counties in Tennessee, which account for over fifty percent of accidents and fatalities statewide. Off duty Troopers were used in an overtime situation in these counties. Operation CARE is a unique program in that it is the single largest law enforcement effort ever undertaken to reduce accidents on our interstates during high volume traffic periods. Troopers were paid overtime to work the three major holiday weekends (Memorial Day, July 4th, and Labor Day) on interstate patrol during peak hours. These two programs greatly aided in the removal of alcohol and drug impaired drivers from our highways.

In January 1980, the Tennessee Bureau of Investigation was removed from the Department of Safety and created as a separate and independent agency. The patrol began its prosecution of vehicular homicide cases when the TBI, which had been investigating such cases, was moved out of the Department of Safety.

In 1980 an intensive program to provide specialized Accident Investigation instruction to troopers was begun. The long-range goal was to train all enforcement personnel in the two-week Basic Accident Investigation course; 30 percent of the personnel in Technical Accident Investigation, and two Accident Reconstructionists per district. The goal was reached of 100 percent completion of the basic accident investigation, the goal of 30 percent for the technical accident investigation has been surpassed and Tennessee is one of the leading states for people trained in Accident Reconstruction.

Training has always been an integral part of the Highway Patrol. Troopers were required to attend a rigid ten-week basic training program as well as, several specialized schools throughout their career. In 1986 the curriculum for the training session was changed considerable due to policies set forth by the new

Utah Highway Patrol

The Utah legislature first authorized the State Road Commission to "patrol or police" the highways of Utah in 1923. A civil engineer, R. Whitney Groo, was given the assignment to organize these special traffic police into "patrols" in 1925. Patrolmen Robert N. Slaughter and Ray Deming were hired on a part-time basis in 1925. Slaughter was moved to full time status in 1926 and Deming in 1927. Three additional patrolmen were hired in 1928. Annual reports refer to this organization as the "state road police patrol" with annual wages of $140 per month.

These patrolmen were issued a forest green dress blouse, with a flying motorcycle wheel insignia sewn on the left shoulder, and forest green motorcycle pants. The daily-wear uniform consisted of a khaki long sleeve shirt with black bow tie and khaki motorcycle pants. Foot wear consisted of black, knee-high leather boots. Patrolmen were issued Harley Davidson motorcycles with red and white spotlights, a siren and a first aid kit. Smith and Wesson .44 special revolvers with cross-draw holsters were issued in 1929. By 1930, all motorcycles were painted white with the words "Utah Highway Patrol" stenciled onto the gas tank. Model A Fords with dual carburetors, which were capable of reaching speeds of 60+ mph, were also issued. Patrolmen were instructed to operate the fuel efficient motorcycles whenever possible and only drive the Model A Fords during inclement weather.

In 1930 the first portable checking station was established in a converted trailer. The trailer was towed to strategic locations throughout northern Utah. In February 1932 the first permanent checking station was built at Santa Clara, near the southern boundary of the state on US 91. A set of Fairbanks-Morse platform scales, 9 feet wide by 28 feet long and capable of weighing 20 tons, were installed. Patrolmen enforced the traffic code and highway revenue laws as well as issued license plates and additional load plates, collected gasoline taxes, and compiled data for the Public Utilities Commission at this location.

By 1932 the uniform was changed to a navy blue dress blouse and cap, with fawn colored motorcycle pants. A white shirt with black tie was worn with the dress blouse. A dark blue long sleeve shirt was worn for daily use. A new fawn colored campaign hat, with circular hat badge of the Utah State Seal, was issued in 1935. Both the campaign hat and the navy blue hat were authorized for wear with the dress uniform. The uniform badge was also changed to include the words "Utah Highway Patrol" and the officer's assigned badge number.

By 1932 the "state road police patrols" consisted of 20 men. Whitney Groo totally reorganized the patrol, adding the ranks of colonel, captain, lieutenant and sergeant. The organization was officially designated as the Utah Highway Patrol at this time. In 1934, the UHP consisted of 30 employees. By 1936 that number had increased to 42.

On March 21, 1935, the Utah Highway Patrol was "vested with the same powers and duties as police officers - except the serving of civil process." The patrol was also made subject to the call of the governor in times of emergency or "other purposes of his discretion."

Many new laws were passed during this period of time which also added to the responsibilities of the Utah Highway Patrol. The first portions of the Uniform Traffic Code were adopted in 1931. Driver license laws became effective in 1934. Members of the UHP issued driver licenses for the next 20 years. In 1935 Utah became one of the first states in the nation to adopt a motor vehicle safety inspection law.

By 1938 the flying motorcycle wheel shoulder insignia was replaced by a beehive. The beehive symbol had been adopted by the Church of Jesus Christ of Latter-day Saints "Mormons" during the 1830s. In the Book of Mormon, the word "Deseret" is found, which means "honeybee" and signifies unity, organization and productivity.

The beehive was adopted as the official emblem of the Utah Highway Patrol in 1947. The beehive was then placed on the doors of the patrol car. A new six-point shirt badge was designed which contained the beehive and the date September 9. The hat badge was also changed to include the beehive.

In 1938 the Utah Highway Patrol determined that more firepower was needed and the duty weapon was changed to a .357 magnum revolver with six inch barrel. The first issued shotguns were Winchester Model 97s.

During World War II, a special governor's proclamation increased the Utah Highway Patrol to 75 officers and 350 volunteer "Deputy Highway Patrolmen" to guard water supplies, railroads, power plants, mines and smelters. The UHP was often called upon to provide

military escorts and additional security at government facilities.

A war speed limit of 35 mph was implemented in October 1942 to conserve gasoline and save on tires. This law was later called the "patriotic speed limit" in an attempt to gain compliance. In April 1944, the National Safety Council awarded Utah the Grand Award for 1943.

On May 31, 1942, the Utah Highway Patrol activated its first dispatch station, KUHP. The first radios provided one-way communication only. The following year, two-way radios were installed in several patrol cars.

In 1945 the Legislature passed the Utah Highway Patrol Civil Service Act establishing a commission to oversee personnel matters such as hiring, firing, promotions, demotions, transfers and pay scales. Effective October 1, 1947, all patrolmen first class were designated as "troopers." The new name applied only to those officers who had completed a one-year probationary period. Officers still in their first year of service were called "patrolmen." The Utah Highway Patrol at this time consisted of 67 men. A new uniform was adopted in 1947, consisting of a cocoa brown shirt with "army pink" epaulets, a new six-point star badge, when the beehive became the official emblem of the Utah Highway Patrol.

New patrol cars were painted a distinctive black and white with a rotating red light mounted on the top in the 1950s. The patrol purchased their first "walkie-talkie" radio in 1950. By 1951 radio communications were completed, linking Salt Lake, Price, Moab, Vernal and Richfield. By 1952 all patrol cars had been equipped with radios capable of receiving and transmitting.

In addition, all officers received advanced training in first aid. This program was called the "Red Cross on the Highways" program. Troopers who completed this training received Red Cross emblems which were sewn on the right sleeve of the long-sleeved shirts, directly above the cuff. Their patrol cars were marked with a metal insignia attached to the front license plate designating the vehicle as a Red Cross Emergency First Aid mobile unit.

The 1951 Legislature created the Department of Public Safety. The Utah Highway Patrol became a division of this new department. Other divisions included Driver License, Financial Responsibility, Bureau of Criminal Identification and the Safety Council.

The damage release sticker program was implemented in 1957. In 1959, Port of Entry and dispatch employees became sworn peace officers. Also in 1959, a dress blouse was again adopted.

In 1959, the Utah Highway Patrol Police Academy was begun. This academy provided two weeks of basic police training which was offered to every agency in the state. The UHP Academy continued to operate until Peace Officer Standards and Training was created in

1967. In the spring of 1961, UHP headquarters moved into a new state office building, directly behind the State Capitol.

The first sections of interstate highway were opened in 1960. In January 1961 the patrol purchased its first aircraft, a single engine, four-seat Piper Comanche. This plane was used for emergency shuttles, search and rescue, executive transportation, traffic control, and other law enforcement activities. In 1963 a second plane was purchased, a 1961 Piper Super Cub, a two-seater craft with a high, fixed wing. This economical plane was specifically designed for slow flight and was extremely effective for search and rescue and traffic patrol.

In March 1965, a helmet and baton for riot duty was implemented. All troopers received riot control training in connection with the issuance of this new equipment.

In 1966 weighmen and dispatchers were designated as troopers and received basic training at the UHP Academy, located at Camp Williams. In 1968 patrol cars were also equipped with the first electronic sirens.

The UHP implemented a radar certification program in 1979. In November 1979 the patrol created an Accident Reconstruction Team (ART.)

The Utah Truck Inspection Program (UTIP) began in 1979. Hazardous materials specialists were added in 1982. Today, UTIP has been expanded and includes the Motor Carrier Safety Assistance Program (MCSAP.)

In 1980 the UHP moved into a new complex which included a new training facility for Peace Officer Standards and Training and office space for the Department of Public Safety and the Department of Transportation. This facility was named the Calvin L. Rampton Complex in recognition of Governor Rampton.

The UHP was selected as the best dressed police organization in the United States in 1982. Also in 1982, the Department of Public Safety created the Medal of Valor to recognize people who risk their life to save the life of another. That same year, DPS implemented "career mobility," allowing troopers to serve in all divisions of the department. In 1983 Utah and Arizona opened the nation's first joint-state Port of Entry.

In 1988 the Utah Highway Patrol Association organized the Utah Hope Project, a community service project. The Utah Hope Project is a charitable, nonprofit organization with the sole purpose of "Making Dreams Come True" for children with life threatening illnesses. Since its creation, the Utah Hope Project has fulfilled over 60 dreams for children.

Also organized in 1988, the UHP Honor Guard provides valuable service during funerals and memorial services. Trained in close order drill, rifle salutes, taps, gravesite dedication and proper flag etiquette, the UHP Honor Guard has been recognized as one of the best in the nation.

In 1988 Utah began training troopers in the Drug Recognition Expert (DRE) program. DRE officers are able to accurately detect impaired drivers by recognizing and documenting the physiological effects of drugs and alcohol on the human body.

In 1991 the Utah Department of Public Safety opened an Emergency Vehicle Operation (EVO) Training Center in Utah County. This facility consists of an emergency response course, skill pad, control tower and an off-road recovery area. Training at this facility includes defensive driving, skid control, emergency response, vehicle dynamics, evasive driving, anti-lock braking systems, pursuit driving, night driving, thresh-hold braking, and the pursuit intervention technique (PIT) maneuver.

In 1992 the UHP Breath Alcohol Testing Program placed a Breath Alcohol Testing Mobile Unit (BAT-mobile) into operation. The BAT-mobile allows an officer to conduct an intoxilyzer test at the scene of an arrest. The large van also provides space for officers to complete reports and is equipped with video to record evidence.

In 1994 the UHP implemented a Civil Disorders Unit (CDU.) The CDU is comprised of 50 troopers and sergeants who are trained in physical fitness, crowd control techniques, arrest control tactics and squad and platoon maneuvers. All members of the department received CDU training during annual in-service training and were issued pepper spray. The UHP CDU has been deployed on several occasions in cooperative efforts with allied law enforcement agencies to defuse potentially violent situations.

Also in 1994, each section of the patrol implemented a Public Information and Education (PI&E) program. Working together with businesses, civic organizations, and schools, the PI&E program goal is to promote safety and reduce crime.

In March 1994 the UHP obtained a computerized Accident Investigation Mapping System (AIMS.) Utilizing infrared and computer technology, the AIMS system is designed to collect large amounts of information at an accident scene in as short a time as possible.

In 1995 the UHP obtained 250 military surplus M-14 rifles. Upon successful completion of a two-day rifle and marksmanship course, troopers were issued these .308 caliber rifles.

During in-service training for 1996-97, all members of the Utah Department of Public Safety were issued a new duty weapon, a .40 caliber semi-automatic pistol known as the Beretta Cougar, model 8040D. Officers received two days of intensive training in nomenclature, maintenance, operation, proper shooting techniques and combat survival with this new weapon.

The current administration of the Utah Department of Public Safety and the Utah Highway Patrol consists of Craig Dearden, commissioner; Ferris E. Groll, deputy commissioner and Richard A. Greenwood, deputy commissioner - colonel, Utah Highway Patrol. Under Colonel Greenwood's command, patrol cars have been equipped with video cameras and computers. Colonel Greenwood has focused on automation, looking for ways to eliminate unnecessary paperwork, and ways to be more productive with limited resources. His administration developed ten areas of emphasis as follows: public service, impaired drivers, occupant restraint usage, criminal interdiction, commercial vehicle safety, safety education, technology, community policing, human resource development and local law enforcement support.

Commissioner Dearden has worked to unify the various divisions within the Utah Department of Public Safety which include the Utah Highway Patrol, Investigations, comprehensive emergency management, Drivers License, Administrative Services, fire marshal, peace officer standards and training and Management Information Services. Also within DPS is the Aero Bureau, Internal Affairs, Public Information, Safety Council, Crime Prevention and Highway Safety. Together, the many employees of the Utah Department of Public Safety comprise the largest, most diversified law enforcement agency in Utah. The members of the Utah Department of Public Safety ensure that Utah is "still the right place."

Vermont Department of Public Safety

The Department of Public Safety is Vermont's largest law enforcement agency. Prior to 1947, Vermont law enforcement was primarily county based. Each of the state's fourteen counties had an elected sheriff responsible for providing law enforcement criminal investigation services to all towns in the county that did not have their own police departments.

On the state level, only the Department of Motor Vehicles Highway Patrol provided centralized, statewide law enforcement services. Members of that Department patrolled the state's roadways on motorcycles enforcing motor vehicle law and investigating accidents. Communication with Highway Patrol members was accomplished through posting of signs in public places. This method of communicating required a strong relationship with the public that was being served. Highway Patrol Officers would routinely have to call for messages about accidents or the status of motor vehicle complaints. Today this close association with the served public would be considered community policing.

The seed of the movement that would become a Department of Public Safety was first planted in 1935 when a special committee was formed to study the feasibility of a state wide police system. The results of this study were positive and support began to grow. The State Grange, at the time a powerful group, and many farmers were among the early supporters of a statewide law enforcement agency. The first bill to establish a Department of Public Safety was introduced in the 1937 Legislature. It was not to be. The defeat of the original proposal has been attributed to lobbying by the sheriffs who perceived a loss of power and a conservative legislature with a tight hold on the purse strings.

The disappearance of an eighteen year old Bennington College student in 1947 resulted in changes to the attitudes of many opponents. Bennington county officials were unsuccessful in locating the student and were forced to call on State Police investigators from Connecticut and New York for assistance. Local investigators and the State Police from Connecticut and New York were at a loss for clues in the case so Vermont's Governor called the FBI. Tragically the case was never solved. This case, plus Governor Gibson's efforts ended a decade-long struggle with the Vermont Legislature passing Act No. 163. On July 1, 1947, the Vermont Department of Public Safety became a reality. There are still some who proudly remember that day.

Major General Merritt A. Edson, a former

U.S. Marine and Medal of Honor winner in World War II, formed the Department of Public Safety and became the first Commissioner. The State Police uniform was modeled after the U.S. Marine Corps uniform and remains a lasting legacy of General Edson. The original strength authorized for the Department was 62, with 7 civilians and 55 troopers. Twenty-seven officers transferred from the Highway Patrol to the Department. This class of Troopers tallied a total of 606 years of service to the people of Vermont before retiring.

Many of the original department members would probably like to forget the working conditions of those first years. The trooper's worked a ninety hour week in 1947-48. Each trooper was responsible for both criminal investigation and routine motor vehicle patrol. They only had one day off a week. No trooper was allowed a vacation between May 15 and September 15. Troopers were on duty Saturdays and Sundays and worked all holidays. They were paid $48.00 a week!

The first Headquarters was established February 9, 1948 at Redstone in Montpelier. For the price of $25,000, the State bought the building and ten acres of land. The photo lab was housed in the basement and equipped with state of the art equipment. Housing the photo laboratory in the basement had a number of unanticipated consequences. Spring thaw and heavy rains flooded the cellar and personnel had to wear rubber boots and wade through the runoff. The fleet was enlarged in 1948. The Department purchased 25 Ford sedans, two

Pontiac sedans, and one Pontiac coupe for a total price of $14,742.41.

The first State Police radio system was completed September 28, 1948. For the first time, a three-way radio system allowed stations to talk to each other and to patrol cars. However, some of the original Troopers and dispatchers will tell you the system was a far cry from today's. The radio system did eliminate the need to post signs in public places. The year 1949 saw the creation of the Fire Prevention Division and the Identification and Records Division. The State Police improved police services through training, public relations and safety education. The Department became visible through appearances at fairs, in schools and civic gatherings. School safety patrols were started. For many years, end of the year school patrol picnics were a well-earned treat for the volunteers. Troopers joined these picnics serving hot dogs and ice cream to the students.

General Edson resigned in mid-1951 after four years of valuable service. William H. Baumann was selected to become Commissioner on July 1, 1951. Commissioner Baumann, only thirty-one years old at the time, became the youngest State Police Commissioner in the nation.

A number of changes came to the growing Department in the mid-1950's. The Field Force Division started using radar as a speed enforcement tool in 1954. Two bloodhounds, "Dutchess" and "Major" joined the force and made significant contributions in searches and rescues. The Crime Lab began to use color photography as an identification tool. A new microwave installation was also completed between Headquarters and the Rutland District Office improving radio communications.

The Department expand into the polygraph field at about the same time. The first polygraph instrument was purchased and Trooper Glenn Davis became the state's first licensed polygrapher. Before this the Department had to use facilities and examiners in neighboring states. The first year of polygraph operation 115 examinations were requested by law enforcement agencies.

The 1960's also saw changes in Vermont that impacted the Department. Vermont changed as new industries, such as IBM and GE, brought new residents to the State. Vermont was no longer a quiet place in the backwater of the country. Socio-economic changes took place with long-term effects on the capacities of law enforcement. The four season recreation industry created economic growth, and resulted in increased out-of-state visitors. Labor Day in the 1940's and 50's meant the end of heavy traffic, but during the early 1960's that changed as Vermont became the destination for fall foliage, hunting, skiing and snowmobiling. The Departmental strength was 118 State Police and 60 civilians at the beginning of 1960. The state's population was 389,881. There were only 41.4 miles of Interstate highway compared with 320 miles in 1998.

Between 1960 and 1970 licensed drivers increased by 35%, the number of registered vehicles increased by 51%, and the interstate system was completed with 320 miles of divided highway.

E.A. Alexander became the third Commissioner of the Department of Public Safety in 1965 with the rank of Colonel. Colonel Alexander was the only appointed Commissioner who had been a Trooper promoted to Commissioner, having begun his career with the Motor Vehicle Highway Patrol in 1929.

The 1960's was the beginning of the drug culture. The Department handled an increased number of complaints involving illegal drugs. By the late 1960's the alleged drug problem had become a significant Vermont problem. The Department and the Legislature recognized the growing drug problem and the Legislature approved a Drug Abuse Control Program. The goal of the program was education, inspection and enforcement. The Department conducted 56 drug investigations in 1968. That number had grown to 374 by 1970.

Also in 1970, the Department went on line with the FBI National Crime Information Center. NCIC messages increased from 430 in 1968 to 1,036 in 1970.

Events of the 60's led to the creation of a number of special teams and programs to meet the diverse needs of the population. A Marine Division was formed and became active in

1960. By 1966 it had five outboard motor patrol boats and a 35 foot cruiser to patrol the State's waterways. A Search and Rescue Team was organized to look for lost persons and conduct rescues in our mountainous terrain.

The Department grew to 193 State Police and 85 civilians by June 30, 1970. E.W. Corcoran was appointed the new Commissioner of the Department of Public Safety on July 1, 1970. The early 70's saw the Crime Lab expanded to offer forensic chemistry. The first civilian, a chemist toxicologist, began to replace sworn police officers in the crime lab. A mobile crime laboratory was constructed to provide forensic services in the field.

The Department had six undercover officers in the 1970's. Long hair, dirty jeans, and thong sandals provided cover while they worked the world of drug culture.

Executive Order Number 35 issued in May, 1971, turned the Pittsford Sanatorium over to the Department for use as a law enforcement training facility. A Canine Unit was established to provide patrol dogs. The Department had only tracking bloodhounds before this. The Identification and Records Division changed its name to the Vermont Criminal Information Center and became the official state repository for all criminal records, photographs, descriptions, and fingerprints. Capturing of this data was all done manually; not until 1976 was computer equipment purchased which allowed statewide access to the information. Data requests averaged 40 a day in the 70's compared to the current 300.

The Department hired the first two women Troopers in 1977. Although the number of women fluctuated during the years, there are a total of 20 female Vermont State Troopers, encompassing various positions to include BCI, Child Abuse and Neglect investigators,

Trooper Ed Hunter and his K-9 "Xerxes".

Vermont State Police scuba team at work, ice dive.

training and recruitment, arson investigator, patrol commander, and patrol Troopers in 1998.

Federal funds allowed for the creation of an Interstate Troop in 1977 to provide the speed enforcement of the 55 mph program. The 70's also saw the organization of a fraud unit to investigate white collar crime as well as a scuba dive team to recover drowning victims or evidence. The Fire Prevention Division was abolished and its functions transferred to the Department of Labor and Industry. An Arson Unit was formed with the responsibility for investigation of all suspicious fires in the State.

By the end of the decade the State's population had grown to 477,427. There were 383,108 registered vehicles and 352,715 licensed drivers. Department strength grew to 259 State Police and 120 civilians.

Headquarters moved to the Waterbury Complex from Montpelier in the Spring of 1983.

The Communications Division had designed and installed a statewide microwave and telecommunications system. These ser-

vices were provided by the Department in support of all state agencies.

In late 1987 the Department was selected to administer a drug control and systems improvement grant from the federal government. This grant funded the first multi-jurisdictional drug task force in Vermont. The State Police transferred the Special Investigations Unit drug investigators into a new task force with a number of local departments supplying full time investigators.

Changes in technology and the organization of the Department of Public Safety in the early 90's helped improve the Department's operating efficiency through reorganization and technology. Reorganization resulted in updating of rank of Trooper, consolidation and reduction in the number of positions, sworn positions being replaced by civilians and the creation of the Criminal Justice Services Division to replace the State Police Support Services Division. The Vermont Criminal Information Center started the automation of criminal records in 1995. Records were automated and included all information on file for a person, eliminating the need for manually searching the files.

Technological advances incorporated by the Department allowed conversion to infrared driving while intoxicated (DWI) processing equipment, establish a DNA analysis capability in the forensic laboratory and install a computer aided dispatch (CAD) records management system.

Changes continue to be made throughout the Department. A recent reorganization resulted in going from five to four Troop areas. Dispatching services are being consolidated with a pilot project in Rockingham/ Brattleboro/Shaftsbury.

The past fifty years have required members of the Department to change. Each change presented new obstacles to overcome. One constant has been the pride and dedication to duty exhibited by members of the Department. Regardless of the position held, uniformed Trooper, communications technician, Emergency Management trainer or planner, laboratory technician, dispatcher, accountant or secretary, the people of the Department of Public Safety have served and will continue to serve the citizens of the state in a competent, professional manner.

Virginia State Police

In its 65-year history, the Virginia State Police has evolved into a modern, efficient organization capable of all aspects of law enforcement.

Troopers have responded to coal strikes, riots, mass demonstrations, natural disasters, airplane crashes, organized crime, drug-related crime, and many other enforcement demands generated by a diverse and ever-changing, fast-paced society.

The mission of the Department of State Police is to provide the Commonwealth of Virginia with a responsive coordinated, composite statewide police department, independent yet supportive of other law enforcement agencies; to preserve law and order; to enforce criminal, traffic and regulatory laws; to meet the goals and objectives of the Governor's Executive Agreement; and to provide security and safety services in the most efficient and effective manner.

Today, with 2,461 employees of the department, 1,829 sworn and 632 non-sworn, carrying out this mission; it is hard to imagine the agency's humble beginnings 65 years ago.

The Virginia Department of State Police evolved from a loosely-knit organization of inspectors vested with the powers to enforce the provisions of The Automobile Acts of 1919.

The inspector positions were incorporated into the newly-created Division of Motor Vehicles in 1923. Inspectors were empowered to enforce the criminal code as well as the motor vehicle code in 1932, and these inspectors gradually came to be identified as troopers.

A uniform for dress wear was adopted in 1931, consisting of gray trousers with a black stripe, blue coat and optional headgear. These colors were chosen to represent the uniforms of both sides in the Civil War.

The title of trooper was adopted in 1938 when the words "State Police" were inscribed on the official badge. Also in that year, radios were installed in patrol cars in Alexandria and Danville, Virginia.

The Virginia State Police became a separate agency of state government in 1942, retaining the responsibility to examine applicants for driver's licenses, in addition to promoting highway safety, supervising inspection stations, determining standards for motor vehicle accessories, and investigating criminal activity. Examination of drivers reverted to the Division of Motor Vehicles in 1948.

In the mid-40s, airplanes joined the surface patrol force. They were used for enforcement, apprehension of fugitives and for finding individuals lost in the forests. Three aircraft were purchased in June 1946.

In 1948 permanent weigh stations were implemented in strategic locations throughout Virginia, staffed by state police and employees of the Department of Highways. These stations were erected on primary highways to weigh trucks and other large commercial vehicles.

Radar was first used as a speed surveying device in 1952. The speed limit on most primary highways was 60 mph. In 1973, as a result of an oil embargo, the speed limit was lowered to 55 mph in Virginia. It was raised in 1988 to 65 mph for passenger vehicles on rural interstate and in 1994 to 65 mph for passenger vehicles and trucks on rural interstate.

In 1969 fatalities on Virginia's highways numbered 1,304. It has never been as high since. The death rate per miles traveled is currently at its lowest level: 1.21 deaths per 100 million vehicle miles traveled on Virginia's streets, roads and highways. This is in sharp contrast to the death rate of 23 persons per 100 million miles of travel in 1934.

The Central Criminal Records Exchange moved from the Attorney General's office in 1970 and brought personnel, equipment and 62,000 criminal history records to administrative headquarters.

The Division of Investigation was organized in 1974 and renamed in 1979, The Bureau of Criminal Investigation.

Virginia State Police Aviation and Medevac.

231

Also in 1974, members of the department joined together to form the Virginia State Police Association with a goal of being "mutually helpful to one another." Today, the association has grown to include 80 percent of the members of the department. It assists members with emergency relief, scholarships for dependents, legal assistance and insurance benefits. The association supports Virginia anti-drug organizations and donates Trooper Teddy bears to the department, so an officer can give a bear to a child who has been in an accident or traumatized in some way.

The largest gift from the Virginia State Police Association to the department was a life-size bronze statue of a uniformed trooper which stands outside the academy in recognition of "The Trooper, Past, Present and Future." The statue was dedicated in March 1990.

Two helicopters were purchased in 1983 for the Virginia State Police to start a medical evacuation plan. Flights are flown by state police aviators with medical attention administered by volunteer fire rescue squads. It is the only private/public cooperative medevac in the nation.

Since its formation, the Virginia State Police has established numerous programs. The organization was recognized as a fully accredited state police agency in 1986, meeting standards pertaining to all aspects of policies, management, operations and support services.

Today, the Virginia State Police organization begins with the superintendent, who carries the rank of colonel and who is appointed by the governor. The superintendent's executive staff includes the directors and deputy directors the Bureau of Criminal Investigation, Field Operations and Administrative and Support Services.

The Bureau of Criminal Investigation is responsible for all investigative matters directed by the superintendent and criminal investigations requested by the governor, attorney general, any sheriff, grand jury, chief of police or commonwealth's attorney.

The bureau coordinates all criminal investigations conducted by the department; provides full-time attention to all major criminal cases under the jurisdiction of the department; and pursues investigations initiated by uniformed personnel when such investigations interfere with other assigned uniformed duties.

The Bureau of Field Operations consists of seven uniformed field divisions with headquarters in Richmond, Culpeper, Appomattox, Wytheville, Chesapeake, Salem and Fairfax. The seven field divisions are divided into 47 area offices.

An eighth division, Safety, headquartered in Richmond, is divided into seven area offices. The Safety Division oversees inspection stations and inspection mechanics and issues yearly inspection decals.

Virginia State Police administrative headquarters is located in Chesterfield County and

Virginia civilian state police garage techs.

includes the superintendent's office, and the offices of Professional Standards and Public Affairs. Most of the personnel assigned to the Bureau of Administrative Support Services are located at administrative headquarters as well.

Also located at the headquarters complex is the Virginia State Police Academy. Trainees undergo 26 weeks of instruction encompassing classroom work and practical exercises. Upon graduation, troopers spend at least eight weeks with a field training officer at their first assignment.

The State Police Academy also provides in-service training for experienced officers from the department and from other police agencies, in addition to workshops and seminars for civilian supervisors and employees.

Becoming a Virginia state trooper means accepting the responsibility of a demanding occupation. Because Virginia State Police are empowered to enforce all laws of the Commonwealth, there is no average day or routine duty for state troopers or special agents.

In addition to patrolling the state's highways, sworn members of the department per-

form a variety of other duties. A trooper may respond to an accident, check commercial vehicles on highways for weight violations or come to the aid of a local police department in a hostage situation, a major accident or a hazardous material spill. A trooper may investigate an airplane accident or traffic fatality, or spend the day in an elementary school talking to students about drugs.

A special agent may investigate a robbery, rape, murder, or embezzlement, analyze a suspicious fire, follow up a criminal investigation, work undercover or conduct surveillance.

Candidates for trooper positions must be 21 years of age with a high school education or equivalent, and must demonstrate competent driving skills. Among other requirements, there is a minimum vision requirement of 20/100 binocular uncorrected vision, correctable to 20/20 with no color deficiencies. The most qualified applicants must pass a battery of tests, including a polygraph exam, a background investigation, medical examination and psychological evaluation.

The department offers a career progression program which allows the choice of either supervisory or non-management tracks. A supervisory career track allows progression to upper ranks for uniformed members in the Bureau of Field Operations through the ranks of sergeant, first sergeant, lieutenant, captain, major and lieutenant colonel.

In the Bureau of Criminal Investigation, members may progress from the rank of special agent to senior special agent, assistant special agent in charge, special agent in charge, investigative manager, deputy assistant director, assistant director, deputy director and director.

In a non-management career track, possibilities include promotion to trooper II, senior trooper, master trooper, special agent and senior special agent.

Virginia is serviced by 63,000 miles of highways, including 1,089 interstate miles, and registers approximately six million vehicles. Since these highways are entrusted for patrol to the state police, traffic safety is a prime concern of the department. Because the department feels that education goes hand in hand with enforcement as a tool for safe highways, it initiates and participates in a variety of programs to promote highway safety.

In addition to patrol, opportunities for troopers include assignments to the tactical team, scuba team, aviation unit, canine unit, motor carrier safety, inspection station supervision, motorcycle patrol, general investigation, fugitive apprehension, narcotics and arson investigation and the executive protective unit.

The tactical team is on call 24 hours a day for emergencies that may require their special training. Tactical team members are prepared to apprehend dangerous criminals, assist local police in potentially hazardous search warrant entries, and to aid in circumstances where an armored car is necessary, such as barricade or hostage situations.

Specially-trained hostage negotiators are on call 24 hours a day, as is the bomb squad disposal unit in each of the field offices. Under-water search and recovery teams are also on call to retrieve bodies, vehicles or stolen objects.

Canine units are proficient in tracking lost children or adults and escaped prisoners. Their presence alone is often helpful in controlling the flow of people in strikes, demonstrations or riots.

Narcotics and explosive detector canines are trained to detect illegal drugs and explosives in cars, suitcases and buildings.

Narcotics is another area in which the Virginia State Police believes that education should go hand in hand with law enforcement. The DARE (Drug Abuse Resistance Education) program is a state police initiative in cooperation with the Department of Education and local law enforcement agencies to combat drug abuse by educating school children about drug involvement.

The core curriculum is geared toward children in the fifth and sixth grades who will enter junior high school during the next two years. Central to the success of the program is the involvement of uniformed police officers as classroom instructors.

The Virginia State Police serves as the coordinating agency for a number of programs undertaken in cooperation with local jurisdictions.

State police headquarters houses the central site for the Commonwealth's automated fingerprint identification system (AFIS). This system contains computerized records of more than a million fingerprints taken during arrest or incarceration. New prints are added daily; prints from the scene of a crime may be compared with those on file, enabling local law enforcement offices with terminals in many parts of the state to cross identify fingerprints in minutes.

The department is the control center for the Virginia Criminal Information Network, a computerized communications system which includes terminals in police and sheriffs' departments, judges' and commonwealth attorneys' offices, and other state agencies such as Department of Motor Vehicles and local FBI offices.

The network enables the state's law enforcement agencies to rapidly receive and transmit messages on escaped criminals, hazardous material spills, severe weather conditions, stolen goods and other pertinent information.

The department also serves as the Virginia point of entry in the National Law Enforcement Telecommunications System, which allows law enforcement agencies throughout the nation to communicate electronically. It is also the Virginia control agency for the National Crime Information Center, which keeps up-to-date records on those wanted for criminal activity.

Crime reports are collected from every law enforcement agency in the state. The department compiles and analyzes the reports and publishes newsletters on the information. Composite reports are filed with the FBI, thereby helping to establish national Uniform Crime Report (UCR) statistics.

The department also coordinates the state's clearinghouse for missing children, compiling and disseminating information it receives from state and local police agencies.

The Department of Virginia State Police is a complex, efficient and highly specialized law enforcement organization. Virginia State Police officers and special agents are an elite group of highly skilled, highly-trained individuals working together to make the Commonwealth one of the safest states in the nation. It's no wonder they have come to be known as "Virginia's finest."

Virginia motor carrier safety officer, Jim Huffman.

Washington State Patrol

June 8, 1921, was the date legislation authorized the appointment of highway police with the power of peace officers in Washington State. The first six patrolmen were commissioned September 1, 1921. The initial appropriation for maintenance of the motorcycle patrol was $70,000.

The first two Highway Patrol directors were called supervisors. The original issue was a badge, cap emblem, and a gun. It wasn't until 1924 that every patrolman became uniformed.

In 1925, the first Chief, William Cole, was appointed and by 1927, the Patrol soon bought its first "paddy wagon" — a Ford panel delivery truck, which was assigned to the major mountain highway at Snoqualmie Pass.

In 1933, the Legislature acknowledged the need for a police organization that was mobile and could be concentrated immediately at any place in the state where the public safety was endangered. The Highway Patrol Division officially became known as the Washington State Patrol, which had been given full police powers. However, the police powers were not to be used unless ordered by the Governor or requested by other law enforcement agencies. The State Patrol was placed directly under the Governor, who was authorized to appoint the Chief.

Communications were haphazard, with patrolmen receiving some of their orders through the mail, some from county sheriffs, and some from their supervisors by telephone. The first radio was installed on a motorcycle in the Vancouver area in 1933. Operating on a City of Portland (Oregon) Police frequency, the unit gave accident and traffic information.

While radio communications had a brilliant future, motorcycles were on their way out by 1933. Light, fast automobiles of the panel delivery type, which could be used as a combination patrol car, mobile jail, and ambulance, were proving much more versatile for all-weather work than the motorcycle.

As the uniform was designed and redesigned, one apparel feature was introduced in 1937 that remains to this day — the bow tie, unique in law enforcement. Originally red, the bow tie was changed to black after a couple of years and has remained a fashion constant as the WSP uniform evolved to its present crisp blue shirt with dark blue pocket flaps, French blue pants striped with dark blue, and royal blue campaign hat.

The Motor Vehicle Inspection Division and Weight Division, created in 1943, were responsible for checking trucks for size, weight,

Mountain passes.

and license violations. Both divisions previously were under the Department of Highways.

It was in 1943 that the Patrol set up its own communications network, completing the installation of two-way sets in all vehicles. Then, in 1947, the Patrol gained its own training center in the former Navy bachelor officers' quarters near the Shelton Airport.

In 1949, the Patrol began to trade away the "paddy wagons" in favor of four-door sedans, with improved police equipment and special engines, transmissions, and high-speed rear ends.

The Patrol began to hire civilian weighmasters in 1955 to work stationary and portable scales. Most of the troopers working weight control in the field were later transferred to traffic duty. The Weight Control Division is now known as the Commercial Vehicle Division.

By the late 1950s, the Patrol began to phase in its current patrol car door design, a diagonal royal blue spear and black and white badge replica.

By 1968, the State Patrol had converted all patrol vehicles to white. The new WSP training academy was built on 23 acres near the existing facility. The Patrol's drive course was constructed on 165 acres adjacent to the Academy and is considered one of the finest in the country.

The Investigative Assistance Division (IAD) was established in 1973, including the Narcotics Section, Organized Crime Intelligence Unit, Missing Children Clearinghouse, and a Clandestine Laboratory Response Team. The Investigative Assistance Division is also the law enforcement contact with Interpol for the state of Washington.

The Identification and Criminal History Section was established in 1974, and two full-service crime laboratories were set up in 1975, in Seattle and Spokane.

The first female troopers were hired by the Patrol in 1975.

In 1981, four more crime laboratories were added in Tacoma, Marysville, Kelso, and Kennewick.

In 1983, an entirely new WACIC (Washington Crime Information Center) data base was brought on-line, providing faster response time as well as access to the FBI's National Crime Information Center computer system and direct entry of missing adults and runaway children.

In 1989, the Legislature passed a bill to incorporate a DNA typing laboratory into the existing Seattle Crime Lab, staffed by specially trained personnel. This also helped in the creation of a DNA data bank to aid future investigations.

The Washington State Patrol gained international recognition for its development of the Mobile Computer Network (MCN), an innovative system linking laptop computers in patrol cars with satellite and land-based radio communication technology. The MCN became operational in 1991.

Chief Annette Sandberg is the first woman to head a state law enforcement agency. She also may have been the youngest of either gender when she was appointed in April 1995 at the age of 33.

The State Fire Marshal's Office joined the agency when the Legislature transferred the Fire Protection Services to the Patrol in July 1995.

In the spring of 1996, commercial vehicle enforcement officers (CVEOs) began special training, which included firearms. CVEOs are being armed for the first time in more than 20 years, when the last of the troopers assigned to weight control returned to traffic duty.

The Problem Oriented Public Safety (POPS) philosophy was initiated by the agency in 1997, following the award of a Community Oriented Policing grant from the federal government. The award added 72 trained POPS officers to the Patrol over the ensuing three years.

POPS signaled the beginning of a new problem-solving philosophy that fosters the development of partnerships among the WSP, citizens, and other stakeholders, who together help solve public safety problems in communities throughout the state. The department made a commitment to bring POPS and Governor Gary Locke's Quality Improvement Initiative together and to train all employees in this new philosophy of public service.

The Criminal Records Division launched a new Web site in January of 1998 called WATCH (Washington Access To Criminal History), where the public can obtain criminal history information online.

In May of 1998, the Patrol published a five-year strategic plan after a year-long effort. As part of this, all organizational units of the department will develop operational plans and performance measures that support the goals of the strategic plan.

Strategic planning was integrated with POPS and a quality philosophy to help the agency meet future demands. By integrating long-range planning with quality business practices, and by developing partnerships, the State Patrol is ensuring that the service needs of Washington's citizens are met.

The Field Operations Bureau is primarily responsible for traffic law enforcement, collision investigation, and motorist assists on 17,524 miles of state and interstate highways.

The bureau oversees patrolling on state highways in eight districts. See our District Overview for more information on regional operations. The bureau also oversees Vessel and Terminal Security (VATS), the Explosives Unit, and the Honor Guard Unit.

The Explosives Unit—or bomb squad— was established to provide assistance to agencies and individuals in the rendering safe of identified explosives or suspected explosive devices and materials. Members provide training in the areas of suspicious letters, packages, devices, and explosives to emergency response personnel and to public and private sector entities.

The Honor Guard was established in 1984 and is available for funerals of active department members, active officers of other agencies, and other functions as the Chief may designate.

VATS was implemented in Districts 2, 7, and 8 to provide a safe environment for all motorists by expanding the scope of traffic control and law enforcement services on Washington State ferry routes. Traffic management and public safety have improved since the Patrol began providing service at ferry terminals and on vessels.

Trooper, graduation day.

L to R: Crime lab, Bomb/drug dog, swat, communications, bicycle, honor guard, pilot, motorcycle, commercial vehicle, trooper and traffic invest. (detective)

West Virginia State Police

The West Virginia State Police is recognized as the fourth oldest state police agency in the nation. The WVSP is a full-service police agency with statewide police authority to: investigate crime, follow up on routine complaints, patrol highways, investigate accidents and restore order in civil disorder or other emergencies. Natural and manmade disasters, labor disputes and prison riots are all occurrences that require the use of state police officers.

The state police force is now 630 members strong, operating from five companies and 61 detachments. Troopers are known and respected for their skills and their wide range of abilities, ranging from investigating crime to controlling traffic and working accidents. The state police are also known for their strong link to the communities they serve.

The state police employs 327 civilians more commonly called non-uniformed members. They provide support services to the uniformed members in the following job classes: computer programmer, fingerprint technician, photo lab technician, nurse, forensic lab analysts/technician, accounting assistant, custodian, electronic technician, building maintenance mechanic, garment worker, automobile mechanic, auto body mechanic, cook, data entry operator, office assistant and administrative clerical personnel, police telecommunicator, graphic artist, media relations specialist and human resources.

Members of the state police receive their training from the West Virginia State Police

Early and essential tools for the West Virginia State Trooper were a horse and a bloodhound.

Academy in Institute. Applicants for trooper must possess one of the following: 75 hours of college credit; an associate's degree; two years active military duty; or two years of continuous law enforcement duty. Applicants must be at least 21 years of age at the time of enlistment and must meet a number of specified medical and psychological criteria.

Cadets are chosen after a number of phases, which include a battery of tests, an interview and a background examination. Applicants are eliminated after each phase in the process. Training covers a 24 week period.

The West Virginia State Police was created in 1919 as a result of violent uprisings surrounding organized labor in the coal industry. Governor John Cornwell signed the bill to create the first statewide police force which arranged for the appointment of a superintendent to a four-year term. This statewide police force would be headquartered in Charleston and the field would consist of two companies. Each company would have one captain, one lieutenant, one first sergeant, four sergeants, four corporals and no more than 55 men.

Officers were recruited and tested for their physical, mental and moral fitness. The first entry requirements were: male, 25-45 years of age, ability to ride horseback, of "sound constitution," of "good moral character" and capable of passing all prescribed tests. They gave the first training in Pickens (Randolph County) and they outfitted and sent the men to post soon afterwards.

The first uniforms were of dark olive drab, similar in color to that of the U.S. Marine Corps. The coats were open at the neck with a cut resembling English Army uniforms. A pistol belt held the firearm and its buckle read "West Virginia Department of Public Safety." A blue, triangular badge was worn on the left side of the coat. Wrap leggings, a black shirt and tie were also standard. A barracks campaign hat, much like the U.S. Army, topped off the uniform dress. The campaign hat has become the most distinguishing characteristic of the state trooper uniform.

The first two companies were located in Clarksburg (Company A) and Kenova (Company B). Each company headquarters contained a barracks with a kitchen and a mess, which provided food and rations for members and their horses. The department provided a $75 per month salary, subsistence pay to members of $15 per month for housing and quarters and 50 cents per meal for rations. Married members were allowed to live with their families but were on call 24 hours a day. Single

members had to obtain the superintendent's permission to move out of a barracks.

Jackson Arnold of Weston was chosen to be the first superintendent. Sam Taylor, a World War I veteran of Wayne County, was the first man to enlist in the state police. Taylor spent his first few months recruiting the first 50 members. After eight years of service, Taylor was riding his state police motorcycle when he tried to stop a drunk driver and was forced into a guardrail. His left leg was seriously injured and had to be amputated as a result. He wore an artificial limb and used a cane the remainder of his life.

In the early years, the state police made an immediate impact in working crimes involving shootings, moonshining and mine-related strikes and violence. The miners fought many battles with mine owners and their employees during this period. Historians commonly call these wars the "Mine Wars." In the early to mid-1920s, the Matewan Massacre, Three Day Battle, Lick Creek Raid and the Battle of Blair Mountain resulted in many deaths. Several "Mine Wars" required U.S. Army intervention.

In 1935 a fingerprint law passed that mandated the fingerprinting of all persons arrested for any offense that required jail. The state police began maintaining these files for the state. The fingerprint identification is now only part of the Criminal Records Section which houses all criminal reports, fingerprint cards and court disposition reports.

The need for training further increased with the onset of World War II. Members were trained as air wardens, auxiliary police and industrial defense plant guards. Captain Charles W. Ray, who enlisted in 1924, had the first early vision of the department's needs for a training facility and worked for years to sell his idea to others and to find ample space.

Captain Ray eventually approached county officials for the use of the Kanawha County Fairgrounds located on a 24-acre tract in Institute. They eventually sold the land to the department for $3,200 and construction took several years. The first class at the State Police Academy was held in 1953.

In 1960 the Criminal Identification Bureau was formed and manned by members of the department who were qualified, through education and experience, to testify as expert witnesses. The chemistry and physics sections processed all criminal investigation evidence. This bureau has evolved into what is now called the Forensic Crime Laboratory that offers a broad range of services to all law enforcement agencies in the state through the processing of evidence and expert trial testimony. Highly-trained experts in documents, biochemistry, trace evidence, drug identification, toxicology, latent prints and firearms/toolmarks staff the laboratory. In 1994 the laboratory was accredited by the American Society of Crime Laboratory Directors which scrutinizes quality assurance, proficiency testing, safety, ethics and management standards. The DNA section of the laboratory is one of only 35 such sections accredited in the world to process such evidence.

In 1972 the department received a new Bell 206/B helicopter and assigned the first pilots, Trooper Wayne Childress and Trooper John Leonard, to the newly created Aviation Division. The department used the helicopter for enforcement of criminal and traffic laws, and transportation in medical emergencies and searches for lost people or aircraft. A special hangar was later constructed beside the State Police Academy, as equipment and manpower were added. The section has since become an effective tool for speed enforcement, rescue, prisoner extradition and suspect and escapee tracking and location.

The Criminal Intelligence Narcotics and Dangerous Drug Division was formed in 1972 in response to the rise in drug possession, trafficking and sales. The unit used plain-clothes officers, many of whom performed their work undercover. The new unit involved 26 officers and has since evolved into what is now called the Bureau of Criminal Investigations (BCI). Along with drug enforcement activity, the unit, now 59 members strong, focuses on violent complex criminal cases and organized crime.

Over the years, the state police has made great strides in providing up-to-date equipment ranging from new semi-automatic weapons and bulletproof vests to new cruisers with new communication equipment so that troopers have the best tools possible to do their jobs.

Vehicles in use by the department are 1994-96 Chevrolet Caprices and 1996-97 Ford Crown Victorias. Also assigned throughout the state are 1994 and 1995 Jeep Cherokee 4x4s and 1997 Ford Expedition 4x4s.

Further enhancements to department programs have included the 1995 addition of a Special Response Team, a highly-trained unit designed to bring a safe and swift conclusion to critical incidents such as: hostage situations, riots, high risk warrant service and large-scale searches.

In 1994, a comprehensive Community Oriented Policing Services (COPS) program was developed that involves a department-wide emphasis on involving citizens in solving problems that affect their communities.

West Virginia State Troopers in the early days on motorcycles.

Governor Underwood has pledged to add 25 new troopers during his four-year term.

The West Virginia State Police Training Academy institute is the primary facility for all law enforcement in the state.

Wisconsin State Patrol

On September 1, 1939, the nucleus of the Wisconsin State Patrol was formed when the Wisconsin Legislature created Chapter 110 of the Wisconsin Statutes. This law created the Motor Vehicle Department, consisting of three divisions: Registration and Licensing, Highway Safety Promotion and Inspection and Enforcement, which eventually evolve into the Wisconsin State Patrol.

The enforcement agencies prior to the State Patrol had a long history in the state: In 1917 the Secretary of State was authorized to ask the Dairy and Food Department and the Oil Inspection Department to make reasonable investigations of the licensing and vehicle sales laws and to appoint additional inspectors. In 1930 he appointed five additional inspectors, who later formed the nucleus of the Wisconsin State Patrol.

During the same period, the Highway Commission was authorized to name up to 10 employees to enforce Chapters 85 and 194 of the Statutes. By 1931 the State Highway engineer to check truck weights and traffic. They also tried to encourage county boards to establish county patrols outside the sheriff's departments which had been authorized by a 1927 law.

Simultaneously, in 1931, the Public Service Commission (formerly the Railroad Commission) was authorized to appoint agents to investigate violations of Chapter 194 relating to the ton-mile tax.

The officers of 1939 purchased their own patrol cars and received $30 reimbursement per month from the state plus gas, oil and grease. Each officer received a siren, flashing red light, and police license plates to display on their car while on duty. When using the car for personal reasons, the officer displayed their own license plates.

There were drawbacks to owning and using personal cars, of course. The official shield on the side of the car was always visible whether they were on or off duty. Of course, the officers had to carry prescribed equipment at all times for emergencies in the small trunks of those cars.

The first uniforms issued to the officers consisted of cadet gray trousers with a navy blue stripe on the outside seam, a navy blue blouse with stripes on the sleeves, a navy blue shirt for summer and a blue reefer for winter. Caps were a military style with a bill. The shoulder patch read "State Traffic Patrol." Each man was required to purchase his own uniform.

While some of the predecessor agencies issued firearms to their agents, the State Patrol did not initially supply them with weapons. Those who had weapons from their previous service continued to use them, but other officers waited until the State Patrol Academy was founded in 1955 to receive a firearm and training in its use.

During World War II and the years immediately following, the fledgling organization added more duties while the small force was reduced even further by the number of officers who joined the services.

In 1939 there was no statutory limit on the size of the Inspection and Enforcement Division. In 1941 state legislation placed a limit of 55 men on the division and called them "traffic officers" for the first time. The state traffic patrol was not to be used in strikes and was now responsible for enforcing the itinerant merchant law. Because the force was so small, they could not be concentrated in areas needing accident prevention services.

Within a county the assigned officer embodied the Motor Vehicle Department; a large part of his time was devoted to such non-enforcement duties as giving driver license tests, taking registration applications and collecting fees on the spot, answering the thousand and one questions on motor vehicle law, and weighing and inspecting trucks.

There were 1,246,000 drivers licensed in Wisconsin in 1941 and legislation required that new drivers had to pass a qualifying exam; there was a new drivers license fee of $1, with 75 cents returned to the local unit of government employing the officer who conducted the examination.

Equipment and training were primitive by today's standards. There was no communication equipment in the original vehicles - if an officer wanted to contact his headquarters, he would have to find a convenient telephone. In emergencies, radio station WIZR at Badger Ordnance would occasionally broadcast an alert when a specific officer needed to contact headquarters during the war. The officers would keep their car radios tuned to that station - then go find the nearest phone to receive their instructions.

The onset of war in 1941 created new duties and regulations for the State Patrol to enforce. For example, in 1941 the national Office of Defense Transportation endorsed a speed limit of 40 mph to conserve the tire and rubber supply; it was later dropped to 35 mph.

In 1943 the State Patrol finally improved its communications system when it put its radio signal on the air for the first time. Station WIZR operated on a frequency of 31.5 MHZ with AM transmission from a ground plane antenna on top of a windmill tower located on a bluff at an altitude above sea level of over, 1,400 feet.

By 1944 the condition of the highways was becoming a critical problem. Roads in bad repair were making travel unsafe. There had virtually been no new roads built and road repair schedules were drastically, restricted during the 1930s due to the Depression. With the coming of the war, these repairs and new roads were again postponed to help with the war effort. So, national and state highway engineers, looking ahead to time when the war would be over and business and tourists would again need improved roads, proposed a national network of Interstate highways which eventually became part of the patrol's responsibility.

In 1945 the fledgling communications system for the patrol took another step forward when additional FM receivers were installed at the control center that allowed headquarters to communicate with adjacent counties and municipal police stations in the area. A home-made radio telegraph, called a CW station, was installed, and CW operators were hired to communicate with the city of Milwaukee and surrounding states. These CW operators checked drivers' licenses by telephone and relayed the information by radio to mobile units and base stations.

The end of World War II brought organizational changes to the patrol. When the Badger Ordnance Plant closed, the patrol's headquarters were moved to the new headquarters in Madison. The communications equipment was controlled with telephone lines.

In 1947 the state trunk highway system was enlarged by 1,000 miles. And another improvement in the communications system occurred: an FM radio station called WWCF east of Baraboo allowed the patrol to use the station's 600-foot tower for a communications center.

Finally in 1949 the patrol received authority to expand in number. In addition to the 55 original traffic officers, legislation added another 15 men to enforce truck weight restrictions.

During the 1950s the patrol underwent major changes. The Legislature expanded the patrol from 70 uniformed officers to 250. Faced with this large influx of untrained recruits with no previous inspection or law enforcement experience, they established an academy on the grounds of Camp McCoy to train all officers.

One innovation that grew out of the war industries was the adaptation of radar to speed checking in the 1950s. In 1952 the patrol set up a speed check experiment near Tomah using a radar unit borrowed from the Highway Commission. They recorded 56 drivers in two hours. Testing the equipment and demonstrating its use was not enough, however; they needed authority to use it as evidence in court against speeders. They got that authority in 1953, when the attorney general agreed that radar evidence was admissible in court.

1955 was a turning point: Wisconsin traffic accidents reached an all-time high of 932 deaths for the year. The state Legislature established a driver licensing point system and authorized state driver examiners to test all applicants for driver licenses.

To meet the need to train these new recruits quickly, an academy was established at Camp McCoy near Tomah. That State Patrol Academy trained not only the 180 new recruits but also the original 70 officers.

The Northwestern University Traffic Institute had an initial contract to run the academy for two years. In 1957 that contract ran out and the patrol took over responsibility for training new recruits and providing annual inservice training for all members.

With the large influx of officers, uniforms were issued for the first time to officers. In 1956 traditional campaign style hats replaced the military style billed cap worn since 1939.

Their patrol cars after the expansion were gray with a black roof and trunk, with 10% of the cars unmarked. The black and gray cruisers remained in use until the mid-60s when they switched to blue and white cruisers, which in turn remained in use until the early '80s when the division switched again to solid blue cruisers in an economy move.

In 1956 the patrol acquired Harley-Davidson motorcycles for their fleet. These gave the officers more mobility - they could ride around traffic jams to reach the scene of an accident more quickly, since they could ride on the shoulder with a cycle.

This new emphasis on highway safety and traffic accident reduction, of course, affected their duty assignments after 1955. When the force tripled, the duties of the officers shifted from serving a resident representative of the Department of Motor Vehicles to performing selective traffic law enforcement based on accident experience.

A new kind of employee was added to the patrol in the mid-50s to help troopers take care of routine duties. Called Traffic Control assistants, these non-uniformed employees were trained to help the officers operate weigh stations and portable scales and handle some of the paperwork involved in truck inspections. In 1956 the first breathalyzers were purchased. These mechanical devices helped identify the level of intoxication of drivers and served as evidence in court that someone was operating under the influence of alcohol.

To keep their special police speedometers accurate, the patrol purchased a special "fifth wheel" trackmeter, a large bicycle-type wheel which attached to the bumper of a cruiser and measured accurately the speed the car was traveling. The measuring device allowed officers to check their own speedometers and remained in use until the '90s when it was finally replaced by "low doppler" radar units.

Communications equipment was slowly being upgraded to keep pace with the changing duties. In 1957 the Wisconsin Law Enforcement Teletype System was inaugurated to connect Milwaukee with the communications center in Madison.

When the additional officers were added to the patrol, their mission was clearly to help improve safety on the highways. A major emphasis of the '60s was to reduce traffic fatalities. Unfortunately, although the number of patrol officers increased, their duties expanded just as fast. Along with heavier traffic and additional traffic laws to enforce, the technological demands on the officers increased, as well.

One major cause of traffic accident deaths was failure to be properly restrained in a vehicle; only automobiles manufactured after 1962 were required to be equipped with seat belts, and there were no laws requiring drivers or passengers to wear them. The patrol established a policy in 1967 that all officers had to use their seat belts while on duty; it was not until 1987 that a safety belt law covering all occupants of motor vehicles was passed.

In 1967 the patrol initiated aerial enforcement. One-eighth mile segments were measured and marked with airplane silhouettes on

A Motor Carrier Enforcement Officer's Specialty vehicle.

high-accident highways. By timing cars with a stopwatch, officers in the plane were able to determine accurately the speed of cars on the highways. Radio communication with the officers on the highway connected the enforcement team. Airplanes are effective in locating disabled motorists, dispatching assistance, spotting and rerouting heavy traffic and sighting accidents as well as detecting other violations.

In 1964, as the patrol celebrated its first 25 years of service, it moved to the Hill Farms State Office Building. By 1969 they had converted the patrol to more sophisticated electronic equipment, they had set up two broadcasting centers to blanket the upper and lower halves of the state, and they had given the dispatchers computer files to look up driver records and motor vehicle registrations.

In 1967 of dedicated technicians had to develop, build and install the network, they had to equip all cruisers with receivers and transmitters, and they had to be available 24 hours a day, 365 days a year for emergency troubleshooting. While the communications staff worked behind the scenes, the troopers on the road in the mid-60s got a new image, when the official color of the patrol's cruisers was changed from gray and black to dark blue with white roof, trunk, and door with a red, white and blue patrol shield.

In 1968 the patrol was increased to 375 uniformed positions and was given the authority to participate in the control of civil disturbances.

In the late '60s, computerization revolutionized Wisconsin's driver license records. Coupled with the implementation in 1969 of the Uniform Traffic Citation and Complaint form, the troopers had a powerful new tool ready to serve them. A driver license search took less time, and the files were more accurate. In 1969 the patrol was assigned computer inquiry terminals so they could check driver and registration files directly.

In 1970 a driver improvement section was established to counsel drivers with bad driving records. That same year, a law was passed requiring vision tests for every licensed driver every four years prior to renewal of the driver's license.

In 1975 the formerly all-male State Patrol hired its first women. Advanced planning was necessary to supply properly fitting uni-

Trooper Don Mayers patrol cruiser.

forms and housing accommodations at the open barracks used at the State Patrol Academy.

New high-band mobile radios were purchased with the aid of more Highway Safety federal money. The 475 units were to augment the patrol's low-band system and help it communicate on the WISPERN channel. This police emergency channel may be used by all law enforcement mobile units in the state, and is also the channel that may be used by law enforcement officers nationwide. In the late '70s, the Communications Bureau was established in the division to coordinate the technological development of the patrol's equipment in the '80s.

The '70s saw a change in the way breath tests and blood alcohol tests were handled in the state. Until 1968 all troopers knew how to operate the Breathalyzer equipment which was a chemical testing device to determine blood alcohol levels; however, most officers did not know how to calibrate or perform routine maintenance on the equipment. In the early 1970s, the Chemical Testing Unit extended its service to local agencies and the staff was expanded to eight technicians. In 1979 the Office of Highway Safety helped the patrol purchase 1,800 pre-arrest breath testers to screen motorists. If they tested positive on the smaller units (which could not be used as evidence in court), they were taken to headquarters where a breathalyzer test was run.

Between 1980-89, the Division of Enforcement and Inspection changed its name to

Division of State Patrol, which better identified its mission, function and activities.

In 1985 the Wisconsin State Patrol became involved in a federally funded program, the Motor Carrier Assistance Program (MCSAP). This doubled the number of motor carrier inspectors in the early 90s. Trooper Joan Germann developed a concept of using a simulated rocking chair to educate kindergartner students of the importance of wearing safety belts. The Wisconsin Troopers Association funded Trooper Germann's invention Administrator Ted Meekma supported allowing Troopers and Inspectors to bring this program to Wisconsin schools while on duty. Trooper Joan Germann was the only Wisconsin State Trooper to be awarded "Officer of the Year" by Attorney General James Doyle.

In 1992 Motor Carrier Inspectors were granted protected retirement status by the Wisconsin Legislature. Troopers and Inspectors obtained full arrest authority in 1993. The Wisconsin Legislature also increased the statutory number of Troopers to 400 in 2000.

This program allows and mandates unsafe Commercial Motor Vehicles and Drivers to be placed out of service until defects are repaired. Drivers exceeding hours limitations are placed out of service until adequate rest. The mission of the MCSAP Program is to remove unsafe vehicles from our highways. This information has been provided by the dedicated officers of the Wisconsin State Patrol.

Wyoming Highway Patrol

The Wyoming Highway Patrol celebrated its golden anniversary in 1983, however, its roots go back another 12 years prior to the traditional founding date of June, 1933. The beginning of the end for the Department of Law Enforcement had come two months earlier in January, 1933 when Governor Leslie Miller axed three agents from Law Enforcement Commissioner George G. "Red" Smith's staff, and announced his recommendation that the Wyoming Legislature, about to convene, abolish the Department entirely.

Legislators agreed with only part of the plan. They went ahead and abolished the Law Enforcement Department but refused to authorize a new Department of Labor and Public Relations. Thus, the Wyoming Department of Law Enforcement, after 12 rather stormy years of existence, passed into the history books at midnight on March 31, 1933.

Possibly realizing that something was needed to fill the void in state law enforcement, Governor Miller went before the Wyoming Highway Commission on April 18; proposing the establishment of a highway patrol. Several other states in the region had recently followed the lead of California, which instituted the first highway patrol among the western states in August of 1929.

Miller suggested that the patrol be composed of a leader or captain and five men; further suggesting that the officers be deputized by the Livestock and Sanitary Board, Public Service Commission and State Treasurer as well as the Highway Department.

The following day, the Commission met again and adopted a resolution which stated in part, "It appears desirable and necessary the State Highway Department should make provisions for a highway patrol in Wyoming to regulate and control the use of motor vehicles on highways and to enforce the laws of this State providing for the collection of taxes and licenses upon trucks used upon the highway of this State and taxes and licenses upon other motor vehicles using the highways of this State and the inspection of livestock being transported in motor vehicles upon the highways of this State, collection of gasoline tax and generally to enforce the laws of this State relative to the use of the highways thereof by motor vehicle and other vehicles."

The Commission also authorized a school of instruction to run for 20 days, with candidates selected by each of the five Highway Commissioners. Of these men, one would be hired as captain, at a monthly salary of $200, while the others would be hired as patrolmen at $175.00 a month.

Speculations about who would head the new patrol centered around former Law Enforcement Commissioner Smith. Indeed, Rex Smith was to become the first head of the patrol. Smith joined the Law Enforcement Department as an agent in January, 1927, and was soon named as deputy commissioner of that agency. He was appointed commissioner of the by-then ill-fated Department of Law Enforcement in May, 1932.

Attempts to kill the Department were common. A scandal involving prohibition conspiracy and graft hit the Department during 1932, bringing with it more calls for reforming or completely doing away with the agency. The speculation about the Law Enforcement Department's demise coinciding with the repeal of the 18th Amendment and therefore the end of America's "noble experiment" - Prohibition - turned out to be at least partially on track. Although liquor sales in Wyoming did not resume fully until April, 1935, two years after the patrol's founding, voters in the Cowboy State, by overwhelmingly approving a liquor referendum in the 1932 general election, made it clear that public sentiment favored repeal.

The first training school for the Wyoming Highway Patrol lasted three weeks and was conducted by Inspector William H. White of the California Highway Patrol. According to the *Tribune*, the schooling consisted of "target practice, contacts with the public, police discipline, traffic law enforcement and other phases of law enforcement work."

At its meeting of May 23, 1933, the day after the conclusion of highway patrol training, the Highway Commission named Smith as patrol captain and selected six patrolmen (not five as was previously planned) from the remaining 14 who had attended the training school.

As suggested in the April meeting, the patrolmen were to be paid a monthly salary of $175 and Smith $200 monthly. Automobiles were furnished by the state, and uniforms were specified as consisting of a forest green military coat, oak brown breeches and caps, Sam Browne belts and brown riding boots. Each officer was to wear the insignia of a buffalo and winged wheel on his arm. The patrolmen got their first uniforms on June 26. By the end of the first year, the patrol had made collections of approximately $83,000 which included state registration fees, county fees, trailer fees, Public Service Commission permit fees, gasoline taxes and fines. The collections totaled about twice as much as the expense reported for operation of the patrol.

Other developments of note during the patrol's first year was the advent of "auto check stations" for inspection of lights and brakes. In this forerunner of the now defunct vehicle

This 1970 photo shows Ptl. T.J. Tittle tuning a stationary radar unit. Passing vehicles' speeds were indicated by a needle and dial mechanism and violators were stopped by calling ahead to other patrolmen down the road.

inspection program, the patrol accredited service stations around the state for the purpose of vehicle safety checks. Windshield stickers were issued to drivers of automobiles deemed in order, and the patrol promised to stop and issue citations to those who didn't have stickers.

Shortly after the Legislature passed the act providing for the official creation of the patrol, the Highway Commission met and approved the addition of five men to the patrol force, bringing the total of patrolmen to 13. After another round of testing and training similar to that carried out in 1933, the five new patrolmen were appointed and assigned to duty beginning in March.

During the early years of the agency, patrolmen had no radios in their cars; instead, messages were left at certain locations, most often service stations. Usually, a red flag was posted so the patrolman would know to stop and get his message. Communication between towns was accomplished by mail or telephone. The system left much to be desired, as urgent messages to patrolmen could take hours or even days to be relayed. To alleviate this problem, Capt. Smith began planning in early 1935 for a statewide short-wave radio system. In April, 1938, Governor Miller, by executive order, declared Wyoming's first speed limit - 60 mph. The order, which went into effect on May 1, also included a provision of a 35 mph speed limit for stretches of highway declared to be particularly hazardous. A significant drop in the accident rate did result, and Smith gave credit to the new speed limits

The winds of political change in the election year of 1938 brought changes to the Wyoming Highway Patrol. Governor Miller, in a bid for an unprecedented third term, was defeated by Republican Nels Smith, who took office on January 2, 1939. Smith began making changes in state government following his inauguration. Rumors were rampant that Red Smith would be replaced by former Sheridan County Sheriff William T. Harwood. The rumors were confirmed in late February when State Republican Chairman James B. Griffith announced that it was the intention of the new administration to install Harwood as head of the patrol.

Red Smith and his patrolmen kept plugging away. They began enforcement of a new law outlawing hitchhiking, and during April, accident report forms, drafted by Capt. Smith, were sent out for the first time. Both developments resulted from the 1939 Legislature's passage of a uniform traffic code.

During 1940, the patrol added two more men to bring its strength to a record 18 members, and the first experimental two-way radios, owned jointly by Laramie County, the city of Cheyenne, and the state of Wyoming were installed in patrol cars.

The stormy political seas calmed for a time, and the patrol managed to get back to more normal operations. Then, in mid-November, Harwood was suddenly dismissed by the Highway Commission. Once again, circumstances surrounding the firing of a patrol chief were murky. Harwood never got a hearing, and Harold H. H. Clark, a Kansas native who was reported to have served in law enforcement in California, was appointed new patrol chief.

No personnel shakeup hit the patrol following Clark's appointment, but the Highway Commission did hand down an order changing the patrol's name to the "Wyoming Courtesy

Cowboy Patrol, with the suggestion that the patrolmen wear cowboy hats, cowboy boots, leather jackets, "frontier style" trousers, a five-pointed star badge, and a low slung holster. Apparently, the plan was toned down, with the only changes in uniform being the introduction of cowboy hats and a circular shoulder patch reading "Cowboy Courtesy Patrol."

Another development during Clark's tenure as patrol captain was the creation of a Safety Education and Instruction Branch with the patrol. In May, 1941, Clark instituted a system of geographical subdivisions known as "districts", with district headquarters located at Cheyenne, Rawlins, Evanston, Riverton, Casper, Sheridan and Basin. Captain Clark's stay in the patrol turned out to be a short one, as he submitted his resignation in August, 1941, after serving just nine months as head of the patrol.

William R. Bradley was named to replace Clark, becoming the fourth patrol captain in just 27 months. However, with Bradley's appointment, the revolving door stopped, as he went on to lead the patrol for the next 24 years until his retirement in June, 1965. A few months after his appointment as patrol captain, the Japanese attack at Pearl Harbor brought the U.S. into World War II. Patrol strength still stood at 18 men when the war started, but sank as low as 9 men in 1943 as several patrolmen were called to the armed forces. By the end of the war, patrol strength had climbed back up to a new high of 22 members.

In 1942, the statewide radio AM network, originally envisioned by Red Smith in 1935, was put into operation by the patrol. In March, 1943, the patrol moved its Cheyenne headquarters into the offices of the defunct KAYN radio station on East Fifth Street in south-east Cheyenne. The availability of radio transmitting equipment in the building made it an ideal site for patrol as it was gearing up its radio system. The patrol offices were later moved back to the State Capitol Building, and then to the Barrett Building south of the Capitol for a few years in the 1950s before finding a home in 1959 at the new Highway Department complex in northwest Cheyenne.

Post war years saw the patrol strength grow to reach 34 men by the end of 1949. Thirteen men joined the patrol in 1947, the most new patrolmen added in any year since the organization was founded. As the patrol grew, so did the biennial appropriation. After being frozen at $180,000 since 1939, the Legislature granted $300,000 in 1947 and $450,000 in 1949.

By 1949, the organization of the patrol had shifted. Capt. Bradley had just two rank- ing subordinates. There were no sergeants or other officers among the other 31 patrol members. Support staff included a chief clerk and seven radio clerks. The patrol's work was steadily increasing. One factor in the increase was the 1947 passage of the driver's license law, which meant that in addition to their other duties, patrolmen were now responsible for conducting drivers' license testing. Other factors were that the highway system in 1949 included about 4,500 miles, an increase in 1,000 miles over the 1933 total, and the number of motor vehicle registrations had reached 140,000, more than double the number during the mid-1930s

A patrol group shot taken in May, 1967 at Laramie.

Commercial traffic was also on the rise, with PSC permits numbering about 20,000 during 1949, compared to only about 7,000 at the end of World War II.

The patrol continued its growth in 1951, when the Legislature granted an appropriation of $650,000, a 45 percent increase from the previous biennium. Authorized strength stood at 40 officers. The biennial appropriation for the patrol in 1953-1954 was again set at $650,000, with authorized strength increasing by one to 41 officers. There were now nine patrol check stations, located in Cheyenne, Laramie, Evanston, Kemmerer, Casper, Sheridan, Newcastle, Lusk and Evanston. These stations were operated 18 hours a day, seven days a week, except for those at Cheyenne, Laramie, and Evanston, which were operated around the clock.

Experimental use of radar began in 1954, with the first operations pursued on US 30 between Cheyenne and Laramie. The next year, the patrol obtained its first "stationary" radar unit.

In 1957, the 34th Legislature voted to increase the patrol's biennial appropriation and manpower again to $1,200,000 and 60 members. Sixteen men were commissioned during 1957; at that point, the most ever in one year. The steadily increasing amounts of vehicles on state roads was a factor in leading legislators to consider the creation of an entire new department in state government, the Department of Revenue and Taxation. The stated goal of the new department would be to take responsibility for all revenue coming into state coffers. Despite objections of the patrol administration, the plan was approved and the Department of Revenue and Taxation came into being in mid-1957. All functions of the Highway Department's Motor Vehicle Division were transferred to the new state agency.

With the demise of the division, the patrol was once again placed under the direct supervision of the Highway Department Superintendent, as had been the case prior to 1949. Thanks to a 42 percent increase in funding voted by the 35th Legislature, the patrol was able to commission 17 recruits during 1959. Patrol Biennial appropriation was $1,700,000 and authorized strength stood at 70 with three more divisions being created during the year. All 17 men who joined the patrol during 1959 attended two weeks of recruit training at Cheyenne.

During the 1963 session, the Legislature appropriated $2,000,000 and authorized a force of 75 officers for the upcoming biennium. A page in patrol history was turned in 1963 when the last two patrol motorcycles were traded in for new cars.

Moving day for the patrol came again in August, 1964, when headquarters personnel took over offices in a new building at the Highway Department complex. The building provided more office space as well as storage

A patrol gambling raid in Casper during WWII netted nearly a dozen slot machines. Capt. Wm. Bradley is at far right, and Ptl. Ed Collier is the man in uniform.

Snowdrifts in excess of 15 feet high helped complicate Patrol duty during the blizzard of '49.

space, communication facilities and a pistol range in the basement.

June 1, 1965, an era in patrol history closed when Col William Bradley retired as director, ending nearly 24 years at the WHP helm. Lt. Fred Wickam was promoted to captain and director of the patrol to succeed Bradley. In addition to Wickam's selection as the fifth patrol director, other milestones during 1965 included the implementation of date processing to handle record keeping and other clerical work, and the initial publication of the *Roadrunner*, the patrol's employee magazine. Also in 1965, the patrol went to the five-day work week for the first time.

Wyoming tied into the National Crime Information Center (NCIC) computer operated by the U.S. Department of Justice in May, 1969. Patrol strength reached a new high of 99 officers in June, 1969 after 8 recruits were commissioned.

In 1972, Douglas was chosen as the site for the new Wyoming Law Enforcement academy. Eighteen patrolmen were graduated from the academy during its first year in operation.

Uniformed patrol strength reached 142 by fall of 1975, with two recruit classes, totaling 28 new patrolmen being trained during the year. At the close of 1975, Col. Fred Wickam retired. During his 10-year tenure as director, the patrol budget nearly tripled and its uniformed strength had almost doubled. On March 18, 1976, Lt. Stan Warne was named as the new director.

Patrol funding increased again in 1976, with a biennial appropriation of $7,733,651 set by the Legislature. The patrol began using aircraft to monitor highways in 1976, and instituted its "Seat Belt Survivor" program the same year, providing the public with an example of the importance of wearing seat belts.

Two hiring firsts were achieved by the patrol during 1979, and 1980. Bonnie Coppock received her commission, thus becoming the first woman to serve on the patrol. Jeff Baltimore became the first black patrolman, commissioned in October, 1980. Change in the patrol hierachy came again at the end of 1981 when Col Warne opted for retirement, and W. O. "Fred" Oyler was chosen to succeed Warne as director.

Tragedy visited the patrol in October of 1981 when Patrolman Pete Visser was fatally njured on Interstate 80 west of Rawlins. Visser was investigating a traffic crash and was seated n his patrol vehicle when it was struck from the rear by a pickup truck driven by an ntoxicated driver. The driver was later convicted of vehicular homicide. Patrolman Visser was he first Wyoming Highway Patrol officer to be killed in the line of duty since the creation of he agency in 1933.

Colonel Fred Oyler retired from the patrol in December 1984. Field operations commander, Major Everette Ayers was named as his successor and remained in the colonel's seat until the spring of 1998. By then the authorized strength of the patrol had grown to 157 sworn positions.

After Colonel Ayers' retirement in the spring of 1998, Colonel John Cox was named as his successor. Colonel Cox originally worked for the patrol in the early seventies, then spent the next 18 years in municipal po-lice service, including 11 years as chief of police in Powell, Wyoming.

Tragedy again visited the Wyoming Highway Patrol in October of 1998 when Trooper Chris Logsdon became the second patrol officer to be killed in the line of duty in the history of the agency. Chris was responding to a report of a driver traveling the wrong direction on the interstate highway near Wheatland, Wyoming when he topped a hill to meet the disoriented driver in his lane. Trooper Logsdon's immediate evasive action avoided a head on collision but resulted in the loss of control of his patrol vehicle which ultimately rolled, taking Chris' life.

In the first three months of 1999, two separate attacks threatened the lives of three Wyoming troopers. In January, Trooper Howard Parkin was shot in the face at point blank range by the driver of a car he had stopped for speeding near Douglas, Wyoming. Parkin was able to return fire hitting the suspect's vehicle as it sped away and then was able to radio for help and give a description of the vehicle. The ensuing man-hunt and chase resulted in the capture of two suspects. Trooper Parkin recovered from a gunshot wound and returned to active duty. In March of 1999, Troopers Bill Kirkman and Delaine Baldwin were involved in a second shooting incident which arose during a traffic stop. During the course of the stop, Trooper Baldwin asked a passenger to step out of the vehicle. As he did so, he pointed a large caliber revolver at Trooper Baldwin's face and fired. Baldwin was able to jerk his head to the side and avoided being shot point blank, but still suffered powder burns and concussion injuries from the shot. Both Baldwin and Kirkman were able to return fire fatally injuring the subject.

December of 1999 ushered in a massive reorganization of the organizational structure of the patrol. A tiered trooper rank structure was introduced which provided for a career track within the rank. Responsibility and authority was pushed deeper into the supervisory ranks resulting in the reclassification of most supervisors to a higher rank. First line supervisors within the patrol are now the rank of lieutenant. The sergeant rank is reserved for officers whose work is primarily confined to management of programs. The reorganization also resulted in the assimilation of the Motor Carrier function and Port of Entry function into the local or divisional supervisory command. A fifth district was created in order to make better use of human resources and concentrate supervisory efforts into more manageable geographical expanses.

The year 2000 saw the inception of the first ever Wyoming Highway Patrol K-9 program. Four K-9 handlers were selected, trained and paired with four single purpose drug detection Labradors. The four K-9 teams were placed along Wyoming's interstate highway system to provide a solid line of defense in Wyoming's highway drug interdiction program.

The Wyoming Highway Patrol continues to address the changing needs of law enforcement in the year 2000. The significant evolution in training, recruitment, technology, continue to pose critical and challenging problems for state law enforcement agencies. Wyoming's rural western lifestyle and broad expanses only serve to magnify the need for the Wyoming Highway Patrol to remain on the cutting edge of law enforcement.

Index

Arizona Peace Officers Memorial. This brass sculpture, a tribute to Arizona peace officers who gave the ultimate sacrifice while protecting the citizens of Arizona stands near the State's capitol in Phoenix, Arizona.